PR
4470
.F69
v. 7
pt. 2

Coleridge, Samuel Taylor

Biographia literaria, or,
Biographical sketches of
my literary life and
opinions

DATE DUE

THE COLLECTED WORKS OF
SAMUEL TAYLOR COLERIDGE · 7

BIOGRAPHIA LITERARIA

General Editor: KATHLEEN COBURN

Associate Editor: BART WINER

THE COLLECTED WORKS

THE COLLECTED WORKS OF

Samuel Taylor Coleridge

Biographia Literaria

OR

*Biographical Sketches of
My Literary Life and Opinions*

II

EDITED BY

James Engell and W. Jackson Bate

ROUTLEDGE & KEGAN PAUL

❧ BOLLINGEN SERIES LXXV
PRINCETON UNIVERSITY PRESS

The Collected Works, sponsored by Bollingen Foundation,
is published in Great Britain
by Routledge & Kegan Paul Ltd
39 Store Street, London WC1
ISBN 0-7100-0896-1
and in the United States of America
by Princeton University Press, 41 William Street
Princeton, New Jersey
ISBN 0-691-09874-3
LCC 68–10201
The Collected Works constitutes
the seventy-fifth publication in Bollingen Series

The present work, number 7, of the Collected Works,
is in 2 volumes, this being 7: II

Printed in the United States of America
by Princeton University Press

CONTENTS

LIST OF ILLUSTRATIONS

BIOGRAPHIA LITERARIA

VOLUME II

CHAPTER 14

Occasion of the Lyrical Ballads, and the objects originally proposed—
Preface to the second edition—The ensuing controversy, its causes and
acrimony—Philosophic definitions of a poem and poetry with scholia[1]

D URING the first year that Mr. Wordsworth and I were
neighbours,[2] our conversations turned frequently on the
two cardinal points of poetry, the power of exciting the sympathy
of the reader by a faithful adherence to the truth of nature, and
the power of giving the interest of novelty by the modifying
colours of imagination.[3] The sudden charm, which accidents of
light and shade, which moon-light or sun-set diffused over a
known and familiar landscape, appeared to represent the practicability of combining both.[4] These are the poetry of nature. The

---

[1] C provides no formal "scholia",
only a few examples (e.g. the book
of Isa as poetry). This suggests that
the title or "argument" of the
chapter was written down before C
wrote or dictated the body of the
chapter and that it was not revised
afterwards in ms or proof.

[2] 1797–8, WW at Alfoxden
House and C at Nether Stowey.

[3] On the ability of "genius" to
bestow "wonder" and "novelty" on
the familiar, see *Friend (CC)* i 110
and ch 4, above, i 81–2.

[4] Cf *Excursion* iv 1058–72:
Within the soul a faculty abides,

. . .

As the ample moon,
In the deep stillness of a summer even
Rising behind a thick and lofty
grove,
Burns, like an unconsuming fire
of light,
In the green trees; and, kindling
on all sides

Their leafy umbrage, turns the
dusky veil
Into a substance glorious as her
own,
Yea, with her own incorporated,
by power
Capacious and serene. Like
power abides
In man's celestial spirit; virtue
thus
Sets forth and magnifies herself
. . .

Cf also the beginning of an annotation on a front flyleaf of Tennemann
Geschichte der Philosophie x: "The
imaginative power (a multiform
power, which acting with its permea-
tive modifying unifying might on the
Thoughts and Images specificates the
Poet, the swimming Crimson of eve
in ⟨Mountain,⟩ Lake, River, Vale,
Village and Village Church, the
flashing or sleeping Moonshine in
Nature's Poesy—which exercising
the same power in moral intuitions
& the representations of worth, or

thought suggested itself (to which of us I do not recollect) that a series of poems might be composed of two sorts. In the one, the incidents and agents were to be, in part at least, supernatural; and the excellence aimed at was to consist in the interesting of the affections by the dramatic truth of such emotions, as would naturally accompany such situations, supposing them real. And real in *this* sense they have been to every human being who, from whatever source of delusion, has at any time believed himself under supernatural agency. For the second class, subjects were to be chosen from ordinary life; the characters and incidents were to be such, as will be found in every village and its vicinity, where there is a meditative and feeling mind to seek after them, or to notice them, when they present themselves.

In this idea originated the plan of the "Lyrical Ballads;" in which it was agreed, that my endeavours should be directed to persons and characters supernatural, or at least romantic; yet so as to transfer from our inward nature a human interest and a semblance of truth sufficient to procure for these shadows of imagination[1] that willing suspension of disbelief for the moment, which constitutes poetic faith.[2] Mr. Wordsworth, on the other

---

baseness in action is the essential Constituent of what is called *a Good heart*—this power cannot be given or taught. It is always an Indigena of the Soil. . . ." *CM (CC)* IV. *BL* (1907) II 264 quotes most of the above.

[1] C echoes Theseus' remark in Shakespeare *A Midsummer Night's Dream* v i 211–12: "The best in this kind are but shadows; and the worst are no worse, if imagination amend them."

[2] Cf ch 22, below, II 134, on "That *illusion,* contradistinguished from *delusion,* that *negative* faith, which simply permits the images presented to work by their own force, without either denial or affirmation of their real existence by the judgment . . .". ". . . Even in the Imitative Arts, that are supposed to have their being in fiction, a well-disciplined mind is offended by actual Delusion". *CN* III 3592 f 136. C's point is enlarged on

in his letter to Stuart 13 May 1816: ". . . Images and Thoughts possess a power in and of themselves, independent of that act of the Judgement or Understanding by which we affirm or deny the existence of a reality correspondent to them. Such is the ordinary state of the mind in Dreams. It is not strictly accurate to say, that we believe our dreams to be actual while we are dreaming. We neither believe it or disbelieve it—with the will the comparing power is suspended, and without the comparing power any act of Judgement, whether affirmation or denial, is impossible. The Forms and Thoughts act merely by their own inherent power: and the strong feelings at times apparently connected with them are in point of fact bodily sensations, which are the causes or occasions of the Images, not (as when we are awake) the effects of them. Add to this a volun-

hand, was to propose to himself as his object, to give the charm of novelty to things of every day, and to excite a feeling analogous to the supernatural, by awakening the mind's attention from the lethargy of custom, and directing it to the loveliness and the wonders of the world before us; an inexhaustible treasure, but for which in consequence of the film of familiarity[1] and selfish solicitude we have eyes, yet see not, ears that hear not, and hearts that neither feel nor understand.[2]

With this view I wrote the "Ancient Mariner," and was preparing among other poems, the "Dark Ladie," and the "Christabel," in which I should have more nearly realized my ideal, than I had done in my first attempt.[3] But Mr. Wordsworth's industry had

---

tary Lending of the Will to this suspension of one of it's own operations (i.e. that of comparison & consequent decision concerning the reality of any sensuous Impression) and you have the true Theory of Stage Illusion—equally distant from the absurd notion of the French Critics, who ground their principles on the presumption of an absolute *Delusion*, and of Dr Johnson who would persuade us that our Judgements are as broad awake during the most masterly representation of the deepest scenes of Othello, as a philosopher would be during the exhibition of a Magic Lanthorn with Punch & Joan, & Pull Devil Pull Baker, &c on it's painted Slides." *CL* IV 641–2. Cf the remarks on dramatic illusion in *Sh C* I 127–31, 199–207, II 321–2, and ch 23, below, II 214. C may be recalling Joseph Priestley's idea of "assent", by which "one single effort of the imagination" gives "assent" to a series of improbable characters and events; see *Lectures on Oratory and Criticism* (1774) 90–2, and Engell *CI* 74. *BL* (1907) II 300 suggests comparison with Schiller's doctrine of "aesthetic semblance". But Schiller states that "our judgement of it should take no account" of any reality the semblance may have; "for inasmuch as it does take account of

it, it is not an aesthetic judgement". This is closer to what C defines (in ch 22) as illusion. See *AE* XXVI pp 192–9.

[1] Shelley, who read *BL* when it appeared, appropriated the phrase near the close of his "Defence of Poetry" (1821): "Poetry . . . purges from our inward sight the film of familiarity which obscures from us the wonder of our being." *Complete Works* ed R. Ingpen and W. E. Peck (1965) VII 137. Cf ". . . the confused multiplicity of seeing with which 'the films of corruption' bewilder us". *Friend (CC)* I 512.

[2] Cf Jer 5.21; Isa 6.10. According to WW, his and C's original intention had been to compose a single poem, which would be sent to the *New Monthly Magazine* and thus pay the expense of their walking tour from Alfoxden to Linton. During the walk they planned *AM*, which "grew and grew till it became too important for our first object . . . and we began to talk of a Volume, which was to consist, as Mr. Coleridge has told the world, of Poems chiefly on natural subjects taken from common life, but looked at, as much as might be, through an imaginative medium". IF note to *We Are Seven*. *WPW* I 360–1.

[3] C's unfinished *Christabel* was not published until 1816, when it

proved so much more successful, and the number of his poems so much greater, that my compositions, instead of forming a balance, appeared rather an interpolation of heterogeneous matter.[1] Mr. Wordsworth added two or three poems written in his own character, in the impassioned, lofty, and sustained diction, which is characteristic of his genius.[2] In this form the "Lyrical Ballads" were published; and were presented by him, as an *experiment*,[3] whether subjects, which from their nature rejected the usual ornaments and extra-colloquial style of poems in general, might not be so managed in the language of ordinary life as to produce the pleasurable interest, which it is the peculiar business of poetry to impart. To the second edition he added a preface of considerable length; in which notwithstanding some passages of apparently a contrary import, he was understood to contend for the extension of this style to poetry of all kinds, and to reject as vicious and indefensible all phrases and forms of style that were not included in what he (unfortunately, I think, adopting an equivocal expression) called the language of *real* life.[4] From this preface, prefixed

---

appeared in *Christabel; Kubla Khan, A Vision; The Pains of Sleep,* published by John Murray. The poem *Love,* in the 2nd ed of *LB* (1800), was intended as an Introduction to *The Dark Ladie,* which was likewise never finished and was left unpublished until HNC included it in *PW* (1834). Cf ch 24, below, II 238 n 3.

[1] In the 1st ed of *LB,* only four of the twenty-three poems were by C: the *Ancient Mariner, The Nightingale, The Foster-Mother's Tale,* and *The Dungeon. Lewti,* originally printed in *LB,* was cancelled, with *The Nightingale* substituted, to preserve the anonymity of the volume. In the 2nd ed (1800) the sole poem added by C was *Love* (see n 3, directly above).

[2] C refers to *Tintern Abbey,* added when *LB* was in the press, and to one or two of the following written by WW "in his own character": *Lines Written at a Small Distance from My House, Lines Written in Early Spring, Expostula-*tion *and Reply,* and *The Tables Turned.*

[3] Cf the Advertisement to *LB* (1798): "The majority of the following poems are to be considered as experiments. They were written chiefly with a view to ascertain how far the language of conversation in the middle and lower classes of society is adapted to the purposes of poetic pleasure." *W Prose* I 116.

[4] The actual phrasing of WW was more qualified than C implies: "a selection of the real language of men in a state of vivid sensation . . . The language too of these men [in rural life] is adopted (purified indeed from what appear to be its real defects, from all lasting and rational causes of dislike or disgust) because such men hourly communicate with the best objects from which the best part of language is originally derived; and because . . . being less under the action of social vanity they convey their feelings and notions in simple and unelaborated

to poems in which it was impossible to deny the presence of original genius, however mistaken its direction might be deemed, arose the whole long continued controversy. For from the conjunction of perceived power with supposed heresy I explain the inveteracy and in some instances, I grieve to say, the acrimonious passions, with which the controversy has been conducted by the assailants.[1]

Had Mr. Wordsworth's poems been the silly, the childish things, which they were for a long time described as being; had they been really distinguished from the compositions of other poets merely by meanness of language and inanity of thought; had they indeed contained nothing more than what is found in the parodies and pretended imitations of them; they must have sunk at once, a dead weight, into the slough of oblivion, and have dragged the preface along with them. But year after year increased the number of Mr. Wordsworth's admirers. They were found too not in the lower classes of the reading public, but chiefly among young men of strong sensibility and meditative minds; and their admiration (inflamed perhaps in some degree by opposition) was distinguished by its intensity, I might almost say, by its *religious* fervour. These facts, and the intellectual energy of the author, which was more or less consciously felt, where it was outwardly and even boisterously denied, meeting with sentiments of aversion to his opinions, and of alarm at their consequences, produced an eddy of criticism, which would of itself have borne up the poems by the violence, with which it whirled them round and round. With many parts of this preface in the sense attributed to them and which the words undoubtedly seem to authorise, I never concurred; but on the contrary objected to them as erroneous in principle, and as contradictory (in appearance at least) both to other parts of the same

expressions. . . . In these Poems I propose to myself to imitate, and, as far as is possible, to adopt the very language of men . . .". *W Prose* I 118, 124, 130.

[1] C refers mainly to the attacks by Francis Jeffrey in *Ed Rev* starting in 1802 (cf ch 4, above, I 71 n 1), "long continued" because they were renewed in the reviews (1814) of WW's *Excursion,* which begins: "This will never do", and the following year of *The White Doe of Rylstone,* beginning: "This, we think, has the merit of being the very worst poem we ever saw imprinted in a quarto volume . . .". *Ed Rev* XXIV (1814) 1–30, XXV (1815) 355–63.

preface, and to the author's own practice in the greater number of the poems themselves.[1] Mr. Wordsworth in his recent collection has, I find, degraded this prefatory disquisition to the end of his second volume, to be read or not at the reader's choice.[2] But he has not, as far as I can discover, announced any change in his poetic creed. At all events, considering it as the source of a controversy, in which I have been honored more, than I deserve, by the frequent conjunction of my name with his, I think it expedient to declare once for all, in what points I coincide with his opinions, and in what points I altogether differ. But in order to render myself intelligible I must previously, in as few words as possible,

[1] Cf C's letter to RS as early as 29 Jul 1802: ". . . Altho' Wordsworth's Preface is half a child of my own Brain/ & so arose out of Conversations, so frequent, that with few exceptions we could scarcely either of us perhaps positively say, which first started any particular Thought . . . yet I am far from going all lengths with Wordsworth/ He has written lately a number of Poems . . . very excellent Compositions/ but here & there a daring Humbleness of Language & Versification, and a strict adherence to matter of fact, even to prolixity, that startled me . . . I rather suspect that some where or other there is a radical Difference in our theoretical opinions respecting Poetry— this I shall endeavor to go to the Bottom of—and acting the arbitrator between the old School & the New School hope to lay down some plain, & perspicuous, tho' not superficial, Canons of Criticism respecting Poetry." *CL* II 830. Somewhat more explicit is his letter to Sotheby 13 Jul 1802: the Preface arose from "the heads of our mutual Conversations &c—& the f[irst pass]ages were indeed partly taken from notes of mine/ for it was at first intended, that the Preface should be written by me". C then goes on to state his differences: "In my opinion every phrase, every metaphor, every personification, should have it's justify-ing cause in some *passion* either of the Poet's mind, or of the Characters described by the poet—But *metre itself* implies a *passion,* i.e. a state of excitement, both in the Poet's mind, & is expected in that of the Reader— and tho' I stated this to Wordsworth, & he has in some sort stated it in his preface, yet he has [not] done justice to it, nor has he in my opinion sufficiently answered it. In my opinion, Poetry justifies, as *Poetry* independent of any other Passion, some new combinations of Language, & *commands* the omission of many others allowable in other compositions/ Now Wordsworth, me saltem judice, has in his system not sufficiently admitted the former, & in his practice has too frequently sinned against the latter.—Indeed, we have had lately some little controversy on this subject . . .". *CL* II 811–12.

[2] *Poems by William Wordsworth: Including Lyrical Ballads, and the Miscellaneous Pieces of the Author. With Additional Poems, a New Preface, and a Supplementary Essay* (2 vols 1815). Here and in succeeding collected editions of his poems WW, having written his new Preface, placed the earlier one at the end of the book, regarding it as less applicable to "the present enlarged and diversified collection". *W Prose* III 26n.

explain my ideas, first, of a POEM; and secondly, of POETRY itself, in *kind*, and in *essence*.

The office of philosophical *disquisition* consists in just *distinction*; while it is the priviledge of the philosopher to preserve himself constantly aware, that distinction is not division.[1] In order to obtain adequate notions of any truth, we must intellectually separate its distinguishable parts; and this is the technical *process* of philosophy. But having so done, we must then restore them in our conceptions to the unity, in which they actually co-exist; and this is the *result* of philosophy.[2] A poem contains the same elements as a prose composition; the difference therefore must consist in a different combination of them, in consequence of a different object proposed.[3] According to the difference of the object will be the difference of the combination. It is possible, that the object may be merely to facilitate the recollection of any given facts or observations by artificial arrangement; and the composition will be a poem, merely because it is distinguished from prose by metre, or by rhyme, or by both conjointly. In this, the lowest sense, a man might attribute the name of a poem to the well known enumeration of the days in the several months;

> Thirty days hath September,
> April, June, and November, &c.

and others of the same class and purpose. And as a particular pleasure is found in anticipating the recurrence of sounds and quantities, all compositions that have this charm superadded, whatever be their contents, *may* be entitled poems.

[1] On the importance to C of "understanding the difference between Division & Distinction" see e.g. an annotation on Marcus Aurelius: *CM* (*CC*) I 175, *Friend* (*CC*) II 104n (I 177n), and *CN* II 3154.

[2] C may be recalling Schiller *AE* XVIII § 4 and n, in which Schiller states that the two opposing conditions of "beauty" must first be philosophically "distinguished with the utmost precision" and then later united at a higher level of thinking. "Nature (sense and intuition) always unites, Intellect always divides; but Reason unites once more. Before he begins to philosophize, therefore, man is nearer to truth than the philosopher who has not yet completed his investigation." *AE* 122–7 (cf clxix–clxxi).

[3] So with "beauty" generally (in which "the *many*, still seen as many, becomes one"). It is by definition a "harmony, and subsists only in composition". *PGC* III: *BL* (1907) II 232–3. That is, it does not characterise a single "element" but the process of harmonising different ones, and exists only as these are brought toegther in "composition" or in "combination".

So much for the superficial *form*. A difference of object and contents supplies an additional ground of distinction. The immediate purpose may be the communication of truths; either of truth absolute and demonstrable, as in works of science; or of facts experienced and recorded, as in history. Pleasure, and that of the highest and most permanent kind, may *result* from the *attainment* of the end; but it is not itself the immediate end.[1] In other works the communication of pleasure may be the immediate purpose; and though truth, either moral or intellectual, ought to be the *ultimate* end, yet this will distinguish the character of the author, not the class to which the work belongs. Blest indeed is that state of society, in which the immediate purpose would be baffled by the perversion of the proper ultimate end; in which no charm of diction or imagery could exempt the Bathyllus even of an Anacreon, or the Alexis of Virgil,[2] from disgust and aversion!

But the communication of pleasure may be the immediate object of a work not metrically composed; and that object may have been in a high degree attained, as in novels and romances. Would then the mere superaddition of metre, with or without rhyme, entitle *these* to the name of poems? The answer is, that nothing can permanently please, which does not contain in itself the reason why it is so, and not otherwise.[3] If metre be super-

---

[1] C is condensing here and throughout the next paragraph what he had put at greater length the previous year in *PGC*. The key word, as he says there, is "immediate". For the *ultimate* aim of poetry and of art as a whole involves "truth", broadly considered. "Beauty", for example, is not a mere subjective state of mind (the "agreeable"). It is a state we experience when the universal (*forma informans*) is conceived as emerging organically through the concrete diversity ("multeity"). It is not "truth" itself but a way of approaching "truth"— "the shorthand hieroglyphic of Truth", a "mediator" between truth and human feeling. MS "Semina Rerum". But the "immediate" purpose, as distinct from that of "science", is the "pleasure" derived from this *means* of approaching the

"truth": from "the pleasurable activity of the mind", as he says below, "excited by the attractions of the journey itself". *PGC* I, II: *BL* (1907) II 221–4. Cf *CN* III 4111 and Lects 2 and 3 of 1811: *Sh C* II 66–7, 74–6.

[2] Bathyllus of Samos, loved by Anacreon: Ode 29 (17)—not to be confused with Bathyllus the mediocre poet, ch 2, above, I 46 n 2—and Alexis, the youth loved by Corydon, in Virgil *Eclogue* 2. A "fine Poem on a hateful subject"—such as these poems—C compared to sweet flowers whose leaves give off a "fetid odor . . . that you start back from . . . thro' disgust". *CN* III 4198. On *Anacreon Odes* see ch 16, below, II 34 n 2.

[3] With C's emphasis that a work of art must "contain in itself" the organic, if it is to please permanently, cf Johnson in *Rambler* No

added, all other parts must be made consonant with it. They must be such, as to justify the perpetual and distinct attention to each part, which an exact correspondent recurrence of accent and sound are calculated to excite. The final definition then, so deduced, may be thus worded. A poem is that species of composition, which is opposed to works of science, by proposing for its *immediate* object pleasure, not truth; and from all other species (having *this* object in common with it) it is discriminated by proposing to itself such delight from the *whole*, as is compatible with a distinct gratification from each component *part*.[1]

Controversy is not seldom excited in consequence of the disputants attaching each a different meaning to the same word; and in few instances has this been more striking, than in disputes concerning the present subject.[2] If a man chooses to call every composition a poem, which is rhyme, or measure, or both, I must leave his opinion uncontroverted. The distinction is at least competent to characterize the writer's intention. If it were subjoined, that the whole is likewise entertaining or affecting, as a tale, or as a series of interesting reflections, I of course admit this as another fit ingredient of a poem, and an additional merit. But if the definition sought for be that of a *legitimate* poem, I answer, it must be one, the parts of which mutually support and explain each other; all in their proportion harmonizing with, and supporting the purpose and known influences of metrical arrangement. The philosophic critics of all ages coincide with the ultimate judgement of all countries, in equally denying the praises of a just

---

154: "That which hopes to resist the blast of malignity, and stand firm against the attacks of time, must contain in itself some original principle of growth."

[1] C's definition of a poem, in *CN* III 4111, 4112, was used in Lects 2 and 4 of 1811: *Sh C* II 68–9, 98. The coalescence of the contributing "parts" of the "whole" is one of the recurring themes of C's discussion of Shakespeare. Cf also the close of C's notes for Lect 13 of 10 Mar 1818: Ultimate form "is without character as Water is purest when without taste, smell or color—but this is the Highest, the Apex, not the whole—& Art is to give *the whole* ad hominem", thus producing a process of "harmonizing" from and through "Chaos", presenting the parts in the act of contributing to the final unity. *CN* III 4397 f 53ᵛ (cf *PA*: *BL*—1907—II 262–3).

[2] "The intelligibility of almost everything he had to say on the subject of poetry would depend [on] his being perspicuous in his definition, because, as he had before said, it often happened that differences between men of good sense arose solely from having attached different ideas to the same words." Lect 3 of 24 Nov 1811: *Sh C* II 75.

poem, on the one hand, to a series of striking lines or distichs, each of which absorbing the whole attention of the reader to itself disjoins it from its context, and makes it a separate whole, instead of an harmonizing part; and on the other hand, to an unsustained composition, from which the reader collects rapidly the general result unattracted by the component parts. The reader should be carried forward, not merely or chiefly by the mechanical impulse of curiosity, or by a restless desire to arrive at the final solution; but by the pleasureable activity of mind excited by the attractions of the journey itself. Like the motion of a serpent, which the Egyptians made the emblem of intellectual power;[1] or like the path of sound through the air; at every step he pauses and half recedes, and from the retrogressive movement collects the force which again carries him onward. Precipitandus est *liber* spiritus, says Petronius Arbiter most happily.[2] The epithet, *liber*, here balances the preceding verb; and it is not easy to conceive more meaning condensed in fewer words.

But if this should be admitted as a satisfactory character of a poem, we have still to seek for a definition of poetry. The writings of PLATO, and Bishop TAYLOR, and the Theoria Sacra of BURNET,[3] furnish undeniable proofs that poetry of the highest kind may exist without metre, and even without the contradistinguishing objects of a poem. The first chapter of Isaiah (indeed a very large proportion of the whole book) is poetry in the most

[1] "The Serpent by which the ancients emblem'd the Inventive faculty appears to me, in its mode of motion most exactly to emblem a writer of Genius." *CN* I 609; cf Barbara Hardy *EIC* IX (1959) 314.

[2] *Satyricon* 118. "The *free* spirit must be hurried onward". Petronius, contrasting the task of the historian with that of the epic poet, is criticising Lucan's historical poem, the *Pharsalia*. *BL* (1847) II 12n.

[3] For references to Plato as poet, see *Friend* (*CC*) I 472, *P Lects* Lect 4 (1949) 158 and n, and an annotation on Thomas Gray *Works* (1814) II: *Misc C* 308–9, *CM* (*CC*) II. Cf McFarland 112–14. On Taylor, see *Friend* (*CC*) I 347n: ". . . the most eloquent of our Writers (I had almost said of our Poets) Jeremy Taylor . . .". In Lect 1 of 18 Nov 1811 C quoted from Taylor, observing that "tho' writing in prose [he] might be considered one of the first of our Poets". *Lects 1808–19* (*CC*) ms. *Telluris theoria sacra* (1681), written in Latin and later translated as *The Sacred Theory of the Earth* (1684–9), by Thomas Burnet (1635–1715), is an imaginative, eloquent work on the structure, character, and future destiny of the earth. C in 1795–6 had contemplated translating it "into blank Verse, the original at the bottom of the page". *CN* I 61.

emphatic sense;[1] yet it would be not less irrational than strange to assert, that pleasure, and not truth, was the immediate object of the prophet. In short, whatever *specific* import we attach to the word, poetry, there will be found involved in it, as a necessary consequence, that a poem of any length neither can be, or ought to be, all poetry.[2] Yet if an harmonious whole is to be produced, the remaining parts must be preserved *in keeping* with the poetry;[3] and this can be no otherwise effected than by such a studied selection and artificial arrangement, as will partake of *one*, though not a *peculiar*, property of poetry. And this again can be no other than the property of exciting a more continuous and equal attention, than the language of prose aims at, whether colloquial or written.

My own conclusions on the nature of poetry, in the strictest use of the word, have been in part anticipated in the preceding disquisition on the fancy and imagination.[4] What is poetry? is so nearly the same question with, what is a poet? that the answer to the one is involved in the solution of the other. For it is a distinction resulting from the poetic genius itself, which sustains and modifies the images, thoughts, and emotions of the poet's own mind. The poet, described in *ideal* perfection, brings the whole soul

---

[1] "Thus taking the first chapter of Isaiah, without more than four or five transpositions and no alteration of words, he had reduced it to complete hexameters—so true it is that wherever passion was, the language became a sort of metre." J. Tomalin's report of Lect 3 of 25 Nov 1811: *Sh C* II 80.

[2] The concept of "pure poetry" is ordinarily associated with E. A. Poe's "The Poetic Principle" (1848), one of the central theses of which is that "a long poem does not exist", the very phrase "long poem" being "a flat contradiction in terms". But Poe is consciously extending the implications of what C states above, and the sentiment was becoming fairly common by C's time. Bate *BP* 74–6, 113.

[3] Cf ". . . Poetry demands a *severer keeping* [than prose]—it admits nothing that Prose may not often admit; but it *oftener* rejects. In other words, it presupposes a more continuous state of Passion." *CN* III 3611. Here and above C italicises "keeping" because he uses the painter's term—"The maintenance of the proper relation between the representations of nearer and more distant objects in a picture . . . the maintenance of harmony of composition" (*OED*). Cf an annotation on *B Poets* IV: *CM* (*CC*) I 58; letters of 9 Apr 1814 and 8 Apr 1820: *CL* III 470, V 34; and *CN* III 3524, 4250.

[4] C could hardly refer to the brief remarks at the close of ch 13, above, I 304–5. More likely he is referring either to the extended discussion he later planned to insert, in what became ch 13, or to the discussion in ch 4, above, I 82–8.

of man into activity,[1] with the subordination of its faculties to each other, according to their relative worth and dignity.[2] He diffuses a tone, and spirit of unity, that blends, and (as it were) *fuses*,[3] each into each, by that synthetic and magical power, to which we have exclusively appropriated the name of imagination.[4] This power, first put in action by the will and understanding,[5] and retained under their irremissive, though gentle and unnoticed, controul (*laxis effertur habenis*)[6] reveals itself in the balance or reconciliation of opposite or discordant qualities:[7] of sameness,

[1] Cf Schiller *AE* xv p 106: man *"ist nur da ganz Mensch, wo er spielt"* (man *"is only fully a human being when he plays"*). C even more closely echoes Schelling *STI* 480 (*SW* III 630): "Die Kunst bringt *den ganzen Menschen*, wie er ist, dahin, nämlich zur Erkenntniss des Höchsten . . ." ("Art brings *the whole man*, as he is inherently constituted, to that point—namely, to the perception of the highest . . ."). For C's stress on the poet or poetry "described in *ideal* perfection" cf *STI* 18–19 (*SW* III 349), in which Schelling discusses "Die idealische Welt der Kunst".

[2] Cf the earlier version of this and the following sentences (May 1810): ". . . Of Poetry commonly so called we might justly call it—A mode of composition that calls into action & gratifies the largest number of the human Faculties in Harmony with each other, & in just proportions. . . . Frame a numeration table of the primary faculties of Man, as Reason, *unified per Ideas, Mater Legum* [mother of law] . . . Judgement, the discriminative, Fancy, the aggregative, Imagination, the modifying & *fusive,* the Senses & Sensations—and from these the different Derivatives of the Agreeable from the Senses, the Beautiful, the Sublime/ the Like and the Different—the spontaneous and the receptive—the Free and the Necessary—And whatever calls into consciousness the greatest number of

these in due proportion & perfect harmony with each other, is the noblest Poem.—Not the mere quantity of pleasure can be any criterion, for that is endlessly dependent on accidents of the Subject receiving it, his age, sensibility, moral habits, &c—but the worth, the permanence, and comparative Independence of the Sources, from which the Pleasure has been derived." *CN* III 3827.

[3] Cf ". . . The fusing power, that fixing unfixes & while it melts & bedims the Image, still leaves in the Soul its living meaning". *CN* III 4066. Cf ch 15, below, II 23 n 2.

[4] From the following sentence to the end of the quotation from Sir John Davies, C is using a notebook entry of Oct–Nov 1811 (*CN* III 4112), which he had also used in Lect 4 of 28 Nov 1811: see *Sh C* II 98–9. On the relation of will to imagination, see ch 13, above, I 304–5.

[5] C's linking of "will" and "understanding" in this context also has a parallel with Jacobi *ULS* 248 and possibly also with Herder *Adrastea* (1801) II 229.

[6] Petrarch *Epistola Barbato Sulmonensi* line 39 (the line before the quotation in ch 10, above, I 222): *Opera* (Basle 1581) III 76. From the passage C had copied into a notebook in 1813: *CN* III 4178. Tr: "carried on with slackened reins".

[7] This is a leading idea in Schiller's *AE*. But cf also Schelling *Abhandlungen: Phil Schrift* 208 (*SW* I 254), though the context is

with difference; of the general, with the concrete; the idea, with the image; the individual, with the representative; the sense of novelty and freshness, with old and familiar objects; a more than usual state of emotion, with more than usual order; judgement ever awake and steady self-possession, with enthusiasm and feeling profound or vehement; and while it blends and harmonizes the natural and the artificial, still subordinates art to nature; the manner to the matter; and our admiration of the poet to our sympathy with the poetry.[1] "Doubtless," as Sir John Davies observes of the soul (and his words may with slight alteration be applied, and even more appropriately to the poetic IMAGINA-TION.)

> Doubtless this could not be, but that she turns
> Bodies to spirit by sublimation strange,
> As fire converts to fire the things it burns,
> As we our food into our nature change.
>
> From their gross matter she abstracts their forms,
> And draws a kind of quintessence from things;
> Which to her proper nature she transforms
> To bear them light, on her celestial wings.
>
> Thus does she, when from individual states
> She doth abstract the universal kinds;
> Which then re-clothed in divers names and fates
> Steal access through our senses to our minds.[2]

different: "Weil z. B. der Begriff von Materie *ursprünglich* aus einer Synthesis entgegengesetzter Kräfte durch die Einbildungskraft hervorgeht . . ." ("Since, for example, the concept of matter *originally* emerges out of a synthesis of opposing powers in the imagination . . .").

[1] C in 1808 had considered writing an essay to "explain my system of balanced opposites—thence the Like in the Unlike". *CN* III 3400. ". . . in all Imitation two elements must exist, and not only exist but must be perceived as existing—Likeness and unlikeness, or Sameness and difference". *CN* III 4397 ff 50–50ᵛ. C's concept of the aesthetic as the balance of "opposites" (especially of "self-possession" and "enthusiasm", and of power and play with control) is indebted to German critical think-

ing generally after Kant and particularly to Schiller's *AE*. See *CN* III 4112n. Cf ch 18, below, II 64 n 2.

[2] Sir John Davies (1570–1626) *Nosce Teipsum: Of the Soule of Man and the Immortalitie Thereof* (1599) IV sts 11–13 (var). C is quoting not from Davies directly but from his own notebook entry of 1811 (*CN* III 4112), in which he had substituted "food" for "meats" (line 4) and had virtually rewritten the third stanza, which in the original reads:

> This does she, when from things
>   particular
> She doth abstract the universall
>   kinds,
> Which bodilesse and immateriall
>   are,
> And can be lodg'd but onely in
>   our minds.

In *B Poets* II 689.

Finally, GOOD SENSE is the BODY of poetic genius, FANCY its DRAPERY, MOTION its LIFE, and IMAGINATION the SOUL that is every where, and in each; and forms all into one graceful and intelligent whole.[1]

[1] The first version of this remark (a notebook entry of 1795–6) illustrates the change that has taken place in C's critical vocabulary, including the distinction between "fancy" and "imagination": "Thought is the *body* of such an Ode, Enthusiasm is the Soul, and Imagination the Drapery!" C in this entry (*CN* I 36) is rephrasing a passage in Edward Young's "On Lyric Poetry" *Works* (1774–8) VI 133–4: ". . . thought, enthusiasm, and picture, which are as the body, soul, and robe of poetry . . .". *CN* I 36n; cf Barbara Hardy *EIC* IX (1959) 314. On "good sense" cf the letters to Thomas Curnick and Sir George Beaumont (9 Mar and 9 Jun 1814): "Poetry must be *more* than good sense, or it is not poetry; but it dare not be less, or discrepant. Good sense is not, indeed, the superstructure; but it is the rock, not only on which the edifice is raised, but likewise the rock-quarry *from* which all its stones have been, by patient toil, dug out." "The sum total of all intellectual excellence is Good Sense & Method. When these have passed into the instinctive readiness of Habit, when the Wheel revolves so rapidly that we can not see it revolve at all, then we call the combination, Genius." *CL* III 470, 504.

CHAPTER 15

The specific symptoms of poetic power elucidated in a critical analysis of Shakspeare's Venus and Adonis, and Lucrece

IN THE application of these principles to purposes of practical criticism[1] as employed in the appraisal of works more or less imperfect, I have endeavoured to discover what the qualities in a poem are, which may be deemed promises and specific symptoms of poetic power, as distinguished from general talent determined to poetic composition by accidental motives, by an act of the will, rather than by the inspiration of a genial and productive nature.[2] In this investigation, I could not, I thought, do better, than keep before me the earliest work of the greatest genius, that perhaps human nature has yet produced, our *myriad-minded** Shakspear. I mean the "Venus and Adonis," and the "Lucrece;" works which give at once strong promises of the strength, and yet obvious proofs of the immaturity, of his genius. From these I abstracted the following marks, as characteristics of original poetic genius in general.

1. In the "Venus and Adonis," the first and most obvious

* Ἀνὴρ μυριόνους, a phrase which I have borrowed from a Greek monk, who applies it to a Patriarch of Constantinople. I might have said, that I have *reclaimed,* rather than borrowed it: [3] for it seems to belong to Shakespear, de jure singulari, et ex privilegio naturæ.[4]

[1] C's phrase, given wide currency by I. A. Richards's *Practical Criticism* (1929), expresses his conviction "how little instructive any criticism can be which does not enter into minutiae". *CN* III 3970; cf 3970n.

[2] On C's distinction between "genius" and "talent" see ch 2, above, I 31, and *Friend (CC)* I 419–21.

[3] From Naucratius' eulogy of St Theodorus Studita (759–826), who was not a patriarch but abbot of Studium. C in 1801 had encountered the eulogy in *Scriptorum ecclesiasticorum historia literaria* (1688–9) I 509–13 (rev ed 1740–3, II 8–11) by the English divine William Cave (1637–1713), and had copied out a few words from it and later applied them to Shakespeare in *Friend (CC)* I 453. *CN* I 1070 and n; III 3285.

[4] "By law/right peculiar to himself, and by a special exception of nature".

19

excellence is the perfect sweetness of the versification;[1] its adaptation to the subject; and the power displayed in varying the march of the words without passing into a loftier and more majestic rhythm, than was demanded by the thoughts, or permitted by the propriety of preserving a sense of melody predominant. The delight in richness and sweetness of sound, even to a faulty excess, if it be evidently original, and not the result of an easily imitable mechanism, I regard as a highly favorable promise in the compositions of a young man. "The man that hath not music in his soul"[2] can indeed never be a genuine poet. Imagery (even taken from nature, much more when transplanted from books, as travels, voyages, and works of natural history); affecting incidents; just thoughts; interesting personal or domestic feelings; and with these the art of their combination or intertexture in the form of a poem; may all by incessant effort be acquired as a trade, by a man of talents and much reading, who, as I once before observed,[3] has mistaken an intense desire of poetic reputation for a natural poetic genius; the love of the arbitrary end for a possession of the peculiar means. But the sense of musical delight, with the power of producing it, is a gift of imagination; and this together with the power of reducing multitude into unity of effect, and modifying a series of thoughts by some one predominant thought or feeling, may be cultivated and improved, but can never be learnt. It is in these that "Poeta nascitur non fit."[4]

2. A second promise of genius is the choice of subjects very remote from the private interests and circumstances of the writer himself.[5] At least I have found, that where the subject is taken immediately from the author's personal sensations and experiences, the excellence of a particular poem is but an equivocal mark, and often a fallacious pledge, of genuine poetic power. We may perhaps

---

[1] Throughout the remainder of the chapter C draws, often almost verbatim, on a notebook entry also used for Lect 4 of 1811. *CN* III 4115 and n; *Sh C* II 87–99.

[2] Shakespeare *Merchant of Venice* v i 83: "The man that hath no music in himself".

[3] See above, I 38.

[4] The source of the proverb ("a poet is born, not made"), which had become common by the seventeenth century, is unknown, though there are possible classical antecedents, notably Florus *De qualitate vitae* frag 8: consuls and proconsuls are made "but not every year is a king or poet born" ("solum aut rex aut poeta non quotannis nascitur"). For a brief history see William S. Walsh *Handy-Book of Literary Curiosities* (Philadelphia 1893) 902–3.

[5] See above, I 44 n 1.

remember the tale of the statuary, who had acquired considerable reputation for the legs of his goddesses, though the rest of the statue accorded but indifferently with ideal beauty; till his wife elated by her husband's praises, modestly acknowledged, that she herself had been his constant model.[1] In the Venus and Adonis, this proof of poetic power exists even to excess. It is throughout as if a superior spirit more intuitive, more intimately conscious, even than the characters themselves, not only of every outward look and act, but of the flux and reflux of the mind in all its subtlest thoughts and feelings,[2] were placing the whole before our view; himself meanwhile unparticipating in the passions, and actuated only by that pleasurable excitement, which had resulted from the energetic fervor of his own spirit in so vividly exhibiting, what it had so accurately and profoundly contemplated. I think, I should have conjectured from these poems, that even then the great instinct, which impelled the poet to the drama, was secretly working in him, prompting him by a series and never broken chain of imagery, always vivid and because unbroken, often minute; by the highest effort of the picturesque in words, of which words are capable, higher perhaps than was ever realized by any other poet, even Dante not excepted; to provide a substitute for that visual language, that constant intervention and running comment by tone, look and gesture, which in his dramatic works he was entitled to expect from the players. His "Venus and Adonis" seem at once the characters themselves, and the whole representation of those characters by the most consummate actors. You seem to be *told* nothing, but to see and hear every thing.[3] Hence it is, that from

---

[1] Cf C's use of the tale in Lect 4 of 1811: *Sh C* II 92. In the lecture the sculptor was an ancient Greek.

[2] Cf *Friend* (*CC*) II 17 ("the Flux and Reflux of my Mind") and below, chs 17, 22, II 48 n 1 and 147 and n 3.

[3] C follows a common distinction in eighteenth-century criticism, especially in the Scottish critics, between mere "description", which obtrudes the poet's own personality and fails to arouse our sympathy with the subject, and actual "representation", which results from genuine sympathetic identification on the part of the poet and also elicits our own. See e.g. Lord Kames *Elements of Criticism* (Edinburgh 1762) II 149–55; Alexander Gerard *Essay on Genius* (1774) 149, 169; W. J. Bate *ELH* XII (1945) 144–64, esp 156–8. Cf Shaftesbury on "the great mimographer" Homer: "He describes no qualities or virtues . . . 'Tis the characters who show themselves". *Characteristics* ed Robertson (1900) I 129–30. Or the discussion of Homer's portrayal of character in Boswell's *Tour to the Hebrides* (21 Aug 1773): "Monboddo: 'Yet no character is described.' Johnson."

the perpetual activity of attention required on the part of the reader; from the rapid flow, the quick change, and the playful nature of the thoughts and images; and above all from the alienation, and, if I may hazard such an expression, the utter *aloofness* of the poet's own feelings, from those of which he is at once the painter and the analyst;[1] that though the very subject cannot but detract from the pleasure of a delicate mind, yet never was poem less dangerous on a moral account. Instead of doing as Ariosto, and as, still more offensively, Wieland has done,[2] instead of degrading and deforming passion into appetite, the trials of love into the struggles of concupiscence; Shakspeare has here represented the animal impulse itself, so as to preclude all sympathy with it, by dissipating the reader's notice among the thousand outward images, and now beautiful, now fanciful circumstances, which form its dresses and its scenery; or by diverting our attention from the main subject by those frequent witty or profound reflections, which the poet's ever active mind has deduced from, or connected with, the imagery and the incidents. The reader is forced into too much action to sympathize with the merely passive of our nature. As little can a mind thus roused and awakened be brooded on by mean and indistinct emotion, as the low, lazy mist can creep upon the surface of a lake, while a strong gale is driving it onward in waves and billows.

'No, they all develop themselves.' " See the discussion in this chapter of Shakespeare as "Proteus", below, ii 27–8 and n 2.

[1] C echoes a well-known review that he probably read, Schiller's "Über Bürgers Gedichte" (1791): "Selbst in Gedichten . . . hatte er damit anfangen müssen, sich selbst fremd zu werden, den Gegenstand seiner Begeisterung von seiner Individualität los zu wickeln, seine Leidenschaft aus einer mildernden Ferne anzuschauen." ("Even in poetry . . . he must have begun so as to become alienated from his own self, to disentangle the object of his enthusiasm from his own individuality, to perceive his passion from a tranquil distance.") The same review, possibly transmitted through C, could also be the source for WW's phrase "emotion recollected in tranquillity". Preface to *LB* (1800). See *AE* clxvii–clxix; *CN* i 787 and n and *CN* i App A (p 453).

[2] Lodovico Ariosto (1474–1533), whose *Orlando furioso* (1532) C at first admired, though he later came to condemn "the gross and disgusting licentiousness, the daring profaneness . . . which poisons Ariosto". *Misc C* 23. Of the style of Christoph Martin Wieland (1733–1813), the first major German translator of Shakespeare and author of the romantic epic *Oberon* (1780), C "spoke highly", said HCR 15 Nov 1810, "but was severe on the want of purity in his *Oberon*". *Misc C* 387; *CN* iii 4115 f 27n. Cf "Satyrane's Letters iii", below, ii 202–3.

3. It has been before observed,[1] that images however beautiful, though faithfully copied from nature, and as accurately represented in words, do not of themselves characterize the poet. They become proofs of original genius only as far as they are modified by a predominant passion; or by associated thoughts or images awakened by that passion;[2] or when they have the effect ✓ of reducing multitude to unity, or succession to an instant;[3] or lastly, when a human and intellectual life is transferred to them from the poet's own spirit,

> Which shoots its being through earth, sea, and air.[4]

In the two following lines for instance, there is nothing objectionable, nothing which would preclude them from forming, in their proper place, part of a descriptive poem:

> Behold yon row of pines, that shorn and bow'd
> Bend from the sea-blast, seen at twilight eve.[5]

But with the small alteration of rhythm, the same words would be equally in their place in a book of topography, or in a descriptive tour. The same image will rise into a semblance of poetry if thus conveyed:

> Yon row of bleak and visionary pines,
> By twilight-glimpse discerned, mark! how they flee
> From the fierce sea-blast, all their tresses wild
> Streaming before them.

I have given this as an illustration, by no means as an instance, of that particular excellence which I had in view, and in which Shakspeare even in his earliest, as in his latest works, surpasses all other poets. It is by this, that he still gives a dignity and a

---

[1] Above, II 20–1; cf Lect 4 of 1811: *Sh C* II 93.

[2] ". . . All Passion unifies as it were by natural Fusion". *CN* II 2012 f 41ᵛ. Cf the remarks on *Lear* and *Venus and Adonis* in *CN* III 3290 ff 14–15, and the phrasing in Lect 4 of 1811: e.g. ". . . Imagination, that capability of reducing a multitude into unity of effect, or by strong passion to modify series of thoughts into one predominant thought or feeling . . .". *Sh C* II 91.

On "fusion" see ch 14, above, II 16 and n 3.

[3] "The most general definition of beauty, therefore, is . . . Multëity in Unity." *PGC* : *BL* (1907) II 232.

[4] *France: an Ode* line 103: "And shot my being thro' earth, sea, and air." *PW* (EHC) I 247.

[5] These and the following lines are by C himself. *CN* III 3290 f 15ᵛ and n; *PW* (EHC) II 1006 (Fragment 40).

passion to the objects which he presents. Unaided by any previous excitement, they burst upon us at once in life and in power.

> Full many a glorious morning have I seen
> *Flatter* the mountain tops with sovereign eye.
> Shakspeare's Sonnet 33rd.

> Not mine own fears, nor the prophetic soul
> Of the wide world dreaming on things to come—
> * * * * * * * * * * * * * *
> * * * * * * * * * * * * * *
> The mortal moon hath her eclipse endur'd,
> And the sad augurs mock their own presage;
> Incertainties now crown themselves assur'd,
> And Peace proclaims olives of endless age.
> Now with the drops of this most balmy time
> My Love looks fresh: and D E A T H to me subscribes!
> Since spite of him, I'll live in this poor rhyme,
> While he insults o'er dull and speechless tribes.
> And thou in this shalt find thy monument,
> When tyrant's crests, and tombs of brass are spent.
> Sonnet 107.[1]

As of higher worth, so doubtless still more characteristic of poetic genius does the imagery become, when it moulds and colors itself to the circumstances, passion, or character, present and foremost in the mind. For unrivalled instances of this excellence, the reader's own memory will refer him to the L E A R, O T H E L L O, in short to which not of the *"great, ever living, dead man's"* dramatic works?[2] Inopem me copia fecit.[3] How true it is to nature, he has himself finely expressed in the instance of love in Sonnet 98.[4]

---

[1] C omits lines 3–4:
Can yet the lease of my true love control,
Suppos'd as forfeit to a confin'd doom.
In his classification of the Sonnets in *B Poets* II C placed Sonnet 107 in the "4th or highest" class for "style and thought": *CM* (*CC*) I 83, 87.

[2] C appears to be quoting from a remark he himself made in Lect 2 of 20 Nov 1811, stating, said Collier, that we should be grateful to possess the works "of Newton of Milton & of Shakspeare, the great *living dead* men of our island & that they would not now be in danger of a second

eruption of the Goths & Vandals". *Lects 1808–19* (*CC*) ms. "Ever-living", which C now adds to the original phrase, echoes the dedication of Thomas Thorpe's 1st ed of Shakespeare's *Sonnets* (1609): "Our Ever-Living Poet". Cf "Shakespere, Milton, Boyle, all the great living-dead men of our Isle." *CN* III 3270 (Feb 1808).

[3] Ovid *Metamorphoses* 3.466. Tr: "Plenty has made me poor." A favourite tag of C's; cf e.g. *CN* I 1383, III 4400.

[4] Cf *CN* III 3303, in which C connected the final line of Sonnet 98 with his love for SH.

From you have I been absent in the spring,
When proud pied April drest in all its trim
Hath put a spirit of youth in every thing;
That heavy Saturn laugh'd and leap'd with him.
Yet nor the lays of birds, nor the sweet smell
Of different flowers in odour and in hue,
Could make me any summer's story tell,
Or from their proud lap pluck them, where they grew:
Nor did I wonder at the lilies white,
Nor praise the deep vermillion in the rose;
They were, tho' sweet, but figures of delight,
Drawn after you, you pattern of all those.
Yet seem'd it winter still, and you away,
As with your shadow I with these did play!

Scarcely less sure, or if a less valuable, not less indispensable mark

Γονίμου μὲν Ποιητοῦ————
————ὅστις ῥῆμα γενναῖον λάκαι,[1]

will the imagery supply, when, with more than the power of the painter, the poet gives us the liveliest image of succession with the feeling of simultaneousness!

With this he breaketh from the sweet embrace
Of those fair arms, that held him to her heart,
And homeward through the dark lawns runs apace:
Look how a bright star shooteth from the sky!
So glides he through the night from Venus' eye.[2]

4. The last character I shall mention, which would prove indeed but little, except as taken conjointly with the former; yet without which the former could scarce exist in a high degree, and (even if this were possible) would give promises only of transitory flashes and a meteoric power; is DEPTH, and ENERGY of THOUGHT. No man was ever yet a great poet, without being at

[1] Aristophanes *Frogs* 96–7 (var). C has changed the grammar to fit his context. Tr: "of a true Poet/Creative Genius . . . such a one as utters noble words".

[2] *Venus and Adonis* lines 811–13, 815–16. In a note of 1808, used in a lecture of that year, C wrote of the last two lines: "How many Images & feelings are here brought together without effort & without discord— the beauty of Adonis—the rapidity of his flight—the yearning yet hopelessness of the enamoured gazer— and a shadowy ideal character thrown over the whole—/ or it acts by impressing the stamp of humanity, of human feeling, over inanimate Objects". *CN* III 3290.

the same time a profound philosopher.[1] For poetry is the blossom and the fragrancy of all human knowledge, human thoughts, human passions, emotions, language.[2] In Shakspeare's *poems*, the creative power, and the intellectual energy wrestle as in a war embrace. Each in its excess of strength seems to threaten the extinction of the other. At length, in the DRAMA they were reconciled, and fought each with its shield before the breast of the other. Or like two rapid streams, that at their first meeting within narrow and rocky banks mutually strive to repel each other, and intermix reluctantly and in tumult; but soon finding a wider channel and more yielding shores blend, and dilate, and flow on in one current and with one voice. The Venus and Adonis did not perhaps allow the display of the deeper passions. But the story of Lucretia seems to favor, and even demand their intensest workings. And yet we find in *Shakspeare's* management of the tale neither pathos, nor any other *dramatic* quality. There is the same minute and faithful imagery as in the former poem, in the same vivid colours, inspirited by the same impetuous vigour of thought, and diverging and contracting with the same activity of the assimilative and of the modifying faculties; and with a yet larger display, a yet wider range of knowledge and reflection; and lastly, with the same perfect dominion, often *domination*, over the whole world of language. What then shall we say? even this; that Shakspeare, no mere child of nature;[3] no automaton of genius; no passive vehicle of inspira-

---

[1] Cf C's notes of 1808: "Energy, depth, and activity of Thought without which a man may be a pleasing and affecting Poet; but never a great one." "Lastly, he [Shakespeare]—previously to his Drama—gave proof of a most profound, energetic & philosophical mind, without which he might have been a very delightful Poet, but not the great dramatic Poet". *CN* III 3247, 3290. C's letter to Sotheby 13 Jul 1802 expresses more precisely and vividly what he is saying here: ". . . A great Poet must be, implicitè if not explicitè, a profound Metaphysician. He may not have it in logical coherence, in his Brain & Tongue; but he must have it by *Tact/* for all sounds, & forms of human nature he must have the *ear* of a wild Arab listening in the silent Desert, the eye of a North American Indian tracing the footsteps of an Enemy upon the Leaves that strew the Forest—; the *Touch* of a blind man feeling the face of a darling Child . . .". *CL* II 810.

[2] C is recalling WW in the Preface to *LB* (1802): "Poetry is the breath and finer spirit of all knowledge; it is the impassioned expression which is in the countenance of all Science." *W Prose* I 141.

[3] In addition to the 1811 version of this sentence (*CN* III 4115; *Sh C* II 95), cf C's remark of 1802: "Great Injury . . . from the supposed Incompatibility of one talent with another/ Judgment with Imagination, & Taste—Good sense with strong feeling &c". *CN* I 1255. What

tion possessed by the spirit, not possessing it;[1] first studied patiently, meditated deeply, understood minutely, till knowledge become habitual and intuitive wedded itself to his habitual feelings, and at length gave birth to that stupendous power, by which he stands alone, with no equal or second in his own class; to that power, which seated him on one of the two glory-smitten summits of the poetic mountain, with Milton as his compeer not rival. While the former darts himself forth, and passes into all the forms of human character and passion, the one Proteus[2] of the fire and the flood; the other attracts all forms and things to himself, into

---

C is objecting to had become far less common in the later eighteenth century. The Scottish school in particular—e.g. Gerard *Essay on Genius* (1774)—had developed a concept of the imagination in which "judgement", far from being in opposition to imagination, was subsumed by it. See above, ɪ lxxxvi, xcvi n, c. Even the conservative Johnson would maintain: "It is ridiculous to oppose judgement to imagination; for it does not appear that men have necessarily less of one as they have more of the other." *Lives* "Roscommon" ɪ 235. Ironically C, in one of his attacks on the conception of Shakespeare as "an ignorant man, a child of nature, a wild genius, a strange medley" (Lect 5 of 2 Dec 1811: *Sh C* ɪɪ 106), attributes the notion to Johnson, whose Preface to Shakespeare is perhaps the supreme tribute to the cleansing sanity and insight of Shakespeare as an objective poet of life.

[1] Cf above, on RS, ch 3, ɪ 66.

[2] Proteus, the sea god who could turn himself into any shape. C and to an even greater extent Hazlitt and Keats, in their approach to Shakespeare, continue, indeed bring to a culmination, one of the major interests of eighteenth-century English and Scottish criticism, especially after 1750: the concept of the "sympathetic imagination"—the ability to enter imaginatively into what we contemplate, to identify with it, to acquire a shared realisation of its character and experience; and along with this a conception of Shakespeare as the greatest literary prototype of this power of the imagination, who, as Hazlitt said, "had only to think of a thing to become that thing, with all the circumstances belonging to it". The modern theory of *Einfühlung* (empathy) is one development of this concept. See ɪɪ 21 n 3, above, and Engell *CI* 8, 153–60, 213, 356. Cf C's letter to Sotheby 13 Jul 1802: "It is easy to cloathe Imaginary Beings with our own Thoughts & Feelings; but to send ourselves out of ourselves, to *think* ourselves in to the Thoughts and Feelings of Beings in circumstances wholly & strangely different from our own/ hoc labor, hoc opus/ and who has atchieved it? Perhaps only Shakespere." *CL* ɪɪ 810. C's first use in a notebook of Proteus as a symbol for Shakespeare was in Nov 1804: ". . . the *imitation* instead of *copy* which is illustrated in very nature *shakespearianized/*— that Proteus Essence that could assume the very form, but yet known & felt not to be the Thing by that difference of the Substance which made every atom of the Form another thing/—that likeness not identity—an exact web, every line of direction miraculously the same, but the one worsted, the other silk". *CN* ɪɪ 2274; cf ɪɪɪ 3247 and n and Lect 3 of 1811: *Sh C* ɪɪ 81.

the unity of his own IDEAL. All things and modes of action shape
themselves anew in the being of MILTON; while SHAKSPEARE
becomes all things, yet for ever remaining himself. O what great
men hast thou not produced, England! my country! truly indeed—

> Must *we* be free or die, who speak the tongue,
> Which SHAKSPEARE spake; the faith and morals hold,
> Which MILTON held. In every thing we are sprung
> Of earth's first blood, have titles manifold!
>
> WORDSWORTH[1]

[1] Sonnets Dedicated to Liberty pt I no XVI lines 11–14 (var).

CHAPTER 16

Striking points of difference between the Poets of the present age and those of the 15th and 16th centuries—Wish expressed for the union of the characteristic merits of both

CHRISTENDOM, from its first settlement on feudal rights, has been so far one great body, however imperfectly organized, that a similar spirit will be found in each period to have been acting in all its members. The study of Shakspeare's *poems* (I do not include his dramatic works, eminently as they too deserve that title) led me to a more careful examination of the contemporary poets both in this and in other countries. But my attention was especially fixed on those of Italy, from the birth to the death of Shakspeare; that being the country in which the fine arts had been most sedulously, and hitherto most successfully cultivated.[1] Abstracted from the degrees and peculiarities of individual genius, the properties common to the good writers of each period seem to establish one striking point of difference between the poetry of the fifteenth and sixteenth centuries, and that of the present age. The remark may perhaps be extended to the sister art of painting. At least the latter will serve to illustrate the former. In the present age the poet (I would wish to be understood as speaking generally, and without allusion to individual names) seems to propose to himself as his main object, and as that which is the most characteristic of his art, new and striking IMAGES; with INCIDENTS that interest the affections or excite the curiosity. Both his characters and his descriptions he renders, as much as possible, specific and individual, even to a degree of portraiture. In his diction and metre, on the other hand, he is comparatively careless. The measure is either constructed on no previous system, and acknowledges no justifying principle but that of the writer's convenience; or else

---

[1] C began studying Italian when he left for Malta in Apr 1804 (*CN* II 2133–2136 and nn). By the following Oct he was becoming pro- ficient in it and had started a close study of Italian metres and versification. On his knowledge of Italian, see *CN* II App A.

29

some mechanical movement is adopted, of which one couplet or stanza is so far an adequate specimen, as that the occasional differences appear evidently to arise from accident, or the qualities of the language itself, not from meditation and an intelligent purpose. And the language from "Pope's translation of Homer," to "Darwin's Temple of Nature," may, notwithstanding some illustrious exceptions, be too faithfully characterized, as claiming to be poetical for no better reason, than that it would be intolerable in conversation or in prose.[1] Though alas! even our prose writings, nay even the stile of our more set discourses, strive to be in the fashion, and trick themselves out in the soiled and over-worn finery of the meretricious muse. It is true, that of late a great improvement in this respect is observable in our most popular writers. But it is equally true, that this recurrence to plain sense, and genuine mother English, is far from being general; and that the composition of our novels, magazines, public harangues, &c. is commonly as trivial in thought, and yet enigmatic in expression, as if E C H O and S P H I N X had laid their heads together to construct it. Nay, even of those who have most rescued themselves from this contagion, I should plead inwardly guilty to the charge of duplicity or cowardice, if I withheld my conviction, that few have guarded the purity of their native tongue with that jealous care, which the sublime Dante in his tract "De la nobile volgare eloquenza," declares to be the first duty of a poet.[2] For language is the armoury

---

[1] I.e. from 1715 to 1803, or roughly the eighteenth century. On Pope and Darwin, see above, ch 1, I 18–20; cf *CN* II 2826.

[2] C was using a Latin–Italian version of *De vulgari eloquentia* in Dante Alighieri *Opere* (5 vols Venice 1793) v. *CN* II 3011n. No particular passage provides the remark C mentions, though the general sentiment is implied, as SC notes, in bk II ch 4, a passage C copied into a notebook and then onto a front flyleaf of RS *Joan of Arc* (1796), which he annotated in the summer of 1814. *BL* (1847) II 31n. Closer is a passage from bk II ch 7: "Consider then, Reader, how much it behoves thee to use the sieve in selecting noble words: for if thou hast regard to the Illustrious Vulgar Tongue, which . . . Poets ought to use when writing in the tragic style in the vernacular (and these are the persons to whom we intend to give information), thou wilt take care that the noblest words alone are in thy sieve." Tr A. G. Ferrers Howell (1890). In a note on p 11 of his copy of *Joan,* C made a similar remark to the one in *BL,* criticising RS's "anguish'd shriek": "Not English. . . . To guard with jealous Care the purity of his native Tongue the sublime Dante declares to be the first Duty of a Poet. It is this conviction more than any other which actuates my severity toward Southey, W. Scott &c—all miserable offenders!—" *CM* (*CC*) IV. For another reference to the Dante work see ch 17, below, II 56 and n 1.

of the human mind; and at once contains the trophies of its past, and the weapons of its future conquests. "Animadverte, quam sit ab improprietate verborum pronum hominibus prolabi in errores circa res!" HOBBES: *Exam. et Emend. hod. Math.*[1]—"Sat vero, in hâc vitæ brevitate et naturæ obscuritate, rerum est, quibus cognoscendis tempus impendatur, ut confusis et multivocis sermonibus intelligendis illud consumere non opus est. Eheu! quantas strages paravere verba nubila, quæ tot dicunt, ut nihil dicunt— nubes potius, e quibus et in rebus politicis et in ecclesiâ turbines et tonitrua erumpunt! Et proinde recte dictum putamus a Platone in Gorgia: ὃς ἂν τὰ ὀνόματα εἰδει, ἴσεται καὶ τὰ πράγματα: et ab Epicteto, ἀρχὴ παιδεύσεως ἡ τῶν ὀνομάτων ἐπίσκεψις: et prudentissime Galenus scribit, ἡ τῶν ὀνομάτων χρῆσις παραχθεῖσα καὶ τὴν τῶν πραγμάτων ἐπιταράττει γνῶσιν, Egregie vero J. C. Scaliger, in Lib. I. de Plantis: Est *primum*, inquit, *sapientis officium, bene sentire, ut sibi vivat: proximum, bene loqui, ut patriæ vivat.*" SENNERTUS *de Puls: Differentiâ*.[2]

---

[1] *Examinatio et emendatio mathematicae hodiernae* (C's ed 1668) Dialogue II (var): *Opera Philosophica* ed Sir W. Molesworth (1839–45) IV 83: "Notice how easily men slip from improper use of words into errors about things themselves." A favourite maxim of C's, he copied it into a notebook early in 1801, used it as a "text" for "a sort of sermon" in the third of the four "philosophical letters" he wrote to Josiah Wedgwood (Feb 1801), and had more recently resurrected it as one of the mottoes for Essay III in *PGC* (1814). *CN* I 911 and n; *CL* II 691; *BL* (1907) II 228.

[2] C is quoting (var, with omissions and an inserted sentence) from the German physician and philosopher, Daniel Sennert (1572–1637), *De chymicorum cum Aristotelicis et Galenicis consensu ac dissensu* ch 5: *Opera* (Lyons 1666) I 193. "There are certainly plenty of things in this short life and dark world which are worth time to study, so that we need not spend time in trying to understand [confused and ambiguous] words. [Alas, what great calamities

have misty words produced, that say so much that they say nothing— clouds, rather, from which hurricanes burst, both in church and state.] I think that what Plato has said in the Gorgias is indeed true: 'Anyone who knows words will know things too'; and as Epictetus [1.17.12] says, 'the study of words is the beginning of education'; and Galen wrote most wisely [in *De simplicium medicamentorum facultatibus* ch 12] 'Confusion in our use of words makes confusion in our knowledge of things.' J. C. Scaliger has indeed said excellently, in Book I of his *Plants:* 'A wise man's first duty is to think well so that he can live for himself; the next is to speak well so that he can live for his country.'" Tr adapted from G. Watson, who points out that the quotation from Plato is not from *Gorgias* but from *Cratylus* 436A. *BL* (1975) 182–3 (though *Cratylus* 435D is closer), whereas SC notes that the second sentence ("Eheu! quantas strages . . ."; enclosed in brackets in the translation above) is not in the original but is probably

Something analogous to the materials and structure of modern poetry[1] I seem to have noticed (but here I beg to be understood as speaking with the utmost diffidence) in our common landscape painters. Their foregrounds and intermediate distances are comparatively unattractive: while the main interest of the landscape is thrown into the back ground, where mountains and torrents and castles forbid the eye to proceed, and nothing tempts it to trace its way back again. But in the works of the great Italian and Flemish masters, the front and middle objects of the landscape are the most obvious and determinate, the interest gradually dies away in the back ground, and the charm and peculiar worth of the picture consists, not so much in the specific objects which it conveys to the understanding in a visual language formed by the substitution of figures for words, as in the beauty and harmony of the colours, lines and expression, with which the objects are represented. Hence novelty of subject was rather avoided than sought for. Superior excellence in the manner of treating the same subjects was the trial and test of the artist's merit.

C's own interpolation. *BL* (1847) II 32n. The puzzling three final words (*de Puls: Differentiâ*) would indicate that the whole passage is from a work by Sennertus with that title. But actually *De pulsuum differentiis* is a work by Galen (129–c 199). A notebook entry of 1801/2 (*CN* I 1000C) records the passage from Sennertus to the end of the remark cited from Galen. Then (still quoting Sennertus, who in turn is quoting Galen) a second paragraph in the notebook entry begins: "Et de Puls. differet c.6. Si nomina propria suppetant . . ." ("If special terms are at hand . . ."), citing a short passage from Bk III ch 6 of *De puls. diff*. After this the passage from Sennertus continues with the quotation from Scaliger. In writing *PGC* years later (1814), and looking for a motto for Essay III, C copied out the passage as it appears above, mistakenly attributing it there to "Sennertus *de Puls. Different*."; in inserting it now in *BL,* he takes it directly from *PGC*. For C's interest in Sennertus 1799–1801, cf *CL* I 531, II 683–4. (Two grammatical errors in the Greek, and the nonsensical παραχθεῖσα [for ταραχθεῖσα] were taken by C from Sennertus and copied again from the notebook without correction.)

[1] C throughout the following two paragraphs and in part of the attached footnote is incorporating and expanding a notebook entry he had written (c May–Aug 1805) on "what appears to me a striking point of difference between the Poetry of the 15 and 16 Centuries, and that of the present Day". *CN* II 2599 and n. From the present account he omits references to three contemporaries, Sir Walter Scott ("careless . . . in his diction and metre"), Matthew Gregory Lewis (1775–1818), and Thomas Campbell (1777–1844) (who adopt "some mechanical measure . . . with a language which claims to be poetical for no better reason, than that it would be intolerable in conversation or prose").

Not otherwise is it with the more polished poets of the 15th and 16th century, especially with those of Italy. The imagery is almost always general: sun, moon, flowers, breezes, murmuring streams, warbling songsters, delicious shades, lovely damsels, cruel as fair, nymphs, naiads, and goddesses, are the materials which are common to all, and which each shaped and arranged according to his judgement or fancy, little solicitous to add or to particularize. If we make an honorable exception in favor of some English poets, the thoughts too are as little novel as the images; and the fable of their narrative poems, for the most part drawn from mythology, or sources of equal notoriety, derive their chief attractions from the manner of treating them; from impassioned flow, or picturesque arrangement. In opposition to the present age, and perhaps in as faulty an extreme, they placed the essence of poetry in the *art*. The excellence, at which they aimed, consisted in the exquisite polish of the diction, combined with perfect simplicity. This their prime object, they attained by the avoidance of every word, which a *gentleman* would *not* use in dignified conversation, and of every word and phrase, which none but a *learned* man *would* use; by the studied position of words and phrases, so that not only each part should be melodious in itself, but contribute to the harmony of the whole, each note referring and conducing to the melody of all the foregoing and following words of the same period or stanza; and lastly with equal labour, the greater because unbetrayed, by the variation and various harmonies of their metrical movement. Their measures, however, were not indebted for their variety to the introduction of new metres, such as have been attempted of late in the "Alonzo and Imogen," and others borrowed from the German, having in their very mechanism a specific overpowering tune,[1] to which the generous reader humours his voice and empha-

[1] *Alonzo the Brave and Fair Imogine,* a ballad by M. G. Lewis in his novel *The Monk* ch 9 (1796), which C reviewed in *C Rev* XIX (1797) 194–200. *CN* I 1128 and n. By "borrowed from the German" C is probably referring less to the stanza than to the metre (amphibrachs or quasi-anapests), both of which are conventional in eighteenth-century English ballads. The galloping rhythm could be exemplified by the following stanza (lines 42–6):

His vizor was closed, and gigantic his height;
His armour was sable to view:
All pleasure and laughter were hushed at his sight;
The dogs as they eyed him drew back in affright;
The lights in the chamber burned blue!

sis, with more indulgence to the author than attention to the meaning or quantity of the words; but which, to an ear familiar with the *numerous*[1] sounds of the Greek and Roman poets, has an effect not unlike that of galloping over a paved road in a German stage-waggon without springs. On the contrary, our elder bards both of Italy and England produced a far greater, as well as more charming variety by countless modifications, and subtle balances of sound in the common metres of their country. A lasting and enviable reputation awaits that man of genius, who should attempt and realize a union. Who should recall the high finish; the appropriateness; the facility; the delicate proportion; and above all, the perfusive and omnipresent grace; which have preserved, as in a shrine of precious amber, the "Sparrow" of Catullus, the "Swallow," the "Grasshopper," and all the other little loves of Anacreon:[2] and which with bright, though diminished glories, revisited the youth and early manhood of christian Europe, in the vales of * Arno, and the groves of Isis and of Cam; and who with

---

* These thoughts were suggested to me during the perusal of the Madrigals of G I O V A M B A T I S T A S T R O Z Z I published in Florence (nella Stamperia del Sermartelli) 1st May 1593, by his sons Lorenzo and Filippo Strozzi, with a dedication to their deceased paternal uncle, "Signor Leone Strozzi, Generale delle battaglie di Santa Chiesa."[3] As I do not remember to have seen either the poems or their author mentioned in any English work, or have found them in any of the common collections of Italian poetry; and as the little work is of rare occurrence; I will transcribe a few specimens. I have seldom met with compositions that possessed, to my feelings, more of that satisfying *entireness*, that complete adequateness of the manner to the matter which so charms us in Anacreon, join'd with the tenderness, and more than the *delicacy* of Catullus. Trifles as they are, they were probably elaborated with great care; yet in the perusal we refer them to a spontaneous energy rather than to voluntary effort. To a cultivated taste there is a delight

---

[1] From "numbers", in the sense of measure, rhythm, harmony. E.g., *Paradise Lost* v 149–50: ". . . prompt eloquence | Flowed from their lips, in prose or numerous verse".

[2] *Anacreon Odes* (or *Anacreontea*) 12 (10), 13 (11), and 33 (25) for the dove, and 43 (34) for the grasshopper. C had these in an English translation by F. Fawkes in *B Poets* XIII, three copies of which work he annotated (though not these poems in vol XIII). In 1808 C had thought

of acquiring the Bodoni edition of *Anacreon Odes,* in Greek and Latin (Parma 1791): *CN* III 3276 f 72ᵛ and n. Of the genuine poems of Anacreon little has survived, but these later imitations had enormous influence on modern poetry.

[3] Giovanni Battista Strozzi the Elder (1504–71), a member of the famous Florentine family, several of whom wrote poetry. A reprint of this extremely rare volume is available in *Bibliotheca Romana* Nos 78–9 (Strasburg 1909).

these should combine the keener interest, deeper pathos, manlier
reflection, and the fresher and more various imagery, which give

---

in *perfection* for its own sake, independent of the material in which it is
manifested, that none but a cultivated taste can understand or appreciate.

After what I have advanced, it would appear presumption to offer a
translation; even if the attempt were not discouraged by the different genius
of the English mind and language, which demands a denser body of thought
as the condition of a high polish, than the Italian. I cannot but deem it
likewise an advantage in the Italian tongue, in many other respects inferior
to our own, that the language of poetry is more distinct from that of prose
than with us. From the earlier appearance and established primacy of the
Tuscan poets, concurring with the number of independent states, and the diversity of written dialects, the Italians have gained a poetic idiom, as the
Greeks before them had obtained from the same causes, with greater and
more various discriminations—ex. gr. the ionic for their heroic verses; the
attic for their iambic; and the two modes of the doric, the lyric or sacerdotal,
and the pastoral, the distinctions of which were doubtless more obvious to
the Greeks themselves than they are to us.

I will venture to add one other observation before I proceed to the
transcription. I am aware, that the sentiments which I have avowed concerning the points of difference between the poetry of the present age, and that of
the period between 1500 and 1650, are the reverse of the opinion commonly
entertained. I was conversing on this subject with a friend, when the servant,
a worthy and sensible woman, coming in, I placed before her two engravings,
the one a pinky-coloured plate of the day, the other a masterly etching by
Salvator Rosa,[1] from one of his own pictures. On pressing her to tell us,
which she preferred, after a little blushing and flutter of feeling, she replied—
why, that, Sir! to be sure! (pointing to the *ware* from the Fleet-street print
shops) It's so *neat* and elegant. T'other is such a *scratchy* slovenly thing." An
artist, whose writings are scarcely less valuable than his works, and to whose
authority more deference will be willingly paid, than I could even wish,
should be shewn to mine, has told us, and from his own experience too, that
good taste must be *acquired*, and like all other good things, is the result of
thought, and the submissive study of the best models.[2] If it be asked, "But

---

[1] Salvator Rosa (1615–73), whose
romantic landscapes, with their
abrupt, rugged forms, had become
especially popular in late eighteenth-
century England as the prototype of
the "picturesque". Cf Uvedale Price
Essay on the Picturesque (1794) 72.
Cf "a grand S. Rosa-Eye" applied
to a drawing of Sir George Beaumont in *CN* II 1899 § 23. For verses
of Rosa's see ch 9, above.

[2] Sir Joshua Reynolds (1723–92),
in his second Discourse (1769): On
whom can the young artist "rely, or
who shall show him the path that
leads to excellence? The answer is
obvious: those great masters who
have travelled the same road with
success . . . The works of those
who have stood the test of ages have
a claim to that respect and venera-
tion to which no modern can pretend. . . . By close inspection, and
minute examination, you will discover, at last, the manner of han-
dling, the artifices of contrast, glaz-
ing, and other expedients . . . With
respect to the pictures that you are to
choose for your models, I could wish
that you would take the world's
opinion rather than your own. In
other words, I would have you

Chapter 16

a value and a name that will not pass away to the poets who have done honor to our own times, and to those of our immediate predecessors.

what shall I deem such?" the answer is; *presume* these to be the best, the *reputation* of which has been matured into *fame* by the consent of ages.[1] For wisdom always has a final majority, if not by conviction, yet by acquiescence. In addition to Sir J. Reynolds I may mention Harris of Salisbury, who in one of his philosophical disquisitions has written on the means of acquiring a just taste with the precision of Aristotle, and the elegance of Quintillian.[2]

MADRIGALE.[3]
Gelido suo ruscel chiaro, e tranquillo
M'insegnò Amor, di state a mezzo'l giorno:

choose those of established reputation . . . If you should not admire them at first, you will, by endeavouring to imitate them, find that the world has not been mistaken. Could we teach taste or genius by rules, they would be no longer taste and genius. But though there neither are, nor can be, any precise invariable rules for the exercise, or the acquisition, of these great qualities, yet we may truly say that they always operate in proportion to our attention in observing the works of nature, to our skill in selecting, and to our care in digesting, methodizing, and comparing our observations." *Discourses* ed Robert R. Wark (San Marino, Cal 1959) 28, 29, 32, 44.

Cf the Advertisement to *LB* (1798): "An accurate taste in poetry, and in all the other arts, Sir Joshua Reynolds has observed, is an acquired talent, which can only be produced by severe thought, and a long continued intercourse with the best models of composition." *W Prose* I 116. C's contribution to the Advertisement? Cf Preface to *LB* (1800): *W Prose* I 156.

[1] On fame vs reputation see ch 2, above, I 33 and n 4.

[2] James Harris (1709–80), born in Salisbury, nephew of the famous Earl of Shaftesbury, and author of *Three Treatises* ["Art", "Music,

Painting, and Poetry", "Happiness"] (1744) and *Hermes, or a Philosophical Inquiry into Universal Grammar* (1751). C, as *BL* (1847) II 37n suggests, is doubtless thinking of the close of *Philological Inquiries* pt II ch 12 in *Works* ed Earl of Malmesbury (1801) II 411–12: ". . . If, while we peruse some Author of high rank, we perceive we don't instantly relish him, let us not be disheartened—let us even FEIGN *a Relish, till we find a Relish come.* A *morsel* perhaps pleases us— Let us cherish it . . . and steadily persevere . . . what began in FICTION, terminates in REALITY. . . . By only seeking and perusing what is *truly* excellent, and by contemplating always *this* and *this alone,* the Mind insensibly *becomes accustomed to it* . . . IF WE CHUSE THE BEST LIFE, USE WILL MAKE IT PLEASANT." The final sentence is an adage of Pythagoras frequently quoted in English religious and moral writing (e.g. Bacon, Jeremy Taylor, John Tillotson). Cf André Dacier *Life of Pythagoras* (1707) 64. (Harris cites Plutarch *Moralia:* "De exilio" 602c.) In using it in this context Harris is partly echoing Addison in *Spectator* No 447. On Harris see *CN* III 4397n.

[3] C here selects nine of the twenty-seven madrigals he had tran-

Ardean le selve, ardean le piagge, e i colli.
Ond 'io, ch' al più gran gielo ardo e sfavillo,
Subito corsi; ma sì puro adorno
Girsene il vidi, che turbar no'l volli:

scribed in *CN* II 2599 (see above, II 32 n 1) partly to exemplify his point about the distinction between Renaissance and "modern" poetic style but also "as mementoes to myself, if ever I should once more be happy enough to resume poetic composition". Tr Beatrice Corrigan in CN II 2599n: (1) "Love showed me his chill stream, clear and tranquil, in summertime at noonday; the woods were burning, the slopes, the hills bere burning. So I, who in the coldest frost burn and sparkle, at once hastened to it; but I saw it flowing on so pure and fair that I did not wish to sully it; I only mirrored myself within it, and on its sweet and shady bank I rested, intent upon the murmuring of its wave." (2) "Breezes, gentle comfort of my tormented life, and so sweet that no longer does burning or death seem grievous to me, but rather desire alone; pray, drive far away the ice, the clouds, the evil weather, now that the clear wave and the shade, no less dear, entice Festivity and Merriment to sport and sing through their groves and meadows." (3) "Oh breezes, peaceful, yet often at amorous war with the flowers and grass, advance softly your green standards of the lily and the rose against the immature season; so that I may find truce or rest, if not peace: and I know well where. Oh charming mild glance, oh ambrosian lips, oh gay laughter!" (4) "Now she stands fixed like a Rock, now like a River she glides away, now she roars like a savage Bear, now sings like a pitying Angel; but into what does she not transform herself? And into what does she not transform me, Stones or Streams, wild beasts or Gods, this my fair— I know not whether Nymph or En-chantress, whether Lady or Goddess, whether sweet or pitiless?" (5) "Weeping you kissed me, and laughing you refused; in grief I found you pitiful, in pleasure I found you cruel; joy was born of weeping, suffering from laughter. Oh wretched lovers, may you always find together Fear and Hope." (6) "Fair flower, you recall to me the dewy cheek of that fair face, and so truly do you resemble it that often I gaze upon you as though upon her: and, blind though I am, contemplate now her charming laugh, now her calm glance. But how lightly, oh Rose, does the morning flee? And who dissolves you like snow, and with you my heart and my very life?" (7) "My Anna, sweet Anna, oh cadence ever fresh and ever brighter, what sweetness do I feel only in saying Anna? [The original has "Filli" instead of "Anna".] I endeavour indeed, but neither here among us nor in the heavens can I find any harmony which is sweeter than her fair name: Heaven, Love, the Echo of my Heart, plays no other tune." (8) "Now that the mead and wood grow dim, beneath your shadowy calm sky move forth, lofty Repose! Ah let me rest one single night, one hour! The wild beasts, the birds, every living thing has sometimes some peace, but I, alas, when do I not wander on, nor weep, nor cry out? and indeed how loudly? But since he does not hear, hear me thou, oh Death." (9) "I laughed and wept with Love, yet never did I write except in flame, in water, or in wind; often I found cruel mercy; ever dead to myself, I lived in another; now I rose from the darkest Abyss to Heaven, now I fell down from it again; wearied at last, here have I made my close."

Sol mi specchiava, e'n dolce ombrosa sponda
Mi stava intento al mormorar dell' onda.

MADRIGALE.

Aure dell' angoscioso viver mio
Refrigerio soave,
E dolce sì, che più non mi par grave
Ne'l arder, ne'l morir, anz' il desio;
Deh voi'l ghiaccio, e le nubi, e'l tempo rio
Discacciatene omai, che l'onda chiara,
E l' ombra non men cara
A scherzare, e cantar per suoi boschetti
E prati Festa ed Allegrezza alletti.

MADRIGALE.

Pacifiche, ma spesso in amorosa
Guerra co'fiori, el' erba
Alla stagione acerba
Verde Insegne del giglio e della rosa
Movete, Aure, pian pian; che tregua o posa,
Se non pace, io ritrove:
E so ben dove—Oh vago, et mansueto
Sguardo, oh labbra d'ambrosia, ah rider lieto!

MADRIGALE.

Hor come un Scoglio stassi,
Hor come un Rio se'n fugge,
Ed hor crud' Orsa rugge,
Hor canta Angelo pio: ma che non fassi?
E che non fammi, O Sassi,
O Rivi, o belve, a Dii, questa mia vaga
Non so, se Ninfa, o Maga,
Non so, se Donna, o Dea,
Non so, se dolce ó rea?

MADRIGALE.

Piangendo mi baciaste,
E ridendo il negaste:
In doglia hebbivi pia,
In festa hebbivi ria:
Nacque Gioia di pianti,
Dolor di riso: O amanti
Miseri, habbiate insieme
Ognor Paura e Speme.

MADRIGALE.

Bel Fior, tu mi rimembri
La rugiadosa guancia del bel viso;
E sì vera l'assembri,
Che'n te sovente, come in lei m'affiso:
Ed hod dell vago riso,
Hor dell sereno sguardo
Io pur cieco risguardo. Ma qual fugge.
O Rosa, il mattin lieve?

E chi te, come neve,
E'l mio cor teco, e la mia vita strugge.

MADRIGALE.

ANNA mia, ANNA dolce, oh sempre nuovo
E più chiaro concento,
Quanta dolcezza sento
In sol ANNA dicendo? Io mi pur pruovo,
Nè quì tra noi ritruovo,
Nè tra cieli armonia,
Che del bel nome suo più dolce sia:
Altro il Cielo, altro Amore,
Altro non suona l'Eco del mio core.

MADRIGALE.

Hor che'l prato, a la selva si scolora,
Al tuo Sereno ombroso
Muovine, alto Riposo!
Deh ch 'io riposi una sol notte, un hora!
Han le fere, e gli augelli, ognun talora
Ha qualche pace; io quando,
Lasso! non vonne errando,
E non piango, e non grido? e qual pur forte?
Mo poiché non sent' egli, odine Morte!

MADRIGALE.

Risi e piansi d'Amor; ne peró mai
Se non in fiamma, ò 'n onda, ò 'n vento scrissi;
Spesso mercè trovai.
Crudel; sempre in me morto, in altri vissi!
Hor da' più scuri abyssi al Ciel m'alzai,
Hor ne pur caddi giuso:
Stanco al fin qui son chiuso!

CHAPTER 17

Examination of the tenets peculiar to Mr. Wordsworth—Rustic life (above all, low and rustic life) especially unfavorable to the formation of a human diction—The best parts of language the product of philosophers, not clowns or shepherds—Poetry essentially ideal and generic— The language of Milton as much the language of real life, yea, incomparably more so than that of the cottager

AS FAR then as Mr. Wordsworth in his preface contended, and most ably contended, for a reformation in our poetic diction, as far as he has evinced the truth of passion, and the *dramatic* propriety of those figures and metaphors in the original poets, which stript of their justifying reasons, and converted into mere artifices of connection or ornament, constitute the characteristic falsity in the poetic style of the moderns;[1] and as far as he has,

[1] In the Appendix added in 1802 to the Preface to *LB* (reprinted in *Poems* 1815 vol II): "The earliest poets of all nations generally wrote from passion excited by real events . . . feeling powerfully as they did, their language was daring, and figurative. In succeeding times, Poets . . . perceiving the influence of such language, and desirous of producing the same effect without being animated by the same passion, set themselves to a mechanical adoption of these figures of speech, and made use of them, sometimes with propriety, but much more frequently applied them to feelings and thoughts with which they had no natural connection whatsoever. A language was thus insensibly produced, differing materially from the real language of men in *any situation*." *W Prose* I 160. Cf C's note of 1805: "A man's Imagination fitfully awaking & sleeping = the odd metaphors & no metaphors of modern

poetry/ Language in its first state without the *inventive* passion." *CN* II 2723. What WW and to a less extent C are saying had become increasingly common in eighteenth-century criticism between Thomas Blackwell's *Enquiry into the Life and Writings of Homer* (1735), which Gibbon praised as "an effort of genius", and William Duff's *Essay on Original Genius* (1767), the last chapter of which is entitled "That Original Poetic Genius Will in general Be Displayed in Its Ultimate Vigour in the Early . . . Periods of Society". See Bate *BP* chs 2–3 passim. Even Johnson, despite his own use of stylised neoclassic diction, would have agreed theoretically. Cf the remark in *Rasselas* (1759) ch 10: "Whatever be the reason, it is commonly observed that the early writers are in possession of nature, and their followers of art: that the first excel in strength and invention, and the latter in elegance

In this volume, my dear Derwent, I have
compressed all I know of the principles of a sober
yet not ungenial Criticism; and most anxiously have
I avoided all mere assertions. All opinions not
followed or preceded by the reasons, on which it has
been grounded. Of one thing I am distinctly conscious
viz. that my main motive and continued impulse
was to secure, as far as in me lay, an intelligent
admiration to Mr Wordsworth's Poems. and while
I frankly avowed what I deemed defects, and why I
deemed them so, yet to evince how very trifling they

Biographia Literaria.

were not only in importance but even in the
proportional space occupied by them; and lastly

BY

S. T. COLERIDGE, Esq.

to satisfy at once a favorite wish as well as favorite
conviction of my own, which I cannot better
express than by adopting the following stanza of
old Gascoigne, in application to Wordsworth's Genius.

Lo! as a Hawk that soareth tow'rd the skies
And climbs aloft for solace of his wing,
The greater gate she getteth up on high,
The truer Stoupe she makes at any thing.

If in so doing I have offended where I shall most
wish and did most expect to please, it is but one
of many proofs that I have been too apt to judge
of the feelings of others by my own.— S. T. C.

1. Note by Coleridge to his son Derwent inscribed on the half-title of
a copy of *Biographia* Volume II. See p 98 n1
Collection the late N. F. D. Coleridge; reproduced by kind permission

with equal acuteness and clearness, pointed out the process in which this change was effected, and the resemblances between that state into which the reader's mind is thrown by the pleasureable confusion of thought from an unaccustomed train of words and images; and that state which is induced by the natural language of empassioned feeling;[1] he undertook a useful task, and deserves all praise, both for the attempt and for the execution. The provocations to this remonstrance in behalf of truth and nature were still of perpetual recurrence before and after the publication of this preface. I cannot likewise but add, that the comparison of such poems of merit, as have been given to the public within the last ten or twelve years, with the majority of those produced previously to the appearance of that preface, leave no doubt on my mind, that Mr. Wordsworth is fully justified in believing his efforts to have been by no means ineffectual. Not only in the verses of those who have professed their admiration of his genius, but even of those who have distinguished themselves by hostility to his theory, and depreciation of his writings, are the impressions of his principles plainly visible. It is possible, that with these principles

---

and refinement"; and his praise of the "natural" language of Shakespeare: ". . . the dialogue of this author . . . is pursued with so much ease and simplicity, that it seems scarcely to claim the merit of fiction . . ."; "his scenes are occupied only by men, who act and speak as the reader thinks that he should himself have spoken or acted . . . Even where the agency is supernatural the dialogue is level with life"; "this style is probably to be sought in the common intercourse of life . . . above grossness and below refinement, where propriety resides". Preface to Shakespeare: *Works* VIII 63–4, 70.

[1] Also in the 1802 Appendix to the Preface to *LB:* "The Reader or Hearer of this distorted language [used by later poets] found himself in a perturbed and unusual state of mind: when affected by the genuine language of passion he had been in a perturbed and unusual state of mind also: in both cases he was willing that his common judgment and understanding should be laid asleep . . . The emotion was in both cases delightful, and no wonder if he confounded the one with the other, and believed them both to be produced by the same, or similar causes. . . . Thus, and from a variety of other causes, this distorted language was received with admiration; and Poets . . . carried the abuse still further, and introduced phrases composed apparently in the spirit of the original figurative language of passion, yet altogether of their own invention . . . [constructing] a phraseology which had one thing, it is true, in common with the genuine language of poetry, namely, that it was not heard in ordinary conversation; that it was unusual." *W Prose* I 160–1. WW is reiterating one of Johnson's arguments about "poetic" language. Cf *Lives* III 341.

others may have been blended, which are not equally evident; and some which are unsteady and subvertible from the narrowness or imperfection of their basis. But it is more than possible, that these errors of defect or exaggeration, by kindling and feeding the controversy, may have conduced not only to the wider propagation of the accompanying truth, but that by their frequent presentation to the mind in an excited state, they may have won for them a more permanent and practical result. A man will borrow a part from his opponent the more easily, if he feels himself justified in continuing to reject a part. While there remain important points in which he can still feel himself in the right, in which he still finds firm footing for continued resistance, he will gradually adopt those opinions, which were the least remote from his own convictions, as not less congruous with his own theory, than with that which he reprobates. In like manner with a kind of instinctive prudence, he will abandon by little and little his weakest posts, till at length he seems to forget that they had ever belonged to him, or affects to consider them at most as accidental and "petty annexments,"[1] the removal of which leaves the citadel unhurt and unendangered.

My own differences from certain supposed parts of Mr. Wordsworth's theory ground themselves on the assumption, that his words had been rightly interpreted, as purporting that the proper diction for poetry in general consists altogether in a language taken, with due exceptions, from the mouths of men in real life, a language which actually constitutes the natural conversation of men under the influence of natural feelings. My objection is, first, that in *any* sense this rule is applicable only to *certain* classes of poetry; secondly, that even to these classes it is not applicable, except in such a sense, as hath never by any one (as far as I know or have read) been denied or doubted; and lastly, that as far as, and in that degree in which it is *practicable*, yet as a *rule* it is useless, if not injurious, and therefore either need not, or ought not to be practised. The poet informs his reader, that he had generally chosen *low and rustic* life;[2] but not *as* low and rustic, or in order to repeat that pleasure of doubtful moral effect, which persons of

---

[1] Cf *Hamlet* iii iii 21–2: "Each small annexment, petty consequence, | Attends the boist'rous ruin".

[2] "Low and rustic life was generally chosen, because . . ." (for the continuation see below, C's quotation): Preface to *LB* (1800), reprinted in *Poems* (1815) vol ii. *W Prose* i 124.

elevated rank and of superior refinement oftentimes derive from a happy *imitation* of the rude unpolished manners and discourse of their inferiors. For the pleasure so derived may be traced to three exciting causes. The first is the naturalness, in *fact*, of the things represented. The second is the apparent naturalness of the *representation*, as raised and qualified by an imperceptible infusion of the author's own knowledge and talent, which infusion does, indeed, constitute it an *imitation* as distinguished from a mere *copy*.[1] The third cause may be found in the reader's conscious feeling of his superiority awakened by the contrast presented to him; even as for the same purpose the kings and great barons of yore retained, sometimes *actual* clowns and fools, but more frequently shrewd and witty fellows in that *character*. These, however, were not Mr. Wordsworth's objects. *He* chose low and rustic life, "because in that condition the essential passions of the heart find a better soil, in which they can attain their maturity, are less under restraint, and speak a plainer and more emphatic language; because in that condition of life our elementary feelings co-exist in a state of greater simplicity, and consequently may be more accurately contemplated, and more forcibly communicated; because the manners of rural life germinate from those elementary feelings; and from the necessary character of rural occupations are more easily comprehended, and are more durable; and lastly, because in that condition the passions of men are incorporated with the beautiful and permanent forms of nature."[2]

Now it is clear to me, that in the most interesting of the poems, in which the author is more or less dramatic, as the "Brothers," "Michael," "Ruth," the "Mad Mother,"[3] &c. the persons introduced are by no means taken *from low or rustic life* in the common

[1] For discussion of the distinction between "imitation" and "copy", see ch 18, below, II 72 and n 4.

[2] See II 42 n 2, above. Preface to *LB* (1800) (var), reprinted in *Poems* (1815). *W Prose* I 124. In his "pantisocratic" days, before he met WW, C had expressed similar sentiments. Cf his remarks to George Dyer 10 Mar 1795 on the extent to which we are "shaped & coloured by surrounding Objects . . . a demonstrative proof, that Man was not made to live in Great Cities! . . .

The pleasures, which we receive from rural beauties, are of little Consequence compared with the Moral Effect of these pleasures— beholding constantly the Best possible we at last become ourselves the best possible. In the country, all around us smile Good and Beauty . . .". *CL* I 154.

[3] The title of *The Mad Mother* (1798) was changed in 1815 to *Her Eyes Are Wild*. The other three poems, not in *LB* (1798), were added in *LB* (1800).

acceptation of those words; and it is not less clear, that the sentiments and language, as far as they can be conceived to have been really transferred from the minds and conversation of such persons, are attributable to causes and circumstances not necessarily connected with "their occupations and abode." The thoughts, feelings, language, and manners of the shepherd-farmers in the vales of Cumberland and Westmoreland, as far as they are actually adopted in those poems, may be accounted for from causes, which will and do produce the same results in *every* state of life, whether in town or country. As the two principal I rank that I N D E P E N - D E N C E , which raises a man above servitude, or daily toil for the profit of others, yet not above the necessity of industry and a frugal simplicity of domestic life; and the accompanying unambitious, but solid and religious E D U C A T I O N , which has rendered few books familiar, but the bible, and the liturgy or hymn book. To this latter cause, indeed, which is so far *accidental*, that it is the blessing of particular countries and a particular age, not the product of particular places or employments, the poet owes the shew of probability, that his personages might really feel, think, and talk with any tolerable resemblance to his representation. It is an excellent remark of Dr. Henry More's (Enthusiasmus triumphatus, Sec. x x x v) that "a man of confined education, but of good parts, by constant reading of the bible will naturally form a more winning and commanding rhetoric than those that are learned; the intermixture of tongues and of artificial phrases debasing *their* style." [1]

It is, moreover, to be considered that to the formation of healthy feelings, and a reflecting mind, *negations* involve impediments not less formidable, than sophistication and vicious intermixture. I am convinced, that for the human soul to prosper in rustic life, a certain vantage-ground is pre-requisite. It is not every man[a] that is likely to be improved by a country life or by country

[a] *BL* (1817): man,

[1] Henry More (1614–87) is speaking of the "enthusiast" David George (d 1556) in *Enthusiasmus Triumphans* § xxxv: *A Collection of Several Philosophical Writings* (1662) ii 24 (var). C had read the work and copied out this among other passages in 1801–2. *CN* i 1000I and n.

He is paraphrasing the first part of the quotation, which in the original reads: "For a man illiterate, as he was [David George], but of good parts, by constant reading of the Bible will naturally contract a more winning . . .".

labours. Education, or original sensibility, or both, must pre-exist, if the changes, forms, and incidents of nature are to prove a sufficient stimulant. And where these are not sufficient, the mind contracts and hardens by want of stimulants; and the man becomes selfish, sensual, gross, and hard-hearted.[1] Let the management of the POOR LAWS in Liverpool, Manchester, or Bristol be compared with the ordinary dispensation of the poor rates in agricultural villages, where the *farmers* are the overseers and guardians of the poor.[2] If my own experience have not been particularly unfortunate, as well as that of the many respectable country clergymen with whom I have conversed on the subject, the result would engender more than scepticism concerning the desirable influences of low and rustic life in and for itself. Whatever may be concluded on the other side, from the stronger local attachments and enterprizing spirit of the Swiss, and other mountaineers, applies to a particular mode of pastoral life, under forms of property, that permit and beget manners truly republican, not to rustic life in general, or to the absence of artificial cultivation. On the contrary the mountaineers, whose manners have been so often eulogized, are in[a] general better educated and greater readers than men of equal rank elsewhere. But where this is not the case, as among the peasantry of North Wales, the ancient mountains, with all their terrors and all their glories, are pictures to the blind, and music to the deaf.

I should not have entered so much into detail upon this passage, but here seems to be the point, to which all the lines of difference converge as to their source and centre. (I mean, as far as, and in whatever respect, my poetic creed *does* differ from the doctrines promulged in this preface.) I adopt with full faith the principle of Aristotle, that poetry as poetry is essentially * *ideal*, that it avoids

---

* Say not that I am recommending abstractions, for these class-characteristics which constitute the instructiveness of a character, are so modified and particularized in each person of the Shaksperian Drama, that life itself does

[a] *BL* (1817): in,

[1] Cf notebook remarks in 1799 and 1803: "People in the country—their vindictive feelings"; and "A curious & more than curious Fact that when the country does not benefit, it depraves. Hence the violent vindictive passions—& the outrageous & dark & wild cruelties—of many country folks." *CN* i 521, 1553.

[2] On the Poor Laws, which C held it "impossible to exaggerate their pernicious tendency and consequences", see *LS* (*CC*) 221–3.

and excludes all *accident*; that its apparent individualities of rank, character, or occupation must be *representative* of a class; and that the *persons* of poetry must be clothed with *generic* attributes, with the *common* attributes of the class; not with such as one gifted individual might *possibly* possess, but such as from his situation it is most probable before-hand, that he *would* possess.[2] If my premises are right, and my deductions legitimate, it follows that there can be no *poetic* medium between the swains of Theocritus and those of an imaginary golden age.

The characters of the vicar and the shepherd-mariner in the poem of the "B ROTHERS," those of the shepherd of Green-head

---

not excite more distinctly that sense of individuality which belongs to real existence. Paradoxical as it may sound, one of the essential properties of Geometry is not less essential to dramatic excellence; and Aristotle has accordingly required of the poet an involution of the universal in the individual. The chief differences are, that in Geometry it is the universal truth, which is uppermost in the consciousness; in poetry the individual form, in which the truth is clothed. With the ancients, and not less with the elder dramatists of England and France, both comedy and tragedy were considered as kinds of poetry. They neither sought in comedy to make us laugh merely; much less to make us laugh by wry faces, accidents of jargon, *slang* phrases for the day, or the clothing of common-place morals in metaphors drawn from the shops or mechanic occupations of their characters. Nor did they condescend in tragedy to wheedle away the applause of the spectators, by representing before them fac-similies of their own mean selves in all their existing meanness, or to work on their sluggish sympathies by a pathos not a whit more respectable than the maudlin tears of drunkenness. Their tragic scenes were meant to *affect* us indeed; but yet within the bounds of pleasure, and in union with the activity both of our understanding and imagination. They wished to transport the mind to a sense of its possible greatness, and to implant the germs of that greatness, during the temporary oblivion of the worthless "thing we are," and of the peculiar state in which each man *happens* to be, suspending our individual recollections and lulling them to sleep amid the music of nobler thoughts.

FRIEND, Pages 251, 252.[1]

[1] No 16, 7 Dec 1809: *Friend* (*CC*) II 217–18 (var). The passage, from "Satryrane's Letters" II, is included again in *BL*, below, II 174.

[2] Aristotle *Poetics* 9.1–4. "1. It is not the function of the poet to relate what has happened, but what may happen—what is possible according to the law of probability or necessity. 2. The poet and the historian differ not by writing in verse or in prose. . . . The true difference is that one relates what has happened, the other what may happen. 3. Poetry, therefore, is a more philosophical and a higher thing than history: for poetry tends to express the universal, history the particular. 4. By the universal I mean how a person of a certain type will on occasion speak or act, according to the law of probability or necessity . . .". Tr S. H. Butcher. On Aristotle cf WW in Preface to *LB* (1800), reprinted in *Poems* (1815): *W Prose* I 139.

Gill in the "MICHAEL," have all the verisimilitude and representative quality, that the purposes of poetry can require. They are
persons of a known and abiding class, and their manners and
sentiments the natural product of circumstances common to the
class. Take "MICHAEL" for instance:

> An old man stout of heart, and strong of limb;
> His bodily frame had been from youth to age
> Of an unusual strength: his mind was keen,
> Intense and frugal, apt for all affairs,
> And in his shepherd's calling he was prompt
> And watchful more than ordinary men.
> Hence he had learnt the meaning of all winds,
> Of blasts of every tone, and oftentimes
> When others heeded not, he heard the South
> Make subterraneous music, like the noise
> Of bagpipers on distant highland hills.
> The shepherd, at such warning, of his flock
> Bethought him, and he to himself would say,
> The winds are now devising work for me!
> And truly at all times the storm, that drives
> The traveller to a shelter, summon'd him
> Up to the mountains. He had been alone
> Amid the heart of many thousand mists,
> That came to him and left him on the heights.
> So liv'd he, till his eightieth year was pass'd.
> And grossly that man errs, who should suppose
> That the green vallies, and the streams and rocks,
> Were things indifferent to the shepherd's thoughts.
> Fields, where with chearful spirits he had breath'd
> The common air; the hills, which he so oft
> Had climb'd with vigorous steps; which had impress'd
> So many incidents upon his mind
> Of hardship, skill or courage, joy or fear;
> Which like a book preserved the memory
> Of the dumb animals, whom he had sav'd,
> Had fed or shelter'd, linking to such acts,
> So grateful in themselves, the certainty
> Of honorable gains; these fields, these hills
> Which were his living being, even more
> Than his own blood—what could they less? had laid
> Strong hold on his affections, were to him
> A pleasurable feeling of blind love,
> The pleasure which there is in life itself.[1]

[1] *Michael, a Pastoral Poem* (1800) lines 42–79 (var).

On the other hand, in the poems which are pitched at a lower note, as the "HARRY GILL," "IDIOT BOY," &c.[1] the *feelings* are those of human nature in general; though the poet has judiciously laid the *scene* in the country, in order to place *himself* in the vicinity of interesting images, without the necessity of ascribing a sentimental perception of their beauty to the persons of his drama. In the "Idiot Boy," indeed, the mother's character is not so much a real and native product of a "situation where the essential passions of the heart find a better soil, in which they can attain their maturity and speak a plainer and more emphatic language,"[2] as it is an impersonation of an instinct abandoned by judgement. Hence the two following charges seem to me not wholly groundless: at least, they are the only plausible objections, which I have heard to that fine poem. The one is, that the author has not, in the poem itself, taken sufficient care to preclude from the reader's fancy the disgusting images of *ordinary, morbid idiocy*, which yet it was by no means his intention to represent. He has even by the "burr, burr, burr," uncounteracted by any preceding description of the boy's beauty, assisted in recalling them. The other is, that the idiocy of the *boy* is so evenly balanced by the folly of the *mother*, as to present to the general reader rather a laughable burlesque[3] on the blindness of anile dotage,

---

[1] Both *Goody Blake and Harry Gill* and *The Idiot Boy*, written in 1798, were published in *LB* (1798). In his 1800 Preface WW felt it necessary to justify each of them: "We see that Pope by the power of verse alone, has contrived to render the plainest common sense interesting, and even . . . with the appearance of passion. In consequence of these convictions I related in metre the Tale of GOODY BLAKE and HARRY GILL, which is one of the rudest of this collection. I wished to draw attention to the truth that the power of the human imagination is sufficient to produce such changes even in our physical nature as might almost appear miraculous. The truth is an important one; the fact (for it is a *fact*) is a valuable illustration of it. And I have the satisfaction of knowing that it has been communicated to many hundreds of people who would never have heard of it, had it not been narrated as a Ballad, and a more impressive metre than is usual in Ballads." Speaking of *The Idiot Boy* and *The Mad Mother*, WW, in accordance with his general aim "to follow the fluxes and refluxes of the mind when agitated by the great and simple affections of our nature", sought in these two poems to trace "the maternal passion through many of its more subtle windings". *W Prose* I 150, 126.

[2] See above, II 43.

[3] C in 1794 had been struck by a remark in Edward Young's "On Lyric Poetry"—". . . the meanest thing in writing, *viz.* an involuntary burlesque"—and had jotted down the last three words as a phrase to remember. *CN* I 33 and n.

than an analytic display of maternal affection in its ordinary workings.

In the "Thorn," the poet himself acknowledges in a note the necessity of an introductory poem, in which he should have pourtrayed the character of the person from whom the words of the poem are supposed to proceed: a superstitious man moderately imaginative, of slow faculties and deep feelings, "a captain of a small trading vessel, for example, who being past the middle age of life, had retired upon an annuity, or small independent income, to some village or country town of which he was not a native, or in which he had not been accustomed to live. Such men having nothing to do become credulous and talkative from indolence." [1] But in a poem, still more in a lyric poem (and the NURSE in Shakspeare's Romeo and Juliet alone prevents me from extending the remark even to dramatic *poetry*, if indeed the Nurse itself can be deemed altogether a case in point) it is not possible to imitate truly a dull and garrulous discourser, without repeating the effects of dulness and garrulity.[2] However this may be, I dare assert, that

[1] WW's note, added to eds of *LB* 1800–5 (var: WW wrote "having little to do"): "This Poem ought to have been preceded by an introductory Poem, which I have been prevented from writing by never having felt myself in a mood when it was probable that I should write it well." He then describes the character speaking in the poem (the passage quoted by C) and adds: ". . . from the same cause [indolence], and other predisposing causes . . . [such men] are prone to superstition. On which account it appeared to me proper to select a character like this to exhibit some of the general laws by which superstition acts upon the mind. Superstitious men are almost always men of slow faculties and deep feelings; their minds are not loose, but adhesive; they have a reasonable share of imagination, by which word I mean the faculty which produces impressive effects out of simple elements; but they are utterly destitute of fancy, the power by which pleasure and surprise are excited by sudden varieties of situation and accumulated imagery. It was my wish to show the manner in which such men cleave to the same ideas; and to follow the turns of passion, always different, yet not palpably different, by which their conversation is swayed." He then describes his attempt in style to attain two ends: to use a language that would be appropriate to such a character and yet at the same time "convey passion to Readers who are not accustomed to sympathize with men feeling in that manner or using such language". He decided therefore to unite simple diction with a "rapid Metre" in order to help the poem to move briskly. *WPW* II 512–13. C is aware of WW's intention. What he is gently saying is that WW's imagination, whatever its greatness otherwise, is fundamentally undramatic. Cf below, ch 22 II 129–30.

[2] ". . . In all her recollections she [the Nurse in *Romeo and Juliet*] entirely assists herself by a remem-

the parts (and these form the far larger portion of the whole) which might as well or still better have proceeded from the poet's own imagination, and have been spoken in his own character, are those which have given, and which will continue to give universal delight; and that the passages exclusively appropriate to the supposed narrator, such as the last couplet of the third stanza; * the seven last lines of the tenth; † and the five following stanzas, with the

* I've measured it from side to side;
'Tis three feet long, and two feet wide.[1]

† Nay, rack your brain—'tis all in vain,
I'll tell you every thing I know;
But to the Thorn, and to the Pond
Which is a little step beyond,
I wish that you would go:
Perhaps, when you are at the place,
You something of her tale may trace.

I'll give you the best help I can:
Before you up the mountain go,
Up to the dreary mountain-top,
I'll tell you all I know.

'Tis now some two-and-twenty years
Since she (her name is Martha Ray)
Gave, with a maiden's true good will,
Her company to Stephen Hill;
And she was blithe and gay,
And she was happy, happy still
Whene'er she thought of Stephen Hill.

brance of visual circumstances. The great difference between the cultivated and the uncultivated mind was this that the cultivated mind will be found to recal the past by certain regular trains of cause & effect whereas with the uncultivated it was wholly done by a coincidence of images or circumstances which happened at the same time". Lect 7 of 9 Dec 1811: *Lects 1808–19* (*CC*) ms. Cf the detailed discussion of this tendency of mind, to which for C Edmund Burke serves as a contrast, in *Friend* (*CC*) i 448–57. Finally, on C's remark that "it is not possible to imitate truly a dull and garrulous discourser, without repeating the effects of dulness and garrulity", Mary Moorman states that C "is really here almost quoting a sentence from Southey's review of the *Ballads*

in the Critical Review". *W Life* (M) i 387n. This somewhat overstates the case. RS's remark is: "The author should have recollected that he who personates tiresome loquacity, becomes tiresome himself". *C Rev* XXIV (1798) 200.

[1] *The Thorn* lines 32–3. WW became defensive about the couplet, which describes "a little muddy Pond". HCR states (9 May 1815): "But on my gently alluding to the lines: 'Three feet long and two feet wide,' and confessing that I dared not read them out in company, he said 'they ought to be liked' ". *CRB* i 166. In 1820 WW replaced the couplet with:

Though but of compass small,
   and bare
To thirsty suns and parching
   air.

exception of the four admirable lines at the commencement of the
fourteenth are felt by many unprejudiced and unsophisticated

> And they had fix'd the wedding-day,
> The morning that must wed them both;
> But Stephen to another maid
> Had sworn another oath;
> And with this other maid to church
> Unthinking Stephen went—
> Poor Martha! on that woeful day
> A pang of pitiless dismay
> Into her soul was sent;
> A fire was kindled in her breast,
> Which might not burn itself to rest.
>
> They say, full six months after this,
> While yet the summer leaves were green,
> She to the mountain-top would go,
> And there was often seen.
>
> 'Tis said, a child was in her womb,
> As now to any eye was plain;
> She was with child, and she was mad;
> Yet often she was sober sad
> From her exceeding pain.
> Oh me! ten thousand times I'd rather
> That he had died, that cruel father!
>
> *   *   *   *   *   *   *   *   *
> *   *   *   *   *   *   *   *   *
> *   *   *   *   *   *   *   *   *
> *   *   *   *   *   *   *   *   *
>
> Last Christmas when we talked of this,
> Old farmer Simpson did maintain,
> That in her womb the infant wrought
> About its mother's heart, and brought
> Her senses back again:
> And when at last her time drew near,
> Her looks were calm, her senses clear.
>
> No more I know, I wish I did,
> And I would tell it all to you;
> For what became of this poor child
> There's none that ever knew:
> And if a child was born or no,
> There's no one that could ever tell;
> And if 'twas born alive or dead,
> There's no one knows, as I have said;
> But some remember well,
> That Martha Ray about this time
> Would up the mountain often climb.[1]

[1] *The Thorn* lines 104–65, omitting lines 144–7 ("the four admirable lines at the commencement of the fourteenth stanza"):

> Sad case for such a brain to hold
> Communion with a stirring child!

hearts, as sudden and unpleasant sinkings[1] from the height to which the poet had previously lifted them, and to which he again re-elevates both himself and his reader.

If then I am compelled to doubt the theory, by which the choice of *characters* was to be directed, not only *a priori*, from grounds of reason, but both from the few instances in which the poet himself *need* be supposed to have been governed by it, and from the comparative inferiority of those instances; still more must I hesitate in my assent to the sentence which immediately follows the former citation; and which I can neither admit as particular fact, or as general rule. "The language too of these men is adopted (purified indeed from what appear[a] to be its real defects, from all lasting and rational causes of dislike or disgust) because such men hourly communicate with the best objects from which the best part of language is originally derived; and because, from their rank in society, and the sameness and narrow circle of their intercourse, being less under the action of social vanity, they convey their feelings and notions in simple and unelaborated expressions."[2] To this I reply; that a rustic's language, purified from all provincialism and grossness, and so far re-constructed as to be made consistent with the rules of grammar (which are in essence no other than the laws of universal logic, applied to Psychological materials) will not differ from the language of any other man of common-sense, however learned or refined he may be, except as far as the notions, which the rustic has to convey, are fewer and more indiscriminate. This will become still clearer, if we add the consideration (equally important though less obvious) that the rustic, from the more imperfect development of his faculties, and from the lower state of their cultivation, aims almost solely to convey *insulated facts*, either those of his scanty experience or his

---

[a] *BL* (1817): appears

Sad case, as you may think, for one
Who had a brain so wild!
In deference to C, WW extensively revised the entire passage C quotes, making it less baldly colloquial.

[1] Cf the remark in 1805 on "sinking" in poetry ("it is a *sink;* one steps into a hole when one was expecting to place the foot on a stair higher": *CN* II 2625 f 99), and its use again as one of the characteristic defects of WW's poetry ("assuredly we seem to sink most abruptly, not to say burlesquely"), below, II 136. The term "sinking" had been popularised for eighteenth-century criticism by Pope's *Peri Bathous: Of the Art of Sinking in Poetry* (1727).

[2] Preface to *LB* (1800): *W Prose* I 124.

traditional belief; while the educated man chiefly seeks to discover and express those *connections* of things, or those relative *bearings* of fact to fact, from which some more or less general law is deducible.[1] For *facts* are valuable to a wise man, chiefly as they lead to the discovery of the indwelling *law*, which is the true *being* of things, the sole solution of their modes of existence, and in the knowledge of which consists our dignity and our power.

As little can I agree with the assertion, that from the objects with which the rustic hourly communicates, the best part of language is formed. For first, if to communicate with an object implies such an acquaintance with it, as renders it capable of being discriminately reflected on; the distinct knowledge of an uneducated rustic would furnish a very scanty vocabulary. The few things, and modes of action, requisite for his bodily conveniences, would alone be individualized;[2] while all the rest of nature would be expressed by a small number of confused, general terms. Secondly, I deny that the words and combinations of words derived from the objects, with which the rustic is familiar, whether with distinct or confused knowledge, can be justly said to form the *best* part of language. It is more than probable, that many classes of the brute creation possess discriminating sounds, by which they can convey to each other notices of such objects as concern their food, shelter, or

[1] "What is that which first strikes us . . . in a man of education? . . . It is the unpremeditated and evidently habitual *arrangement* of his words, grounded on the habit of foreseeing, in each integral part, or (more plainly) in every sentence, the whole that he then intends to communicate. However irregular and desultory his talk, there is *method* in the fragments." By contrast in "the ignorant man . . . his memory alone is called into action . . . objects and events recur in the narration in the same order, and with the same accompaniments, however accidental or impertinent, as they had first occurred to the narrator". *Friend* (*CC*) I 448–9. C's special example of the latter is Dame Quickly's speech telling Falstaff when and where he offered her marriage (*2 Henry IV* II i 74–86).

C, in his extensive argument on this in *The Friend,* draws on J. J. Engel, who uses the same illustration in *Anfangsgründe einer Theorie der Dichtungsarten: Schriften* XII (Berlin 1806) 554–8. See *Friend* (*CC*) I 451 n 1. Cf above, ch 10, I 191, and below, II 58.

[2] C in 1800 had taken issue with Adam Smith's opinion (*Wealth of Nations*—1776—bk I ch 1) that agricultural work, involving many different kinds of things, was by definition less restricting than making one kind of thing (e.g. pins) in a factory. "Farmers", said C, "talk always of their own occupations— Mechanics on abstracter things". *CN* I 735 and n. C's prejudice, which leads him to miss the point Smith makes, is in part a reaction to his own early "pantisocratic" enthusiasm.

safety. Yet we hesitate to call the aggregate of such sounds a language, otherwise than metaphorically. The best part of human language, properly so called, is derived from reflection on the acts of the mind itself.[1] It is formed by a voluntary appropriation of fixed symbols to internal acts, to processes and results of imagination, the greater part of which have no place in the consciousness of uneducated man; though in civilized society, by imitation and passive remembrance of what they hear from their religious instructors and other superiors, the most uneducated share in the harvest which they neither sowed or reaped. If the history of the phrases in hourly currency among our peasants were traced, a person not previously aware of the fact would be surprized at finding so large a number, which three or four centuries ago were the exclusive property of the universities and the schools; and at the commencement of the Reformation had been transferred from the school to the pulpit, and thus gradually passed into common life. The extreme difficulty, and often the impossibility, of finding words for the simplest moral and intellectual processes in the languages of uncivilized tribes has proved perhaps the weightiest obstacle to the progress of our most zealous and adroit missionaries. Yet these tribes are surrounded by the same nature, as our peasants are; but in still more impressive forms; and they are, moreover, obliged to *particularize* many more of them. When therefore Mr. Wordsworth adds, "accordingly such a language" (meaning, as before, the language of rustic life purified from provincialism) "arising out of repeated experience and regular feelings is a more permanent, and a far more philosophical language, than that which is frequently substituted for it by poets, who think they are conferring honor upon themselves and their art in proportion as they indulge in arbitrary and capricious habits of expression;"[2] it may be answered, that the language, which he has in view, can be attributed to rustics with no greater right, than the style of Hooker or Bacon to Tom Brown or Sir Roger L'Estrange.[3] Doubtless, if what is peculiar to each were omitted

---

[1] Cf ". . . elevates the Mind by making its feelings the Objects of its reflection" (a function of Schiller's modern [i.e. "sentimental" as distinct from "naïve"] poet). *CN* III 4397 f 48; cf *PA: BL* (1907) II 254.

[2] Preface to *LB* (1800), con-tinuing from the passage above (with the omission of a clause toward the end): *W Prose* I 124.

[3] Thomas Brown (1663–1704), associated with Addison's famous phrase "of facetious memory", was a prolific writer of satiric poems,

in each, the result must needs be the same. Further, that the poet, who uses an illogical diction, or a style fitted to excite only the low and changeable pleasure of wonder by means of groundless novelty, substitutes a language of *folly* and *vanity*, not for that of the *rustic*, but for that of *good sense* and *natural feeling*.

Here let me be permitted to remind the reader, that the positions, which I controvert, are contained in the sentences—"*a selection of the* REAL *language of men*;"—"*the language of these men* (i.e. men in low and rustic life) *I propose to myself to imitate, and as far as possible, to adopt the very language of men.*" "*Between the language of prose and that of metrical composition, there neither is, nor can be any essential difference.*"[1] It is against these exclusively, that my opposition is directed.

I object, in the very first instance, to an equivocation in the use of the word "real." Every man's language varies, according to the extent of his knowledge, the activity of his faculties, and the depth or quickness of his feelings. Every man's language has, first, its *individualities*; secondly, the common properties of the *class* to which he belongs; and thirdly, words and phrases of *universal* use. The language of Hooker, Bacon, Bishop Taylor, and Burke, differ from the common language of the learned class only by the superior number and novelty of the thoughts and relations which they had to convey. The language of Algernon Sidney[2] differs not at all

letters, and dialogues, noted for their scurrilous humour and knowledge of London low life. He is also remembered for the lines beginning "I do not love thee, Dr Fell". Sir Roger L'Estrange (1616–1704), translator and Royalist pamphleteer, was the first English journalist of distinction, publishing the *Public Intelligencer*, the *News*, the *London Gazette*, and the *Observator*. Cf C's ms notes on Jeremy Collier's tr of *The Picture of Cebes* in *The Emperor Marcus Antoninus His Conversation with Himself . . . to which is added The Mythological Picture of Cebes the Theban* (1701): ". . . the *Blackguard Slang*, which passed for *easy* writing from the Restoration of Charles to the accession of Queen Anne. . . . I believe, Sir Roger L'Estrange was the Introducer of this

Thames-Waterman's Language—was ably discipled by the facetious Tom Brown, & his Grub-Street imitator, Edward Ward . . .". *CM* (*CC*) I 182. Cf *Friend* (*CC*) I 359, *TT* 3 Jul 1833.

[1] Preface to *LB* (1800): *W Prose* I 123 (var), 130 (var), 134.

[2] Algernon Sidney (1622–83), grand-nephew of Sir Philip, is "the later Sidney" referred to in WW's sonnet "Great men have been among us" (line 3). He was accused of complicity at the discovery of the "Rye House Plot" (reputedly a scheme to assassinate Charles II). He was tried before Judge Jeffreys, condemned, and executed. He was denied counsel; the jury was packed; and the evidence consisted of testimony from a perjured reformer, hearsay, and extracts out of context

from that, which every well educated gentleman would wish to write, and (with due allowances for the undeliberateness, and less connected train, of thinking natural and proper to conversation) such as he would wish to talk. Neither one or the other differ half as much from the general language of cultivated society, as the language of Mr. Wordsworth's homeliest composition differs from that of a common peasant. For "real" therefore, we must substitute *ordinary*, or *lingua communis*. And this, we have proved, is no more to be found in the phraseology of low and rustic life, than in that of any other class. Omit the peculiarities of each, and the result of course must be common to all. And assuredly the omissions and changes to be made in the language of rustics, before it could be transferred to any species of poem, except the drama or other professed imitation, are at least as numerous and weighty, as would be required in adapting to the same purpose the ordinary language of tradesmen and manufacturers. Not to mention, that the language so highly extolled by Mr. Wordsworth varies in every county, nay in every village, according to the accidental character of the clergyman, the existence or non-existence of schools; or even, perhaps, as the exciseman, publican, or barber happen to be, or not to be, zealous politicians, and readers of the weekly newspaper *pro bono publico*. Anterior to cultivation the lingua communis of every country, as Dante has well observed, exists every where in parts, and no where as a whole.[1]

Neither is the case rendered at all more tenable by the addition of the words, "*in a state of excitement*."[2] For the nature of a man's words, when he is strongly affected by joy, grief, or anger, must necessarily depend on the number and quality of the general

---

from some of Sidney's writings, particularly his then-unpublished *Discourses Concerning Government,* which was published in 1698, fifteen years after his death. C refers to him frequently in *The Friend* (*CC*) I 68, 79, 92, 215, 217, 266, 324. His annotations on Sidney's *Works* (1772) were published, though not completely, in *NTP* 189–93. *CM* (*CC*) IV. See also *CN* II 3117, 3118 and n.

[1] C apparently refers to *De vulgari eloquentia* bk I ch 7: "The language, then, which we are proceeding to treat of is three-fold . . . And that this language was uniform at first after the beginning of the Confusion [of tongues, i.e. Babel] . . .". Tr A. G. Ferrers Howell. For C's use of the work, cf ch 16, above, II 30, and esp *CN* II 3011 and n, III 3611 and n.

[2] WW's actual words are: "the real language of men in a state of vivid sensation". See above, ch 14, II 8 and n 4.

truths, conceptions and images, and of the words expressing them, with which his mind had been previously stored. For the property of passion is not to *create*; but to set in increased activity. At least, whatever new connections of thoughts or images, or (which is equally, if not more than equally, the appropriate effect of strong excitement) whatever generalizations of truth or experience, the heat of passion may produce; yet the terms of their conveyance must have pre-existed in his former conversations, and are only collected and crowded together by the unusual stimulation. It is indeed very possible to adopt in a poem the unmeaning repetitions, habitual phrases, and other blank counters, which an unfurnished or confused understanding interposes at short intervals, in order to keep hold of his subject which is still slipping from him, and to give him time for recollection; or in mere aid of vacancy, as in the scanty companies of a country stage the same player pops backwards and forwards, in order to prevent the appearance of empty spaces, in the procession of Macbeth, or Henry VIIIth. But what assistance to the poet, or ornament to the poem, these can supply, I am at a loss to conjecture. Nothing assuredly can differ either in origin or in mode more widely from the *apparent* tautologies of intense and turbulent feeling, in which the passion is greater and of longer endurance, than to be exhausted or satisfied by a single representation of the image or incident exciting it. Such repetitions I admit to be a beauty of the highest kind; as illustrated by Mr. Wordsworth himself from the song of Deborah. *"At her feet he bowed, he fell, he lay down; at her feet he bowed, he fell; where he bowed, there he fell down dead."* 1

---

1 Judges 5.27, which WW cites in his note to *The Thorn* (see above, II 49 n 1) to illustrate that "repetition and apparent tautology are frequently beauties of the highest kind". *WPW* II 513. Cf *CN* III 3247, 4113, 4116 and n.

CHAPTER 18

Language of metrical composition, why and wherein essentially different from that of prose—Origin and elements of metre—Its necessary consequences, and the conditions thereby imposed on the metrical writer in the choice of his diction

I CONCLUDE therefore, that the attempt is impracticable; and that, were it not impracticable, it would still be useless. For the very power of making the selection implies the previous possession of the language selected. Or where can the poet have lived? And by what rules could he direct his choice, which would not have enabled him to select and arrange his words by the light of his own judgement? We do not adopt the language of a class by the mere adoption of such words exclusively, as that class would use, or at least understand; but likewise by following the *order*, in which the words of such men are wont to succeed each other. Now this order, in the intercourse of uneducated men, is distinguished from the diction of their superiors in knowledge and power, by the greater *disjunction* and *separation* in the component parts of that, whatever it be, which they wish to communicate. There is a want of that prospectiveness of mind, that *surview*, which enables a man to foresee the whole of what he is to convey, appertaining to any one point; and by this means so to subordinate and arrange the different parts according to their relative importance, as to convey it at once, and as an organized whole.[1]

Now I will take the first stanza, on which I have chanced to open, in the Lyrical Ballads. It is one the most simple and the least peculiar in its language.

> In distant countries I have been,
> And yet I have not often seen
> A healthy man, a man full grown,
> Weep in the public road alone.
> But such a one, on English ground,

[1] See ch 10, above, I 191, and esp ch 17, II 53 and n 1.

And in the broad highway I met;
Along the broad highway he came,
His cheeks with tears were wet.
Sturdy he seem'd, though he was sad,
And in his arms a lamb he had.[1]

The words here are doubtless such as are current in all ranks of life; and of course not less so, in the hamlet and cottage, than in the shop, manufactory, college, or palace. But is this the *order*, in which the rustic would have placed the words? I am grievously deceived, if the following less *compact* mode of commencing the same tale be not a far more faithful copy. "I have been in a many parts far and near, and I don't know that I ever saw before a man crying by himself in the public road; a grown man I mean, that was neither sick nor hurt," &c. &c. But when I turn to the following stanza in "The Thorn:"

At all times of the day and night
This wretched woman thither goes,
And she is known to every star
And every wind that blows:
And there beside the thorn she sits,
When the blue day-light's in the skies;
And when the whirlwind's on the hill,
Or frosty air is keen and still;
And to herself she cries,
Oh misery! Oh misery!
Oh woe is me! Oh misery![2]

and[a] compare this with the language of ordinary men; or with that which I can conceive at all likely to proceed, in *real* life, from *such* a narrator, as is supposed in the note to the poem; compare it either in the succession of the images or of the sentences;[b] I am reminded of the sublime prayer and hymn of praise, which MILTON, in opposition to an established liturgy, presents as a fair *specimen* of common extemporary devotion, and such as we might expect to hear from every self-inspired minister of a conventicle![3] And I reflect with delight, how little a mere theory,

---

[a] *BL* (1817) begins new paragraph: And   [b] *BL* (1817): sentences,

[1] *The Last of the Flock* (1798) lines 1–10 (var).
[2] *The Thorn* (1798) lines 67–77.
[3] C refers to the prayer of Adam and Eve in *Paradise Lost* v 153–208, preceded by the description (144–9):

Lowly they bow'd adoring, and began
Their Orisons, each Morning duly paid
In various style, for neither various style

though of his own workmanship, interferes with the processes of genuine imagination in a man of true poetic genius, who possesses, as Mr. Wordsworth, if ever man did, most assuredly does possess,

THE VISION AND THE FACULTY DIVINE.[1]

One point then alone remains, but that the most important; its examination having been, indeed, my chief inducement for the preceding inquisition. *"There neither is or can be any essential difference between the language of prose and metrical composition."* [2] Such is Mr. Wordsworth's assertion. Now prose itself, at least, in all argumentative and consecutive works,[a] differs, and ought to differ, from the language of conversation; even as *

* It is no less an error in teachers, than a torment to the poor children, to inforce the necessity of reading as they would talk. In order to cure them of *singing* as it is called; that is, of too great a [b]difference, the [c] child is made to repeat the words with his eyes from off the book; and then indeed, his tones resemble talking, as far as his fears, tears and trembling will permit. But as soon as the eye is again directed to the printed page, the spell begins anew; for an instinctive sense tells the child's feelings, that to utter its own momentary thoughts, and to recite the written thoughts of another, as of another, and a far wiser than himself, are two widely different things; and as the two acts are accompanied with widely different feelings, so must they justify different modes of enunciation. Joseph Lancaster, among his other sophistications of the excellent Dr. Bell's invaluable system, cures this fault of *singing*, by hanging fetters and chains on the child, to the music of which, one of his school fellows who walks before, dolefully chaunts out the child's last speech and confession, birth, parentage, and education.[3] And this soul-

---

[a] *BL* (1817) omits comma   [b-c] *BL* (1817): difference. The

---

Nor holy rapture wanted they
    to praise
Their Maker, in fit strains
    pronounc't or sung
Unmeditated . . .
C may also be recalling Milton's defence of extemporary devotion in preference to liturgical forms in *Eikonoklastes* ch 16: *Works* (Columbia ed 1931–40) v 219–25.

  1 *Excursion* I 79; cf ch 12, above, I 241.

  2 See above, II 55.

  3 Andrew Bell (1753–1832), while superintendent of a large orphanage asylum in Madras and facing a scarcity of teachers, introduced a system in which the older students participated in the teaching. Its

success convinced him of its general value as an educational method, and he wrote about it in *An Experiment in Education* (1797). The system was quickly adopted with some changes by Joseph Lancaster (1778–1838), a Quaker, in a large school in Southwark. Lancaster was given such enthusiastic support by the Nonconformists that the Church of England asked Bell to organise some schools in a similar way. Thereafter, especially because religious differences fanned it, the men were thrown into the position of rivals. Bell's system naturally appealed to C as a "dynamic principle", one that could arouse active participation by the "whole individual". Cf his praise

reading ought to differ from talking. Unless therefore the difference denied be that of the mere *words*, as materials common to all styles of writing, and not of the *style* itself in the universally admitted sense of the term, it might be naturally presumed that there must exist a still greater between the ordonnance of poetic composition and that of prose, than is expected to distinguish prose from ordinary conversation.

There are not, indeed, examples wanting in the history of literature, of apparent paradoxes that have summoned the public wonder as new and startling truths, but which on examination have shrunk into tame and harmless *truisms*; as the eyes of a cat, seen in the dark, have been mistaken for flames of fire. But Mr. Wordsworth is among the last men, to whom a delusion of this

---

benumbing ignominy, this unholy and heart-hardening burlesque on the last fearful infliction of outraged law, in pronouncing the sentence to which the stern and familiarized judge not seldom bursts into tears, has been extolled as a happy and ingenious method of remedying—what? and how?—why, one extreme in order to introduce another, scarce less distant from good sense, and certainly likely to have worse moral effects, by enforcing a semblance of petulant ease and self-sufficiency, in repression, and possible after-perversion of the natural feelings. I have to beg Dr. Bell's pardon for this connection of the two names, but he knows that contrast is no less powerful a cause of association than likeness.

---

of Bell in *Friend* (*CC*) II 69–70 (I 102–3 and n 4), to which Bell had been a subscriber (II 414). Meeting Bell early in 1808, C read the proof-sheets of Bell's *The Madras School, or Elements of Tuition* (Chelsea 1808), and as a warm Anglican supported Bell soon afterwards in a lecture on education in which, by needlessly attacking Lancaster, HCR said, he gave "great offence". *CN* III 3291n; *Sh C* II 18. C, singling out Lancaster's methods of discipline, continued to dwell on them until, said De Q, people were asking "Have you heard Coleridge lecture on Bel and the Dragon?" *De Q Works* v 196. In Lect 6 of 5 Dec 1811 he was supposed to discuss "*Romeo and Juliet* and Shakespeare's female characters" but digressed to the subject of Lancaster, stating what he says above about the punishment of pupils for reading poetry in a "singsong" way. Lamb whispered to HCR, "It is a pity he did not leave this till he got to *Henry VI* and then he might say he could not help taking part against the Lancastrians"; and later, as C continued running from topic to topic, added: "This is not so much amiss. Coleridge said in his advertisement he would speak about the nurse in *Romeo and Juliet,* and so he is delivering the lecture in the character of the nurse." *CRB* I 53. In his Lect 7 of 18 Nov 1813 in Bristol, C described the "new system of education", praising Bell and attacking Lancaster for his modes of punishment: "to load a boy with fetters . . . to expose him to the sneers and insults of his peers, because forsooth he reads his lessons in a *singing tone,* was a pitiful mockery of human nature". *Lects 1808–19* (*CC*) ms.

kind would be attributed by any one, who had enjoyed the slightest opportunity of understanding his mind and character. Where an objection has been anticipated by such an author as natural, his answer to it must needs be interpreted in some sense which either is, or has been, or is capable of being controverted. My object then must be to discover some other meaning for the term "*essential difference*" in this place, exclusive of the indistinction and community of the words themselves. For whether there ought to exist a class of words in the English, in any degree resembling the poetic dialect of the Greek and Italian, is a question of very subordinate importance. The number of such words would be small indeed, in our language; and even in the Italian and Greek, they consist not so much of different words, as of slight differences in the *forms* of declining and conjugating the same words; forms, doubtless, which having been, at some period more or less remote, the common grammatic flexions of some tribe or province, had been accidentally appropriated to poetry by the general admiration of certain master intellects, the first established lights of inspiration, to whom that dialect happened to be native.

Essence, in its primary signification, means the principle of *individuation*, the inmost principle of the *possibility*, of any thing, *as* that particular thing. It is equivalent to the *idea* of a thing, whenever we use the word idea, with philosophic precision. Existence, on the other hand, is distinguished from essence, by the superinduction of *reality*.[1] Thus we speak of the essence, and essential properties of a circle; but we do not therefore assert, that any thing, which really *exists*, is mathematically circular. Thus too, without any tautology we contend for the *existence* of the Supreme Being; that is, for a reality correspondent to the idea.[2] There is, next, a *secondary* use of the word essence, in which it signifies the point or ground of contra-distinction between two modifications of the same substance or subject. Thus we should be allowed to say, that the style of architecture of Westminster Abbey is *essentially*

---

[1] Similarly the imagination, as the counterpart in the finite mind of the creative process of nature, is "the Laboratory, in which Thought elaborates Essence into Existence". *CN* II 3158. On the concept of life itself as "the principle of individuation" see *TL* (1848) 42–50 and *C Life* (B) 193–5.

[2] Cf ". . . that law of conscience, which . . . unconditionally *commands* us [to] attribute *reality*, and actual *existence*, to those ideas and to those only, without which the conscience itself would be baseless and contradictory, to the ideas of Soul, of Free-will, of Immortality, and of God!" *Friend* (*CC*) II 79 (I 112).

different from that of Saint Paul, even though both had been built with blocks cut into the same form, and from the same quarry. Only in this latter sense of the term must it have been *denied* by Mr. Wordsworth (for in this sense alone is it *affirmed* by the general opinion) that the language of poetry (i.e. the formal construction, or architecture, of the words and phrases) is *essentially* different from that of prose. Now the burthen of the proof lies with the oppugner, not with the supporters of the common belief. Mr. Wordsworth, in consequence, assigns as the proof of his position, "that not only the language of a large portion of every good poem, even of the most elevated character, must necessarily, except with reference to the metre, in no respect differ from that of good prose; but likewise that some of the most interesting parts of the best poems will be found to be strictly the language of prose, when prose is well written. The truth of this assertion might be demonstrated by innumerable passages from almost all the poetical writings even of Milton himself." He then quotes Gray's sonnet—

> In vain to me the smiling mornings shine,
> And reddening Phœbus lifts his golden fire;
> The birds in vain their amorous descant join,
> Or cheerful fields resume their green attire;
> These ears alas! for other notes repine;
> *A different object do these eyes require;*
> *My lonely anguish melts no heart but mine,*
> *And in my breast the imperfect joys expire!*
> Yet morning smiles the busy race to cheer,
> And new born pleasure brings to happier men:
> The fields to all their wonted tributes bear,
> To warm their little loves the birds complain.
> *I fruitless mourn to him that cannot hear,*
> *And weep the more because I weep in vain;* [1]

and adds the following remark:—"It will easily be perceived, that the only part of this Sonnet which is of any value, is the lines printed in italics. It is equally obvious, that except in the rhyme, and in the use of the single word 'fruitless' for fruitlessly, which is so far a defect, the language of these lines does in no respect differ from that of prose." [2]

An idealist defending his system by the fact, that when asleep we often believe ourselves awake, was well answered by his plain

---

[1] Thomas Gray *Sonnet on the Death of Richard West.*   [2] Preface to *LB* (1800): *W Prose* I 132–4.

neighbour, "Ah, but when awake do we ever believe ourselves asleep?"—Things identical must be convertible. The preceding passage seems to rest on a similar sophism. For the question is not, whether there may not occur in prose an order of words, which would be equally proper in a poem; nor whether there are not beautiful lines and sentences of frequent occurrence in good poems, which would be equally becoming as well as beautiful in good prose; for neither the one or the other has ever been either denied or doubted by any one. The true question must be, whether there are not modes of expression, a *construction*, and an *order* of sentences, which are in their fit and natural place in a serious prose composition, but would be disproportionate and heterogeneous in metrical poetry; and, vice versa, whether in the language of a serious poem there may not be an arrangement both of words and sentences, and a use and selection of (what are called) *figures of speech*, both as to their kind, their frequency, and their occasions, which on a subject of equal weight would be vicious and alien in correct and manly prose. I contend, that in both cases this unfitness of each for the place of the other frequently will and ought to exist.

And first from the *origin* of metre. This I would trace to the balance in the mind effected by that spontaneous effort which strives to hold in check the workings of passion.[1] It might be easily explained likewise in what manner this salutary antagonism is assisted by the very state, which it counteracts; and how this balance of antagonists became organized into *metre* (in the usual acceptation of that term) by a supervening act of the will and judgement, consciously and for the foreseen purpose of pleasure.[2] Assuming these principles, as the data of our argument, we deduce

[1] "What is MUSIC? . . . Passion and order aton'd!" ". . . Order and Passion—*N.b.* how by excitement of the Associative Power Passion itself imitates Order, and the *order* resulting produces a pleasurable *Passion* (whence Metre) . . .". *CN* II 3231 f 14, III 4397 f 48ᵛ. Cf WW's own remark in the Preface to *LB* (1800): ". . . the co-presence of something regular, something to which the mind has been accustomed when in an unexcited or a less excited state, cannot but have great efficacy in tempering and restraining the passion by an intertexture of ordinary feeling". *W Prose* I 146.

[2] Cf the parallel with Schiller's general theme in *Aesthetische Briefe* Nos 12–14, and also C's letter to Davy (9 Sept 1807) on his proposed lectures in which C intends to speak of his "many years' continued reflection" on, among other subjects, "the source of our pleasures in the fine Arts in the *antithetical* balance-loving nature of man, & the connection of such pleasures with moral excellence". *CL* III 30. *BL* (1907) II 278. Cf ch 14, above, II 17.

from them two legitimate conditions, which the critic is entitled to expect in every metrical work. First, that as the *elements* of metre owe their existence to a state of increased excitement, so the metre itself should be accompanied by the natural language of excitement.[1] Secondly, that as these elements are formed into metre *artificially*, by a *voluntary* act, with the design and for the purpose of blending *delight* with emotion, so the traces of present *volition* should throughout the metrical language be proportionally discernible. Now these two conditions must be reconciled and co-present. There must be not only a partnership, but a union; an interpenetration of passion and of will, of *spontaneous* impulse and of *voluntary* purpose. Again, this union can be manifested only in a frequency of forms and figures of speech (originally the offspring of passion, but now the adopted children of power)[2] greater[a] than would be desired or endured, where the emotion is not voluntarily encouraged, and kept up for the sake of that pleasure, which such emotion so tempered and mastered by the will is found capable of communicating.[3] It not only dictates, but of itself tends to produce, a more frequent employment of picturesque and vivifying language, than would be natural in any other case, in which there did not exist, as there does in the present, a previous and well understood, though tacit, *compact* between the poet and

---

[a] *BL* (1817): greater,

[1] ". . . *Metre itself* implies a *passion,* i.e. a state of excitement, both in the Poet's mind, & is expected in that of the Reader—and tho' I stated this to Wordsworth, & he has in some sort stated it in his preface, yet he has [not] done justice to it, nor has he in my opinion sufficiently answered it." To Sotheby 13 Jul 1802: *CL* ɪɪ 812. WW (Appendix to the 1802 Preface), in speaking of the early language of poetry, had stated: "To this language it is probable that metre of some sort or other was early superadded. . . . Metre is but adventitious to composition . . .". *W Prose* ɪ 161, 164. Cf the remarks on the connection of metre and passion in Lect 3 of 24 Nov 1811: *Sh C* ɪɪ 79–80.

[2] Cf ". . . the *inventive* passion". *CN* ɪɪ 2723, quoted above, ɪɪ 40

n 1. Cf also "'But tho' the *Metaphor* began in *Poverty,* it did not *end* there . . . the *Metaphor* was cultivated, not out of *Necessity,* but for *Ornament*". Harris *Philological Inquiries* pt ɪɪ ch 10: *Works* ɪɪ 385.

[3] "In my opinion, Poetry justifies, as *Poetry* independent of any other Passion, some new combinations of Language, & *commands* the omission of many others allowable in other compositions". C's letter to Sotheby 13 Jul 1802: *CL* ɪɪ 812. HCR records him saying of WW (15 Nov 1810: *CRD* ɪ 304–5): "He should have recollected that verse being the language of passion, and passion dictating energetic expressions, it became him to make his subjects and style accord. One asks why tales so simple were not in prose." *BL* (1907) ɪɪ 278.

his reader, that the latter is entitled to expect, and the former bound to supply this species and degree of pleasurable excitement. We may in some measure apply to this union the answer of POLIXENES, in the Winter's Tale, to PERDITA'S neglect of the streaked gilly-flowers, because she had heard it said,

> There is an art which in their piedness shares
> With great creating nature.
> > *Pol:* Say there be:
> Yet nature is made better by no mean,
> But nature makes that mean. So ev'n that art,
> Which you say adds to nature, is an art,
> That nature makes! You see, sweet maid, we marry
> *A gentler scyon to the wildest stock:*
> And make conceive a bark of ruder kind
> By bud of nobler race. This is an art,
> Which does mend nature—change it rather; but
> The art itself is nature.[1]

Secondly, I argue from the EFFECTS of metre. As far as metre acts in and for itself, it tends to increase the vivacity and susceptibility both of the general feelings and of the attention. This effect it produces by the continued excitement of surprise, and by the quick reciprocations of curiosity still gratified and still re-excited, which are too slight indeed to be at any one moment objects of distinct consciousness, yet become considerable in their aggregate influence. As a medicated atmosphere, or as wine during animated conversation; they act powerfully, though themselves unnoticed. Where, therefore, correspondent food and appropriate matter are not provided for the attention and feelings thus roused, there must needs be a disappointment felt; like that of leaping in the dark from the last step of a stair-case, when we had prepared our muscles for a leap of three or four.[2]

The discussion on the powers of metre in the preface is highly ingenious and touches at all points on truth. But I cannot find any statement of its powers considered abstractly and separately. On the contrary Mr. Wordsworth seems always to estimate metre by the powers, which it exerts during (and, as I think, in *consequence*

---

[1] Shakespeare *Winter's Tale* IV iv 87–97 (var).

[2] Cf in C's discussion of a passage in Marino's sonnets: "one steps into a hole when one was expecting to place the foot on a stair higher". *CN* II 2625 f 99. The statement about the sense of anticlimax, if the expectations aroused by metre are unfulfilled, is repeated below, II 122–3.

of) its combination with other elements of poetry. Thus the previous difficulty is left unanswered, *what* the elements are, with which it must be combined in order to produce its own effects to any pleasureable purpose. Double and tri-syllable rhymes, indeed, form a lower species of wit, and attended to exclusively for their own sake may become a source of momentary amusement;[1] as in poor Smart's distich to the Welch 'Squire who had promised him a hare:

> Tell me thou son of great Cadwallader!
> Hast sent the hare? or hast thou swallow'd her?[2]

But for any *poetic* purposes, metre resembles (if the aptness of the simile may excuse its meanness) yeast, worthless or disagreeable by itself, but giving vivacity and spirit to the liquor with which it is proportionally combined.

The reference to the "Children in the Wood" by no means satisfies my judgement.[3] We all willingly throw ourselves back for awhile into the feelings of our childhood. This ballad, therefore, we read under such recollections of our own childish feelings, as would equally endear to us poems, which Mr. Wordsworth himself would regard as faulty in the opposite extreme of gaudy and technical ornament. Before the invention of printing, and in a still greater degree, before the introduction of writing, metre, especially *alliterative* metre, (whether alliterative at the beginning of the words, as in "Pierce Plouman," or at the end as in rhymes) possessed an independent value as assisting the recollection, and consequently the preservation, of *any* series of truths or incidents. But I am not convinced by the collation of facts, that the *"Children*

[1] Cf, above, on trisyllable rhymes, i 62 and n 3.

[2] Christopher Smart (1722–71), mentally unstable and unfortunate in life, in his *To the Rev. Mr. Powell on the Non-Performance of a Promise He Made the Author of a Hare* (1752) lines 13–14 ("Thou valiant son of great Cadwallader, | Hast thou a hare, or hast thou swallow'd her?"). In *B Poets* xi 180. C is here quoting from a notebook entry (1801) in which he had jotted down these lines. *CN* i 967 and n.

[3] WW in the Preface had contrasted Johnson's parody of the ballad stanza (see below, ii 76 and n 3) with the following stanza from *Babes in the Wood*: "Those pretty Babes with hand in hand | Went wandering up and down; | But never more they saw the Man | Approaching from the town." The difference, says WW, is "not from the metre, not from the language . . . but the *matter* expressed . . .". *Children in the Wood* is the title of the familiar version in Percy's *Reliques*. WW is apparently quoting from a recently published pamphlet (1800?). *W Prose* i 154, 186.

in the Wood" owes either its preservation, or its popularity, to its metrical form. Mr. Marshal's repository affords a number of tales in prose inferior in pathos and general merit, some of as old a date, and many as widely popular. TOM HICKATHRIFT, JACK THE GIANT-KILLER, GOODY TWO-SHOES, and LITTLE RED RIDING-HOOD are formidable rivals.[1] And that they have continued in prose, cannot be fairly explained by the assumption, that the comparative meanness of their thoughts and images precluded even the humblest forms of metre. The scene of GOODY TWO-SHOES in the church is perfectly susceptible of metrical narration;[2] and among the Θαύματα θαυμαστότατα[3] even of the present age, I do not recollect a more astonishing image than that of the *"whole rookery, that flew out of the giant's beard"* scared by the tremendous voice, with which this monster answered the challenge of the heroic TOM HICKATHRIFT![4]

If from these we turn to compositions universally, and independently of all early associations, beloved and admired; would the MARIA, THE MONK, or THE POOR MAN'S ASS of STERNE,[5] be read with more delight, or have a better chance of immortality, had they without any change in the diction been composed in rhyme, than in their present state? If I am not grossly mistaken, the general reply would be in the negative. Nay, I will confess, that in Mr. Wordsworth's own volumes the ANECDOTE FOR FATHERS, SIMON LEE, ALICE FELL, THE BEGGARS, and[a] THE SAILOR'S MOTHER,[6] notwithstanding the beauties

[a] BL (1817): AND

[1] C refers to a collection of penny chapbooks published by John Marshall, 4 Aldermary Churchyard, Bow Lane: *Marshall's Cheap Repository. Tracts* (1796–7).

[2] The scene in which, after being locked in the church all night, Goody sees ghosts but refuses to be frightened (ch 7). *The History of Little Goody Two-Shoes* (1765), alleged to have been written by Oliver Goldsmith, was probably by Griffith Jones (1722–86) and his brother Giles (fl 1760–70).

[3] "Marvels most marvellous".

[4] The story of Tom Hickathrift, a young cart-maker who slew giants, was frequently reprinted in chapbooks in the seventeenth and eighteenth centuries. See the Introduction by G. L. Gomme (ed) *The History of Thomas Hickathrift* (Villon Society 1885). The description C quotes of the giant's beard has not been found in either pt I or II of the tale.

[5] Three stories in Laurence Sterne's *Sentimental Journey Through France and Italy* (1768), the third of which was actually entitled "The Dead Ass".

[6] The first two were published in *LB* (1798) and the last three in *Poems* (1807).

which are to be found in each of them where the poet interposes the music of his own thoughts, would have been more delightful to me in prose, told and managed, as by Mr. Wordsworth they would have been, in a moral essay, or pedestrian tour.

Metre in itself is simply a stimulant of the attention, and therefore excites the question: Why is the attention to be thus stimulated? Now the question cannot be answered by the pleasure of the metre itself: for this we have shown to be *conditional*, and dependent on the appropriateness of the thoughts and expressions, to which the metrical form is superadded.[1] Neither can I conceive any other answer that can be rationally given, short of this: I write in metre, because I am about to use a language different from that of prose. Besides, where the language is not such, how interesting soever the reflections are, that are capable of being drawn by a philosophic mind from the thoughts or incidents of the poem, the metre itself must often become feeble. Take the three last stanzas of the SAILOR'S MOTHER, for instance. If I could for a moment abstract from the effect produced on the author's feelings, as a man, by the incident at the time of its real occurrence, I would dare appeal to his own judgement, whether in the *metre* itself he found a sufficient reason for *their* being written *metrically*?

> And thus continuing, she said
> I had a son, who many a day
> Sailed on the seas; but he is dead;
> In Denmark he was cast away
> And I have travelled far as Hull, to see
> What clothes he might have left, or other property.

> The bird and cage, they both were his;
> 'Twas my son's bird; and neat and trim
> He kept it; many voyages
> This singing bird hath gone with him;
> When last he sailed he left the bird behind;
> As it might be, perhaps, from bodings of his mind.

> He to a fellow-lodger's care
> Had left it, to be watched and fed,

[1] C, though he might not have cared to admit it, has been siding with Johnson's celebrated discussions of metre and against the prevailing opinion of most eighteenth-century metrists. Johnson argues that most of the effects of metre are interwoven with and depend on the sense and imagery, and to illustrate his point uses exactly the same rhythms Pope uses in describing the labours of Sisyphus, but now with a different thought and imagery, and produces an almost opposite result. *Lives* "Pope" III 230–2; *Rambler* Nos 92, 94.

Till he came back again; and there
I found it when my son was dead;
And now, God help me for my little wit!
I trail it with me, Sir! he took so much delight in it.[1]

If disproportioning the emphasis we read these stanzas so as to
make the rhymes perceptible, even *tri-syllable* rhymes could
scarcely produce an equal sense of oddity and strangeness, as we
feel here in finding *rhymes at all* in sentences so exclusively colloquial. I would further ask whether, but for that visionary state,
into which the figure of the woman and the susceptibility of his
own genius had placed the poet's imagination (a state, which
spreads its influence and coloring over all, that co-exists with the
exciting cause, and in which

> The simplest, and the most familiar things
> Gain a strange power of spreading awe around * them)

> * Altered from the description of Night-Mair in the Remorse.
> Oh Heaven 'twas frightful! Now run-down and stared at,
> By hideous shapes that cannot be remembered;
> Now seeing nothing and imagining nothing;
> But only being afraid—stifled with fear!
> While every goodly or familiar form
> Had a strange power of spreading terror round me.[2]

N.B. Though Shakspeare has for his own *all-justifying* purposes introduced
the Night-*Mare* with her own foals, yet Mair means a Sister or perhaps a
Hag.[3]

[1] *The Sailor's Mother* (1802; pub 1807) lines 19–36. In response to C's criticism WW later altered several lines in the attempt to make them less bald.

[2] *Remorse* IV i 68–73 (var): *PW* (EHC) II 861. Cf the discussions of "nightmair" in *CN* III 3322 (in 1808), in which C quotes the same passage ("From my Mss Tragedy"), and (in 1811) in *CN* III 4046 and n. *BL* (1907) II 280 cites C's marginal note to the corresponding section of *Osorio* (IV i): "Prophetical dreams are things of nature, and explicable by that law of the mind in which, where dim ideas are connected with vivid feelings, Perception and Imagination insinuate themselves and mix with the forms of Recollection, till the Present appears to exactly correspond with the Past. Whatever is partially like, the Imagination will gradually represent as wholly like . . .". *PW* (EHC) II 566.

[3] C is correct in thinking that the "mare" in "nightmare" is not a female horse (from OE *mere*) but a goblin or monster (from OE *mare*), usually thought of as female, that settles on people or animals at night, inducing suffocation. The reference to Shakespeare is to Edgar's charm in *Lear* III iv 120–1: "Swithold footed twice the 'old [wold], | He met the night-mare and her nine-fold". Though the obvious interpretation is that he has met the nightmare multiplied nine-fold, it is frequently argued that the meaning is "nine foals" and that it is put as "fold" for the sake of the rhyme. See also *CN* I 174 (no 12) and n.

I[a] would ask the poet whether he would not have felt an abrupt down-fall in these verses from the preceding stanza?

> The ancient spirit is not dead;
> Old times, thought I, are breathing there!
> Proud was I, that my country bred
> Such strength, a dignity so fair!
> She begged an alms, like one in poor estate;
> I looked at her again, nor did my pride abate.[1]

It must not be omitted, and is besides worthy of notice, that those stanzas furnish the only fair instance that I have been able to discover in all Mr. Wordsworth's writings, of an *actual* adoption, or true imitation, of the *real* and *very* language of *low and rustic life,* freed from provincialisms.

Thirdly, I deduce the position from all the causes elsewhere assigned, which render metre the proper form of poetry, and poetry imperfect and defective without metre. Metre therefore having been connected with *poetry* most often and by a peculiar fitness, whatever else is combined with *metre* must, though it be not itself *essentially* poetic, have nevertheless some property in common with poetry, as an intermedium of affinity, a sort (if I may dare borrow a well-known phrase from technical chemistry) of *mordaunt*[2] between it and the superadded metre. Now poetry, Mr. Wordsworth truly affirms, does always imply PASSION;[3] which word must be here understood in its most general sense, as an excited state of the feelings and faculties. And as every passion has its proper pulse, so will it likewise have its characteristic modes of expression.[4] But where there exists that degree of genius and talent which entitles a writer to aim at the honors of a poet, the very *act* of poetic composition *itself* is, and is *allowed*

---

[a] *BL* (1817) begins new paragraph

[1] *The Sailor's Mother* lines 7–12.
[2] A substance used in dyeing to fix colours. Cf C's use of the word in *Friend (CC)* I 463 and *CN* III 4301 f 54ᵛ.
[3] C apparently refers to the remarks "For all good poetry is the spontaneous overflow of feelings . . ."; "I have said that Poetry is the spontaneous overflow of powerful feelings . . .". Preface to *LB* (1800): *W Prose* I 126, 148.

[4] C is recalling a passage in Sir Kenelm Digby's *Treatise on Bodies* that he had noted in 1801: "This change of motion and different beating of the heart, is that which properly is called passion. . . . Conformable whereunto, Physicians do tell us, that every passion hath a distinct pulse." *Two Treatises . . .* (1645) 377. See *CN* I 105 and n.

to imply and to produce, an unusual state of excitement, which of course justifies and demands a correspondent difference of language, as truly, though not perhaps in as marked a degree, as the excitement of love, fear, rage, or jealousy. The vividness of the descriptions or declamations in DONNE, or DRYDEN, is as much and as often derived from the force and fervour of the describer, as from the reflections,[a] forms or incidents which constitute their subject and materials. The wheels take fire from the mere rapidity of their motion.[1] To what extent, and under what modifications, this may be admitted to act, I shall attempt to define in an after remark on Mr. Wordsworth's reply to this objection, or rather on his objection to this reply, as already anticipated in his preface.[2]

Fourthly, and as intimately connected with this, if not the same argument in a more general form, I adduce the high spiritual instinct of the human being impelling us to seek unity by harmonious adjustment, and thus establishing the principle, that *all* the parts of an organized whole must be assimilated to the more *important* and *essential* parts.[3] This and the preceding arguments may be strengthened by the reflection, that the composition of a poem is among the *imitative* arts; and that imitation, as opposed to copying, consists either in the interfusion of the SAME throughout the radically DIFFERENT, or of the different throughout a base radically the same.[4]

[a] *BL* (1817) omits comma

[1] C refers to the vision of the wheels in Ezek 1.15–21 and 10. 1–22, which he had entered into a notebook in 1799 and was to use in *SM* as a symbol of "the living *educts* of the imagination" ("Whithersoever the spirit was to go, they [the wheels] went, thither was their spirit to go . . . for the spirit of the living creature was in the wheels"). *CN* I 425 and n; *SM* (*CC*) 29.

[2] See below, II 80–1.

[3] Kathleen Coburn cites as relevant to the above and to C's discussion of metre generally J. A. Eberhard's article on rhythm ("Takt") in *Charaktere der vornehmsten Dichter aller Nationen* (*Nachträge zu Sulzers allgemeiner Theorie der schönen Künste*) ed J. G. Dyk and G. Schatz (5 vols Leipzig 1792–1806) I 45–8, a work C read at Göttingen in 1799: "Rhythm affords pleasure through the consonance of its parts to each other, and the consonance of these with the predominant passion". *CN* I 406n.

[4] One of C's favourite distinctions. In general, as he uses the term, a "copy" tries to duplicate the original so closely that it can be almost mistaken for it (e.g. wax figures or wax fruit). The act of "copy" is doomed since art, conceived thus, can never compete with nature itself. On the other hand, a true "imitation", as distinct from a copy, starts out with "an acknowledged total difference" in the medium and the materials used (e.g.

Lastly, I appeal to the practice of the best poets, of all countries and in all ages, as *authorizing* the opinion, (*deduced* from all the foregoing) that in every import of the word ESSENTIAL, which would not here involve a mere truism, there may be, is, and ought to be, an *essential* difference between the language of prose and of √ metrical composition.

In Mr. Wordsworth's criticism of GRAY's Sonnet, the reader's

the two-dimensional canvas in painting; words in a poem; or the musical scale and the sounds inevitable and appropriate to musical instruments); and the "form" drawn out from these materials will be peculiar to those materials and to that medium and hence make the imitation more of a "living" thing, with its own "unity working through diversity"—something in "kind" from the original, yet at the same time analogous to it. Thus a true "imitation" duplicates the process of nature itself by presenting, in itself, the organising spirit (*natura naturans*). Still another process of unity working through diversity also takes place within our own minds when we see or respond to a good "imitation". For accepting at the start an "acknowledged" difference (the flat canvas in painting, the obduracy and limitations of stone in sculpture, the stylised movements of the dance, etc), we then find ourselves noticing similarities: our own act of mind, in short, is one that moves from diversity toward unity and/or similarity. In observing a "copy", this act of mind is reversed. We start out with an idea of similarity (so great that we may almost confuse "copy" and "original"— again as in wax figures), but then begin to note differences. This is the opposite of the aesthetic process, which is to move toward harmony or integration (unity from and through "multeity") rather than away from it. C's most complete discussion of the distinction is in *PA: BL* (1907) II 255–6, which is indebted not only to

Schelling *Über das Verhältniss der bildenden Künste zu der Natur: Phil Schrift* 356, but also to Kant and especially Schiller. *CN* III 4397 ff 49–50n. But there is a traditional distinction behind this that goes back, as Raysor says, to Aristotle's more developed conception of imitation in contrast to Plato's. *Sh C* I 200. By the 1750s English criticism was seeking to broaden the concept of imitation and contrast it to routine copying. Edward Young extended it to creative imitation of great writers and models ("He that imitates the divine *Iliad,* does not imitate Homer"), and Reynolds followed him. Young *Conjectures on Original Composition* (1759) ed E. J. Morley (1918) 11; Reynolds *Discourses* XI (1782) ed Wark (1959) 203–4. Meanwhile, reverting to the concept of art as an "imitation of nature" critical discussion stressed the need for what C calls "an acknowledged total difference". Typical is Adam Smith's celebrated "Of the Imitative Arts": the pleasure is greater in proportion to the "degree of disparity between the imitating and the imitated object"; hence artificial fruits and flowers please less than a painting of them; etc. *Essays on Philosophical Subjects* (1795) 137–41. C himself was using the distinction in 1804, though in a simpler way before he had read Schelling. *CN* II 2271, 2274. For other instances, see above, I 76 (C's n), and below, II 84 n 2; *Sh C* I 128, II 80–1, 117, 159–60, 201, 263, 313, 321; *Misc C* 49; *TT* 3 Jul 1833.

sympathy with his praise or blame of the different parts is taken
for granted rather perhaps too easily.[1] He has not, at least, attempted to win or compel it by argumentative analysis. In *my*
conception at least, the lines rejected as of no value do, with the
exception of the two first, differ as much and as little from the
language of common life, as those which he has printed in italics
as possessing genuine excellence. Of the five lines thus honorably
distinguished, two of them differ from prose even more widely,
than the lines which either precede or follow, in the *position* of
the words.

> *A different object do these eyes require;*
> My lonely anguish melts no heart but mine;
> *And in my breast the imperfect joys expire.*

But were it otherwise, what would this prove, but a truth, of
which no man ever doubted? Videlicet, that there are sentences,
which would be equally in their place both in verse and prose.
Assuredly it does not prove the point, which alone requires proof;
namely, that there are not passages, which would suit the one, and
not suit the other. The first line of this sonnet is distinguished
from the ordinary language of men by the epithet to morning.[2]
(For we will set aside, at present, the consideration, that the
particular word "*smiling*" is hackneyed, and (as it involves a sort
of personification) not quite congruous with the common and
material attribute of *shining*.) And, doubtless, this adjunction of
epithets for the purpose of additional description, where no particular attention is demanded for the quality of the thing, would
be noticed as giving a poetic cast to a man's conversation. Should
the sportman exclaim, "*come boys! the rosy morning calls you
up*," he will be supposed to have some song in his head. But no one
suspects this, when he says, "A wet morning shall not confine us
to our beds." This then is either a defect in poetry, or it is not.
Whoever should decide in the *affirmative*, I would request him to
reperuse any one poem, of any confessedly great poet from Homer

---

[1] WW, after making the remarks
quoted above, II 63, had added in
1802: "By the foregoing quotation
[Gray's Sonnet] I have shown that
the language of Prose may yet be
well adapted to Poetry; and it was
previously asserted, that a large
portion of the language of every
good poem can in no respect differ
from that of good Prose." *W Prose*
I 135.

[2] "In vain to me the smiling
mornings shine".

to Milton, or from Eschylus to Shakspeare; and to strike out (in thought I mean) every instance of this kind. If the number of these fancied erasures did not startle him; or if he continued to deem the work improved by their total omission; he must advance reasons of no ordinary strength and evidence, reasons grounded in the essence of human nature. Otherwise I should not hesitate to consider him as a man not so much *proof against* all authority, as *dead to* it.

The second line,

> And reddening Phœbus lifts his golden fire,[a]

has indeed almost as many faults as words. But then it is a bad line, not because the language is distinct from that of prose; but because it conveys incongruous images, because it confounds the cause and the effect, the real *thing* with the personified *representative* of the thing; in short, because it differs from the language of GOOD SENSE! That the "Phœbus" is hacknied, and a school-boy image,[1] is an *accidental* fault, dependent on the age in which the author wrote, and not deduced from the nature of the thing. That it is part of an exploded mythology, is an objection more deeply grounded. Yet when the torch of ancient learning was re-kindled, so cheering were its beams, that our eldest poets, cut off by christianity from all *accredited* machinery, and deprived of all *acknowledged* guardians and symbols of the great objects of nature, were naturally induced to adopt, as a *poetic* language, those fabulous personages, those forms of the * supernatural in nature, which had given them such dear delight in the poems

---

* But still more by the mechanical system of philosophy which has needlessly infected our theological opinions, and teaching us to consider the world in its relation to God, as of a building to its mason,[b] leaves the idea of omnipresence a mere abstract notion in the state-room of our reason.[2]

[a] *BL* (1817) fire.   [a] *BL* (1817) omits comma

[1] Cf ch 1, on Boyer's condemnation of school-boy images, I 9–11.
[2] Cf C's hope (Sept 1817) to "demonstrate the hollowness and falsehood" of any philosophy that "substitutes the Lockian, and Newtonian—From God we *had* our Being—for the Pauline—*In* whom we move and live and *have* our Being". The "moderns" regard the Deity as a "Watch-maker" and degrade the Divine, or God-created, "into a piece of Clock-Work—they live without God in the world", whereas the ancients often tended to the other extreme: they are aware of the Divine in creation but "make the world the total God". To C. A. Tulk: *CL* IV 768.

of their great masters.[1] Nay, even at this day what scholar of genial taste will not so far sympathize with them, as to read with pleasure in PETRARCH, CHAUCER, or SPENSER, what he would perhaps condemn as puerile in a modern poet?

I remember no poet, whose writings would safelier stand the test of Mr. Wordsworth's theory, than SPENSER. Yet will Mr. Wordsworth say, that the style of the following stanzas is either undistinguished from prose, and the language of ordinary life? Or that it is vicious, and that the stanzas are *blots* in the Faery Queen?

> By this the northern waggoner had set
> His sevenfold teme behind the stedfast starre,
> That was in ocean waves yet never wet,
> But firm is fixt and sendeth light from farre
> To all that in the wild deep wandering are.
> And chearful chanticleer with his note shrill
> Had warned once that Phœbus's fiery carre
> In haste was climbing up the easterne hill,
> Full envious that night so long his room did fill.
>
> *Book I. Can. 2. St.* 2.[2]

> At last the golden oriental gate
> Of greatest heaven gan to open fayre,
> And Phœbus fresh as brydegrome to his mate,
> Came dauncing forth, shaking his deawie hayre,
> And hurl'd his glist-ring beams through gloomy ayre;
> Which when the wakeful elfe perceived, streightway
> He started up, and did him selfe prepayre
> In sun-bright armes, and battailous array;
> For with that pagan proud he combat will that day.
>
> *B. I. Can.* 5, *St.* 2.

On the contrary to how many passages, both in hymn books and in blank verse poems, could I (were it not invidious) direct the reader's attention, the style of which is most *unpoetic*, *because*, and only because, it is the style of *prose*? He will not suppose me capable of having in my mind such verses, as

> I put my hat upon my head
> And walk'd into the strand;
> And there I met another man,
> Whose hat was in his hand.[3]

---

[1] Cf C's comments on Boccaccio's and Ariosto's christianising Jupiter and Apollo: *CN* II 2670, III 4388 f 146ᵛ.

[2] Actually st 1.

[3] The opening of Johnson's spontaneous parody of the ballad-form when Thomas Percy was lavishly

To such specimens it would indeed be a fair and full reply, that these lines are not bad, because they are *unpoetic*; but because they are empty of all sense and feeling; and that it were an idle attempt to prove that an ape is not a Newton, when it is evident that he is not a man.[1] But the sense shall be good and weighty, the language correct and dignified, the subject interesting and treated with feeling; and yet the style shall, notwithstanding all these merits, be justly blameable as *prosaic*, and solely because the words and the order of the words would find their appropriate place in prose, but are not suitable to *metrical* composition. The "Civil Wars" of Daniel is an instructive, and even interesting work; but take the following stanzas (and from the hundred instances which abound I might probably have selected others far more striking)

> And to the end we may with better ease
> Discern the true discourse, vouchsafe to shew
> What were the times foregoing near to these,
> That these we may with better profit know.
> Tell how the world fell into this disease;
> And how so great distemperature did grow;
> So shall we see with what degrees it came;
> How things at full do soon wax out of frame.

praising the "beautiful simplicity" of the ballads. The most complete account of the incident is by George Steevens *European Magazine* (1785): *Johnsonian Miscellanies* ed G. B. Hill (Oxford 1897) II 314–15. C quotes the version WW in his Preface had quoted from *London Magazine* (Apr 1785). *W Prose* I 152–4, 186. The nineteenth-century legend of Johnson's supposed scorn of the ballad-form, based on WW's and C's remarks, still persists. Actually Johnson was seriously interested in Percy's work, helping him with a Glossary and writing the Dedication for the *Reliques of Ancient English Poetry* (1765). On this occasion, a tea at Frances Reynolds's house, he was simply teasing his friend Percy, stating that the ballad-metre was so easy that one could use it in common conversation. He then proceeded to do so for several stanzas until Percy begged him to stop. Cf W. J. Bate *Samuel Johnson* (1977) 392–3.

[1] C is paraphrasing what WW said in the Preface to *LB* (1800): "The proper method of treating trivial and simple verses, to which Dr. Johnson's stanza would be a fair parallelism, is not to say this is a bad kind of poetry, or this is not poetry, but this wants sense; it is neither interesting in itself, nor can *lead* to anything interesting; the images neither originate in that sane state of feeling which arises out of thought, nor can excite thought or feeling in the Reader. This is the only sensible manner of dealing with such verses: Why trouble yourself about the species till you have previously decided upon the genus? Why take pains to prove that an Ape is not a Newton when it is self-evident that he is not a man." *W Prose* I 154.

Ten kings had from the Norman conqu'ror reign'd
With intermixt and variable fate,
When England to her greatest height attain'd
Of power, dominion, glory, wealth, and state;
After it had with much ado sustain'd
The violence of princes with debate
For titles, and the often mutinies
Of nobles for their ancient liberties.

For first the Norman, conqu'ring all by might,
By might was forced to keep what he had got;
Mixing our customs and the form of right
With foreign constitutions, he had brought;
Mastering the mighty, humbling the poorer wight,
By all severest means that could be wrought;
And making the succession doubtful rent
His new-got state and left it turbulent.

B. I. St. VII. VIII. & IX.[1]

Will it be contended,[a] on the one side, that these lines are mean and senseless? Or on the other, that they are not prosaic, and for *that* reason unpoetic? This poet's well-merited epithet is that of the *"well-languaged Daniel;"* but likewise and by the consent of his contemporaries no less than of all succeeding critics, the "prosaic Daniel."[2] Yet those, who thus designate this wise and amiable writer from the frequent incorrespondency of his diction to his metre in the majority of his compositions, not only deem them valuable and interesting on other accounts; but willingly admit, that there are to be found throughout his poems, and especially in his *Epistles* and in his *Hymen's Triumph*, many and exquisite specimens of that style which, as the *neutral ground* of prose and verse, is common to both.[3] A fine and almost faultless extract,

---

[a] *BL* (1817) omits comma

[1] *Civile Wars* (1595) I sts 7–9 (var: "with" for "by" in st 7 line 7). In *B Poets* IV 117.

[2] "Well-languag'd" is the epithet given Samuel Daniel (1562–1619) by William Browne (c 1590–c 1645) in *Britannia's Pastorals* (1613–16) II ii 303. In *B Poets* IV 309, also quoted in "The Life of Daniel" in IV 113. Michael Drayton (1563–1631) states that Daniel was regarded as "too much historian in verse; | His rhymes were smooth, his meters well did close, | But yet his manner better fitted prose." *To My Dearly-Beloved Friend Henry Reynolds* (1627) lines 126–8.

[3] Cf C's remark to Lamb on a front flyleaf of Lamb's copy of Daniel *Poetical Works* (2 vols 1718) II: "Thousands even of educated men would become more sensible, fitter to be members of Parliament, or Ministers, by reading Daniel".

eminent as for other beauties, so for its perfection in this species of diction, may be seen in L A M B ' s Dramatic Specimens, &c.,[a] a work of various interest from the nature of the selections themselves (all from the plays of Shakspeare's contemporaries) and deriving a high additional value from the notes, which are full of just and original criticism, expressed with all the freshness of originality.[1]

Among the possible effects of practical adherence to a theory, that aims to *identify* the style of prose and verse (if it does not indeed claim for the latter a yet nearer resemblance to the average style of men in the vivâ voce intercourse of real life) we might anticipate the following as not the least likely to occur. It will happen, as I have indeed before observed, that the metre itself, the sole acknowledged difference, will occasionally become metre to the eye only. The existence of *prosaisms*, and that they detract from the merit of a poem, *must* at length be conceded,[2] when a number of successive lines can be rendered, even to the most delicate ear, unrecognizable as verse, or as having even been intended for verse, by simply transcribing them as prose: when if the poem be in blank verse, this can be effected without any alteration, or at most by merely restoring one or two words to their

[a] *BL* (1817) omits comma

CM (CC) II. "Read Daniel—the admirable Daniel—in his 'Civil Wars', and 'Triumphs of Hymen'. The style and language are just such as any very pure and manly writer of the present day—Wordsworth, for example—would use; it seems quite modern in comparison with the style of Shakespeare." *TT* 15 Mar 1834. C in 1804 considered including a sonnet from Daniel in his projected "Comforts and Consolations" (*CN* I 1796n) and used him as a source of mottoes in *Friend* (*CC*) I 91, 100, 114, 129. For C's annotations on Daniel see *CM* (*CC*) I 44–7, 58–9 (on *B Poets*) and II (on Chalmers *English Poets* and Daniel *Poetical Works*). For his comparison of WW and Daniel see ch 22, below, II 146–8.

[1] Lamb *Specimens of English Dramatic Poets* (1808) 266–71 prints extracts from Daniel's *Hymen's Triumph* (1615). The "fine and almost faultless extract" to which C refers is doubtless the story of Isulia (lines 1476–1631), which so appealed to C that he used the name Isulia for SH. *CN* III 3291 f 3 and n.

[2] Cf Preface to *LB* (1800): ". . . a numerous class of critics who, when they stumble upon these prosaisms as they call them, imagine that they have made a notable discovery, and exult over the Poet as over a man ignorant of his own profession". *W Prose* I 132. Cf *OED*, which cites the above passage from *BL* for "prosaism" in this sense, but WW in 1850.

proper places, from which they had been* transplanted for no assignable cause or reason but that of the author's convenience; but if it be in rhyme, by the mere exchange of the final word of each line for some other of the same meaning, equally appropriate, dignified and euphonic.

The answer or objection in the preface to the anticipated remark "that metre paves the way to other distinctions," is contained in the

---

* As the ingenious gentleman under the influence of the Tragic Muse contrived to dislocate, "I wish you a good morning, Sir! Thank you, Sir, and I wish you the same," into two blank-verse heroics:—

> To you a morning good, good Sir! I wish.
> You, Sir! I thank: to you the same wish I.

In those parts of Mr. Wordsworth's works which I have thoroughly studied, I find fewer instances in which this would be practicable than I have met in many poems, where an approximation of prose has been seduously and on system guarded against. Indeed excepting the stanzas already quoted from the *Sailor's Mother*, I can recollect but one instance: viz. a short passage of four or five lines in T H E B R O T H E R S, that model of English pastoral, which I never yet read with unclouded eye.—"James, pointing to its summit, over which they had all purposed to return together, informed them that he would wait for them there. They parted, and his comrades passed that way some two hours after, but they did not find him at the appointed place, *a circumstance of which they took no heed*: but one of them going by chance into the house, which at this time was James's house, learnt *there*, that nobody had seen him all that day."[1] The only change which has been made is in the position of the little word *there* in two instances, the position in the original being clearly such as is not adopted in ordinary conversation. The other words printed in *italics* were so marked because, though good and genuine English, they are not the phraseology of common conversation either in the word put in apposition, or in the connection by the genitive pronoun. Men in general would have said, "but that was a circumstance they paid no attention to, or took no notice of," and the language is, on the theory of the preface, justified only by the narrator's being the *Vicar*. Yet if any ear *could* suspect, that these sentences were ever printed as metre, on those very words alone could the suspicion have been grounded.

[1] *The Brothers* (1800; published 1800) lines 362–71. C quotes from the 1800 ed, possibly from memory, since there are four minor variants in addition to the two that he states he is making. However, in an errata list WW had already made some changes, which were incorporated in 1802 and later editions, and in 1827 he completely revised the passage, in deference to C, to read (lines 369–76):

> Upon its aëry summit crowned
> with heath,

> The loiterer, not unnoticed by
> his comrades,
> Lay stretched at ease; but,
> passing by the place
> On their return, they found
> that he was gone.
> No ill was feared; till one of
> them by chance
> Entering, when evening was far
> spent, the house
> Which at that time was James's
> home, there learned
> That nobody had seen him all
> that day.

following words. "The distinction of rhyme and metre is voluntary and uniform, and not like that produced by (what is called) poetic diction, arbitrary and subject to infinite caprices, upon which no calculation whatever can be made. In the one case the reader is utterly at the mercy of the poet respecting what imagery or diction he may choose to connect with the passion."[1] But is this a *poet*, of whom a poet is speaking? No surely! rather of a fool or mad-man: or at best of a vain or ignorant phantast! And might not brains so wild and so deficient make just the same havock with rhymes and metres, as they are supposed to effect with modes and figures of speech? How is the reader at the *mercy* of such men? If he continue to read their nonsense, is it not his own fault? The ultimate end of criticism is much more to establish the principles of writing, than to furnish *rules* how to pass judgement on what has been written by others; if indeed it were possible that the two could be separated. But if it be asked, by what principles the poet is to regulate his own style, if he do not adhere closely to the sort and order of words which he hears in the market, wake, high-road, or plough-field? I reply; by principles, the ignorance or neglect of which would convict him of being no *poet*, but a silly or presumptu-ous usurper of the name! By the principles of grammar, logic, psychology! In one word by such a knowledge of the facts, material and spiritual, that most appertain to his art, as if it have been governed and applied by *good sense*, and rendered instinctive by habit, becomes the representative and reward of our past conscious reasonings, insights, and conclusions, and acquires the name of T A S T E.[2] By what *rule* that does not leave the reader at the poet's

[1] Preface to *LB* (1800): *W Prose* I 144 (var). C's quotation breaks off before the close of the sentence, which continues: "whereas in the other [rhyme and versification] the metre obeys certain laws, to which the Poet and Reader both willingly submit because they are certain, and because no interference is made by them with the passion but such as the concurring testimony of ages has shewn to heighten and improve the pleasure which co-exists with it".

[2] On "good sense" see ch 14, above, II 18, and, on Shakespeare, ch 15, above, II 26–8 ("knowledge, become habitual and intuitive,

wedded itself to his habitual feel-ings"). "The Ideal of Human Na-ture . . . [is] to judge & create by Principles, vital indeed & ab intra, but yet Principles as certain tho—& here is the distinction, here is that which brings Poetry so close to Religion, and Philosophy—an hand-maid of the same family at least—not so ascertainable.—Of Mathe-matics the motto is—all may if they will—of Poetry & Philosophy, all *may* who *can*." *CN* III 4301 f 65. More specifically on taste as the emotional response to intellectual perception and value, thus indicating knowledge assimilated into "habitual

mercy, and the poet at his own, is the latter to distinguish between
the language suitable to *suppressed,* and the language, which is
characteristic of *indulged,* anger?[1] Or between that of rage and
that of jealousy? Is it obtained by wandering about in search of
angry or jealous people in uncultivated society, in order to copy
their words? Or not far rather by the power of imagination proceeding upon the *all in each* of human nature? By *meditation,*
rather than by *observation?*[2] And by the latter in consequence

feeling", cf C's ms notes for Lect 1
of 15 Jan 1808: ". . . In its metaphorical Sense as applied to the fine
arts, Taste implies an intellectual
perception of any object blended
with a distinct consciousness of pain
or pleasure conceived as resulting
from that Object—or vice versâ a
sense of Enjoyment or Dislike instantly combined with & appearing
to proceed from some intellectual
perception of the Object." Berg MS
Portions of Four Lectures f 3v:
Lects 1808–19 (CC) ms. Cf also
PGC and "Fragment of an Essay on
Taste" (1810): *BL* (1907) II 224–7,
248–9. C's phrasing in the *BL* text
is a distilled statement of the concept
of taste developed in later eighteenth-century criticism (in reaction
to the common earlier notion of it
as based either on "reason" or on
mere individual "feeling"): that it is
the accumulated response of experience and study "digested" into
habitual feeling and imaginative insight. Typical are Reynolds's later
Discourses (esp XII and XIII), in
which the concept becomes a central
theme. For background see W. J.
Bate *From Classic to Romantic*
(Cambridge, Mass 1946) 85–91,
172–6. Cf also the passage from the
Advertisement to *LB* (1798), var in
Preface to *LB* (1800), quoted above,
II 35 n 2 (end of n on p 36).

[1] C is commenting on WW's
"Essay, Supplementary to the Preface" in *Poems* (1815): "Passion,
it must be observed, is a word which
signifies *suffering;* but the connection
which suffering has with effort, with

exertion, and *action,* is immediate
and inseparable. How strikingly is
this property of human nature exhibited by the fact, that, in popular
language, to be in a passion is to be
angry! . . . To be moved, then, by
a passion, is to be excited, often to
external, and always to internal,
effort; whether for the continuance
and strengthening of the passion, or
for its suppression . . .". *W Prose*
III 81–2.

[2] Cf the Preface to WW *Poems*
(1815) I viii: "The powers requisite
for the production of poetry are:
first, those of Observation and Description,—*i.e.,* the ability to observe
with accuracy things as they are in
themselves, and with fidelity to
describe them, unmodified by any
passion or feeling existing in the
mind of the describer . . .". *W
Prose* III 26. The contrast of "meditation" (which involves dwelling on a
subject with a full and active mind)
with mere "observation" is, as Shawcross and Raysor point out, a recurring theme of C's in the Shakespeare lectures. *BL* (1907) II 281–2;
Sh C II 117n. Cf Lect 6 of 5 Dec
1811, on Shakespeare's ability to
create "a vast multiplicity of characters by simple meditation; he had
only to imitate such parts of his
character, or to exaggerate such as
existed in possibility and they were
at once nature & fragments of
Shakespeare. . . . When he used the
term meditation he did not mean to
say that Shakespeare was without
observation. Mere observation might
be able to produce an accurate

only of the former? As eyes, for which the former has pre-determined their field of vision, and to which, as to *its* organ, it communicates a microscopic power?[1] There is not, I firmly believe, a man now living, who has from his own inward experience a clearer intuition, than Mr. Wordsworth himself, that the last mentioned are the true sources of *genial* discrimination. Through the same process and by the same creative agency will the poet distinguish the degree and kind of the excitement produced by the very act of poetic composition. As intuitively will he know, what differences of style it at once inspires and justifies; what intermixture of conscious volition is natural to that state; and in what instances such figures and colors of speech degenerate into mere creatures of an arbitrary purpose, cold technical artifices of ornament or connection. For even as truth is its own light and evidence, discovering at once itself and falsehood, so is it the prerogative of poetic genius to distinguish by parental instinct its proper offspring from the changelings, which the gnomes of vanity or the fairies of fashion may have laid in its cradle or called by its names. Could a rule be given from *without*, poetry would cease to be poetry, and sink into a mechanical art.[2] It would be

---

copy . . . & even furnish . . . more ideas than even the copyist possessed, but they would only be in parts and in fragments . . .". *Lects 1808–19* (*CC*) ms. Or on *The Tempest:* "Shakspeare's characters are all *genera* intensely individualized; the results of meditation, of which observation supplied the drapery and the colours necessary to combine them with each other. He had virtually surveyed all the great component powers and impulses of human nature,—had seen that their different combinations and subordinations were in fact the individualizers of men, and showed how their harmony was produced by reciprocal disproportions of excess or deficiency. The language in which these truths are expressed was not drawn from any set fashion, but from the profoundest depths of his moral being . . .". *Sh C* i 137, reprinted from *LR,* probably an

expanded version of C's lecture notes for Lect 6 of 16 Nov 1813 in Bristol: *Lects 1808–19* (*CC*) ms. As the above quotations show, the distinction is a counterpart to that between "imitation" and "copy" (see above, ii 72 n 4). Raysor (*Sh C* ii 117n) points out the parallels in Richter *Vorschule der Aesthetik* (1804) § 57 and Schelling *Über das Verhältniss: SW* vii 301. For analogous uses of "meditation" in *Friend,* cf "the eye of the meditative imagination"; "discoveries . . . preconcerted by meditation". *Friend* (*CC*) i 349 (ii 178), i 530.

[1] Cf discussion of "the armed vision", ch 7, above, i 118 n 3.

[2] Cf "Rules are . . . but Means to Ends . . . therefore the end, the nature, the Idea of a work must be first known and appreciated, before we can discover, much more apply, the Rules, according to which we are to judge of its merits or defects".

μόρφωσις, not ποίησις.[1] The *rules* of the IMAGINATION are
themselves the very powers of growth and production. The *words*,
to which they are reducible, present only the outlines and external
appearance of the fruit. A deceptive counterfeit of the superficial
form and colors may be elaborated; but the marble peach feels
cold and heavy, and *children* only put it to their mouths.[2] We
find no difficulty in admitting as excellent, and the legitimate
language of poetic fervor self-impassioned, DONNE'S apostrophe
to the Sun in the second stanza of his "Progress of the Soul."

> Thee, eye of heaven! this great soul envies not:
> By thy male force is all, we have, begot.
> In the first East thou now beginn'st to shine,
> Suck'st early balm and island spices there;
> And wilt anon in thy loose-rein'd career
> At Tagus, Po, Seine, Thames, and Danow dine,
> And see at night this western world of mine:
> Yet hast thou not more nations seen, than she,
> Who before thee one day began to be,
> And, thy frail light being quenched, shall long, long outlive thee![3]

CN III 4384 f 158ᵛ. Cf the remark, translated and condensed from A. W. Schlegel: "The form is mechanic when on any given material we impress a pre-determined form, not necessarily arising out of the properties of the material—as when to a mass of wet clay we give whatever shape we wish it to retain when hardened—The organic form on the other hand is innate, it shapes as it developes itself from within . . .". MS Egerton 2800 f 24ᵛ, probably used in Lect 8 of 1812–13 at the Surrey Institution: *Lects 1808–19* (*CC*) ms. Cf also *Sh C* I 231; II 36, 170.

[1] A "fashioning", not a "creation".

[2] "What a marble peach on a mantel-piece, that you take up deluded . . . is compared with a fruit-piece of Vanhuysen's, even such is a mere *Copy* of nature compared with a true histrionic *Imitation*." To Charles Mathews 30 May 1814: *CL* III 501. Cf *TT* 6 Jul 1833. On "copy" contrasted with "imitation" see above, II 72 n 4.

[3] Lines 11–20 (var) and (below) 31–7 (var). On the latter passage, cf Baron Hatherley's account of a visit he and Basil Montagu made to C (29 Jan 1829): "He had been seized with a fit of enthusiasm for Donne's poetry, which I think somewhat unaccountable. There was great strength, however, in some passages which he read. One stanza or rather division of his poem, on the 'Progress of the Soul', struck me very much; it was, I think, the fourth, in which he addresses Destiny as the 'Knot of Causes' ". *Memoir of the Right Hon. William Page Wood, Baron Hatherley* ed W. R. W. Stephens (2 vols 1883) I 175. "After all, there is but one Donne! & now tell me yet, wherein *in his own kind* he differs from the *similar* power in Shakespere? Sh. was all men potentially except Milton—& they differ from him by negation, or privation, or both. . . ." Annotation on *Womans Constancy* in Donne *Poems* (1669) 4–5: *CM* (*CC*) II. On Donne's "wit" cf ch 1, above, I 23 n 3.

Or the next stanza but one:

> Great destiny, the commissary of God,
> That hast marked out a path and period
> For ev'ry thing! Who, where we offspring took,
> Our ways and ends see'st at one instant: thou
> Knot of all causes! Thou, whose changeless brow
> Ne'er smiles or frowns! O vouchsafe thou to look,
> And shew my story in thy eternal book, &c.

As little difficulty do we find in excluding from the honors of unaffected warmth and elevation the madness prepense of Pseudo-poesy, or the startling *hysteric* of weakness over-exerting itself, which bursts on the unprepared reader in sundry odes and apostrophes to abstract terms. Such are the Odes to Jealousy, to Hope, to Oblivion, and the like in Dodsley's collection[1] and the magazines of that day, which seldom fail to remind me of an Oxford copy of verses on the two S U T T O N S,[2] commencing with

> I N O C U L A T I O N, heavenly maid! descend![3]

[1] Robert Dodsley (1703–64), who published works of Johnson, Burke, Goldsmith, Akenside, Chesterfield, and many other noted writers. His *Select Collection of Old Plays* (12 vols 1744) contributed to the revival of interest in Elizabethan and Jacobean drama. In *A Collection of Poems by Various Hands* (3 vols 1748, enlarged in later eds), to which C refers, Dodsley made an effort to secure contributions from every well-known poet of the time. C exaggerates the number of odes there of the type he mentions. In the enlarged 5-vol ed (1765) only fifteen have abstractions in the title (Ambition, Indolence, Health, Memory, Wisdom—none, incidentally, is addressed to Jealousy, Hope, or Oblivion). On the other hand, such poems abound in magazines of the later 1700s.

[2] The "two Suttons" were Daniel and Robert, sons of a surgeon at Debenham, Suffolk. In the 1760s they improved on the process of inoculation for smallpox introduced from Turkey earlier in the century. ("Inoculation" involved deliberate infection from mild cases of smallpox as contrasted with "vaccination" through cow-pox advocated by Edward Jenner [1749–1823] in 1793.) Daniel Sutton in particular had considerable success with inoculation, which was often risky, and in 1769 adopted the title of "Professor of Inoculation in the kingdom of Great Britain, and in all the dominions of his Britannic Majesty". R. Hingston Fox *Dr. John Fothergill and His Friends* (1919) 81; cited in *BL* (1920) 310.

[3] William Lipscomb (1754–1842) *Beneficial Effects of Inoculation* II 39–40:

> I NOCULATION, heaven-instructed maid;
> She woo'd from Turkey's shores to Britain's aid.

("She" in the second line refers not to Inoculation but to Lady Mary Wortley Montagu [1689–1762], who introduced inoculation into Britain from Turkey.) The poem, delivered at Oxford in 1772, won the Chancellor's prize; it was not "on the two Suttons". Published in *G Mag* LIII pt 2 (1783) 782–3, 869, it was

It is not to be denied that men of undoubted talents, and even
poets of true, though not of first-rate, genius, have from a mistaken
theory deluded both themselves and others in the opposite extreme.
I once read to a company of sensible and well-educated women the
introductory period of Cowley's preface to his *Pindaric Odes,
written in imitation of the style and manner of the odes of Pindar.*
"If (says Cowley) a man should undertake to translate Pindar,
word for word, it would be thought that one madman had translated another; as may appear, when he, that understands not the
original, reads the verbal traduction of him into Latin prose, than
which nothing seems more raving."[1] I then proceeded with his
own free version of the second Olympic composed for the charitable purpose of *rationalizing* the Theban Eagle.

> Queen of all harmonious things,
> Dancing words and speaking strings,
> What God, what hero, wilt thou sing?
> What happy man to equal glories bring?
> Begin, begin thy noble choice,
> And let the hills around reflect the image of thy voice.
> Pisa does to Jove belong,
> Jove and Pisa claim thy song.
> The fair first-fruits of war, th' Olympic games,
> Alcides offer'd up to Jove;
> Alcides too thy strings may move!
> But oh! what man to join with these can worthy prove?
> Join Theron boldly to their sacred names;
> Theron the next honor claims;
> Theron to no man gives place;
> Is first in Pisa's and in Virtue's race;
> Theron there, and he alone,
> Ev'n his own swift forefathers has outgone.[2]

One of the company exclaimed, with the full assent of the rest,
that if the original were madder than this, it must be incurably
mad. I then translated the ode from the Greek, and as nearly as
possible, word for word; and the impression was, that in the general
movement of the periods, in the form of the connections and
transitions, and in the sober majesty of lofty sense, it appeared to
them to approach more nearly, than any other poetry they had

---

republished separately in 1793. In
the revised version in *Oxford Prize
Poems* (1807) 29–38 the above lines
were omitted.
    [1] The opening sentence of Cow-
ley's Preface, in C's annotated
Cowley *Poetical Works* (1681) iii
p⁻2.
    [2] Lines 1–18: *Poetical Works* iii
1–2.

heard, to the style of our bible in the prophetic books. The first strophe will suffice as a specimen:

> Ye harp-controuling hymns! (or) ye hymns the sovereigns
>   of harps!
> What God? what Hero?
> What Man shall we celebrate?
> Truly Pisa indeed is of Jove,
> But the Olympiad (or the Olympic games) did Hercules
>   establish,
> The first-fruits of the spoils of war.
> But Theron for the four-horsed car,
> That bore victory to him,
> It behoves us now to voice aloud:
> The Just, the Hospitable,
> The Bulwark of Agrigentum,
> Of renowned fathers
> The Flower, even him
> Who preserves his native city erect and safe.

But are such rhetorical caprices condemnable only for their deviation from the language of real life? and are they by no other means to be precluded, but by the rejection of all distinctions between prose and verse, save that of metre? Surely good sense, and a moderate insight into the constitution of the human mind, would be amply sufficient to prove, that such language and such combinations are the native produce neither of the fancy nor of the imagination; that their operation consists in the excitement of surprize by the juxta-position and *apparent* reconciliation of widely different or incompatible things. As when, for instance, the hills are made to reflect the image of a *voice*. Surely, no unusual taste is requisite to see clearly, that this compulsory juxta-position is not produced by the presentation of impressive or delightful forms to the inward vision, nor by any sympathy with the modifying powers with which the genius of the poet had united and inspirited all the objects of his thought; that it is therefore a species of *wit*,[1] a pure work of the *will*, and implies a leisure and self-possession both of thought and of feeling, incompatible with the steady

[1] Cf Lect 6 of 5 Dec 1811: "The Lecturer here drew a distinction between *Wit* & *Fancy*. When the whole pleasure received was derived from surprise at an unexpected turn of expression then he called it *Wit:* But when the pleasure was produced not only by surprise but likewise by an image which remained with us and gratified us for its own sake then he called it *Fancy*." *Lects 1808–19 (CC)* ms. Cf *CN* iii 4503 ff 135ᵛ–135.

fervour of a mind possessed and filled with the grandeur of its subject. To sum up the whole in one sentence. When a poem, or a part of a poem, shall be adduced, which is evidently vicious in the figures and contexture of its style, yet for the condemnation of which no reason can be assigned, except that it differs from the style in which men actually converse, then, and not till then, can I hold this theory to be either plausible, or practicable, or capable of furnishing either rule, guidance, or precaution, that might not, more easily and more safely, as well as more naturally, have been deduced in the author's own mind from considerations of grammar, logic, and the truth and nature of things, confirmed by the authority of works, whose fame is not of ONE country, nor of ONE age.

CHAPTER 19

Continuation—Concerning the real object which, it is probable, Mr. Wordsworth had before him, in his critical preface—Elucidation and application of this[a]—The neutral style, or that common to Prose and Poetry, exemplified by specimens from Chaucer, Herbert, &c[b]

IT M I G H T appear from some passages in the former part of Mr. Wordsworth's preface, that he meant to confine his theory of style, and the necessity of a close accordance with the actual language of men, to those particular subjects from low and rustic life, which by way of experiment he had purposed to naturalize as a new species in our English poetry. But from the train of argument that follows; from the reference to Milton; and from the spirit of his critique on Gray's sonnet; those sentences appear to have been rather courtesies of modesty, than actual limitations of his system. Yet so groundless does this system appear on a close examination; and so strange and* over-whelming in its conse-

---

* I had in my mind the striking but untranslatable epithet, which the celebrated Mendelssohn applied to the great founder of the Critical Philosophy "*Der alleszermalmende* K A N T ," i.e. the all-becrushing, or rather the *all-to-nothing-crushing* K A N T .[1] In the facility and force of compound epithets, the German from the number of its cases and inflections approaches to the Greek: that language so

Bless'd in the happy marriage of sweet words.[2]

[a–b] *BL* (1817) printed at end of heading to ch 20, after "*continued*"

[1] Moses Mendelssohn (1729–86), the philosopher and grandfather of the composer, in the preface to his *Morgenstunden* (Frankfort & Leipzig 1790) iv, in which he mentions his interest in what he had read and heard about the works of Lambert, Tetens, Platner, and "des alles zermalmenden *Kants*". *CN* iii 4046n, which also points out that HCR had quoted the phrase in his "Letters on the Philosophy of Kant from an Undergraduate in the University of Jena" *Monthly Register* i (1802) 415.

[2] "The learned Greek rich in fit epithets, | Blest in the lovely marriage of pure words". From Thomas Tomkis (fl 1614) *Lingua: or the Combat of the Tongue and the Five Senses for Superiority* i i 60–1, which appears in Robert Dodsley *Select Collection of Old Plays* (1744) v 7. *CN* ii 2964n, where it is also noted that, two years after reading the line (1806), C quoted it in a letter to SH

quences, that I cannot, and I do not, believe that the poet did ever himself adopt it in the unqualified sense, in which his expressions have been understood by others, and which indeed according to all the common laws of interpretation they seem to bear. What then did he mean? I apprehend, that in the clear perception, not unaccompanied with disgust or contempt, of the gaudy affectations of a style which passed too current with too many for poetic diction, (though in truth it had as little pretensions to poetry, as to logic or common sense) he narrowed his view for the time; and feeling a justifiable preference for the language of nature, and of good-sense, even in its humblest and least ornamented forms, he suffered himself to express, in terms at once too large and too exclusive, his predilection for a style the most remote possible from the false and showy splendor which he wished to explode. It is possible, that this predilection, at first merely comparative, deviated for a time into direct partiality. But the real object, which he had in view, was, I doubt not, a species of excellence which had been long before most happily characterized by the judicious and amiable G A R V E ,[1] whose works are so justly beloved and esteemed by the Germans, in his remarks on G E L L E R T (see Sammlung Einiger Abhandlungen von Christian Garve) from which the following is literally translated. "The talent, that is required in order to make excellent verses, is perhaps greater than the philosopher is ready to admit, or would find it in his power to acquire: the talent to seek only the apt expression of the thought, and yet to

---

It is in the woeful harshness of its sounds alone that the German need shrink from the comparison.

---

accompanying a copy of Chapman's *Homer* that he presented to her (*CM—CC—*II) and used both lines in Lect 6 of 5 Dec 1811 (*Sh C* II 119). However, as the ed of *Lects 1808–19* (*CC*) notes, the lines do not appear in the longhand transcript of Collier's shorthand notes; *LR* I 259 first printed the letter to SH.

[1] Christian Garve (1742–98), who succeeded the poet C. F. Gellert (see ch 10, above, I 211 n 2) as professor of philosophy at Leipzig, translated Adam Smith, Adam Ferguson, and Burke's *Sublime and Beautiful,* and was known for the lucid style of his own moral and critical writings. C owned and annotated several of his works, but the annotations were apparently unrecorded and the volumes have not been traced. C copied out this particular passage in Dec 1803 from Garve "Vermischten Anmerkungen über Gellerts Moral, dessen Schriften überhaupt, und Charakter" *Sammlung einiger Abhandlungen* . . . (Leipzig 1799) 233–4. C is not translating the passage as "literally" as he claims but rather freely. *CN* I 1702 and n; cf I 1675 and n.

find at the same time with it the rhyme and the metre. Gellert possessed this happy gift, if ever any one of our poets possessed it; and nothing perhaps contributed more to the great and universal impression which his fables made on their first publication, or conduces more to their continued popularity. It was a strange and curious phenomenon, and such as in Germany had been previously unheard of, to read verses in which every thing was expressed, just as one would wish to talk, and yet all dignified, attractive, and interesting; and all at the same time perfectly correct as to the measure of the syllables and the rhyme. It is certain, that poetry when it has attained this excellence makes a far greater impression than prose. So much so indeed, that even the gratification which the very rhymes afford, becomes then no longer a contemptible or trifling gratification."

However novel this phenomenon may have been in Germany at the time of Gellert, it is by no means new, nor yet of recent existence in our language. Spite of the licentiousness with which Spenser*a* occasionally compels the orthography of his words into a subservience to his rhymes, the whole Fairy Queen is an almost continued instance of this beauty. Waller's song "Go, lovely Rose, &c." is doubtless familiar to most of my readers; but if I had happened to have had by me the Poems of COTTON, more but far less deservedly celebrated as the author of the "Virgil travestied,"*b* I should have indulged myself, and I think have gratified many who are not acquainted with his serious works, by selecting some admirable specimens of this style.[1] There are not a few poems in that volume, replete with every excellence of thought, image, and passion, which we expect or desire in the poetry of the

---

a BL (1817): Spencer   *b BL* (1817) omits quotation marks

[1] Charles Cotton (1630–87), translator of Montaigne and friend of Izaak Walton. His *Scarronides, or Virgil Travestie* (1664–70), to which C refers, a burlesque of *Aeneid* bks I and IV, ran through fifteen editions. The lyrics in his posthumous *Poems on Several Occasions* (1689) interested not only C (whose poem *Separation* [1809–10] is based on one of Cotton's odes) but also WW, who praised Cotton's ode *Winter* in the 1815 Preface for its "profusion of *fanciful* comparisons, which indicate on the part of the poet extreme activity of intellect, and a correspondent hurry of delightful feeling". *W Prose* III 38. Probably the interest of both WW and C in Cotton's poems had been aroused by Lamb, who had written enthusiastically about him to WW (5 Mar 1803), quoting the greater part of *Winter,* and later in "New Year's Eve" quoted the whole of Cotton's *New Year* as an example of "the purging sunlight of clear poetry". *LL* II 98–103.

milder muse; and yet so worded, that the reader sees no one reason
either in the selection or the order of the words, why he might not
have said the very same in an appropriate conversation, and
cannot conceive how indeed he could have expressed such thoughts
otherwise, without loss or injury to his meaning.

But in truth our language is, and from the first dawn of poetry
ever has been, particularly rich in compositions distinguished by
this excellence. The final *e*, which is now mute, in Chaucer's age
was either sounded or dropt indifferently.[1] We ourselves still use
either *beloved* or *belov'd* according as the rhyme, or measure,
or the purpose of more or less solemnity may require. Let the
reader then only adopt the pronunciation of the poet and of the
court, at which he lived, both with respect to the final *e* and to
the accentuation of the last syllable: I would then venture to ask,
what even in the colloquial language of elegant and unaffected
women (who are the peculiar mistresses of "pure English and
undefiled,")[2] what could we hear more natural, or seemingly more
unstudied, than the following stanzas from Chaucer's "Troilus and
Creseide"? [a]

> And after this forth to the gate he went,
> Ther as Creseide out rode a full gode paas:
> And up and doun there made he many a wente,
> And to himselfe ful oft he said, Alas!
> Fro hennis rode my blisse and my solas:
> As wouldè blisful God now for his joie,
> I might her sene agen come in to Troie!
>   And to the yondir hill I gan her guide,
> Alas! and there I toke of her my leave:
> And yond I saw her to her fathir ride;
> For sorrow of which mine hearte shall to-cleve;
> And hithir home I came when it was eve;
> And here I dwel; out-cast from allè joie,
> And shall, til I maie sene her efte in Troie.
>   And of himselfe imaginid he ofte
> To ben defaitid, pale and waxen lesse
> Than he was wonte, and that men saidin softe,

---

[a] *BL* (1817) omits quotation marks and has full stop for question mark

[1] Not "dropt indifferently" but
according to specific rules that had
been clarified by Thomas Tyrwhitt
(1730–86) in the "Essay on the
Language and Versification of Chaucer" included in his ed of *The*
Canterbury Tales (1775–8) IV 93–
102. Later C showed himself quite
aware of this (*TT* 15 Mar 1834).

[2] Alluding to Spenser's tribute to
"Dan Chaucer, well of English un-
defyled". *Faerie Queene* IV ii st 32.

What may it be? who can the sothè guess,
Why Troilus hath al this heviness?
And al this n' as but his melancholie,
That he had of himselfe suche fantasie.
Another time imaginin he would
That every wight, that past him by the wey
Had of him routhe, and that they saien should,
I am right sorry, Troilus will die!
And thus he drove a daie yet forth or twey
As ye have herde; suche life gan he to lede
As he that stode betwixin hope and drede:
For which him likid in his songis shewe
Th' encheson of his wo as he best might,
And made a songe of wordis but a fewe,
Somwhat his woefull herté for to light,
And when he was from every mann'is sight
With softé voice he of his lady dere,
That absent was, gan sing as ye may hear:

  *   *   *   *   *   *   *   *

This song when he thus songin had, full soon
He fell agen into his sighis olde:
And every night, as was his wonte to done,
He stodè the bright moonè to beholde
And all his sorrowe to the moone he tolde,
And said: I wis, when thou art hornid newe,
I shall be glad, if al the world be trewe![1]

Another exquisite master of this species of style, where the scholar and the poet supplies the material, but the perfect well-bred gentleman the expressions and the arrangement, is George Herbert. As from the nature of the subject, and the too frequent quaintness of the thoughts, his "Temple; or Sacred Poems and Private Ejaculations" are comparatively but little known, I shall extract two poems.[2] The first is a Sonnet, equally admirable for

[1] *Troilus and Criseyde* v 603–37, 645–51 (var). In *B Poets* I 398. One of C's projected works in 1803, suggested by the forthcoming publication that year of William Godwin's *Life of Chaucer,* was a general critique of Chaucer, studying him in relation to his contemporaries and comparing him with major poets of other periods. Letter to Godwin 10 Jun 1803: *CL* II 505. Cf *CN* I 1646 and *CL* II 1054, and above, ch 2, I 33.

[2] *The Temple* (1633) by George Herbert (1593–1633), published shortly after his death, remained little known in the middle and later eighteenth century until C's own time. No ed was published between 1709 and 1799 except for John Wesley's *Select Parts of Mr. Herbert's Sacred Poems* (1773), though some of his poems were included in more general collections, usually of hymns, psalms, and other religious verse. K. Williamson *PQ* 41

the weight, number, and expression of the thoughts, and for the simple dignity of the language. (Unless indeed a fastidious taste should object to the latter half of the sixth line.) The second is a poem of greater length, which I have chosen not only for the present purpose, but likewise as a striking example and illustration of an assertion hazarded in a former page of these sketches: 1 namely, that the characteristic fault of our elder poets is the reverse of that, which distinguishes too many of our more recent versifiers; the one conveying the most fantastic thoughts in the most correct and natural language; the other in the most fantastic language conveying the most trivial thoughts.2 The latter is a riddle of words; the former an enigma of thoughts. The one reminds me of an odd passage in Drayton's IDEAS:

SONNET IX.

As other men, so I myself do muse,
Why in this sort I wrest invention so;
And why these *giddy metaphors* I use,
Leaving the path the greater part do go?
I will resolve you: *I am lunatic!* 3

The other recalls a still odder passage in the "SYNAGOGUE: *or the Shadow of the Temple*," a connected series of poems in imitation of Herbert's "TEMPLE," and in some editions annexed to it.

(1962) 769–72. C's discussion of Herbert and quotations from him in this chapter did much to increase Herbert's reputation. C's own serious interest in Herbert seems to have begun in 1809. *CN* III 3532–3, 3580, 3735; and *Friend* (*CC*) II 44 (I 45), in which he states: ". . . The quaintness of some of his thoughts (not of his diction, than which nothing can be more pure, manly, and unaffected,) has blinded modern readers to the great general merit of his Poems, which are for the most part exquisite in their kind". Cf C's letter to William Collins 6 Dec 1818: "I find more substantial comfort, now, in pious George Herbert's 'Temple,' which I used to read to amuse myself with his quaintness— in short, only to laugh at—than in all

the poetry, since the poems of Milton." *CL* IV 893. For C's annotations on Herbert and Harvey (see below) see *CM* (*CC*) II.

1 See ch 1, above, I 23.

2 C, as George Watson suggests, echoes Dryden's comparison of Donne's satires with Cleveland's: "the one gives us deep thoughts in common language, though rough cadence; the other gives us common thoughts in abstruse words". *Essay on Dramatic Poesy* (1668): *Essays* ed W. P. Ker (Oxford 1926) I 52. *BL* (1975) 226n.

3 No IX (lines 1–5) in the sonnet sequence *Idea* (1619), by Michael Drayton (1563–1631), not to be confused with his earlier *Ideas Mirrour* (1594). In *B Poets* III 551.

O how my mind
　　Is gravell'd!
　　　Not a thought,
That I can find,
　　But's ravell'd
　　　All to nought!
Short ends of threds,
　　And narrow shreds
　　　Of lists;
Knot's snarled ruffs,
　　Loose broken tufts
　　　Of twists;
Are my torn meditations ragged cloathing,
Which wound, and woven shape a sute for nothing:
One while I think, and then I am in pain
To think how to unthink that thought again![1]

Immediately after these burlesque passages I cannot proceed to the extracts promised, without changing the ludicrous tone of feeling by the interposition of the three following stanzas of Herbert's.

VIRTUE.

Sweet day so cool, so calm, so bright,
The bridal of the earth and sky:
The dew shall weep thy fall to night,
　　For thou must dye!

Sweet rose, whose hue angry and brave
Bids the rash gazer wipe his eye:
Thy root is ever in its grave,
　　And thou must dye!

Sweet spring, full of sweet days and roses,
A nest, where sweets compacted lie:
My musick shews, ye have your closes,
　　And all must dye![2]

THE BOSOM SIN:

A SONNET BY GEORGE HERBERT.

Lord, with what care hast thou begirt us round!
Parents first season us; then schoolmasters

[1] Christopher Harvey (or Harvie, 1597–1663) *Confusion* lines 1–16. His *The Synagogue,* a series of poems that includes the one C cites, was bound up with the 6th (1641) and several later eds of Herbert's *Temple.* In C's ed of Herbert's *Temple* (10th ed 1674), bound with Harvey's *Synagogue* (6th ed 1673), both of which he annotated, the poem appears on ii 51.

[2] C prints the first three of four stanzas (substituting "nest" for "box" in line 10). In his annotated copy, *Temple* (1674) i 80, C deleted the printed "box" and inserted "Nest" (as in *BL*) and drew a line after the third stanza.

Deliver us to laws; they send us bound
To rules of reason, holy messengers,
Pulpits and Sundays, sorrow dogging sin,
    Afflictions sorted, anguish of all sizes,
    Fine nets and stratagems to catch us in,
Bibles laid open, millions of surprizes;
Blessings before hand, ties of gratefulness,
    The sound of glory ringing in our ears:
    Without, our shame; within,*a* our consciences;
Angels and grace, eternal hopes and fears!
    Yet all these fences, and their whole array
    One cunning BOSOM-SIN blows quite away.1

LOVE UNKNOWN.

Dear friend, sit down, the tale is long and sad:
And in my faintings, I presume, your love
Will more comply than help. A Lord I had,
And have, of whom some grounds, which may improve,
I hold for two lives, and both lives in me.
To him I brought a dish of fruit one day
And in the middle placed my HEART. But he
                              (I sigh to say)
Lookt on a servant who did know his eye,
Better than you knew me, or (which is one)
Than I myself. The servant instantly,
Quitting the fruit, seiz'd on my *heart* alone,
And threw it in a font, wherein did fall
A stream of blood, which issued from the side
Of a great rock: I well remember all,
And have good cause: there it was dipt and dy'd,
And washt, and wrung! the very wringing yet
Enforceth tears. *Your heart was foul, I fear.*
Indeed 'tis true. I did and do commit
Many a fault, more than my lease will bear;
Yet still ask'd pardon, and was not deny'd.
But you shall hear. After my heart was well,
And clean and fair, as I one eventide,
                              (I sigh to tell)
Walkt by myself abroad, I saw a large
And spacious furnace flaming, and thereon
A boiling caldron, round about whose verge
Was in great letters set AFFLICTION.
The greatness shew'd the owner. So I went

a BL (1817) omits comma

1 *Sin: Temple* (1674) i 37–8. On   a front flyleaf of his copy C noted:
                                        "a good sonnet".

To fetch a sacrifice out of my fold,
Thinking with that, which I did thus present,
To warm his love, which, I did fear, grew cold.
But as my heart did tender it, the man
Who was to take it from me, slipt his hand,
And threw my *heart* into the scalding pan;
My heart that brought it (do you understand?)
The *offerer's* heart. *Your heart was hard, I fear.*
Indeed 'tis true. I found a callous matter
Began to spread and to expatiate there:
But with a richer drug than scalding water
I bath'd it often, ev'n with holy blood,
Which at a board, while many drank bare wine,
A friend did steal into my cup for good,
Ev'n taken inwardly, and most divine
To supple hardnesses. But at the length
Out of the caldron getting, soon I fled
Unto my house, where to repair the strength
Which I had lost, I hasted to my bed;
But when I thought to sleep out all these faults,
                                        (I sigh to speak)
I found that some had stuff'd the bed with thoughts,
I would say *thorns*. Dear, could my heart not break,
When with my pleasures even my rest was gone?
Full well I understood who had been there:
For I had given the key to none but one:
It must be he. *Your heart was dull, I fear.*
Indeed a slack and sleepy state of mind
Did oft possess me; so that when I pray'd,
Though my lips went, my heart did stay behind.
But all my scores were by another paid,
Who took my guilt upon him. *Truly, friend;*
For ought I hear, your master shows to you
More favour than you wot of. Mark the end!
The font did only what was old renew:
The caldron suppled what was grown too hard:
The thorns did quicken what was grown too dull:
All did but strive to mend what you had marr'd.
Wherefore be cheer'd, and praise him to the full
Each day, each hour, each moment of the week,
Who fain would have you be new, tender, quick![1]

---

[1] *Love Unknown* (var: reading,   "my debt"): *Temple* (1674) i 121–3.
line 61, "my guilt" for Herbert's

CHAPTER 20

The former subject continued[a]

I HAVE no fear in declaring my conviction, that the excellence defined and exemplified in the preceding Chapter is not the characteristic excellence of Mr. Wordsworth's style; because I can add with equal sincerity, that it is precluded by higher powers.[1] The praise of uniform adherence to genuine, logical English is undoubtedly his; nay, laying the main emphasis on the word *uniform* I will dare add that, of all contemporary poets, it is *his alone*. For in a less absolute sense of the word, I should certainly

---

[a] See ch 19 n[a-b]

[1] In particular, those stressed in ch 22, below. Relevant to the whole of vol II, esp chs 20–2, is a note on the half-title of *BL* II C addressed to DC c Jul 1817: "In this volume, my dear Derwent, I have compressed all I know of the principles of a sober yet not ungenial Criticism: and most anxiously have I avoided all mere *assertions*—all *opinion* not followed or preceded by the reasons, on which it has been grounded. Of one thing I am distinctly conscious, viz. that my main motive and continued impulse was to secure, as far as in me lay, an intelligent admiration to Mr Wordsworth's Poems— and while I frankly avowed what I deemed defects, and why I deemed them so, yet to evince how *very* trifling they were not only in importance but even in the proportional space occupied by them; and lastly to satisfy at once a favorite wish as well as favorite conviction of my own, which I cannot better express than by adopting the following stanza of old Gascoigne's, in application to Wordsworth's Genius

> Lo! as a Hawk that soareth
> tow'rd the sky
> And climbs aloft for solace of
> hir wing,
> The greater Gate she getteth up
> on high,
> The truer stoupe she makes at
> any thing.

If in so doing I have offended where I should most wish and did most expect to please, it is but one of many proofs that I have been too apt to judge of the feelings of others by my own.—

S. T. C."

The note, on a copy of *BL* formerly in the possession of the Rev N. F. D. Coleridge, is reproduced above, facing II 40. The lines from George Gascoigne—*The Fruites of Warre* st 34 lines 1–4 (var): in *Works of the English Poets* ed Alexander Chalmers (1810) II 516— C had copied into a notebook in Apr 1817. *CN* III 4353 and n.

include MR. BOWLES, LORD BYRON,[1] and, as to all his later writings, MR. SOUTHEY, the exceptions in their works being so few and unimportant. But of the specific excellence described in the quotation from Garve,[2] I appear to find more, and more undoubted specimens in the works of others; for instance, among the minor poems of Mr. Thomas Moore, and of our illustrious Laureate.[3] To me it will always remain a singular and noticeable fact; that a theory which would establish this *lingua communis*, not only as the best, but as the only commendable style, should have proceeded from a poet, whose diction, next to that of Shakspeare and Milton, appears to me of all others the most *individualized* and characteristic.[4] And let it be remembered too, that I am now interpreting the controverted passages of Mr. W.'s critical preface by the purpose and object, which he may be supposed to have intended, rather than by the sense which the words themselves must convey, if they are taken without this allowance.

A person of any taste, who had but studied three or four of Shakspeare's principal plays, would without the name affixed scarcely fail to recognize as Shakspeare's, a quotation from any other play, though but of a few lines. A similar peculiarity, though in a less degree, attends Mr. Wordsworth's style, whenever he

---

[1] In Mar 1815 C, at Bowles's suggestion, wrote Byron an embarrassed letter of self-introduction asking him to look over the volume of his poems later published as *SL* (1817) and, if he thought well of them, to recommend them "to some respectable Publisher". Byron agreed and (having a hand at this time in managing Drury Lane) also suggested that C write another tragedy like *Remorse*. C continued to think of this while writing *BL,* reopened his correspondence with Byron in Oct, and, unable to begin a tragedy, wrote *Zapolya* (1817) as a substitute. *CL* IV 559–63, 597–606, 622–3, 626–8; *C Life* (B) 138–40. But cf C's later remark, speaking of Scott and Byron: ". . . in less than a century, the Baronet's & the

Baron's Poems will lie on the same shelf of oblivion". Annotation on Samuel Pepys *Memoirs* (2 vols 1825) II i 125: *CM (CC)* III.

[2] Ch 19, above, II 90.

[3] RS, who had recently (1813) been appointed poet laureate to succeed Henry James Pye (1745–1813). In a letter of 15 Jun 1817 to HCR, criticising Moore's *Lalla Rookh,* C exclaimed: "Why, there are not 3 lines together without some adulteration of common English. . .". *CL* IV 740. For similar remarks on Bowles, Byron, Moore, and RS see ch 22, below, II 144.

[4] "But in imaginative power, he stands nearest of all modern writers to Shakespear and Milton; and yet in a kind perfectly unborrowed and his own." See below, II 151.

speaks in his own person; or whenever, though under a feigned name, it is clear that he himself is still speaking, as in the different dramatis personæ of the "RECLUSE."[1] Even in the other poems in which he purposes to be most dramatic, there are few in which it does not occasionally burst forth. The reader might often address the poet in his own words with reference to the persons introduced;

> It seems, as I retrace the ballad line by line
> That but half of it is theirs, and the better half is thine.[2]

Who, having been previously acquainted with any considerable portion of Mr. Wordsworth's publications, and having studied them with a full feeling of the author's genius, would not at once claim as Wordsworthian the little poem on the rainbow?

> The child is father of the man, &c.[3]

Or in the "Lucy Gray"?

> No mate, no comrade Lucy knew;
> She dwelt on a wide moor;
> *The sweetest thing that ever grew*
> *Beside a human door.*[4]

Or in the "Idle Shepherd-boys"?

> Along the river's stony marge
> The sand-lark chaunts a joyous song;
> The thrush is busy in the wood,
> And carols loud and strong.

[1] WW's projected *magnum opus,* which he describes in the Preface to *The Excursion* (1814) as "a philosophical poem, containing views of Man, Nature, and Society . . . The preparatory poem [*The Prelude*] is biographical, and conducts the history of the Author's mind to the point when he was emboldened to hope that his faculties were sufficiently mature for entering upon the arduous labour which he had proposed to himself; and the two Works have the same kind of relation to each other, if he may so express himself, as the ante-chapel has to the body of a gothic church." There were to be three major parts of *The Recluse.* Pts I and III were to "consist chiefly of meditations in the Author's own person". Of these only a portion of pt I was written (*WPW* v 313–39). It is the intermediate part—the recently published *Excursion* (1814)—to which C refers above. Here, by contrast to pts I and III, "the intervention of characters speaking is employed, and something of a dramatic form adopted". *W Prose* III 5–6.

[2] Adapted from *The Pet-Lamb* (1800) lines 63–4: "And it seemed, as I retraced the ballad line by line, | That but half of it was hers, and one half of it was *mine.*"

[3] "My heart leaps up . . ." (1802); pub 1807) line 7.

[4] *Lucy Gray* (1799; pub 1800) lines 5–8.

> A thousand lambs are on the rock
> All newly born! both earth and sky
> Keep jubilee, and more than all,
> Those boys with their green coronal,
> They never hear the cry,
> That plaintive cry which up the hill
> Comes from the depth of Dungeon Gill.[1]

Need I mention the exquisite description of the Sea Loch in the "Blind Highland Boy." Who but a poet tells a tale in such language to the little ones by the fire-side as—

> Yet had he many a restless dream
> Both when he heard the eagle's scream,
> And when he heard the torrents roar,
> And heard the water beat the shore
> Near where their cottage stood.
>
> Beside a lake their cottage stood,
> Not small like ours a peaceful flood;
> But one of mighty size, and strange
> That rough or smooth is full of change
> And stirring in its bed.
>
> For to this lake by night and day,
> The great sea-water finds its way
> Through long, long windings of the hills,
> And drinks up all the pretty rills;
> And rivers large and strong:
>
> Then hurries back the road it came—
> Returns on errand still the same;
> This did it when the earth was new;
> And this for evermore will do,
> As long as earth shall last.
>
> And with the coming of the tide,
> Come boats and ships that sweetly ride,
> Between the woods and lofty rocks;
> And to the shepherd with their flocks
> Bring tales of distant lands.[2]

I might quote almost the whole of his "RUTH," but take the following stanzas:

> But as you have before been told,
> This stripling, sportive gay and bold,
> And with his dancing crest,

---

[1] *The Idle Shepherd-Boys* (1800; pub 1800) lines 23–33 (var).
[2] *The Blind Highland Boy* (1806; pub 1807) lines 46–70 (substituting "eagle's" for "eagles" in the first stanza quoted).

So beautiful, through savage lands
Had roam'd about with vagrant bands
Of Indians in the West.

The wind, the tempest roaring high,
The tumult of a tropic sky,
Might well be dangerous food
For him, a youth to whom was given
So much of earth, so much of heaven,
And such impetuous blood.

Whatever in those climes he found
Irregular in sight or sound,
Did to his mind impart
A kindred impulse; seem'd allied
To his own powers, and justified
The workings of his heart.

Nor less to feed voluptuous thought
The beauteous forms of nature wrought,
Fair trees and lovely flowers;
The breezes their own languor lent,
The stars had feelings, which they sent
Into those magic bowers.

Yet in his worst pursuits, I ween,
That sometimes there did intervene
Pure hopes of high intent:
For passions, link'd to forms so fair
And stately, needs must have their share
Of noble sentiment.[1]

But from Mr. Wordsworth's more elevated compositions, which already form three-fourths of his works;[2] and will, I trust, constitute hereafter a still larger proportion;—from these, whether in rhyme or blank-verse, it would be difficult and almost superfluous to select instances of a diction peculiarly his own, of a style which cannot be imitated without its being at once recognized, as originating in Mr. Wordsworth. It would not be easy to open on any one of his loftier strains, that does not contain examples of this; and more in proportion as the lines are more excellent, and most like the author. For those, who may happen to have been less familiar with his writings, I will give three specimens taken with little choice. The first from the lines on the "BOY OF WINANDER-MERE,"[3]—who

---

[1] *Ruth* (1799; pub 1800) lines 115–44.

[2] Cf ch 4, above, I 69, and ch 22, below, II 126.

[3] "There was a Boy . . ." (1798; pub 1800) lines 10–25 (var, in particular omitting line 13, "Responsive to his call,—-with quivering peals");

Blew mimic hootings to the silent owls,
That they might answer him. And they would shout,
Across the watery vale and shout again
With long halloos, and screams, and echoes loud
Redoubled and redoubled, concourse wild
Of mirth and jocund din. And when it chanc'd,
That pauses of deep silence mock'd his skill,
Then sometimes in that silence, while he hung
Listening, a gentle shock of mild surprize
Has carried far into his heart the voice
Of mountain torrents; or the visible scene *
Would enter unawares into his mind
With all its solemn imagery, its rocks,

* Mr. Wordsworth's having judiciously adopted "*concourse wild*" in this passage for "*a wild scene*" as it stood in the former edition, encourages me to hazard a remark, which I certainly should not have made in the works of a poet less austerely accurate in the use of words, than he is, to his own great honor.[1] It respects the propriety of the word, "*scene*," even in the sentence in which it is retained. D RYDEN, and he only in his more careless verses, was the first as far as my researches have discovered, who for the convenience of rhyme used this word in the vague sense, which has been since too current even in our best writers,[2] and which (unfortunately, I think) is given as its first explanation in Dr. Johnson's Dictionary, and therefore would be taken by an incautious reader as its proper sense.[3] In Shakspeare and Milton the word is never used without some clear reference, proper or metaphorical, to the theatre. Thus Milton;

> Cedar and pine, and fir and branching palm
> A Sylvan *scene*; and as the ranks ascend
> Shade above shade, a woody *theatre*
> Of stateliest view.[4]

I object to any extension of its meaning because the word is already more equivocal than might be wished; inasmuch as in the limited use, which I recommend, it may still signify two different things; namely, the scenery, and the characters and actions presented on the stage during the presence of particular scenes. It can therefore be preserved from *obscurity* only by keeping the original signification full in the mind. Thus Milton again,

> Prepare thou for another scene.[5]

C's italics. The lines were later inserted in *Prelude* (1805–6) v 397–413.

[1] "A wild scene" was the reading in 1800 and 1802.

[2] *OED* traces uses of "scene" in this sense to the sixteenth century.

[3] C is as usual unfair to Johnson. The first of Johnson's six definitions of "scene" emphasises the more literal and traditional sense ("The stage; the theatre of dramatick poetry") that C himself is emphasising. It is the second definition that broadens it metaphorically to "The general appearance of any action; the whole contexture of objects; a display . . ."; and interestingly Johnson's first two examples for this second meaning are the two quotations C gives from Milton below, which are then followed by four from Dryden.

[4] *Paradise Lost* IV 139–42.

[5] *Paradise Lost* XI 637 (substituting "thou" for "thee").

Its woods, and that uncertain heaven, received
Into the bosom of the steady lake.

The second shall be that noble imitation of Drayton * (if it was not rather a coincidence) in the "JOANNA."

When I had gazed perhaps two minutes' space,
Joanna, looking in my eyes, beheld
That ravishment of mine, and laugh'd aloud.
The rock, like something starting from a sleep,
Took up the lady's voice, and laugh'd again!
That ancient woman seated on *Helm-crag*
Was ready with her cavern! *Hammar-scar,*
And the tall steep of SILVER-HOW sent forth
A noise of laughter: southern LOUGHRIGG heard,
And FAIRFIELD answered with a mountain tone.
HELVELLYN far into the clear blue sky
Carried the lady's voice!—old SKIDDAW blew
His speaking trumpet!—back out of the clouds
From GLARAMARA southward came the voice:
And KIRKSTONE tossed it from his misty head!²

The third which is in rhyme I take from the "Song at the feast of Brougham Castle, upon the restoration of Lord Clifford the shepherd to the estates of his ancestors."

"Now another day is come,ª
Fitter hope, and nobler doom:
He hath thrown aside his crook,
And hath buried deep his book;
Armour rusting in the halls

* Which COPLAND scarce had spoke, but quickly every hill
Upon her verge that stands, the neighbouring vallies fill;
HELVILLON from his height, it through the mountains
     threw.
From whom as soon again, the sound DUNBALRASE drew,
From whose stone-trophied head, it on the WENDROSS
     went,
Which, tow'rds the sea again, resounded it to DENT.
That BROADWATER, therewith within her banks astound,
In sailing to the sea told it to EGREMOUND,
Whose buildings, walks and streets, with echoes loud and
     long
Did mightily commend old COPLAND for her song!
     DRAYTON'S POLYOLBION: *Song XXX.*¹

ª *BL* (1817) omits comma

¹ Lines 155–64. In *B Poets* III 538.

² *To Joanna* (1800; pub 1800) lines 51–65 (substituting "From" for "Of" in the next to the last line).

On the blood of Clifford calls;
Quell the Scot, exclaims the lance!
Bear me to the heart of France
Is the longing of the shield—
Tell thy name, thou trembling field!
Field of death, where'er thou be,
Groan thou with our victory!
Happy day, and mighty hour,
When our shepherd, in his power,
Mailed and horsed with lance and sword,
To his ancestors restored,
Like a re-appearing star,
Like a glory from afar,
First shall head the flock of war!"
Alas! the fervent harper did not know,
That for a tranquil soul the lay was framed,
Who, long compelled in humble walks to go
Was softened into feeling, soothed, and tamed.
Love had he found in huts where poor men lie:
His daily teachers had been woods and rills,
The silence that is in the starry sky,
The sleep that is among the lonely hills.[1]

The words themselves in the foregoing extracts, are, no doubt, sufficiently common for the greater part. (But in what poem are they not so? if we except a few misadventurous attempts to translate the arts and sciences into verse?) In the "Excursion" the number of polysyllabic (or what the common people call, *dictionary*) words is more than usually great. And so must it needs be, in proportion to the number and variety of an author's conceptions, and his solicitude to express them with precision. But are those words *in those places* commonly employed in real life to express the same thought or outward thing? Are they the style used in the ordinary intercourse of spoken words? No! nor are the modes of connections: and still less the breaks and transitions. Would any but a poet—at least could any one without being conscious that he had expressed himself with noticeable vivacity— have described a bird singing loud by, "The thrush is *busy* in the wood?" Or have spoken of boys with a string of club-moss round their rusty hats, as the boys "*with their green coronal?*" Or have translated a beautiful May-day into "*Both earth and sky keep jubilee?*" Or have brought all the different marks and circum-

---

[1] *Song, at the Feast of Brougham Castle* (1807; pub 1807) lines 138– 64 (in *Poems* 1815 lines 142–68); C's italics.

stances of a sea-loch before the mind, as the actions of a living and acting power? Or have represented the reflection of the sky in the water, as "*That uncertain heaven received into the bosom of the steady lake?*" Even the grammatical construction is not unfrequently peculiar; as "The wind, the tempest roaring high, the tumult of a tropic sky, might well be *dangerous food to him*, a youth to whom was given, &c." [1] There is a peculiarity in the frequent use of the ἀσυνάρτητον [2] (i.e. the omission of the connective particle before the last of several words, or several sentences used grammatically as single words, all being in the same case and governing or governed by the same verb) and not less in the construction of words by apposition (*to him, a youth*.) In short, were there excluded from Mr. Wordsworth's poetic compositions all, that a literal adherence to the theory of his preface *would* exclude, two-thirds at least of the marked beauties of his poetry must be erased. [3] For a far greater number of lines would be sacrificed, than in any other recent poet; because the pleasure received from Wordsworth's poems being less derived either from excitement of curiosity or the rapid flow of narration, the *striking* passages form a larger proportion of their value. I do not adduce it as a fair criterion of comparative excellence, nor do I even think it such; but merely as matter of fact. I affirm, that from no contemporary writer could so many lines be quoted, without reference to the poem in which they are found, for their own independent weight or beauty. [4] From the sphere of my own experience I can bring to my recollection three persons of no every-day powers and acquirements, who had read the poems of others with more and more unallayed pleasure, and had thought more highly of their authors, as poets; who yet have confessed to me, that from no modern work had so many passages started up anew in their minds at different times, and as different occasions had awakened a meditative mood.

---

[1] The phrases and lines quoted in the three preceding sentences are from *The Idle Shepherd-Boys* lines 25, 30, 28–9; "There was a Boy . . ." lines 24–5; *Ruth* lines 121–4 (var).

[2] Literally "unarticulated". A synonym for "asyndeton". *Greek–English Lexicon* ed H. G. Liddell and R. Scott refers it to Dionysius of Halicarnassus *Thucydides* 6 and Galen 15.468.

[3] Cf above, I 69, and below, II 126.

[4] Cf ch 22, below, II 144.

CHAPTER 21

Remarks on the present mode of conducting critical journals [1]

ONG have I wished to see a fair and philosophical inquisition
into the character of Wordsworth, as a poet, on the evidence
of his published works; and a positive, not a comparative, apprecia-
tion of their *characteristic* excellencies, deficiencies, and defects.
I know no claim, that the mere *opinion* of any individual can
have to weigh down the *opinion* of the author himself; against the
probability of whose parental partiality we ought to set that of his
having thought longer and more deeply on the subject. But I should
call that investigation fair and philosophical, in which the critic
announces and endeavors to establish the principles, which he holds
for the foundation of poetry in general, with the specification of
these in their application to the different *classes* of poetry. Having
thus prepared his canons of criticism for praise and condemnation,
he would proceed to particularize the most striking passages to
which he deems them applicable, faithfully noticing the frequent
or infrequent recurrence of similar merits or defects, and *as* faithfully distinguishing what is characteristic from what is accidental,
or a mere flagging of the wing. Then if his premises be rational, his
deductions legitimate, and his conclusions justly applied, the
reader, and possibly the poet himself, may adopt his judgement in
the light of judgement and in the independence of free-agency.
If he has erred, he presents his errors in a definite place and
tangible form, and holds the torch and guides the way to their
detection.

---

[1] Ch 21, as Kathleen Coburn says,
is largely "an attack on Francis
Jeffrey as a necessary clearing of the
way to the high estimate of WW in
the following chapter". *CN* III 3337n.
In particular C has in mind Jeffrey's
most recent attack on WW, the
famous review of WW's *Excursion* in
Ed Rev XXIV (1814) 1–30, which
had affected C the more because he
himself was rather disappointed in
the poem. See his letter to WW of 3
May 1815. *CL* IV 572–6. For discussion of the controversy between
C and Jeffrey, see esp David Erdman
and Paul Zall *SIR* XIV (1975) 75–83.
In what C says of reviewing generally, cf chs 2 and 3, above, I 42–4,
60–2, and on Jeffrey in particular, I
50–3, above, and II 108, below.

I most willingly admit, and estimate at a high value, the services which the EDINBURGH REVIEW, and others formed afterwards on the same plan, have rendered to society in the diffusion of knowledge.[1] I think the commencement of the Edinburgh Review an important epoch in periodical criticism; and that it has a claim upon the gratitude of the literary republic, and indeed of the reading public at large, for having originated the scheme of reviewing those books only, which are susceptible and deserving of argumentative criticism. Not less meritorious, and far more faithfully and in general far more ably executed, is their plan of supplying the vacant place of the trash or mediocrity, wisely left to sink into oblivion by their own weight, with original essays on the most interesting subjects of the time, religious, or political; in which the titles of the books or pamphlets prefixed furnish only the name and occasion of the disquisition. I do not arraign the keenness, or asperity of its damnatory style, in and for itself, as long as the author is addressed or treated as the mere impersonation of the work then under trial. I have no quarrel with them on this account, as long as no personal allusions are admitted, and no re-commitment (for new trial) of juvenile performances, that were published, perhaps forgotten, many years before the commencement of the review: [2] since for the forcing back of such works to public notice no motives are easily assignable, but such as are

[1] *Ed Rev*, the first important review completely independent of publishers, had been founded Oct 1802 primarily by Jeffrey, Sydney Smith (1771–1845), Henry Peter (later Lord) Brougham (1778–1868), and Francis Horner (1778–1817) the economist. Smith, after editing the first three numbers, left for London and was succeeded by Jeffrey (1803).

[2] Cf C's letter to Jeffrey 23 May 1808: "Without knowing me you have been, perhaps rather unwarrant[ab]ly, severe on my morals and Understanding—inasmuch as you have, I understand—for I have not seen the Reviews, frequently introduced *my* name when I had never brought any publication within your court—With one slight exception—a shilling pamphlet [*Conciones ad Populum*] that never obtained the least notice—I have not published any thing with my name, or known to be mine, for 13 years—surely, I might quote against you the complaint of Job as to those who brought against him 'the iniquities of his Youth'. . .". *CL* III 116–17. During the same month he confided to a notebook his thought that "the High & Mighty Edingburghers &c." had been "elevated into Guardians & Overseers of Taste & Poetry for much the same Reason, as St Cecilia was chosen as the guardian Goddess of Music"—namely her inability to compose or play music herself. *CN* III 3337. Cf above, I 59.

furnished to the critic by his own personal malignity; or what is
still worse, by a *habit* of malignity in the form of mere wantonness.

> No private grudge they need, no personal spite:
> The *viva sectio* is its own delight!
> All enmity, all envy, they disclaim,
> Disinterested thieves of our good name:
> Cool, sober murderers of their neighbour's fame!
>
> S. T. C.[1]

Every censure, every sarcasm respecting a publication which
the critic, with the criticised work before him, can make good, is the
critic's right. The writer is authorised to reply, but not to complain.
Neither can any one prescribe to the critic, how soft or how hard;
how friendly, or how bitter, shall be the phrases which he is to
select for the expression of such reprehension or ridicule. The
critic must know, what effect it is his object to produce; and with a
view to this effect must he weigh his words. But as soon as the
critic betrays, that he knows more of his author, than the author's
publications could have told him; as soon as from this more
intimate knowledge, elsewhere obtained, he avails himself of the
slightest trait *against* the author; his censure instantly becomes
personal injury, his sarcasms personal insults. He ceases to be a
CRITIC, and takes on him the most contemptible character to
which a rational creature can be degraded, that of a gossip, back-
biter, and pasquillant:[2] but with this heavy aggravation, that he

---

[1] C apparently wrote the verses for this occasion. *PW* (EHC) II 972.

[2] The paragraph to this point, as George Watson notes (*BL*—1975—239n), is a translation of Lessing's *Briefe, antiquarischen Inhalts* No 57, except for the second sentence, which C inserts ("The writer is authorised to reply, but not to complain"): "Jeder Tadel, jeder Spott, den der Kunstrichter mit dem kritisierten Buche in der Hand gut machen kann, ist dem Kunstrichter erlaubt. Auch kann ihm niemand vorschreiben, wie sanft oder wie hart, wie lieblich oder wie bitter, er die Ausdrücke eines solchen Tadels oder Spottes wählen soll. Er muss wissen, welche Wirkung er damit hervor bringen will, und es ist nothwendig, dass er seine Worte nach dieser Wirkung abwäget. Aber so bald der Kunstrichter verräth, dass er von seinem Autor mehr weiss, als ihm die Schriften desselben sagen können; so bald er sich aus dieser nähern Kenntniss des geringsten nachtheiligen Zuges wider ihn bedienet: sogleich wird sein Tadel persönliche Beleidigung. Er höret auf, Kunstrichter zu seyn, und wird —das verächtlichste, was ein vernünftiges Geschöpf werden kann— Klätscher, Anschwärzer, Pasquillant." *Sämmtliche Schriften* (1784–96) XII 160–1. See C's acknowledgement to Lessing in his subsequent paragraph.

steals the unquiet, the deforming passions of the World into the Museum; into the very place which, next to the chapel and oratory, should be our sanctuary, and secure place of refuge; offers abominations on the altar of the muses; and makes its sacred paling the very circle in which he conjures up the lying and prophane spirit.

This determination of unlicensed personality, and of permitted and legitimate censure (which I owe in part to the illustrious LESSING, himself a model of acute, spirited, sometimes stinging, but always argumentative and honorable, criticism) is beyond controversy the true one: and though I would not myself exercise all the rights of the latter, yet, let but the former be excluded, I submit myself to its exercise in the hands of others, without complaint and without resentment.[1]

Let a communication be formed between any number of learned men in the various branches of science and literature;[2] and whether the president and central committee be in London, or Edinburgh, if only they previously lay aside their individuality, and pledge themselves inwardly as well as ostensibly, to administer judgement according to a constitution and code of laws; and if by grounding this code on the two-fold basis of universal morals and philosophic reason, independent of all foreseen application to particular works

[1] Cf "Be minute, & assign your Reasons often, & your first impressions always—& then blame or praise—I care not which—I shall be gratified". To Sotheby 10 Sept 1802 *CL* II 863.

[2] Cf C's proposal to John Murray (4 Jul 1816) of "a Review of old Books (i.e. of all works important or remarkable the Authors of which are deceased) with a probability of a tolerable Sale". *CL* IV 648–9. Or, speaking of a model review generally: "Notwithstanding what you say, I am persuaded that a review would amply succeed even now, which should be started upon a published code of principles, critical, moral, political, and religious; which should announce what sort of books it would review, namely, works of *literature* as contradistinguished from all that offspring of the press, which in the present age supplies food for the craving caused by the extended ability of reading without any correspondent education of the mind, and which formerly was done by conversation, and which should really give a fair account of what the author *intended* to do, and in his own words, if possible, and in addition, afford one or two fair specimens of the execution,—itself never descending for one moment to any personality. . . . You see the great reviewers are now ashamed of reviewing works in the old style, and have taken up essay writing instead. Hence arose such publications as the 'Literary Gazette' and others, which are set up for the purpose—not a useless one—of advertising new books of all sorts for the circulating libraries. A mean between the two extremes still remains to be taken." *TT* 7 June 1830.

and authors, they obtain the right to speak each as the representative of their body corporate; they shall have honor and good wishes from me, and I shall accord to them their fair dignities, though self assumed, not less chearfully than if I could enquire concerning them in the herald's office, or turn to them in the book of peerage. However loud may be the outcries for prevented or subverted reputation, however numerous and impatient the complaints of merciless severity and insupportable despotism, I shall neither feel, nor utter ought but to the defence and justification of the critical machine. Should any literary Quixote find himself provoked by its sounds and regular movements, I should admonish him with Sancho Panza, that it is no giant but a windmill; there it stands on its own place, and its own hillock, never goes out of its way to attack any one, and to none and from none either gives or asks assistance. When the public press has poured in any part of its produce between its mill-stones, it grinds it off, one man's sack the same as another, and with whatever wind may happen to be then blowing. All the two and thirty winds are alike its friends.[1] Of the whole wide atmosphere it does not desire a single finger-breadth more than what is necessary for its sails to turn round in. But this space must be left free and unimpeded. Gnats, beetles, wasps, butterflies, and the whole tribe of ephemerals and insignificants, may flit in and out and between; may hum, and buzz, and jarr; may shrill their tiny pipes, and wind their puny horns, unchastised and unnoticed. But idlers and bravadoes of larger size and prouder show must beware, how they place themselves within its sweep. Much less may they presume to lay hands on the sails, the strength of which is neither greater or less than as the wind is, which drives them round. Whomsoever the remorseless arm[2] slings aloft, or whirls along with it in the air, he has himself alone to blame; though when the same arm throws him from it, it will more often double than break the force of his fall.

Putting aside the too manifest and too frequent interference of NATIONAL PARTY, and even PERSONAL predilection or aversion; and reserving for deeper feelings those worse and more criminal intrusions into the sacredness of private life, which not seldom merit legal rather than literary chastisement,[3] the two

[1] "Two and thirty" because of the number of points on the compass card of the mariner's compass.

[2] Of the windmill.

[3] C, as noted above (I 67, C's n, and n 3), had smarted for years at

principal objects and occasions which I find for blame and regret in the conduct of the review in question are: first, its unfaithfulness to its own announced and excellent plan, by subjecting to criticism works neither indecent or immoral, yet of such trifling importance even in point of size and, according to the critic's own verdict, so devoid of all merit, as must excite in the most candid mind the suspicion, either that dislike or vindictive feelings were at work; or that there was a cold prudential pre-determination to increase the sale of the Review by flattering the malignant passions of human nature.[1] That I may not myself become subject to the charge, which I am bringing against others, by an accusation without proof, I refer to the article on Dr. Rennell's sermon in the very first number of the Edinburgh Review as an illustration of my meaning.[2] If in looking through all the succeeding volumes the reader should find this a solitary instance, I must submit to that painful forfeiture of esteem, which awaits a groundless or exaggerated charge.

The second point of objection belongs to this review only in

the charge that he had deserted his family. When this was resurrected by John Wilson's vitriolic review of *BL* in *Blackwood's* II (1817) 3–18, describing him in the process as "both a wicked and pernicious member of society", C wrote to HCR (3 Dec 1817) asking his advice about "bringing to legal Justice the Publisher of the atrocious Calumny". Both HCR and WW persuaded C not to pursue the matter. *CL* IV 785–6 and n.

[1] The editors of *Ed Rev* stated in their Advertisement to the first number (Oct 1802) that "it forms no part of their object, to take notice of every production that issues from the Press; and that they wish their Journal to be distinguished, rather for the selection, than for the number, of its articles. Of the books that are daily presented to the world, a very large proportion is evidently destined to obscurity, by the insignificance of their subjects, or the defects of their execution; and it seems unreasonable to expect that

the Public should be interested by any account of performances, which have never attracted any share of its attention. A review of such productions, like the biography of private individuals, could afford gratification only to the partiality of friends, or the malignity of enemies." On the "complete deviation" of the "original plan" of *Ed Rev* cf *EOT* (*CC*) I 101.

[2] Thomas Rennell *Discourses on Various Subjects* (1801), reviewed in *Ed Rev* I (1802) 83–90 immediately after the review of RS's *Thalaba*, in which Jeffrey launched his first attack on the "Lake School" of poetry. The review indeed censures Rennell's *Discourses* as of minor value, "putting obvious truths into vehement language", and says that Rennell "is apt to put on the appearance of a holy bully, an evangelical swaggerer, as if he could carry his point against infidelity by big words and strong abuse, and kick and cuff men into Christians. . . . This affectation of contempt will not do."

common with all other works of periodical criticism; at least, it applies in common to the general system of all, whatever exception there may be in favor of particular articles. Or if it attaches to the Edinburgh Review, and to its only corrival (the Q U A R T E R L Y) [1] with any peculiar force, this results from the superiority of talent, acquirement, and information which both have so undeniably displayed; and which doubtless deepens the regret though not the blame. I am referring to the substitution of assertion for argument; to the frequency of arbitrary and sometimes petulant verdicts, not seldom unsupported even by a single quotation from the work condemned, which might at least have explained the critic's meaning, if it did not prove the justice of his sentence. Even where this is not the case, the extracts are too often made without reference to any general grounds or rules from which the faultiness or inadmissibility of the qualities attributed may be deduced; and without any attempt to show, that the qualities *are* attributable to the passage extracted. I have met with such extracts from Mr. Wordsworth's poems, annexed to such assertions, as led me to imagine, that the reviewer, having written his critique before he had read the work, had then *pricked with a pin* for passages, wherewith to illustrate the various branches of his preconceived opinions. By what principle of rational choice can we suppose a critic to have been directed (at least in a christian country, and himself, we hope, a christian) who gives the following lines, portraying the fervor of solitary devotion excited by the magnificent display of the Almighty's works, as a proof and example of an author's tendency to *downright ravings*, and absolute unintelligibility?

> O then what soul was his, when on the tops
> Of the high mountains he beheld the sun
> Rise up, and bathe the world in light! He looked—
> Ocean and earth, the solid frame of earth,
> And ocean's liquid mass, beneath him lay
> In gladness and deep joy. The clouds were touch'd,
> And in their silent faces did he read
> Unutterable love! Sound needed none,
> Nor any *voice* of joy: his spirit drank
> The spectacle! sensation, soul, and form,

[1] The *Quarterly Review* was founded in Feb 1809 by the publisher John Murray, who was encouraged by Scott to create a Tory counterpart to the Whig *Ed Rev.* Its first editor was William Gifford (1756–1826), followed briefly (1824–5) by C's nephew John Taylor Coleridge (1790–1876) and then J. G. Lockhart (1794–1854).

All melted into him. They swallowed up
His animal being: in them did he live,
And by them did he live: they were his life.

                                    (EXCURSION.)[1]

Can it be expected, that either the author or his admirers, should
be induced to pay any serious attention to decisions which prove
nothing but the pitiable state of the critic's own taste and sensibility? On opening the Review they see a favorite passage, of the
force and truth of which they had an intuitive certainty in their
own inward experience confirmed, if confirmation it could receive,
by the sympathy of their most enlightened friends; some of whom
perhaps, even in the world's opinion, hold a higher intellectual
rank than the critic himself would presume to claim. And this very
passage they find selected, as the characteristic effusion of a mind
deserted by reason; as furnishing evidence that the writer was
raving, or he could not have thus strung words together without
sense or purpose! No diversity of taste seems capable of explaining
such a contrast in judgement.

That I had *over-rated* the merit of a passage or poem, that I had
erred concerning the *degree* of its excellence, I might be easily
induced to believe or apprehend. But that lines, the sense of which
I had analysed and found consonant with all the best convictions
of my understanding; and the imagery and diction of which had

[1] *Excursion* I 219–31, which C
naturally quotes from the 1814 text.
The passage as revised in 1827
begins:
    Such was the Boy—but for the
        growing Youth
    What soul was his, when, from
        the naked top
    Of some bold headland . . .
Actually, Jeffrey in his review, *Ed
Rev* XXIV (1814) 1–30, does not
single out the passage as C quotes
it but rather I 224–39, beginning at
the sixth line ("The clouds were
touched") of the passage above and
extending for another eight lines.
Jeffrey, after quoting I 148–61,
remarks: "We should like extremely
to know what is meant by tracing an
ebbing and flowing mind in the fixed
lineaments of naked crags?—but this
is but the beginning of the raving fit.
The young pedlar's sensations at
sunrise are thus naturally recorded."
He then quotes I 224–39. Cf C's
letter to Lady Beaumont 3 Apr
1815: "From this state of mind, in
which I was comparing Wordsworth
with himself [stating that *The Excursion* was not equal to *The Prelude*], I was roused by the infamous
Edingburgh Review of the Poem.
If ever Guilt lay on a Writer's head,
and if malignity, slander, hypocrisy
and self-contradicting Baseness can
constitute Guilt, I dare openly, and
openly (please God!) I will, im-
peach the Writer of that Article of
it." *CL* IV 564. Presumably the discussion in *BL* above and the references to Jeffrey elsewhere constitute
the "impeachment".

collected round those convictions my noblest as well as my most delightful feelings; that I should admit such lines to be mere nonsense or lunacy, is too much for the most ingenious *arguments* to effect. But that such a revolution of taste should be brought about by a few broad assertions, seems little less than impossible.[1] On the contrary, it would require an effort of charity not to dismiss the criticism with the aphorism of the wise man, in animam malevolam sapientia haud intrare potest.[2]

What then if this very critic should have cited a large number of single lines and even of long paragraphs, which he himself acknowledges to possess eminent and original beauty?[3] What if he himself has owned, that beauties as great are scattered in abundance throughout the whole book? And yet, though under this impression, should have commenced his critique in vulgar exultation with a prophecy meant to secure its own fulfilment? With a "THIS WON'T DO!"[4] What? if after such acknowledgements extorted from his own judgement he should proceed from charge to charge of tameness, and raving; flights and flatness; and at length, consigning the author to the house of incurables, should conclude with a strain of rudest contempt evidently grounded in the distempered state of his own moral associations? Suppose too all this done without a single leading principle established or even announced, and without any one attempt at argumentative deduc-

---

[1] Cf C's remark to Allsop (2 Dec 1818) on "the broad predetermined Abuse of the Edingburgh Review". *CL* IV 889.

[3] Wisd 1.4, in the Apocrypha: "Into a malicious soul wisdom cannot enter". In *CN* II 2906 C quoted the Vulgate version, "in animam malevolam non introibit ["will not enter"] sapientia".

[3] In fact, the latter half of the review is largely devoted to extracts singled out for praise: "But the truth is, that Mr Wordsworth, with all his perversities, is a person of great powers; and has frequently a force in his moral declamations, and a tenderness in his pathetic narratives, which neither his prolixity nor his affectation can altogether deprive of their effect. . . . Besides those more extended passages of interest or

beauty, which we have quoted, and omitted to quote, there are scattered up and down the book, and in the midst of its most repulsive portions, a very great number of single lines and images, that sparkle like gems in the desart, and startle us with an intimation of the great poetic powers that lie buried in the rubbish that has been heaped around them." *Ed Rev* XXIV (1814) 16, 28.

[4] Jeffrey's review begins: "This will never do. It bears no doubt the stamp of the author's heart and fancy; but unfortunately not half so visibly as that of his peculiar system . . . but this, we suspect, must be recommended by the system—and can only expect to succeed where it has been previously established."

tion, though the poet had presented a more than usual opportunity for it, by having previously made public his own principles of judgement in poetry, and supported them by a connected train of reasoning!

The office and duty of the poet is to select the most dignified as well as

> The happiest, gayest, attitude of things.[1]

The reverse, for in all cases a reverse is possible, is the appropriate business of burlesque and travesty, a predominant taste for which has been always deemed a mark of a low and degraded mind. When I was at Rome, among many other visits to the tomb of Julius II, I went thither once with a Prussian artist, a man of genius and great vivacity of feeling. As we were gazing on Michael Angelo's M O S E S, our conversation turned on the horns and beard of that stupendous statue;[2] of the necessity of each to support the other; of the super-human effect of the former, and the necessity of the existence of both to give a harmony and *integrity* both to the image and the feeling excited by it. Conceive them removed, and the statue would become *un*-natural, without being *super*-natural. We called to mind the horns of the rising sun, and I repeated the noble passage from Taylor's Holy Dying.[3] That horns were the emblem of power and sovereignty among the Eastern nations,[4] and are still retained as such in Abyssinia; the Achelous

[1] Mark Akenside (1721–70) *The Pleasures of Imagination* (1744) I 30. C apparently quotes from memory (the line reads "The gayest, happiest attitude of things"). For his frequent references to Akenside see *CN* I 123n.

[2] Cf C's praise of the *Moses* to Samuel Rogers (25 May 1815). *CL* IV 569.

[3] ". . . For the life of a man comes upon him slowly and insensibly. But as when the Sun approaches towards the gates of the morning, he first opens a little eye of Heaven, and sends away the spirits of darknesse, and gives light to a cock, and calls up the lark to Mattins, and by and by gilds the fringes of a cloud and peeps over the Eastern hills, thrusting out his golden horns, like those which decked the browes of

Moses when he was forced to wear a vail, because himself had seen the face of God. . .". *The Rule and Exercise of Holy Dying* I iii 2 (1651) 22; *Works* ed R. Heber (1839) IV 350. Cf *CN* III 3925 and n.

[4] The association of Moses with horns comes from the Vulgate version of Exod 34.29, which relates that, when Moses descended from Mt Sinai with the tablets, he "wist not that the skin of his face shone". The Hebrew *kāran* (to shine) is connected with *keren* (horn). The Vulgate translated the verb as "to be horned" ("ignorabat quod cornuta esset facies sua"). The interpretation was probably influenced by the fact that throughout the Bible (and in the Near East generally, as C says in the next sentence) the horn is the

of the ancient Greeks;[1] and the probable ideas and feelings, that originally suggested the mixture of the human and the brute form in the figure, by which they realized the idea of their mysterious Pan, as representing intelligence blended with a darker power, deeper, mightier, and more universal than the conscious intellect of man; than intelligence;—all these thoughts and recollections passed in procession before our minds. My companion who possessed more than his share of the hatred, which his countrymen bore to the French, had just observed to me, "*a Frenchman, Sir! is the only animal in the human shape, that by no possibility can lift itself up to religion or poetry:*" When, lo! two French officers of distinction and rank entered the church! *Mark you*, whispered the Prussian, "*the first thing, which those scoundrels—will notice (for they will begin by instantly noticing the statue in parts, without one moment's pause of admiration impressed by the whole) will be the horns and the beard. And the associations, which they will immediately connect with them will be those of a* HE-GOAT *and a* CUCKOLD." Never did man guess more luckily. Had he inherited a portion of the great legislator's prophetic powers, whose statue we had been contemplating, he could scarcely have uttered words more coincident with the result: for even as he had said, so it came to pass.[2]

In the EXCURSION the poet has introduced an old man, born in humble but not abject circumstances, who had enjoyed more

symbol of strength. E.g. 1 Kings 22.11; Amos 6.13; Zech 1.18; Ps 75.4. Hence the "horns of the altar" (e.g. 1 Kings 1.50), originally bull's horns and symbolising the strength of God, were the most sacred part of the altar. Cf C on Fichte grasping "the Horns of the Altar, but with nerve-palsied hand—and blind". *CL* IV 875.

[1] In Greek mythology the river Achelous appeared to human beings in the body of a bull and with the head of a bearded horned man. After Hercules broke off one of his horns in wrestling with him, Achelous, in order to retrieve it, gave Hercules the horn of plenty. According to one myth, the Sirens were born of the drops of blood that fell to earth from Achelous' broken horn.

[2] Cf "Vulgar minds generalize every thing, because they cannot think, they never attempt to think except in words, and are the passive Slaves of Association.—It is out of the power of a Frenchman to look at the sublime *Moses* of Michael Angelo Buonarotti and not think these words—It has a pair of Horns on its Head—and as much out of his power, he having thought these words, not to think of Horns in general, Cows' Horns, Goats' Horns, and (as 9 out of 10 of them are cursed with animalcular Wits) probably Cuckoldism and so forth. He pronounces the Statue mean and ludicrous." Egerton MS 2800 f 186.

than usual advantages of education, both from books and from the more awful discipline of nature. This person he represents, as having been driven by the restlessness of fervid feelings, and from a craving intellect, to an itinerant life; and as having in consequence passed the larger portion of his time, from earliest manhood, in villages and hamlets from door to door,

> A vagrant merchant bent beneath his load.[1]

Now whether this be a character appropriate to a lofty didactick poem, is perhaps questionable. It presents a fair subject for controversy; and the question is to be determined by the congruity or incongruity of such a character with what shall be proved to be the essential constituents of poetry. But surely the critic who, passing by all the opportunities which such a mode of life would present to such a man; all the advantages of the liberty of nature, of solitude and of solitary thought; all the varieties of places and seasons, through which his track had lain, with all the varying imagery they bring with them; and lastly, all the observations of men,

> Their manners, their enjoyment and pursuits,
> Their passions and their feelings[2]

which the memory of these yearly journies must have given and recalled to such a mind—the critic, I say, who from the multitude of possible associations should pass by all these in order to fix his attention exclusively on *the pin-papers*, and *stay-tapes*, which *might* have been among the wares of his pack;[3] this critic in my opinion cannot be thought to possess a much higher or much healthier state of moral feeling, than the FRENCHMEN above recorded.

---

[1] *Excursion* I 335 in 1814, altered to "A vagrant Merchant under a heavy load | Bent as he moves. . .".
[2] *Excursion* I 354–5 (var).
[3] C refers to the close of Jeffrey's long review: "Why should Mr Wordsworth have made his hero a superannuated Pedlar? . . . Did Mr Wordsworth really imagine, that his favourite doctrines were likely to gain any thing in point of effect or authority by being put into the mouth of a person accustomed to higgle about tape, or brass sleeve-buttons? . . . Is there any thing in his learned, abstracted, and logical harangues, that savours of the calling that is ascribed to him? . . . A man who went about selling flannel and pocket-handkerchiefs in this lofty diction, would soon frighten away all his customers; and would infallibly pass for either a madman, or for some learned and affected gentleman, who, in a frolic, had taken up a character which he was peculiarly ill qualified for supporting." *Ed Rev* XXIV (1814) 29–30.

CHAPTER 22

The characteristic defects of Wordsworth's poetry, with the principles from which the judgement, that they are defects, is deduced—Their proportion to the beauties—For the greatest part characteristic of his theory only

IF Mr. Wordsworth have set forth principles of poetry which his arguments are insufficient to support, let him and those who have adopted his sentiments be set right by the confutation of those arguments, and by the substitution of more philosophical principles. And still let the due credit be given to the portion and importance of the truths, which are blended with his theory: truths, the too exclusive attention to which had occasioned its errors, by tempting him to carry those truths beyond their proper limits. If his mistaken theory have at all influenced his poetic compositions, let the effects be pointed out, and the instances given. But let it likewise be shewn, how far the influence has acted; whether diffusively, or only by starts; whether the number and importance of the poems and passages thus infected be great or trifling compared with the sound portion; and lastly, whether they are inwoven into the texture of his works, or are loose and separable. The result of such a trial would evince beyond a doubt, what it is high time to announce decisively and aloud, that the *supposed* characteristics of Mr. Wordsworth's poetry, whether admired or reprobated; whether they are simplicity or simpleness; faithful adherence to essential nature, or wilful selections from human nature of its meanest forms and under the least attractive associations; are as little the *real* characteristics of his poetry at large, as of his genius and the constitution of his mind.

In a comparatively small number of poems, he chose to try an experiment; and this experiment we will suppose to have failed. Yet even in these poems it is impossible not to perceive, that the natural *tendency* of the poet's mind is to great objects and elevated conceptions. The poem intitled "Fidelity" is for the greater part written in language, as unraised and naked as any perhaps in the

119

two volumes.[1] Yet take the following stanza and compare it with
the preceding stanzas of the same poem.

> There sometimes does a leaping fish
> Send through the tarn a lonely cheer;
> The crags repeat the Raven's croak
> In symphony austere;
> Thither the rainbow comes—the cloud,
> And mists that spread the flying shroud;
> And sun-beams; and the sounding blast,
> That if it could would hurry past,
> But that enormous barrier binds it fast.[2]

Or compare the four last lines of the concluding stanza with the
former half:

> Yet proof was plain that since the day
> On which the traveller thus had died,
> The dog had watch'd about the spot,
> Or by his master's side:
> *How nourish'd there for such long time*
> *He knows who gave that love sublime,*
> *And gave that strength of feeling great*
> *Above all human estimate.*[3]

Can any candid and intelligent mind hesitate in determining,
which of these best represents the tendency and native character
of the poet's genius? Will he not decide that the one was written
because the poet *would* so write, and the other because he could
not so entirely repress the force and grandeur of his mind, but that
he must in some part or other of *every* composition write otherwise? In short, that his only disease is the being out of his element;
like the swan, that having amused himself, for a while, with
crushing the weeds on the river's bank, soon returns to his own

---

[1] Of *Poems* (1815).

[2] *Fidelity* (1805; pub 1807) lines
25–33. One of the preceding stanzas,
the third, exemplifies the "unraised"
language with which C is contrasting
the present stanza:

> It was a Cove, a huge Recess,
> That keeps till June December's
> snow
> A lofty Precipice in front,
> A silent Tarn below!
> Far in the bosom of Helvellyn,
> Remote from public Road or
> Dwelling,

> Pathway, or cultivated land;
> From trace of human foot or
> hand.

[3] *Fidelity* lines 58–65 (var).
Possibly thinking of the contrast C
is stressing, WW later told IF:
". . . the sentiment in the last four
lines of the last stanza in my verses
was uttered by a shepherd with such
exactness, that a traveller, who
afterwards reported his account in
print, was induced to question the
man whether he had read them,
which he had not". *WPW* iv 417.

majestic movements on its reflecting and sustaining surface. Let it be observed, that I am here supposing the imagined judge, to whom I appeal, to have already decided against the poet's theory, as far as it is different from the principles of the art, generally acknowledged.

I cannot here enter into a detailed examination of Mr. Wordsworth's works; but I will attempt to give the main results of my own judgement, after an acquaintance of many years, and repeated perusals. And though, to appreciate the defects of a great mind it is necessary to understand previously its characteristic excellences, yet I have already expressed myself with sufficient fulness, to preclude most of the ill effects that might arise from my pursuing a contrary arrangement. I will therefore commence with what I deem the prominent *defects* of his poems hitherto published.

The first *characteristic, though only occasional* defect, which I appear to myself to find in these poems is the INCONSTANCY of the *style*. Under this name I refer to the sudden and unprepared transitions from lines or sentences of peculiar felicity (at all events striking and original) to a style, not only unimpassioned but undistinguished. He sinks too often and too abruptly to that style, which I should place in the second division of language, dividing it into the three species; *first*, that which is peculiar to poetry; *second*, that which is only proper in prose; and *third*, the neutral or common to both. There have been works, such as Cowley's essay on Cromwell, in which prose and verse are intermixed (not as in the Consolation of Boetius, or the Argenis of Barclay, by the insertion of poems supposed to have been spoken or composed on occasions previously related in prose, but) the poet passing from one to the other as the nature of the thoughts or his own feelings dictated.[1] Yet this mode of composition does not satisfy a culti-

---

[1] *De consolatione philosophiae,* written by Anicius Manlius Severinus Boethius (c 480–524) in prison before he was executed, is alternately in prose and verse. The procedure imitates that of *De nuptiis Philologiae et Mercurii* by Martianus Capella (fl 410), who in turn follows the Menippean satires of Publius Varro (c 82–36 B.C.). The *Argenis* (1621) by John Barclay (1582–1621), the Scottish Latin poet, is a long romance concerned with the dangers of political intrigue. C annotated both his own copy of it (Amsterdam 1659) and RS's copy of the English translation (1629). Cf above, ch 9, I 166 and n 1, C's comments on the *Argenis* in *CM (CC)* I 217–21, and his quote above, I 166. The Cowley work to which C refers is his *A Discourse by Way of Vision, Concerning the Government of Oliver Cromwel: Works*

vated taste. There is something unpleasant in the being thus obliged to alternate states of feeling so dissimilar, and this too in a species of writing, the pleasure from which is in part derived from the preparation and previous expectation of the reader. A portion of that awkwardness is felt which hangs upon the introduction of songs in our modern comic operas; and to prevent which the judicious Metastasio (as to whose exquisite *taste* there can be no hesitation, whatever doubts may be entertained as to his *poetic genius*) uniformly placed the ARIA at the end of the scene, at the same time that he almost always raises and impassions the style of the recitative immediately preceding.[1] Even in real life, the difference is great and evident between words used as the *arbitrary marks* of thought, our smooth market-coin of intercourse with the image and superscription worn out by currency; and those which convey pictures either borrowed from *one* outward object to enliven and particularize some *other*; or used allegorically to body forth the inward state of the person speaking; or such as are at least the exponents of his peculiar turn and unusual extent of faculty. So much so indeed, that in the social circles of private life we often find a striking use of the latter put a stop to the general flow of conversation, and by the excitement arising from concentered attention produce a sort of damp and interruption for some minutes after.[2] But in the perusal of works of literary *art*, we *prepare* ourselves for such language; and the business of the writer, like that of a painter whose subject requires unusual splendor and

---

(1681) vi 52–78, the interspersed verses of which C describes as typifying "good sense, & the common feelings of *all* good & sensible men; but without the passion, or the peculiar feelings, & stronger excitements of the poetic character". *CN* I 829.

[1] Pietro Bonaventura Trapassi (1698–1782) as a boy so impressed G. V. Gravina (1664–1718), the noted jurist and head of the Arcadian Academy, that Gravina adopted him and gave him the name Metastasio ("transformation"). His numerous lyric dramas and libretti —among them *Didone abbandonata* (1752), *Artaserse* (1730), and *La Clemenza di Tito* (1734)—were put

to music by most of the leading composers of his time, including Gluck, Handel, and Mozart. Cf *CN* II 2826 and n. For WW's tr of five of his lyrics see *WPW* IV 369–70.

[2] Cf C's 1802 remark in a notebook: "Ill effect of a fine & apposite Quotation in *damping* easy commerce of sensible Chit Chat.—So a good Story—". *CN* I 1314. C may be recalling Johnson's essay on the subject (*Rambler* No 188) in which he states that learning, like brilliance of wit, intimidates company into silence, whereas stories "are for the most part heard without envy, because they are not supposed to imply any intellectual qualities above the common rate".

prominence, is so to raise the lower and neutral tints, that what in a different style would be the *commanding* colors, are here used as the means of that gentle *degradation* requisite in order to produce the effect of a *whole.* Where this is not atchieved in a poem, the metre merely reminds the reader of his claims in order to disappoint them; and where this defect occurs frequently, his feelings are alternately startled by anticlimax and hyperclimax.[1]

I refer the reader to the exquisite stanzas cited for another purpose from the blind Highland Boy;[2] and then annex as being in my opinion instances of this *disharmony* in style the two following:

> And one, the rarest, was a shell,
> Which he, poor child, had studied well:
> The shell of a green turtle, thin
> And hollow;—you might sit therein,
> It was so wide, and deep.

> Our Highland Boy oft visited
> The house which held this prize, and led
> By choice or chance did thither come
> One day, when no one was at home,
> And found the door unbarred.[3]

[1] Cf C's earlier remark on the effects of metre: where "correspondent food and appropriate matter are not provided for the attention and feelings thus roused, there must needs be a disappointment felt; like that of leaping in the dark from the last step of a stair-case, when we had prepared our muscles for a leap of three or four". Ch 18, above, II 66. *OED* cites C and the above passage for "hyperclimax".

[2] See ch 20, above, II 101.

[3] C quotes from the revised *Blind Highland Boy* (1815) lines 116–20, 136–40. In 1807 the vessel had been
—A Household Tub, like one of
    those
Which women use to wash their
    clothes,
This carried the blind Boy.
As C stated (*CN* III 3240 and n), he hoped to persuade WW to substitute something less homely than the tub, and told him of a passage in William Dampier *Collection of Voyages* (1729) I 105–6, in which

a boy used the shell of a large green turtle as a boat. WW made the change, appending a note in which he still maintained the veracity of his original version: "Upon the suggestion of a Friend, I have substituted such a Shell for that less elegant vessel in which my blind voyager did actually intrust himself to the dangerous current of Loch Levin, as was related to me by an Eye-witness." *Poems* (1815) I 339. In reaction to C's remark in *BL*, above, about "*disharmony* in style" directed primarily at the lines ". . . you might sit therein, | It was so wide, and deep", WW finally revised the stanza (1827) into the conventionally decorative mode he had earlier condemned:
The rarest was a Turtle-shell
Which he, poor Child, had
    studied well;
A shell of ample size, and light
As the pearly car of Amphitrite,
That sportive dolphins drew.

Or page 172, vol. I.[1]

'Tis gone forgotten, *let me do*
My best. There was a smile or two—
I can remember them, I see
The smiles worth all the world to me.
Dear Baby, I must lay thee down:
Thou troublest me with strange alarms!
Smiles hast thou, sweet ones of thine own;
I cannot keep thee in my arms,
For they confound me: *as it is,*
I have forgot those smiles of his![2]

Or page 269, vol. I.

Thou hast a nest, for thy love and thy rest,
And though little troubled with sloth
Drunken lark! thou would'st be loth
To be such a traveller as I.
  Happy, happy liver
With a soul as strong as a mountain river
Pouring out praise to th' Almighty giver!
Joy and jollity be with us both,
Hearing thee or else some other,
  As merry a brother
I on the earth will go plodding on
By myself chearfully till the day is done.[3]

The incongruity, which I appear to find in this passage, is that of the two noble lines in italics with the preceding and following. So vol. II, page 30.

[1] The references from here on are to *Poems* (1815).

[2] *The Emigrant Mother* (1802; pub 1807) lines 55–64 (var; C's italics). In deference to C, WW revised the opening of the stanza to read (1820):
'Tis gone—like dreams that we forget;
There was a smile or two— yet—yet
I can remember them . . .
In 1836 the final lines were changed to
For they confound me;—where —where is
That last, that sweetest smile of his.

[3] *To a Skylark* (1802?; pub 1807) lines 18–29 (C's italics). In 1820 WW completely dropped the final four lines, substituting a different passage, which was further revised in 1827 to:
Alas! my journey, rugged and uneven,
Through prickly moors or dusty ways must wind;
But hearing thee, or others of thy kind,
As full of gladness and as free of heaven,
I, with my fate contented, will plod on,
And hope for higher raptures, when life's day is done.

> Close by a pond, upon the further side
> He stood alone; a minute's space I guess,
> I watch'd him, he continuing motionless;
> To the pool's further margin then I drew;
> He being all the while before me full in view.[1]

Compare this with the repetition of the same image, in the next stanza but two.

> And still as I drew near with gentle pace,
> Beside the little pond or moorish flood
> Motionless as a cloud the old man stood;
> That heareth not the loud winds as they call
> And moveth altogether, if it move at all.[2]

Or lastly, the second of the three following stanzas, compared both with the first and the third.

> My former thoughts returned, the fear that kills;
> And hope that is unwilling to be fed;
> Cold, pain, and labour, and all fleshly ills;
> And mighty poets in their misery dead.
> But now, perplex'd by what the old man had said,
> My question eagerly did I renew,
> How is it that you live, and what is it you do?

> He with a smile did then his tale repeat;
> And said, that, gathering leeches far and wide
> He travelled; stirring thus about his feet
> The waters of the ponds where they abide.
> "Once I could meet with them on every side,
> But they have dwindled long by slow decay;
> Yet still I persevere, and find them where I may."

> While he was talking thus, the lonely place,[a]
> The old man's shape, and speech, all troubled me:
> In my mind's eye I seemed to see him pace
> About the weary moors continually,
> Wandering about alone and silently.[3]

[a] *BL* (1817) omits comma

[1] *Resolution and Independence* (1802; pub 1807) lines 59–63. The whole stanza, of which these are the last five lines, was dropped in 1820.

[2] Lines 80–4 (var); lines 73–7 in 1820 and later, with "Beside the little pond or moorish flood" altered to "Upon the margin of that moorish flood". The final three lines were quoted by WW in Preface (1815) as part of an extended example (lines 57–77) of "the conferring, the abstracting, and the modifying powers of the Imagination . . . all brought into conjunction". See *W Prose* III 33.

[3] Lines 120–38 (var).

Indeed this fine poem is *especially* characteristic of the author. There is scarce a defect or excellence in his writings of which it would not present a specimen. But it would be unjust not to repeat that this defect is only occasional. From a careful reperusal of the two volumes of poems, I doubt whether the objectionable passages would amount in the whole to one hundred lines; not the eighth part of the number of pages.[1] In the EXCURSION the feeling of incongruity is seldom excited by the diction of any passage considered in itself, but by the sudden superiority of some other passage forming the context.

The second defect I could generalize with tolerable accuracy, if the reader will pardon an uncouth and new coined word. There is, I should say, not seldom a *matter-of-factness* in certain poems.[2] This may be divided into, *first*, a laborious minuteness and fidelity in the representation of objects, and their positions, as they appeared to the poet himself; *secondly*, the insertion of accidental circumstances, in order to the full explanation of his living characters, their dispositions and actions; which circumstances might be necessary to establish the probability of a statement in real life, where nothing is taken for granted by the hearer, but appear superfluous in poetry, where the reader is willing to believe for his own sake. To this *accidentality*, I object, as contravening the essence of poetry, which Aristotle pronounces to be σπουδαιότατον καὶ φιλοσοφώτατον γένος,[3] the most intense, weighty and philosophical product of human art; adding, as the *reason*, that it is the most catholic and abstract. The following passage from Davenant's prefatory letter to Hobbs well expresses this truth. "When I considered the actions which I meant to describe (those inferring the persons) I was again persuaded rather to choose those of a former age, than the present; and in a century so far removed as might preserve me from their improper examinations, who know not the

---

[1] Cf ch 4, above, I 69, and ch 20, II 102.

[2] ". . . Here & there [in WW's recent poems] a daring Humbleness of Language & Versification, and a strict adherence to matter of fact, even to prolixity, that startled me". To RS 29 Jul 1802: *CL* II 830. Cf WW's remark to IF, speaking of *Lucy Gray*, about "the imaginative influences which I have endeavoured to throw over common life with Crabbe's matter of fact style of treating subjects of the same kind". *WPW* I 360. *OED* cites J. W. Croker (1816), but not C, for "matter-of-factness".

[3] Adapted from *Poetics* 9.3. "The noblest and most philosophical form of writing". See ch 17, above, II 46 n 2.

requisites of a poem, nor how much pleasure they lose (and even the pleasures of heroic poesy are not unprofitable) who take away the liberty of a poet, and fetter his feet in the shackles of an historian. For why should a poet doubt in story to mend the intrigues of fortune by more delightful conveyances of probable fictions, because austere historians have entered into bond to truth? An obligation, which were in poets as foolish and unnecessary, as is the bondage of false martyrs, who lie in chains for a mistaken opinion. *But by this I would imply, that truth, narrative and past is the idol of historians (who worship a dead thing) and truth operative, and by effects continually alive, is the mistress of poets, who hath not her existence in matter, but in reason."* [1]

For this minute accuracy in the painting of local imagery, the lines in the E X C U R S I O N, p. 96, 97, and 98, may be taken, if not as a striking instance yet as an illustration of my meaning.[2] It must be some strong motive (as, for instance, that the description was necessary to the intelligibility of the tale) which could induce me to describe in a number of verses what a draftsman could present to the eye with incomparably greater satisfaction by half a dozen strokes of his pencil, or the painter with as many touches of his brush. Such descriptions too often occasion in the mind of a reader, who is determined to understand his author, a feeling of labor, not very dissimilar to that, with which he would construct a diagram, line by line, for a long geometrical proposition. It seems to be like taking the pieces of a dissected map out of its box. We first look at one part, and then at another, then join and dove-tail them; and when the successive acts of attention have been completed, there is a retrogressive effort of mind to behold it as a whole. The Poet should paint to the imagination, not to the fancy; and I know no happier case to exemplify the distinction between these two faculties. Master-pieces of the former mode of poetic painting abound in the writings of Milton, ex. gr.

> The fig tree, not that kind for fruit renown'd,
> But such as at this day to Indians known
> In Malabar or Decan, spreads her arms
> Branching so broad and long, that in the ground

---

[1] Sir William Davenant (1606–68) *Preface to Gondibert* (1651) 13–14; C's italics. In *B Poets* IV 768. C in 1810 had copied out the italicised part of the quotation into a notebook: *CN* III 3769.

[2] *Excursion* III 23–73.

The bended twigs take root, *and daughters grow*
About the mother-tree, a pillar'd shade
High over-arched, and E C H O I N G   W A L K S   B E T W E E N :
There oft the Indian Herdsman shunning heat
Shelters in cool, and tends his pasturing herds
At loop holes cut through thickest shade.

MILTON, *P. L.* 9, 1100.[1]

This is *creation* rather than *painting*, or if painting, yet such,
and with such co-presence of the whole picture flash'd at once
upon the eye, as the sun paints in a camera obscura.[2] But the poet
must likewise understand and command what Bacon calls the
vestigia communia of the senses, the latency of all in each, and
more especially as by a magical *penna duplex*, the excitement of
vision by sound and the exponents of sound.[3] Thus, "THE

[1] *Paradise Lost* IX 1101–10.

[2] Cf "The power of genius was not shewn in elaborating a picture of which many specimens were given in Poems of modern date, where the work was so dutchified by minute touches that the reader naturally asked why words & not painting were used? . . . The power of Poetry is by a single word to produce that energy in the mind as compels the imagination to produce the picture. Thus when Prospero says

> one midnight
> Fated to his purpose did
>   Antonio open
> The gates of Milan & i' the dead
>   of darkness
> The Ministers for his purpose
>   hurried thence
> Me & thy crying self.

"Thus by introducing the simple happy epithet *crying* in the last line a complete picture is present to the mind & in this the power of true poetry consists." Lect 9 of 16 Dec 1811: *Lects 1808–19* (*CC*) ms.

[3] Cf *CN* III 3587: ". . . Lord Bacon's impressio communis—unum vestigium in sensus varios" ("common impression—one print upon various senses"). See *CN* III 3587n. The reference in Bacon has not been found, though there are extended passages in *Sylva Sylvarum* Centu-

ries II and III that touch on the relation of sound and sight. *Works* ed James Spedding et al (1870) II 385–436, esp 428–30. In his metaphor of the "double pen" C may be thinking of the simple machine (stylographic pen or pennaepolygraph) patented in 1808 by Ralph Wedgwood, in which two pens are moved by the same action of the hand.

On the excitement of one sense by another, cf Hazlitt's conception of "gusto" as an intensity of imaginative conception in which "the impressions made on one sense excite by affinity those of another". Hence his complaint of Claude Lorrain's landscapes: "They do not interpret one sense by another . . . That is, his eye wanted imagination: it did not strongly sympathise with his other faculties. He saw the atmosphere, but he did not feel it." *H Works* IV 79. Both C and Hazlitt here (and it is typical of the aspiration of "high Romanticism" generally in the arts) are continuing the eighteenth-century psychological and critical interest in the interplay of the senses (of which the nineteenth- and twentieth-century concept of "synaesthesia" is a further development) and in the importance of "suggestiveness" in exciting this interplay.

ECHOING WALKS BETWEEN," may be almost said to reverse the fable in tradition of the head of Memnon, in the Egyptian statue.[1] Such may be deservedly entitled the *creative words* in the world of imagination.

The second division respects an apparent minute adherence to *matter-of-fact* in character and incidents; *a biographical* attention to probability, and an *anxiety* of explanation and retrospect. Under this head I shall deliver, with no feigned diffidence, the results of my best reflection on the great point of controversy between Mr. Wordsworth, and his objectors; namely, on THE CHOICE OF HIS CHARACTERS.[2] I have already declared, and, I trust justified, my utter dissent from the mode of argument which his critics have hitherto employed. To *their* question, why did you chuse such a character, or a character from such a rank of life? the Poet might in my opinion fairly retort: why, with the conception of my character did you make wilful choice of mean or ludicrous associa-

---

Relevant writers in the eighteenth century include Burke, Hume, Uvedale Price, and Archibald Alison. For background see W. J. Bate *From Classic to Romantic* (Cambridge, Mass 1946) 148–59, and, for the broader thinking about the relations of the arts generally, Jean Hagstrum *The Sister Arts* (Chicago 1958) and Lawrence Lipking *The Ordering of the Arts* (Princeton 1970).

[1] One of the colossal statues of Amenhotep III near Thebes. When the rays of the morning sun first struck it, a sound occurred, usually described as like the twang of a harp. Popular legend interpreted it as the voice of Memnon greeting his mother Eos. It is thought to have been caused by the movement of air through the crevices of the stone because of the rising change of temperature at dawn. When the statue was restored by Septimius Severus (A.D. 170) the sounds ceased. C's point is that as light (vision) striking Memnon produced sound so, in reverse, the phrase of Milton is an example of sound or of the suggestion of it prompting an imagina-

tive sense of sight. Cf "the sweet sounds, that issued from the Head of Memnon at the Touch of Light". *SM (CC)* 98.

[2] C is probably thinking in particular of Jeffrey's remarks on WW's choice of the Pedlar in *The Excursion* (ch 21, above, II 118 n 3). Cf No V of C's letters in *Bl Mag* X (Oct 1821) 259; repr *CW* IV 431: "Here and there . . . [WW] may be thought to betray a preference of mean or trivial instances for grand morals, a capricious predilection for incidents that contrast with the depth and novelty of the truths they are to exemplify. But still to the principle, to the habit of tracing the presence of the high in the humble, the mysterious Dii Cabiri, in the form of the dwarf Miner, with hammer and spade, and week-day apron, we must attribute Wordsworth's *peculiar* power, his *leavening* influence on the opinions, feelings, and pursuits of his admirers,—most on the young of most promise and highest acquirements; and that, while others are read with delight, his works are a *religion*."

tions not furnished by me, but supplied from your own sickly and fastidious feelings? How was it, indeed, probable, that such arguments could have any weight with an author, whose plan, whose guiding principle, and main object it was to attack and subdue that state of association, which leads us to place the chief value on those things on which man DIFFERS from man, and to forget or disregard the high dignities, which belong to HUMAN NATURE, the sense and the feeling, which *may* be, and *ought* to be, found in *all* ranks? The feelings with which, as christians, we contemplate a mixed congregation rising or kneeling before their common maker: Mr. Wordsworth would have us entertain at *all* times as men, and as readers; and by the excitement of this lofty, yet prideless impartiality in *poetry*, he might hope to have encouraged its continuance in *real life*. The praise of good men be his! In real life, and, I trust, even in my imagination, I honor a virtuous and wise man, without reference to the presence or absence of artificial advantages. Whether in the person of an armed baron, a laurel'd bard, &c. or of an old pedlar, or still older leachgatherer, the same qualities of head and heart must claim the same reverence. And even in poetry I am not conscious that I have ever suffered my feelings to be disturbed or offended by any thoughts or images, which the poet himself has not presented.

But yet I object nevertheless, and for the following reasons. First, because the object in view, as an *immediate* object, belongs to the moral philosopher, and would be pursued, not only more appropriately, but in my opinion with far greater probability of success, in sermons or moral essays, than in an elevated poem. It seems, indeed, to destroy the main fundamental distinction, not only between a *poem* and *prose*, but even between philosophy and works of fiction, inasmuch as it proposes *truth* for its immediate object, instead of *pleasure*.[1] Now till the blessed time shall come, when truth itself shall be pleasure, and both[2] shall be so united, as to be distinguishable in words only, not in feeling, it will remain the poet's office to proceed upon that state of association, which actually exists as *general*; instead of attempting first to *make* it what it ought to be, and then to let the pleasure follow. But here

[1] See above, II 12–13.
[2] At this point, *BL* (1817) II 144 (the end of the page), the sheets printed in Bristol for *BL* (1817) stop. See Introd, above, I lxii n 2, and *CL* IV 659.

is unfortunately a small *Hysteron–Proteron*.[1] For the communication of pleasure is the introductory means by which alone the poet must expect to moralize his readers. Secondly: though I were to admit, for a moment, *this* argument to be groundless: yet how is the moral effect to be produced, by merely attaching the name of some low profession to powers which are *least* likely, and to qualities which are assuredly not *more* likely, to be found in it? The poet, speaking in his own person, may at once delight and improve us by sentiments, which teach us the independence of goodness, of wisdom, and even of genius, on the favors of fortune. And having made a due reverence before the throne of Antonine, he may bow with equal awe before Epictetus among his fellow-slaves—[2]

　　　　——————————————— and rejoice
In the plain presence of his dignity.[3]

Who is not at once delighted and improved, when the P O E T Wordsworth himself exclaims,

> O many are the poets that are sown
> By Nature; men endowed with highest gifts,
> The vision and *a* the faculty divine,
> Yet wanting the accomplishment of verse,
> Nor having e'er, as life advanced, been led
> By circumstance to take unto the height
> The measure of themselves, these favor'd beings,
> All but a scatter'd few, live out their time
> Husbanding that which they possess within,
> And go to the grave unthought of. Strongest minds
> Are often those of whom the noisy world
> Hears least.
>
> 　　　　　EXCURSION, B. 1.[4]

a BL (1817): send

1 "Latter–Former": i.e. reversing the normal order. See *CN* III 3421 and n, *SM* (*CC*) 104.

2 The Emperor Marcus Aurelius Antoninus (121–80) and his great fellow-Stoic, the slave Epictetus (c 55–c 135), whose writings strongly influenced Marcus Aurelius. On C's copies of the Marcus Aurelius *Meditations* and of Jeremy Collier's tr see *CN* II 2077n, III 4314n; and *CM* (*CC*) I 155–96. C found it "surprizing" that neither Marcus Aurelius nor Epictetus was "in the Lists of School Books at any of the Public Schools". *CM* (*CC*) I 161.

3 *Excursion* (1814) I 79–80 (var).

4 I 81–4, 90–7.

To use a colloquial phrase, such sentiments, in such language, do one's heart good; though I for my part, have not the fullest faith in the *truth* of the observation. On the contrary I believe the instances to be exceedingly rare; and should feel almost as strong an objection to introduce such a character in a poetic fiction, as a pair of black swans on a lake, in a fancy-landscape. When I think how many, and how much better books, than Homer, or even than Herodotus, Pindar or Eschylus, could have read, are in the power of almost every man, in a country where almost every man is instructed to read and write;[1] and how restless, how difficultly hidden, the powers of genius are; and yet find even in situations the most favorable, according to Mr. Wordsworth, for the formation of a pure and poetic language; in situations which ensure familiarity with the grandest objects of the imagination; but *one* BURNS, among the shepherds of *Scotland*, and not a single poet of humble life among those of *English* lakes and mountains; I conclude, that POETIC GENIUS is not only a very delicate but a very rare plant.

But be this as it may, the feelings with which,

[1] C here essentially rephrases a notebook entry of Nov 1808, in which he suggests to himself that he write an "essay" on the theme in Gray's *Elegy* of unfulfilled talent ("Full many a flower is born to blush unseen" lines 51ff): "Full many a flower &c—. Essay. To examine & whether there be truth in this—Take the present age/ Every Boy who strongly wished it, might learn to read—3 out of 4 are now taught reading—it is scarce possible that he might not procure the Bible, & many religious Books, which at all events would give him the best & most natural Language—here quote Dr H. More [see above, ch 17, II 44]—probably, Milton, Gray, Thomson, &c/ how much more than Pindar ever read!—and yet no great Geniuses start up from the Multitude now more than 100 years back—Difference between Burns and Bloomfield [Robert Bloomfield (1766–1823), the self-taught author of the wide-selling poem *The Farm-* er's *Boy* (1800) and *Good Tidings or News from the Farm* (1804)]—Lessings (von dem Leben und den Werken des M. A. Plautus) says—Das Glück mag einen Grossen Geist aus einem Stande entspringen lassen, aus welchem es will, er wird sich allezeit hervordringen und zur Bewunderung der Welt werden. [The quotation is from Lessing's article on Plautus in *Sämmtliche Schriften* (Berlin 1794) XXII 269: "Fortune may let a great mind emerge from whatever class it chooses. Such a mind will always force its way to the front and become the admiration of the world."] *Genius* a *very* rare production, but to write verses very easy, and the good sense & modesty and occupation forming Habits opposite to idleness, not the want of equal Genius, prevent *Ducks* & like Poets from being more numerous." The reference here is to Stephen Duck (1705–56), the self-educated "thresher poet". *CN* III 3415; 3415n gives full detail.

I think of C H A T T E R T O N , the marvellous boy,
The sleepless soul, that perish'd in his pride:
Of B U R N S , that walk'd in glory and in joy
Behind his plough upon the mountain-side— 1

are widely different from those with which I should read a *poem*,
where the author, having occasion for the character of a poet and
a philosopher in the fable of his narration, had chosen to make
him a *chimney-sweeper*; and then, in order to remove all doubts on
the subject, had *invented* an account of his birth, parentage and
education, with all the strange and fortunate accidents which had
concurred in making him at once poet, philosopher, and sweep!
Nothing, but biography, can justify this. If it be admissible even
in a *Novel*, it must be one in the manner of De Foe's, that were
meant to pass for histories, not in the manner of Fielding's: in the
life of Moll Flanders, or Colonel Jack, not in a Tom Jones or even
a Joseph Andrews.2 Much less then can it be legitimately introduced in a *poem*, the characters of which, amid the strongest
individualization, must still remain representative. The precepts of
Horace, on this point, are grounded on the nature both of poetry
and of the human mind.3 They are not more peremptory, than
wise and prudent. For in the first place a deviation from them
perplexes the reader's feelings, and all the circumstances which
are feigned in order to make such accidents less improbable, divide
and disquiet his faith, rather than aid and support it. Spite of all
attempts, the fiction *will* appear, and unfortunately not as *fictitious*
but as *false*. The reader not only *knows*, that the sentiments and
language are the poet's own, and his own too in his *artificial*
character, *as poet*; but by the fruitless endeavours to make him
think the contrary, he is not even suffered to *forget* it. The effect
is similar to that produced by an epic poet, when the fable and the
characters are *derived* from Scripture history, as in the *Messiah* of
Klopstock, or in *Cumberland's Calvary:*4 and not merely *sug-*

---

1 *Resolution and Independence*
lines 43–6 (1815 text var, substituting "Burns, that walk'd" for "Him
who walked"). Cf C's early poem
written at Christ's Hospital, *Monody
on the Death of Chatterton* (1790).
2 For C on Defoe and Fielding
see esp his annotations on *Robinson
Crusoe* and on *Tom Jones* in CM
(*CC*) II.

3 *Ars poetica* lines 114–19, 153–
78, on "decorum" or "preserving the
representative" in character portrayal.
4 Friedrich Gottlieb Klopstock
(1724–1803), whose epic *Der
Messias* (1748–73) C was fond of
contrasting with those of Milton.
"The inferiority of Klopstock's
Messiah is inexpressible. . . . The

gested by it as as in the Paradise Lost of Milton. That *illusion*, contradistinguished from *delusion*, that *negative* faith,[1] which simply permits the images presented to work by their own force, without either denial or affirmation of their real existence by the judgment, is rendered impossible by their immediate neighbourhood to words and facts of known and absolute truth. A faith, which transcends even historic belief, must absolutely *put out* this mere poetic Analogon[2] of faith, as the summer sun is said to extinguish our household fires, when it shines full upon them. What would otherwise have been yielded to as pleasing fiction, is repelled as revolting falsehood. The effect produced in this latter case by the solemn belief of the reader, is in a less degree brought about in the instances, to which I have been objecting, by the baffled attempts of the author to *make* him believe.

Add to all the foregoing the seeming uselessness both of the project and of the anecdotes from which it is to derive support. Is there one word for instance, attributed to the pedlar in the EXCURSION, characteristic of a *pedlar*? One sentiment, that might not more plausibly, even without the aid of any previous explanation, have proceeded from any wise and beneficent old man, of a rank or profession in which the language of learning and refinement are natural and to be expected? Need the rank have been at all particularized, where nothing follows which the knowledge of that rank is to explain or illustrate? When on the contrary this information renders the man's language, feelings, sentiments, and information a riddle, which must itself be solved by episodes of anecdote? Finally when this, and this alone, could have induced a genuine *poet* to inweave in a poem of the loftiest style, and on subjects the loftiest and of most universal interest, such minute matters of fact, (not unlike those furnished for the obituary of a magazine by the friends of some obscure *ornament of society lately deceased* in some obscure town,) as

---

feigned speeches and events in the Messiah shock us like falsehoods; but nothing of that sort is felt in the Paradise Lost, in which no particulars, at least very few indeed, are touched which can come into collision or juxtaposition with recorded matter." *Misc C* 162; cf 164, 392, 438, *CL* II 811, and below, II 194. The forgotten blank-verse *Calvary:*

or the Death of Christ (1792) by the dramatist Richard Cumberland (1732–1811) was a laboured imitation of Milton. For discussion of it see SC in *BL* (1847) II 148–9n. C wrote an obituary of Cumberland for the *Courier* 9 May 1811: *EOT* (*CC*) II 134–5.

1 See ch 14, above, II 6 and n 2.
2 See ch 2, above, I 37 and n 4.

Among the hills of Athol he was born.
There on a small hereditary farm,
An unproductive slip of rugged ground,
His Father dwelt; and died in poverty:
While he, whose lowly fortune I retrace,
The youngest of three sons, was yet a babe,
A little one—unconscious of their loss.
But 'ere he had outgrown his infant days
His widowed mother, for a second mate,
Espoused the teacher of the Village School;
Who on her offspring zealously bestowed
Needful instruction.

From his sixth year, the Boy of whom I speak,
In summer, tended cattle on the hills;
But through the inclement and the perilous days
Of long-continuing winter, he repaired
To his step-father's school.—&c.[1]

For all the admirable passages interposed in this narration, might, with trifling alterations, have been far more appropriately, and with far greater verisimilitude, told of a poet in the character of a poet; and without incurring another defect which I shall now mention, and a sufficient illustration of which will have been here anticipated.

Third; an undue predilection for the *dramatic* form in certain poems, from which one or other of two evils result. Either the thoughts and diction are different from that of the poet, and then there arises an incongruity of style; or they are the same and indistinguishable, and then it presents a species of ventriloquism,[2] where two are represented as talking, while in truth one man only speaks.

The fourth class of defects is closely connected with the former;

[1] *Excursion* I 112–23, 134–8. In response to C's criticism, WW rewrote the fourth line in the first of the two passages above, omitted the rest, and inserted a new passage (about the youth's parents) generally lacking in the "minute matters of fact" C is censuring.

[2] "Ventriloquism" is one of C's favourite terms (e.g. *Sh C* I 82, II 162; *Misc C* 54, 90, 394, 411), indicating the reverse of the truly "dramatic", in which the poet, Proteus-like, becomes the character.

See ch 15, on sympathetic identification (above, II 27 and n 2). As in his discussion of *The Thorn* (above, II 59, or again, below, II 150), C is stating that WW's gifts, however great, do not include genuine empathy and hence are inapplicable to the "dramatic". ". . . It seems to me that he ought never to have abandoned the contemplative position which is peculiarly—perhaps I might say exclusively—fitted for him. His proper title is *Spectator ab extra*." *TT* 21 Jul 1832.

but yet are such as arise likewise from an intensity of feeling disproportionate to *such* knowledge and value of the objects described, as can be fairly anticipated of men in general, even of the most cultivated classes; and with which therefore few only, and those few particularly circumstanced, can be supposed to sympathize: In this class, I comprize occasional prolixity, repetition, and an eddying[1] instead of progression of thought. As instances, see page 27, 28, and 62 of the Poems, Vol. I.[2] and the first eighty lines of the Sixth Book of the Excursion.

Fifth and last; thoughts and images too great for the subject. This is an approximation to what might be called *mental* bombast, as distinguished from verbal: for, as in the latter there is a disproportion of the expressions to the thoughts,[a] so in this there is a disproportion of thought to the circumstance and occasion. This, by the bye, is a fault of which none but a man of genius is capable. It is the awkwardness and strength of Hercules with the distaff of Omphale.[3]

It is a well known fact, that bright colours in motion both make and leave the strongest impressions on the eye. Nothing is more likely too, than that a vivid image or visual spectrum, thus originated, may become the link of association in recalling the feelings and images that had accompanied the original impression. But if we describe this in such lines, as

> They flash upon that inward eye,
> Which is the bliss of solitude![4]

in what words shall we describe the joy of retrospection, when the images and virtuous actions of a whole well-spent life, pass before

---

[a] *BL* (1817) omits comma

[1] Cf the *M Post* version of *Dejection* (4 Oct 1802), "Their life the eddying of thy living soul" (*PW*—EHC—I 369n), I. A. Richards's praise of the word in *Coleridge on Imagination* (3rd ed 1962) 152, and "Eddy of Contradictory feelings" in *CN* III 3766.

[2] *Poems* (1815) I 27–8 contains *Anecdote for Fathers* sts 4–13, later altered (1827); I 62 is a blank page, but C may mean the facing page, also unnumbered, containing "Extract from the conclusion of a poem". SC suggests that C refers to II 62,

containing *Song at the Feast of Brougham Castle* lines 80–103, because she had heard her father object to the passage "on account of its too much retarding the impassioned flow of the poem". *BL* (1847) II 152–3n.

[3] As punishment for slaying Iphitus, Hercules was condemned for three years to bondage to Omphale, Queen of Lydia, who dressed him in woman's clothes and set him to spinning wool with the female slaves. Cf *Friend* (*CC*) I 36.

[4] "I wandered lonely . . ." (1804; pub 1807) lines 21–2.

that conscience which is indeed the *inward* eye: which is indeed *"the bliss of solitude?"* Assuredly we seem to sink [1] most abruptly, not to say burlesquely, and almost as in a *medly* [2] from this couplet to—

> And then my heart with pleasure fills,
> And dances with the *daffodils.*
> Vol. I. p. 329.[a] [3]

The second instance is from Vol. II. page 12, where the poet having gone out for a day's tour of pleasure, meets early in the morning with a knot of *gypsies*, who had pitched their blanket-tents and straw-beds, together with their children and asses, in some field by the road-side. At the close of the day on his return our tourist found them in the same place. "Twelve hours," says he,

> Twelve hours, twelve bounteous hours, are gone while I
> Have been a traveller under open sky,
> Much witnessing of change and cheer,
> Yet as I left I find them here! [4]

Whereat the poet, without seeming to reflect that the poor tawny wanderers might probably have been tramping for weeks together through road and lane, over moor and mountain, and consequently must have been right glad to rest themselves, their children and cattle, for one whole day; and overlooking the obvious truth, that such repose might be quite as necessary for *them*, as a walk of the same continuance was pleasing or healthful for the more fortunate poet; expresses his indignation in a series of lines, the diction and imagery of which would have been rather above, than below the mark, had they been applied to the immense empire of China improgressive for thirty centuries:

> The weary S U N betook himself to rest,
> —Then issued V E S P E R from the fulgent west,

a BL (1817): 320

---

[1] See above, II 52 n 1.

[2] Presumably used as it applies to a musical composition consisting of detached parts of different works. *OED* definition 6.

[3] "I wandered lonely . . ." lines 23–4.

[4] *Gipsies* (1807; pub 1807) lines 9–12 and (below) 13–24. In the second passage the last three lines were altered and expanded in 1820 and 1827. "Coleridge censured the disproportion in the machinery of the poem on the Gipsies. Had the whole world been standing idle, more powerful arguments to expose the evil could not have been brought forward." HCR 15 Nov 1810. *CRD* I 305.

Outshining, like a visible God,
The glorious path in which he trod!
And now ascending, after one dark hour,
And one night's diminution of her power,
Behold the mighty M o o n! this way
She looks, as if at them—but they
Regard not her:—oh, better wrong and strife,
Better vain deeds or evil than such life!
The silent H e a v e n s have goings on:
The S t a r s have tasks!—but *these* have none!

The last instance of this defect, (for I know no other than these already cited) is from the Ode, page 351. Vol. I I. where, speaking of a child, "a six year's darling of a pigmy size," [1] he thus addresses him:

Thou best philosopher who yet dost keep
Thy heritage! Thou eye among the blind,
That, deaf and silent, read'st the eternal deep,
Haunted for ever by the Eternal Mind—
Mighty Prophet! Seer blest!
On whom those truths do rest,
Which we are toiling all our lives to find!
Thou, over whom thy immortality
Broods like the day, a master o'er the slave.
A presence that is not to be put by! [2]

Now here, not to stop at the daring spirit of metaphor which connects the epithets "deaf and silent," with the apostrophized *eye*: or (if we are to refer it to the preceding word, philosopher) the faulty and equivocal syntax of the passage; and without examining the propriety of making a "master *brood* o'er a slave," or the *day* brood *at all*; we will merely ask, what does all this mean? In what sense is a child of that age a *philosopher*? In what sense does he *read* "the eternal deep?" In what sense is he declared to be "*for ever haunted* by the Supreme Being? or so inspired as to deserve the splendid titles of a *mighty prophet*, a *blessed seer*? By reflection? by knowledge? by conscious intuition? or by *any* form or modification of consciousness?" These would be tidings indeed; but such as would pre-suppose an immediate revelation to the inspired communicator, and require miracles to authenticate his inspiration. Children at this age give us no such information of themselves; and at what time were we dipt in the Lethe, which has

[1] *Ode. Intimations of Immortality* (1802–4; pub 1807) line 86.   [2] Ibid lines 110–19 (var).

produced such utter oblivion of a state so godlike? There are many of us that still possess some remembrances, more or less distinct, respecting themselves at six years old; pity that the worthless straws only should float, while treasures, compared with which all the mines of Golconda and Mexico were but straws, should be absorbed by some unknown gulf into some unknown abyss.

But if this be too wild and exorbitant to be suspected as having been the poet's meaning; if these mysterious gifts, faculties, and operations, are *not* accompanied with consciousness; who *else* is conscious of them? or how can it be called the child, if it be no part of the child's conscious being? For aught I know, the thinking Spirit within me may be *substantially* one with the principle of life, and of vital operation. For aught I know, it may be employed as a secondary agent in the marvellous organization and organic movements of my body. But, surely, it would be strange language to say, that *I* construct my *heart*! or that *I* propel the finer influences through my *nerves*! or that *I* compress my brain, and draw the curtains of sleep round my own eyes! [1] S P I N O Z A and B E H M E N were on different systems both Pantheists; and among the ancients there were philosophers, teachers of the E N K A I Π A N, who not only taught, that God was All, but that this All constituted God.[2] Yet not even these would confound the *part*, as a part, with the Whole, *as* the whole. Nay, in no system is the distinction

[1] In italicising "I" throughout the paragraph, C is making a distinction between the kind of pantheism that identifies the self with all things, and hence with God, and the kind that assumes one spirit working throughout the whole, both in external nature and the self.

[2] Cf ch 12, above, I 246, in which C names Parmenides and Plotinus in connection with the "One and All". To quote a work that C read and annotated, Thomas Stanley *History of Philosophy* (1701) 446: "Xenophanes held that God is one and incorporeal, eternal . . . that he is all things . . .". Johann Jakob Brucker *Historia critica philosophiae* (1766–7), which C read in early 1797, I 1148 has a similar interpretation of Diogenes Laertius 9.2 (see also Aristotle *Metaphysics* 986b).

Xenophanes and his pupil Parmenides (who in his turn taught Zeno and Melissus) are both discussed by Brucker (I 1148–9, 1160) as possible forerunners of Spinoza as pantheists.

For a history of the Greek phrase see McFarland 341–2. He points out that the precise wording first appears in Stobaeus (fifth century A.D.): "Zeno and Melissus [said] that [God was] the one and all, alone eternal and infinite". After Jacobi published his famous conversation with Lessing (*ULS;* see esp xi, 22–5), the term "became almost universally current as a synonym for pantheism". See also McFarland 77–82. Cf C's use of the Greek phrase in the title of his burlesque ode in ch 9, above, I 159n.

between the individual and God, between the Modification, and the one only Substance, more sharply drawn, than in that of SPINOZA. JACOBI indeed relates of LESSING, that after a conversation with him at the house of the poet, GLEIM (the Tyrtæus and Anacreon of the German Parnassus)[1] in which conversation L. had avowed privately to Jacobi his reluctance to admit any *personal* existence of the Supreme Being, or the *possibility* of personality except in a finite Intellect, and while they were sitting at table, a shower of rain came on unexpectedly. Gleim expressed his regret at the circumstance, because they had meant to drink their wine in the garden: upon which Lessing in one of his half-earnest, half-joking moods, nodded to Jacobi, and said, "It is *I*, perhaps, that am doing *that*," i.e. *raining*! and J. answered, "or perhaps I"; Gleim contented himself with staring at them both, without asking for any explanation.[2]

So with regard to this passage. In what sense can the magnificent attributes, above quoted, be appropriated to a *child*, which would not make them equally suitable to a *bee*, or a *dog*, or a *field of corn*; or even to a ship, or to the wind and waves that propel it? The omnipresent Spirit works equally in *them*, as in the child; and the child is equally unconscious of it as they. It cannot surely be, that the four lines, immediately following, are to contain the explanation?

> To whom the grave
> Is but a lonely bed without the sense or sight
> Of day or the warm light,
> A place of thought where we in waiting lie.[3]

Surely, it cannot be that this wonder-rousing apostrophe is but a comment on the little poem of "We are Seven"?[4] that the whole

---

[1] Johann Wilhelm Ludwig Gleim (1719–1803), a warm-hearted patron and encourager of younger poets. In speaking of him as at once the Tyrtaeus (fl 650 B.C., and celebrated for his poems on warlike themes and Spartan virtues) and the pleasure-loving Anacreon (fl 580 B.C.) of Germany, C is referring particularly to Gleim's *Preussische Kriegslieder von einem Grenadier* (1758), songs both patriotic and Anacreontic in their praise of drinking, and also to

his *Lieder nach dem Anakreon* (1766).

[2] C's anecdote is taken from Jacobi *ULS* 51.

[3] *Ode. Intimations of Immortality* lines 120–3. In response to C's criticism WW omitted these lines in all eds after 1815, substituting the single line "In darkness lost, the darkness of the grave".

[4] *We Are Seven* (1798; pub 1800).

meaning of the passage is reducible to the assertion, that a *child*, who by the bye at six years old would have been better instructed in most christian families, has no other notion of death than that of lying in a dark, cold place? And still, I hope, not as *in a place of thought*! not the frightful notion of lying *awake* in his grave![1] The analogy between death and sleep is too simple, too natural, to render so horrid a belief possible for children; even had they not been in the habit, as all christian children are, of hearing the latter term used to express the former. But if the child's belief be only, that "he is not dead, but sleepeth":[2] wherein does it differ from that of his father and mother, or any other adult and instructed person? To form an idea of a thing's becoming nothing; or of nothing becoming a thing; is impossible to all finite beings alike, of whatever age, and however educated or uneducated. Thus it is with splendid paradoxes in general. If the words are taken in the common sense, they convey an absurdity; and if, in contempt of dictionaries and custom, they are so interpreted as to avoid the absurdity, the meaning dwindles into some bald truism. Thus you must at once understand the words *contrary* to their common import, in order to arrive at any *sense*; and *according* to their common import, if you are to receive from them any feeling of *sublimity* or *admiration*.

Though the instances of this defect in Mr. Wordsworth's poems are so few, that for themselves it would have been scarcely just to attract the reader's attention toward them; yet I have dwelt on it, and perhaps the more for this very reason. For being so very few, they cannot sensibly detract from the reputation of an author, who is even characterized by the number of profound truths in his writings, which will stand the severest analysis; and yet few as they are, they are exactly those passages which his *blind* admirers would be most likely, and best able, to imitate. But WORDSWORTH, where he is indeed Wordsworth, may be mimicked by Copyists, he may be plundered by Plagiarists; but he can not be imitated,

---

[1] Shawcross points out that for WW and DW the notion was less frightful. Cf *DWJ* I 139–40 (29 Apr 1802): "We then went to John's Grove . . . William lay, and I lay, in the trench under the fence—he with his eyes shut, and listening to the waterfalls and the birds. . . .

He thought that it would be as sweet thus to lie so in the grave, to hear the *peaceful* sounds of the earth, and just to know that our dear friends were near." *BL* (1907) II 291.

[2] Matt 9.24 (var); Mark 5.39 (var); Luke 8.52 (var).

except by those who are not born to be imitators. For without his depth of feeling and his imaginative power his *Sense* would want its vital warmth and peculiarity; and without his strong sense, his *mysticism* would become *sickly*—mere fog, and dimness!

To these defects which, as appears by the extracts, are only occasional, I may oppose with far less fear of encountering the dissent of any candid and intelligent reader, the following (for the most part correspondent) excellencies. First, an austere purity of language both grammatically and logically; in short a perfect appropriateness of the words to the meaning. Of how high value I deem this, and how particularly estimable I hold the example at the present day, has been already stated:[1] and in part too the reasons on which I ground both the moral and intellectual importance of habituating ourselves to a strict accuracy of expression. It is noticeable, how limited an acquaintance with the master-pieces of art will suffice to form a correct and even a sensitive taste, where none but master-pieces have been seen and admired: while on the other hand, the most correct notions, and the widest acquaintance with the works of excellence of all ages and countries, will not perfectly secure us against the contagious familiarity with the far more numerous offspring of tastelessness or of a perverted taste. If this be the case, as it notoriously is, with the arts of music and painting, much more difficult will it be, to avoid the infection of multiplied and daily examples in the practice of an art, which uses words, and words only, as its instruments. In poetry, in which every line, every phrase, may pass the ordeal of deliberation and deliberate choice, it is possible, and barely possible, to attain that ultimatum which I have ventured to propose as the infallible test of a blameless style; namely; its *untranslatableness* in words of the same language without injury to the meaning.[2] Be it observed, however, that I include in the *meaning* of a word not only its correspondent object, but likewise all the associations which it recalls. For language is framed to convey not the object alone, but likewise the character, mood and intentions of the person who is representing it. In poetry it *is* practicable to preserve the diction uncorrupted by the affectations and misappropriations, which promiscuous authorship, and reading not promiscuous only because it is disproportionally most conversant with the compositions

[1] Ch 16, above, II 29–30.   [2] Cf ch 1, above, I 23.

of the day, have rendered general. Yet even to the poet, composing in his own province, it is an arduous work: and as the result and pledge of a watchful good sense, of fine and luminous distinction, and of complete self-possession, may justly claim all the honor which belongs to an attainment equally difficult and valuable, and the more valuable for being rare. It is at *all* times the proper food of the understanding; but in an age of corrupt eloquence it is both food and antidote.

In prose I doubt whether it be even possible to preserve our style wholly unalloyed by the vicious phraseology which meets us every where, from the sermon to the newspaper, from the harangue of the legislator to the speech from the convivial chair, announcing a *toast* or sentiment. Our chains rattle, even while we are complaining of them. The poems of Boetius rise high in our estimation when we compare them with those of his contemporaries, as Sidonius Apollinaris, &c.[1] They might even be referred to a purer age, but that the prose, in which they are set, as jewels in a crown of lead or iron, betrays the true age of the writer. Much however may be effected by education. I believe not only from grounds of reason, but from having in great measure assured myself of the fact by actual though limited experience, that to a youth led from his first boyhood to investigate the meaning of every word and the reason of its choice and position, Logic presents itself as an old acquaintance under new names.[2]

On some future occasion, more especially demanding such disquisition,[3] I shall attempt to prove the close connection between veracity and habits of mental accuracy; the beneficial after-effects of verbal precision in the preclusion of fanaticism, which masters the feelings more especially by indistinct watchwords; and to display the advantages which language alone, at least which language with incomparably greater ease and certainty than any other means, presents to the instructor of impressing

[1] For Boethius see above, II 121 and n 1. Caius Sollius Apollinaris Sidonius (c 430–88), bp of Clermont, whose surviving poems have little interest other than historical. C on 19 Nov 1796 had ordered a copy of his works through John Thelwall. *CL* I 262.

[2] C apparently refers to the teaching of Boyer. See ch 1, above, I 9.

[3] Probably a reference to C's projected work on logic for students. In the *Logic* as we now have it, C treats of some of the subjects mentioned below, e.g. "distinguishing the similar from the same": *Logic* (*CC*) 15–16.

modes of intellectual energy so constantly, so imperceptibly, and as it were by such elements and atoms, as to secure in due time the formation of a second nature. When we reflect, that the cultivation of the judgment is a positive command of the moral law, since the reason can give the *principle* alone, and the conscience bears witness only to the *motive*, while the application and effects must depend on the judgment: when we consider, that the greater part of our success and comfort in life depends on distinguishing the similar from the same, that which is peculiar in each thing from that which it has in common with others, so as still to select the most probable, instead of the merely possible or positively unfit, we shall learn to value earnestly and with a practical seriousness a mean, already prepared for us by nature and society, of teaching the young mind to think well and wisely by the same unremembered process and with the same never forgotten results, as those by which it is taught to speak and converse. Now how much warmer the interest is, how much more genial the feelings of reality and practicability, and thence how much stronger the impulses to imitation are, which a *contemporary* writer, and especially a contemporary *poet*, excites in youth and commencing manhood, has been treated of in the earlier pages of these sketches.[1] I have only to add, that all the praise which is due to the exertion of such influence for a purpose so important, joined with that which must be claimed for the infrequency of the same excellence in the same perfection, belongs in full right to Mr. WORDSWORTH. I am far however from denying that we have poets whose *general* style possesses the same excellence, as Mr. Moore, Lord Byron, Mr. Bowles, and in all his later and more important works our laurel-honoring Laureate.[2] But there are none, in whose works I do not appear to myself to find *more* exceptions, than in those of Wordsworth. Quotations or specimens would here be wholly out of place, and must be left for the critic who doubts and would invalidate the justice of this eulogy so applied.

The second characteristic excellence of Mr. W's works is: a correspondent weight and sanity of the Thoughts and Sentiments,— won, not from books; but—from the poet's own meditative obser-

[1] See the more extended remarks, ch 1, above, in which C speaks of the influence on him of Bowles's sonnets, I 12–17, 24.

[2] Cf the similar remarks, above, II 99.

vation. They are *fresh* and have the dew upon them.[1] His muse, at least when in her strength of wing, and when she hovers aloft in her proper element,

> Makes audible a linked lay of truth,
> Of truth profound a sweet continuous lay,
> Not learnt, but native, her own natural notes!
>
> S. T. C.[2]

Even throughout his smaller poems there is scarcely one, which is not rendered valuable by some just and original reflection.

See page 25, vol. 2nd:[3] or the two following passages in one of his humblest compositions.

> O Reader! had you in your mind
> Such stores as silent thought can bring,
> O gentle Reader! you would find
> A tale in every thing.

and

> I have heard of hearts unkind, kind deeds
> With coldness still returning:
> Alas! the gratitude of men
> Has oftener left *me* mourning.[4]

or in a still higher strain the six beautiful quatrains, page 134.

> Thus fares it still in our decay:
> And yet the wiser mind
> Mourns less for what age takes away
> Than what it leaves behind.
>
> The Blackbird in the summer trees,
> The Lark upon the hill,
> Let loose their carols when they please,
> Are quiet when they will.
>
> With nature never do *they* wage
> A foolish strife; they see
> A happy youth, and their old age
> Is beautiful and free!

[1] Cf C's statement about Thomas Poole, whose remarks present "truths plucked as they are growing, and delivered to you with the dew on them, the fair earnings of an observing eye, armed and kept on the watch by thought and meditation". *C&S (CC)* 92–3n.

[2] *To William Wordsworth* lines 58–60: *PW* (EHC) i 406.

[3] In *Poems* (1815): *Star-Gazers* (1806; pub 1807) lines 9–20.

[4] *Simon Lee* (1798; pub 1798) lines 73–6, 101–4 (var).

But we are pressed by heavy laws;
And often, glad no more,
We wear a face of joy, because
We have been glad of yore.

If there is one, who need bemoan
His kindred laid in earth,
The household hearts that were his own,
It is the man of mirth.

My days, my Friend, are almost gone,
My life has been approved,
And many love me; but by none
Am I enough beloved.[1]

or the sonnet on Buonaparte, page 202, vol. 2;[2] or finally (for a volume would scarce suffice to exhaust the instances,) the last stanza of the poem on the withered Celandine, vol. 2, p. 312.[a]

To be a prodigal's favorite—then, worse truth,
A miser's pensioner—behold our lot!
Oh man! that from thy fair and shining youth
Age might but take the things, youth needed not.[3]

Both in respect of this and of the former excellence, Mr. Wordsworth strikingly resembles Samuel Daniel, one of the golden writers of our golden Elizabethan age, now most causelessly neglected: Samuel Daniel, whose diction bears no mark of time, no distinction of age, which has been, and as long as our language shall last, will be so far the language of the to-day and for ever, as that it is more intelligible to us, than the transitory fashions of our own particular age.[4] A similar praise is due to his sentiments. No frequency of perusal can deprive them of their freshness. For though they are brought into the full day-light of every reader's comprehension; yet are they drawn up from depths which few in any age are

[a] *BL* (1817): 212.

[1] *The Fountain* (1799; pub 1800) lines 33–56.

[2] "I grieved for Buonaparte . . ." (1802; pub 1802).

[3] *The Small Celandine* (1804; pub 1807) lines 21–4.

[4] Cf "We find both in his poetry and prose such a legitimate rational flow of language, as approaches nearer the style of the 18th than the 16th century; and of which we may safely assert, that it will never become obsolete." "Life of Daniel" (quoting Headley) in *B Poets* iv 114. On Daniel's language, see ch 18, above, ii 78 and n 2. WW himself was interested in Daniel and studied him carefully. Cf e.g. *Excursion* iv 324–31 and WW's note *WPW* v 118–19, 424–5; Reed ii 130, 216, 385, 486; *BL* (1907) ii 292.

priviledged to visit, into which few in any age have courage or inclination to descend. If Mr. Wordsworth is not equally with Daniel alike intelligible to all readers of average understanding in all passages of his works, the comparative difficulty does not arise from the greater impurity of the ore, but from the nature and uses of the metal. A poem is not necessarily obscure, because it does not aim to be popular. It is enough, if a work be perspicuous to those for whom it is written, and*ᵃ*

> Fit audience find, though few.[1]

To the "Ode on the intimation of immortality from recollections of early childhood" the poet might have prefixed the lines which Dante addresses to one of his own Canzoni—

> Canzon, io credo, che saranno radi
> Che tua ragione intendan bene:
> Tanto lor sei faticoso ed alto.

> O lyric song, there will be few, think I,
> Who may thy import understand aright:
> Thou art for *them* so arduous and so high![2]

But the ode was intended for such readers only as had been accustomed to watch the flux and reflux of their inmost nature.[3] to venture at times into the twilight realms of consciousness, and to feel a deep interest in modes of inmost being, to which they know that the attributes of time and space are inapplicable and alien, but which yet can not be conveyed, save in symbols of time and space. For such readers the sense is sufficiently plain, and they will be as little disposed to charge Mr. Wordsworth with believing the platonic pre-existence in the ordinary interpretation of the words, as I am to believe, that Plato himself ever meant or taught it.[4]

ᵃ BL (1817): and,

[1] Milton *Paradise Lost* VII 31.

[2] *Convivio* II Canzone I 53–5 (var). C had been struck by the lines and copied them into a notebook 1807–8. *CN* II 3219 and n. In the copy of *BL* C sent to DC (see ch 20, above, n 1) he altered "intendan bene" to "bene intenderrano", as in the 1818 *Friend* (*CC*) I 511n, perhaps to adjust the

metre ("Color" at the beginning of line 54 C had omitted).

[3] C echoes WW's statement in Preface to *LB* (1800) that one of his purposes "is to follow the fluxes and refluxes of the mind when agitated by the great and simple affections of our nature". *W Prose* I 126.

[4] Cf WW's remark to IF that in the ode he "took hold of the notion

Πολλά οἱ ὑπ' ἀγκῶ-
νος ὠκέα βέλη
῎Ενδον ἐντὶ φαρέτρας
Φωνᾶντα συνετοῖσιν· ἐς
Δὲ τὸ πᾶν ἑρμηνέως
Χατίζει. Σοφὸς ὁ πολ-
λὰ εἰδὼς φυᾷ.
Μαθόντες δέ, λάβροι
Παγγλωσσίᾳ, κόρακες ὣς
῎Ακραντα γαρύετον
Διὸς πρὸς ὄρνιχα θεῖον.[1]

Third (and wherein he soars far above Daniel) the sinewy
strength and originality of single lines and paragraphs: the frequent
curiosa felicitas[2] of his diction, of which I need not here give
specimens, having anticipated them in a preceding page. This
beauty, and as eminently characteristic of Wordsworth's poetry,
his rudest assailants have felt themselves compelled to acknowledge
and admire.

Fourth; the perfect truth of nature in his images and descriptions
as taken immediately from nature, and proving a long and genial
intimacy with the very spirit which gives the physiognomic expression to all the works of nature. Like a green field reflected in a
calm and perfectly transparent lake, the image is distinguished
from the reality only by its greater softness and lustre. Like the
moisture or the polish on a pebble, genius neither distorts nor
false-colours its objects; but on the contrary brings out many a
vein and many a tint, which escape the eye of common observation,
thus raising to the rank of gems, what had been often kicked away

---

of pre-existence as having sufficient
foundation in humanity [human
experience generally] for authorizing
me to make for my purpose the
best use of it I could as a Poet".
WPW iv 464.

[1] Pindar *Olympian Odes* 2.83–8
(or in the old numbering 150–9).
C has altered the first person pronoun to the third, to apply the
passage to WW, and has "inter-
preter" in the singular instead of the
plural. A reading in the penultimate
line suggests the source to be *Poetae
graeci veteres* II 6. "Full many a

swift arrow [has he] beneath [his]
arm, within [his] quiver, many an
arrow that is vocal to the wise; but
for the crowd they need [an inter-
preter]. The true poet is he who
knoweth much by gift of nature,
but they that have only learnt the
lore of song, and are turbulent and
intemperate of tongue, like a pair of
crows, chatter in vain against the
god-like bird of Zeus." Tr LCL.

[2] "Studied felicity". Petronius
(speaking of Horace) *Satyricon* 118.
BL (1920) 324n.

by the hurrying foot of the traveller on the dusty high road of custom.

Let me refer to the whole description of skating, vol. I, page 44 [a] to 47, especially to the lines

> So through the darkness and the cold we flew,
> And not a voice was idle: with the din
> Meanwhile the precipices rang aloud;
> The leafless trees and every icy crag
> Tinkled like iron; while the distant hills
> Into the tumult sent an alien sound
> Of melancholy, not unnoticed, while the stars
> Eastward were sparkling clear, and in the west
> The orange sky of evening died away.[1]

Or to the poem on the green linnet, vol. I. p. 244. What can be more accurate yet more lovely than the two concluding stanzas?

> Upon yon tuft of hazel trees,
> That twinkle to the gusty breeze,
> Behold him perched in ecstasies,
>   Yet seeming still to hover,
> There! where the flutter of his wings
> Upon his back and body flings
> Shadows and sunny glimmerings
>   That cover him all over.
>
> While thus before my eyes he gleams,
> A brother of the leaves he seems;
> When in a moment forth he teems
>   His little song in gushes:
> As if it pleased him to disdain
> And mock the form when he did feign
> While he was dancing with the train
>   Of leaves among the bushes.[2]

Or the description of the blue-cap, and of the noon-tide silence, p. 284; or the poem to the cuckoo, p. 299;[3] or, lastly, though I might multiply the references to ten times the number, to the poem so completely Wordsworth's commencing

> Three years she grew in sun and shower, &c.[4]

[a] *BL* (1817): 42

[1] *Influence of Natural Objects* (1798; published in *Friend* 28 Dec 1809 and meanwhile incorporated in *Prelude* I 401–89) lines 38–46.

[2] *The Green Linnet* (1803; pub 1807) lines 25–40.

[3] *The Kitten and the Falling Leaves* (1804; pub 1807) lines 63–88; and *To the Cuckoo* (1802; pub 1807) lines 1–16.

[4] "Three years she grew . . ." (1799; pub 1800).

Fifth: a meditative pathos, a union of deep and subtle thought
with sensibility; a sympathy with man as man; the sympathy indeed
of a contemplator, rather than a fellow-sufferer or co-mate, (spectator, haud particeps) [1] but of a contemplator, from whose view
no difference of rank conceals the sameness of the nature; no
injuries of wind or weather, of toil, or even of ignorance, wholly
disguise the human face divine. The superscription and the image
of the Creator still remain legible to *him* under the dark lines, with
which guilt or calamity had cancelled or cross-barred it. Here the
man and the poet lose and find themselves in each other, the one
as glorified, the latter as substantiated. In this mild and philosophic
pathos, Wordsworth appears to me without a compeer. Such he *is*:
so he *writes*. See vol. I. page 134 to 136, or that most affecting
composition, the "Affliction of Margaret———of———," page 165
to 168,[2] which no mother, and if I may judge by my own experience, no parent can read without a tear. Or turn to that genuine
lyric, in the former edition, entitled, the "Mad Mother," page 174
to 178, of which I can not refrain from quoting two of the stanzas,
both of them for their pathos, and the former for the fine transition in the two concluding lines of the stanza, so expressive of
that deranged state, in which from the increased sensibility the
sufferer's attention is abruptly drawn off by every trifle, and in the
same instant plucked back again by the one despotic thought, and
bringing home with it, by the blending, *fusing* power of Imagination and Passion,[3] the alien object to which it had been so abruptly
diverted, no longer an alien but an ally and an inmate.

> Suck, little babe, oh suck again!
> It cools my blood; it cools my brain:
> Thy lips, I feel them, baby! they
> Draw from my heart the pain away.
> Oh! press me with thy little hand;
> It loosens something at my chest;
> About that tight and deadly band
> I feel thy little fingers prest.

---

[1] "A spectator, not a participant".
Cf above, II 135 n 2, on WW as a
"Spectator ab extra". C later stated
that WW and Goethe, however
different in other ways, "both have
this peculiarity of utter non-sym-
pathy with the subjects of their
poetry. They are always, both of

them, spectators *ab extra*,—feeling
for, but never *with*, their characters."
TT 16 Feb 1833.

[2] " 'Tis said, that some have died
for love" (1800; pub 1800) and
The Affliction of Margaret ————
(1801?; pub 1807).

[3] Cf above, II 16, 64–5.

The breeze I see is in the tree!
It comes to cool my babe and me.

Thy father cares not for my breast,
'Tis thine, sweet baby, there to rest,
'Tis all thine own!—and, if its hue,
Be changed, that was so fair to view,
'Tis fair enough for thee, my dove!
My beauty, little child, is flown,
But thou wilt live with me in love,
And what if my poor cheek be brown?
'Tis well for me, thou can'st not see
How pale and wan it else would be.[1]

Last, and pre-eminently,[a] I challenge for this poet the gift of IMAGINATION in the highest and strictest sense of the word. In the play of *Fancy*, Wordsworth, to my feelings, is not always graceful, and sometimes *recondite*.[2] The *likeness* is occasionally too strange, or demands too peculiar a point of view, or is such as appears the creature of predetermined research, rather than spontaneous presentation. Indeed his fancy seldom displays itself, as mere and unmodified fancy. But in imaginative power, he stands nearest of all modern writers to Shakespear and Milton; and yet in a kind perfectly unborrowed and his own.[3] To employ his own words, which are at once an instance and an illustration, he does indeed to all thoughts and to all objects—

———————————add the gleam,
The light that never was on sea or land,
The consecration, and the poet's dream.[4]

I shall select a few examples as most obviously manifesting this faculty; but if I should ever be fortunate enough to render my analysis of imagination, its origin and characters thoroughly intelligible to the reader, he will scarcely open on a page of this poet's works without recognizing, more or less, the presence and the influences of this faculty.

---

[a] *BL* (1817) omits comma

[1] "Her eyes are wild . . ." (1798; pub 1798) lines 31–40, 61–70. Cf *CN* II 2112 and n.

[2] On "fancy" see Introd and chs 4 and 13, above, I xcvii–civ, 82–8, 304–5.

[3] Cf on WW's poetic language, which, "next to that of Shakspeare and Milton, appears to me of all others the most *individualized* and characteristic", above, II 99.

[4] *Elegiac Stanzas, Suggested by a Picture of Peele Castle* (1805; pub 1807) lines 14–16.

From the poem on the Yew Trees, vol. I. page 303, 304.

> But worthier still of note
> Are those fraternal four of Borrowdale,
> Joined in one solemn and capacious grove:
> Huge trunks!—and each particular trunk a growth
> Of intertwisted fibres serpentine
> Up-coiling, and inveterately convolved,—
> Not uninformed with phantasy, and looks
> That threaten the prophane;—a pillared shade,
> Upon whose grassless floor of red-brown hue,
> By sheddings from the pinal umbrage tinged
> Perennially—beneath whose sable roof
> Of boughs, as if for festal purpose decked
> With unrejoicing berries, ghostly shapes
> May meet at noontide—FEAR and trembling HOPE,
> SILENCE and FORESIGHT—DEATH, the skeleton,
> And TIME, the shadow—there to celebrate,
> As in a natural temple scattered o'er
> With altars undisturbed of mossy stone,
> United worship; or in mute repose
> To lie, and listen to the mountain flood
> Murmuring from Glaramara's inmost caves.[1]

The effect of the old man's figure in the poem of Resignation and Independence, vol. II. page 33.

> While he was talking thus, the lonely place,[a]
> The old man's shape, and speech, all troubled me:
> In my mind's eye I seemed to see him pace
> About the weary moors continually,
> Wandering about alone and silently.[2]

Or the 8th, 9th, 19th, 26th, 31st, and 33d, in the collection of miscellaneous sonnets—the sonnet on the subjugation of Switzerland, page 210,[3] or the last ode from which I especially select the two following stanzas or paragraphs, page 349 to 350.

a BL (1817) omits comma

[1] *Yew-Trees* (1803?; pub 1815) lines 13–33 (var). In *BL* (1847) SC commented on the variant in line 22: " '*Pining* umbrage' in all the editions. I have left my Father's substitution as a curious instance of a possible different reading. 'Piny shade' and 'piny verdure' we read of in the poets; but 'pinal' I believe is new. *Pining,* which has quite a different sense, is doubtless still better, but

perhaps my Father's ear shrank from it after the word '*sheddings*' at the beginning of the line."
[2] *Resolution and Independence* (1802; pub 1807) lines 134–8 (in 1815); also quoted above, II 125.
[3] In the order mentioned: "Where lies the land . . ." (1802–4; pub 1807); "Even as a dragon's eye . . ." (1807–14; pub 1815); *To the River Duddon* ("O Mountain Stream")

Our birth is but a sleep and a forgetting:
The soul that rises with us, our life's star
Hath had elsewhere its setting,
    And cometh from afar.
Not in entire forgetfulness,
And not in utter nakedness,
But trailing clouds of glory do we come
From God who is our home:
Heaven lies about us in our infancy!
Shades of the prison-house begin to close
    Upon the growing boy;
But he beholds the light, and whence it flows,
    He sees it in his joy!
The youth who daily further from the east
Must travel, still is nature's priest,
    And by the vision splendid
    Is on his way attended;
At length the man perceives it die away,
And fade into the light of common day.[1]

And page 352 to 354 of the same ode.

O joy that in our embers
Is something that doth live,
That nature yet remembers
What was so fugitive!
The thought of our past years in me doth breed
Perpetual benedictions: not indeed
For that which is most worthy to be blest;
Delight and liberty the simple creed
Of childhood, whether busy or at rest,
With new-fledged hope still fluttering in his breast:—
Not for these I raise
The song of thanks and praise;
But for those obstinate questionings
Of sense and outward things,
Fallings from us, vanishings;
Blank misgivings of a creature
Moving about in worlds not realized,
High instincts, before which our mortal nature
Did tremble like a guilty thing surprised!
But for those first affections,
Those shadowy recollections,

(1806; pub 1807); *Composed upon Westminster Bridge* (1802; pub 1807); "Methought I saw the footsteps . . ." (1802–4; pub 1807); "It is a beauteous Evening . . ." (1802; pub 1807); "Two Voices are there . . ." (1806–7; pub 1807).

[1] *Ode. Intimations of Immortality* lines 58–76.

> Which, be they what they may,
> Are yet the fountain light of all our day,
> Are yet a master light of all our seeing;
> Uphold us—cherish—and have power to make
> Our noisy years seem moments in the being
> Of the eternal silence; truths that wake
>   To perish never:
> Which neither listlessness, nor mad endeavour
> Nor man nor boy
> Nor all that is at enmity with joy
> Can utterly abolish or destroy!
> Hence, in a season of calm weather,
> Though inland far we be,
> Our souls have sight of that immortal sea
> Which brought us hither,
> Can in a moment travel thither—
> And see the children sport upon the shore,
> And hear the mighty waters rolling evermore.[1]

And since it would be unfair to conclude with an extract, which though highly characteristic must yet from the nature of the thoughts and the subject be interesting, or perhaps intelligible, to but a limited number of readers; I will add from the poet's last published work a passage equally Wordsworthian; of the beauty of which, and of the imaginative power displayed therein, there can be but one opinion, and one feeling. See White Doe, page 5.

> Fast the church-yard fills;—anon
> Look again and they are gone;
> The cluster round the porch, and the folk
> Who sate in the shade of the prior's oak!
> And scarcely have they disappear'd
> Ere the prelusive hymn is heard:—
> With one consent the people rejoice,
> Filling the church with a lofty voice!
> They sing a service which they feel
> For 'tis the sun-rise of their zeal
> And faith and hope are in their prime
> In great Eliza's golden time.
>
> A moment ends the fervent din
> And all is hushed without and within;
> For though the priest more tranquilly
> Recites the holy liturgy,
> The only voice which you can hear
> Is the river murmuring near.
> When soft!—the dusky trees between

[1] *Ode* lines 133–171.

And down the path through the open green,
Where is no living thing to be seen;
And through yon gateway, where is found,
Beneath the arch with ivy bound,
Free entrance to the church-yard ground;
And right across the verdant sod
Towards the very house of God;
Comes gliding in with lovely gleam,
Comes gliding in serene and slow,
Soft and silent as a dream,
A solitary doe!
White she is as lily of June,
And beauteous as the silver moon
When out of sight the clouds are driven
And she is left alone in heaven!
Or like a ship some gentle day
In sunshine sailing far away—
A glittering ship that hath the plain
Of ocean for her own domain.

* * * * * * * * * * * * * *

What harmonious pensive changes
Wait upon her as she ranges
Round and round this pile of state
Overthrown and desolate!
Now a step or two her way
Is through space of open day,
Where the enamoured sunny light
Brightens her that was so bright:
Now doth a delicate shadow fall,
Falls upon her like a breath
From some lofty arch or wall,
As she passes underneath.[1]

The following analogy will, I am apprehensive, appear dim and fantastic, but in reading Bartram's Travels I could not help transcribing the following lines as a sort of allegory, or connected simile and metaphor of Wordsworth's intellect and genius.—"The soil is a deep, rich, dark mould, on a deep stratum of tenacious clay; and that on a foundation of rocks, which often break through both strata, lifting their back above the surface. The trees which chiefly grow here are the gigantic, black oak; magnolia magniflora; fraxinus excelsior; platane; and a few stately tulip trees."[2] What

---

[1] *The White Doe of Rylstone* (1807–8; pub 1815) I 31–68, 81–92 (in 1815). The following couplet was omitted in 1832 and thereafter: "And right across the verdant sod | Towards the very house of God".
[2] William Bartram (1739–1823) *Travels Through North & South*

Mr. Wordsworth *will* produce, it is not for me to prophesy: but I could pronounce with the liveliest convictions what he is capable of producing. It is the FIRST GENUINE PHILOSOPHIC POEM.[1]

The preceding criticism will not, I am aware, avail to overcome the prejudices of those, who have made it a business to attack and ridicule Mr. Wordsworth's compositions.

Truth and prudence might be imaged as concentric circles. The poet may perhaps have passed beyond the latter, but he has confined himself far within the bounds of the former, in designating these critics, as too petulant to be passive to a genuine poet, and too feeble to grapple with him;—"men of palsied imaginations, in whose minds all healthy action is languid;—who, therefore, feel as the many direct them, or with the many are greedy after vicious provocatives."[2]

Let not Mr. Wordsworth be charged with having expressed himself too indignantly, till the wantonness and the systematic and malignant perseverance of the aggressions have been taken into fair consideration.[3] I myself heard the commander in chief

---

Carolina, Georgia, East & West Florida . . . (Philadelphia 1791) 36–7. See *RX* 7–8, 452–3, and C's remark about the book when he gave his copy to SH: *CM* (*CC*) I 227. C on 26 Mar 1801 had copied a condensed version of the description, adding "I applied this by a fantastic analogue & similitude to Wordsworth's Mind". In *BL*, above, he is quoting from that condensed version, with the addition of "magniflora" after "magnolia". *CN* I 926 and n; Barbara Hardy *EIC* IX (1959) 314.

[1] Cf the remark to Richard Sharp 15 Jan 1804: ". . . I dare affirm that he [WW] will hereafter be admitted as the first & greatest philosophical Poet—the only man who has effected a compleat and constant synthesis of Thought & Feeling and combined them with Poetic Forms . . . and I prophesy immortality to his *Recluse,* as the first & finest philosophical Poem . . .". So eleven years later (30 May 1815)

C told WW, after expressing mild disappointment in *The Excursion:* ". . . In the very Pride of confident Hope I looked forward to the Recluse, as the *first* and *only* true Phil. Poem in existence". *CL* II 1034, IV 574.

[2] WW's "Essay, Supplementary to the Preface" (1815): *W Prose* III 66 (var).

[3] This sentence, the rest of the paragraph, and the footnote were omitted by SC in *BL* (1847) "for the same reason which led the late editor [HNC] to suppress a note on the subject in Vol. I.—namely this; that as those passages contain *personal* remarks, right or wrong, they were anomalies in my Father's writings, unworthy of them [Jeffrey and other critics] and of him, and such as I feel sure he would not himself have reprinted". *BL* (1847) I clviii. On the suppressed note and Jeffrey's visit to Cumberland, see ch 3, above, I 50 and n 2.

of this unmanly warfare make a boast of his private admiration of Wordsworth's genius. I have heard him declare, that whoever came into his room would probably find the Lyrical Ballads lying open on his table, and that (speaking exclusively of those written by Mr. Wordsworth himself,) he could nearly repeat the whole of them by heart.[1] *But* a Review, in order to be a saleable article, must be *personal, sharp,* and *pointed*: and, *since then,* the Poet has made himself, and with himself all who were, or were supposed to be, his friends and admirers, the object of the critic's revenge— how? by having spoken of a work so conducted in the terms which it deserved! I once heard a clergyman in boots and buckskin avow, that he would cheat his own father *in a horse*.[2] A moral system of a similar nature seems to have been adopted by too many anonymous critics. As we used to say at school, in reviewing they *make* being rogues: and he, who complains, is to be laughed at for his ignorance of *the game*. With the pen out of their hand they are *honorable men*. They exert indeed power (which is to that of the injured party who should attempt to expose their glaring perversions and misstatements, as twenty to one) to write down, and (where the author's circumstances permit) to *impoverish* the man, whose learning and genius they themselves in private have repeatedly admitted. They knowingly strive to make it impossible for the man even to publish * any future work without exposing himself to all the wretchedness of debt and embarrassment. But this

---

* Not many months ago an eminent bookseller was asked what he thought of —————? The answer was: "I have heard his powers very highly spoken of by some of our first-rate men; but I would not have a work of his if any one would give it me: for he is spoken but slightly of, or not at all in the Quarterly Review: and the Edinburgh, you know, is decided, to cut him up!"—[3]

[1] Cf HCR 14 Nov 1810: C "related to us that Jeffrey . . . had lately called on him, and assured him that he was a great admirer of Wordsworth's poetry, that the Lyrical Ballads were always on his table, and that Wordsworth had been attacked in the *Review* simply because the errors of men of genius ought to be exposed." *CRD* i 304. Again, 8 Jul 1825 to Daniel Stuart: "I give you my honor, that Jeffray himself told me, that *he* was himself an enthusiastic Admirer of Wordsworth's Poetry—but it was necessary that a Review should have a character." *CL* v 475. Cf *CN* iii 3496 and n.

[2] Cf the same account, which identifies him as a clergyman "at Salisbury", in Allsop ii 99.

[3] Cf the similar account in a letter to Francis Wrangham (5 Jun 1817), in which the "first-rate men" are identified as Byron and Scott. *CL* iv 736.

is all *in their vocation*: and bating what they do in their *vocation*, "*who can say that black is the white of their eye?*" [1]

So much for the detractors from Wordsworth's merits. On the other hand, much as I might wish for their fuller sympathy, I dare not flatter myself, that the freedom with which I have declared my opinions concerning both his theory and his defects, most of which are more or less connected with his theory either as cause or effect, will be satisfactory or pleasing to *all* the poet's admirers and advocates. More indiscriminate than mine their admiration may be: deeper and more sincere it can not be. But I have advanced no opinion either for praise or censure, other than as texts introductory to the reasons which compel me to form it. Above all, I was fully convinced that such a criticism was not only wanted; but that, if executed with adequate ability, it must conduce in no mean degree to Mr. Wordsworth's *reputation*. His *fame* belongs to another age, and can neither be accelerated or retarded.[2] How small the proportion of the defects are to the beauties, I have repeatedly declared; and that no one of them originates in deficiency of poetic genius. Had they been more and greater, I should still, as a friend to his literary character in the present age, consider an analytic display of them as *pure gain*; if only it removed, as surely to all reflecting minds even the foregoing analysis must have removed, the strange mistake so slightly grounded, yet so widely and industriously propagated, of Mr. Wordsworth's turn for SIMPLICITY! I am not half as much irritated by hearing his enemies abuse him for vulgarity of style, subject, and conception; as I am disgusted with the gilded side of the same meaning, as displayed by some affected admirers with whom he is, forsooth, a *sweet, simple poet!* and *so* natural, that little master Charles, and

---

[1] Proverbial for "to find fault with". E.g. Francis Grose *Dictionary of the Vulgar Tongue* (3rd ed 1796) 181: "Black Eye. He cannot say black is the white of my eye; he cannot point out a blot in my character." See *OED* "White" 2.

[2] "If in one instance (in my Literary Life) I have appeared to deviate from this rule ["never to admit the *faults* of a work of Genius to those who denied or were incapable of feeling and understanding the *Beauties*"], first, it was not till the fame of the Writer (which I had been for 14 years successively toiling, like a second Ali, to build up) had been established: and secondly and chiefly, with the purpose and, I may safely add, with the *effect* of rescuing the necessary task from malignant Defamers and in order to set forth the excellences and the trifling proportion which the Defects bore to the excellences." To Thomas Allsop 2 Dec 1818: *CL* IV 888. On fame vs reputation see ch 2, above, I 33 and n 4.

his younger sister, are *so* charmed with them, that they play at "Goody Blake," or at "Johnny and Betty Foy!"

Were the collection of poems published with these biographical sketches, important enough, (which I am not vain enough to believe) to deserve such a distinction: EVEN AS I HAVE DONE, SO WOULD I BE DONE UNTO.

For more than eighteen months have the volume of Poems, entitled SIBYLLINE LEAVES, and the present volumes up to this page been printed, and ready for publication.[1] But ere I speak of myself in the tones, which are alone natural to me under the circumstances of late years, I would fain present myself to the Reader as I was in the first dawn of my literary life:

> When Hope grew round me, like the climbing vine,
> And fruits and foliage not my own seem'd mine![2]

For this purpose I have selected from the letters which I wrote home from Germany, those which appeared likely to be most interesting, and at the same time most pertinent to the title of this work.

---

[1] Somewhat exaggerated. The ms had been submitted to the printer on 19 Sept 1815, though not as far as "this page" in ch 22. The printing, begun in Oct, continued till the following Jul. See Introd, above, I lviii–lxi.

[2] *Dejection* lines 80–1 (var): *PW* (EHC) I 366.

SATYRANE'S LETTERS[1]

LETTER I

O N Sunday morning, September 16, 1798, the Hamburg Pacquet set sail from Yarmouth: and I, for the first time in my life, beheld my native land retiring from me. At the moment of its disappearance—in all the kirks, churches, chapels, and meeting-houses, in which the greater number, I hope, of my countrymen were at that time assembled, I will dare question whether there was one more ardent prayer offered up to heaven, than that which I then preferred for my country. Now then (said I to a gentleman who was standing near me) we are out of our country. Not yet, not yet! he replied, and pointed to the sea; "This, too, is a Briton's country." This bon mot gave a fillip to my spirits, I rose and looked round on my fellow-passengers, who were all on the deck. We were eighteen in number, videlicet, five Englishmen, an English lady, a French gentleman and his servant, an Hanoverian and his servant, a Prussian, a Swede, two Danes, and a Mulatto boy, a German tailor and his wife (the smallest couple I ever beheld) and a Jew. We were all on the deck; but in a short time I observed marks of dismay. The lady retired to the cabin in some confusion, and many of the faces round me assumed a very doleful and frog-coloured appearance; and within an hour the number of those on deck was lessened by one half. I was giddy, but not sick,

[1] For general discussion of C's reasons for inserting the following three "Letters" about his trip to Germany (1798-9) see Introd, above, I lxii–lxiii. The letters, here slightly revised, were first published in three issues of *The Friend:* No 14 (23 Nov 1809), No 16 (7 Dec 1809), No 18 (21 Dec 1809). *Friend* (*CC*) II 187–96, 209–21, 236–47. For the name, which C defines as "the Idoloclast, or breaker of Idols", see the opening of *Friend* No 14 (1809), to which he also prefixes a poem on "Satyrane" later called *A Tombless Epitaph. Friend (CC)* II 184–5. In Spenser's *Faerie Queene,* "Sir Satyrane" is the son of a satyr but is faithful to Una (Truth). Many of the notes for this section are paraphrased or quoted directly from *Friend (CC).* In order to save space the letter *"F"* is printed in parentheses for such notes. Letter I was essentially a revision of a letter to Mrs C 3 Oct 1798: *CL* I 420–8. (*F*). For details of the sea trip see Reed I 248–9.

and the giddiness soon went away, but left a feverishness and want of appetite, which I attributed, in great measure, to the *sæva Mephitis*[1] of the bilge-water; and it was certainly not decreased by the exportations from the cabin. However, I was well enough to join the able-bodied passengers, one of whom observed not inaptly, that Momus[2] might have discovered an easier way to see a man's inside, than by placing a window in his breast. He needed only have taken a salt-water trip in a pacquet-boat.

I am inclined to believe, that a pacquet is far superior to a stage-coach, as a means of making men open out to each other. In the latter the uniformity of posture disposes to dozing, and the definiteness of the period at which the company will separate, makes each individual think more of those, *to* whom he is going, than of of those *with* whom he is going. But at sea, more curiosity is excited, if only on this account, that the pleasant or unpleasant qualities of your companions are of greater importance to you, from the uncertainty how long you may be obliged to house with them. Besides, if you are countrymen, that now begins to form a distinction and a bond of brotherhood; and if of different countries, there are new incitements of conversation, more to ask and more to communicate. I found that I had interested the Danes in no common degree. I had crept into the boat on the deck and fallen asleep; but was awaked by one of them about three o'clock in the afternoon, who told me that they had been seeking me in every hole and corner, and insisted that I should join their party and drink with them. He talked English with such fluency, as left me wholly unable to account for the singular and even ludicrous incorrectness with which he spoke it. I went, and found some excellent wines and a desert of grapes with a pine apple. The Danes had christened me Doctor Teology, and dressed as I was all in black, with large shoes and black worsted stockings, I might certainly have passed very well for a Methodist missionary. However I disclaimed my title. What then may you be? A man of fortune? No!—A merchant? No! A merchant's traveller? No!—A clerk? No! un Philosophe, perhaps? It was at that time in my life, in which of all possible names and characters I had the greatest

---

[1] "Dreadful, noxious exhalation". Cf *Aeneid* 7.84 ("saevamque exhalat opaca mephitim").

[2] The god of censure and ridicule, who objected to the creation of man because, without a window in his breast, his heart could not be seen.

disgust to that of "un Philosophe."[1] But I was weary of being questioned, and rather than be nothing, or at best only the abstract idea of a man, I submitted by a bow, even to the aspersion implied in the word "un philosophe."—The Dane then informed me, that all in the present party were philosophers likewise. Certes we were not of the stoic school. For we drank and talked and sung, till we talked and sung all together; and then we rose and danced on the deck a set of dances, which in *one* sense of the word at least, were very intelligibly and appropriately intitled *reels*. The passengers who lay in the cabin below in all the agonies of sea-sickness, must have found our bacchanalian merriment

> ————————————————a tune
> Harsh and of dissonant mood for their complaint.[2]

I thought so at the time; and (by way, I suppose, of supporting my newly assumed philosophical character) I thought too, how closely the greater number of our virtues are connected with the fear of death, and how little sympathy we bestow on pain, where there is no danger.

The two Danes were brothers. The one was a man with a clear white complexion, white hair, and white eye-brows, looked silly, and nothing that he uttered gave the lie to his looks. The other, whom, by way of eminence I have called THE DANE, had likewise white hair, but was much shorter than his brother, with slender limbs, and a very thin face slightly pock-fretten. This man convinced me of the justice of an old remark, that many a faithful portrait in our novels and farces has been rashly censured for an outrageous caricature, or perhaps nonentity. I had retired to my station in the boat—he came and seated himself by my side, and appeared not a little tipsy. He commenced the conversation in the most magnific style, and as a sort of pioneering to his own vanity, he flattered me with *such* grossness! The parasites of the old comedy were modest in the comparison. His language and accentuation were so exceedingly singular, that I determined for once in my life to take notes of a conversation. Here it follows, somewhat

---

[1] Cf C's remark of the preceding Mar (1798) to his brother George, deprecating "those men both in England & France, who have modestly assumed to themselves the exclusive title of Philosophers". *CL* I 395. (*F*).

[2] Milton *Samson Agonistes* lines 661–2 (var). (*F*).

abridged indeed, but in all other respects as accurately as my memory permitted.

THE DANE. Vat imagination! vat language! vat vast science! and vat eyes! vat a milk-vite forehead!—O my heafen! vy, you're a Got!

ANSWER. You do me too much honour, Sir.

THE DANE. O me! if you should dink I is flattering you!—No, no, no! I haf ten tousand a year—yes, ten tousand a year—yes, ten tousand pound a year! Vell—and vat is dhat? a mere trifle! I 'ouldn't gif my sincere heart for ten times dhe money.—Yes, you're a Got! I a mere man! But, my dear friend! dhink of me, as a man! Is, is—I mean to ask you now, my dear friend—is I not very eloquent? Is I not speak English very fine?

ANSW. Most admirably! Believe me, Sir! I have seldom heard even a native talk so *fluently.*

THE DANE. (*squeezing my hand with great vehemence*) My *dear* friend! vat an affection and fidelity we have for each odher! But tell me, do tell me,—Is I not, now and den, speak some fault? Is I not in some wrong?

ANSW. Why, Sir! perhaps it might be observed by nice critics in the English language, that you occasionally use the word "Is" instead of "am." In our best companies we generally say I am, and not I is or Ise. Excuse me, Sir! it is a mere trifle.

THE DANE. O!—is, is, am, am, am. Yes, yes—I know, I know.

ANSW. I am, thou art, he is, we are, ye are, they are.

THE DANE. Yes, yes—I know, I know—Am, am, am, is dhe presens, and Is is dhe perfectum—yes, yes—and are is dhe plusquam perfectum.

ANSW. And "Art," Sir! is——?

THE DANE. My dear friend! it is dhe plusquam perfectum, no, no—dhat is a great lie. "Are" is the plusquam perfectum—and "art" is dhe plusquam plueperfectum—(*then swinging my hand to and fro, and cocking his little bright hazel eyes at me, that danced with vanity and wine*) You see, my dear friend! that I too have *some* lehrning.

ANSW. Learning, Sir? Who dares suspect it? Who can listen to you for a minute, who can even look at you, without perceiving the extent of it?

THE DANE. My *dear* friend!—(*then with a would-be humble*

look, and in a tone of voice as if he was reasoning) I could not talk so of presens and imperfectum, and futurum and plusquamplue perfectum, and all dhat, my dear friend! without *some* lehrning?

ANSW. Sir! a man like you cannot talk on any subject without discovering the depth of his information.

THE DANE. Dhe grammatic Greek, my friend! ha! ha! ha! (*laughing, and swinging my hand to and fro—then with a sudden transition to great solemnity*) Now I will tell you, my dear friend! Dhere did happen about me vat de whole historia of Denmark record no instance about nobody else. Dhe bishop did ask me all dhe questions about all dhe religion in dhe Latin grammar.

ANSW. The grammar, Sir? The language, I presume——

THE DANE. (*a little offended.*) Grammar is language, and language is grammar—

ANSW. Ten thousand pardons!

THE DANE. Vell, and I was only fourteen years—

ANSW. Only fourteen years old?

THE DANE. No more. I vas fourteen years old—and he asked me all questions, religion and philosophy, and all in dhe Latin language—and I answered him all every one, my dear friend! all in dhe Latin language.

ANSW. A Prodigy! an absolute prodigy!

THE DANE. No, no, no! he was a bishop, a great superintendent.

ANSW. Yes! a bishop.

THE DANE. A bishop—not a mere predicant, not a prediger—

ANSW. My dear Sir! we have misunderstood each other. I said that your answering in Latin at so early an age was a prodigy, that is, a thing that is wonderful, that does not often happen.

THE DANE. Often! Dhere is not von instance recorded in dhe whole historia of Denmark.

ANSW. And since then Sir——?

THE DANE. I was sent ofer to dhe Vest Indies—to our Island, and dhere I had no more to do vid books. No! no! I put my genius another way—and I haf made ten tousand pound a year. Is not dhat *ghenius*, my dear friend!—But vat is money! I dhink the poorest man alive my equal. Yes, my dear friend! my little fortune is pleasant to my generous heart, because I can do good—no man with so little a fortune ever did so much generosity—no person, no man person, no woman person ever denies it. But we are all Got's children.

Here the Hanoverian interrupted him, and the other Dane, the Swede, and the Prussian, joined us, together with a young Englishman who spoke the German fluently, and interpreted to me many of the Prussian's jokes. The Prussian was a travelling merchant, turned of threescore, a hale man, tall, strong, and stout, full of stories, gesticulations, and buffoonery with the soul as well as the look of a mountebank, who, while he is making you laugh, picks your pocket.[1] Amid all his droll looks and droll gestures, there remained one look untouched by laughter; and that one look was the true face, the others were but its mask. The Hanoverian was a pale, fat, bloated young man, whose father had made a large fortune in London, as an army-contractor. He seemed to emulate the manners of young Englishmen of fortune. He was a good-natured fellow, not without information or literature; but a most egregious coxcomb. He had been in the habit of attending the House of Commons, and had once spoken, as he informed me, with great applause in a debating society. For this he appeared to have qualified himself with laudable industry: for he was perfect in Walker's Pronouncing Dictionary,[2] and with an accent, which forcibly reminded me of the Scotchman in Roderic Random, who professed to teach the English pronunciation,[3] he was constantly *deferring* to my superior judgment, whether or no I had pronounced this or that word with propriety, or "the true delicacy." When he spoke, though it were only half a dozen sentences, he always rose; for which I could detect no other motive, than his partiality to that elegant phrase so liberally introduced in the orations of our British legislators, "While I am on my legs." The Swede, whom for reasons that will soon appear, I shall distinguish by the name of "Nobility," was a strong-featured, scurvy-faced man, his complexion resembling, in colour, a red hot poker beginning to cool. He appeared miserably dependent on the Dane; but was however incomparably the best informed and most rational of the party. Indeed his manners and conversation discovered him to be both a

[1] A favourite C image: see *EOT* (*CC*) I 54 and n.
[2] John Walker (1732–1807) *Dictionary of the English Language, Answering at Once the Purpose of* *Rhyming, Spelling, and Pronouncing* (1775).
[3] The Scottish schoolmaster in Tobias Smollett *Adventures of Roderick Random* (1748) ch 14.

man of the world and a gentleman. The Jew was in the hold: the French gentleman was lying on the deck so ill, that I could observe nothing concerning him, except the affectionate attentions of his servant to him. The poor fellow was very sick himself, and every now and then ran to the side of the vessel, still keeping his eye on his master, but returned in a moment and seated himself again by him, now supporting his head, now wiping his forehead and talking to him all the while in the most soothing tones. There had been a matrimonial squabble of a very ludicrous kind in the cabin, between the little German tailor and his little wife. He had secured two beds, one for himself, and one for her. This had struck the little woman as a very cruel action; she insisted upon their having but one, and assured the mate in the most piteous tones, that she was his lawful wife. The mate and the cabin boy decided in her favour, abused the little man for his want of tenderness with much humour, and hoisted him into the same compartment with his sea-sick wife. This quarrel was interesting to me, as it procured me a bed, which I otherwise should not have had.

In the evening, at 7 o'clock, the sea rolled higher, and the Dane, by means of the greater agitation, eliminated enough of what he had been swallowing to make room for a great deal more. His favourite potation was sugar and brandy, i.e. a very little warm water with a large quantity of brandy, sugar, and nutmeg. His servant boy, a black-eyed Mulatto, had a good-natured round face, exactly the colour of the skin of the walnut-kernel. The Dane and I were again seated, tete a tete, in the ship's boat. The conversation, which was now indeed rather an oration than a dialogue, became extravagant beyond all that I ever heard. He told me that he had made a large fortune in the island of Santa Cruz,[1] and was now returning to Denmark to enjoy it. He expatiated on the style in which he meant to live, and the great undertakings which he proposed to himself to commence, till the brandy aiding his vanity, and his vanity and garrulity aiding the brandy, he talked like a madman—entreated me to accompany him to Denmark—there I should see his influence with the government, and he would introduce me to the king, &c. &c. Thus he went on dreaming aloud, and then passing with a very lyrical transition to the subject of general politics, he declaimed, like a member of the Corresponding

---

[1] St Croix in the Virgin Islands, then a Danish possession.

Society,[1] *about* (not concerning) the Rights of Man, and assured me that notwithstanding his fortune, he thought the poorest man alive his equal. "All are equal, my dear friend! all are equal! Ve are all Got's children. The poorest man haf the same rights with me. Jack! Jack! some more sugar and brandy. Dhere is dhat fellow now! He is a Mulatto—but he is my equal.—That's right, Jack! (*taking the sugar and brandy*) Here you Sir! shake hands with dhis gentleman! Shake hands with me, you dog! Dhere, dhere!—We are all equal my dear friend!——Do I not speak like Socrates, and Plato, and Cato—they were all philosophers, my dear philosophe! all very great men!—and so was Homer and Virgil—but they were poets, yes, yes! I know all about it!—But what can any body ⁄ say more than this? we are all equal, all Got's children. I haf ten thousand a year, but I am no more than the meanest man alive. I haf no pride; and yet, my dear friend! I can say, do! and it is done. Ha! ha! ha! my dear friend! Now dhere is dhat gentleman (*pointing* to "Nobility") he is a Swedish baron—you shall see. Ho! (*calling to the Swede*) get me, will you, a bottle of wine from the cabin. SWEDE.—Here, Jack! go and get your master a bottle of wine from the cabin. *Dane.* No, no, no! do *you* go now—you go yourself—*you* go now! *Swede.* Pah!—*Dane.* Now go! Go, I pray you." AND THE SWEDE WENT!!

After this the Dane commenced an harangue on religion, and mistaking me for "un philosophe" in the continental sense of the word, he talked of Deity in a declamatory style, very much resembling the devotional rants of that rude blunderer, Mr. Thomas Paine, in his Age of Reason,[2] and whispered in my ear, what damned *hypocrism*[3] all Jesus Christ's business was. I dare aver, that few men have less reason to charge themselves with indulging in *persiflage* than myself. I should hate it if it were only that it is a Frenchman's vice, and feel a pride in avoiding it because our own language is too honest to have a word to express it by. But in this instance the temptation had been too powerful, and I have placed it on the list of my offences. Pericles answered one of his dearest friends who had solicited him on a case of life and death, to take

[1] A working-men's society founded in response to the French Revolution, led and encouraged by British Jacobins, who frequently gave speeches in Hyde Park.
[2] Thomas Paine (1737–1809), whose deistic *Age of Reason* (1794–5) C also attacks in *Friend* (*CC*) 1 32.
[3] Obsolete: *OED* cites only Josuah Sylvester's tr of Du Bartas (1591) 1 ii 938. (*F*).

an equivocal oath for his preservation: *Debeo amicis opitulari, sed usque ad Deos.** [1] Friendship herself must place her last and boldest step on this side the altar. What Pericles would not do to save a friend's life, you may be assured I would not hazard merely to mill the chocolate-pot of a drunken fool's vanity till it frothed over. Assuming a serious look, I professed myself a believer, and sunk at once an hundred fathoms in his good graces. He retired to his cabin, and I wrapped myself up in my great coat, and looked at the water. A beautiful white cloud of foam at momently intervals coursed by the side of the vessel with a roar, and little stars of flame danced and sparkled and went out in it: and every now and then light detachments of this white cloud-like foam darted off from the vessel's side, each with its own small constellation, over the sea, and scoured out of sight like a Tartar troop over a wilderness.[2]

It was cold, the cabin was at open war with my olfactories, and I found reason to rejoice in my great coat, a weighty high-caped, respectable rug, the collar of which turned over, and played the part of a night-cap very passably. In looking up at two or three bright stars, which oscillated with the motion of the sails, I fell asleep, but was awakened at one o'clock Monday morning, by a shower of rain. I found myself compelled to go down into the cabin, where I slept very soundly, and awoke with a very good appetite at breakfast time, my nostrils, the most placable of all the senses, reconciled to or indeed insensible of the mephitis.

Monday, September 17th, I had a long conversation with the Swede, who spoke with the most poignant contempt of the Dane, whom he described as a fool, purse-mad; but he confirmed the boasts of the Dane respecting the largeness of his fortune, which he had acquired in the first instance as an advocate, and afterwards as a planter. From the Dane and from himself I collected that he was indeed a Swedish nobleman, who had squandered a fortune, that was never very large, and had made over his property to the Dane, on whom he was now utterly dependent. He seemed to suffer

---

* *Translation.* It behoves me to side with my friends but only as far as the gods.

[1] Aulus Gellius *Noctes Atticae* 1.3.20, which quotes the words in Greek. (*F*).

[2] An observation (first noted in *CN* I 335 f 1ᵛ) that led C to revise a line in *AM:* see *CN* I 335n and *PW* (EHC) I 190n (revision for *SL* of *AM* line 104).

very little pain from the Dane's insolence. He was in high degree humane and attentive to the English lady, who suffered most fearfully, and for whom he performed many little offices with a tenderness and delicacy which seemed to prove real goodness of heart. Indeed, his general manners and conversation were not only pleasing, but even interesting; and I struggled to believe his insensibility respecting the Dane philosophical fortitude. For though the Dane was now quite sober, his character oozed out of him at every pore. And after dinner, when he was again flushed with wine, every quarter of an hour or perhaps oftener he would shout out to the Swede, "Ho! Nobility, go—do such a thing! Mr. Nobility!—tell the gentlemen such a story, and so forth," with an insolence which must have excited disgust and detestation, if his vulgar rants on the sacred rights of equality, joined to his wild havoc of general grammar no less than of the English language, had not rendered it so irresistibly laughable.

At four o'clock I observed a wild duck swimming on the waves, a single solitary wild duck. It is not easy to conceive, how interesting a thing it looked in that round objectless desert of waters. I had associated such a feeling of immensity with the ocean, that I felt exceedingly disappointed, when I was out of sight of all land, at the narrowness and *nearness*, as it were, of the circle of the horizon. So little are images capable of satisfying the obscure feelings connected with words. In the evening the sails were lowered, lest we should run foul of the land, which can be seen only at a small distance. And at four o'clock, on Tuesday morning, I was awakened by the cry of land! land! It was an ugly island rock at a distance on our left, called Heiligeland,[1] well known to many passengers from Yarmouth to Hamburg, who have been obliged by stormy weather to pass weeks and weeks in weary captivity on it, stripped of all their money by the exorbitant demands of the wretches who inhabit it. So at least the sailors informed me.—About nine o'clock we saw the main land, which seemed scarcely able to hold its head above water, low, flat, and dreary, with light-houses and land-marks which seemed to give a character and language to the dreariness. We entered the mouth of the Elbe, passing Neu-werk; though as yet the right bank only of the river was visible to us. On this I saw a church, and thanked

[1] Heligoland, in the North Sea. (*F*).

God for my safe voyage, not without affectionate thoughts of those I had left in England. At eleven o'clock on the same morning we arrived at Cuxhaven, the ship dropped anchor, and the boat was hoisted out, to carry the Hanoverian and a few others on shore. The captain agreed to take us, who remained, to Hamburg for ten guineas, to which the Dane contributed so largely, that the other passengers paid but half a guinea each. Accordingly we hauled anchor, and passed gently up the river. At Cuxhaven both sides of the river may be seen in clear weather; we could now see the right bank only. We passed a multitude of English traders that had been waiting many weeks for a wind. In a short time both banks became visible, both flat and evidencing the labour of human hands by their extreme neatness. On the left bank I saw a church or two in the distance; on the right bank we passed by steeple and windmill and cottage, and windmill and single house, windmill and windmill, and neat single house, and steeple. These were the objects and in the succession. The shores were very green and planted with trees not inelegantly. Thirty-five miles from Cuxhaven, the night came on us, and as the navigation of the Elbe is perilous, we dropped anchor.

Over what place, thought I, does the moon hang to *your* eye, my dearest friend? To me it hung over the left bank of the Elbe.[1] Close above the moon was a huge volume of deep black cloud, while a very thin fillet crossed the middle of the orb, as narrow and thin and black as a ribbon of crape. The long trembling road of moonlight, which lay on the water and reached to the stern of our vessel, glimmered dimly and obscurely. We saw two or three lights from the right bank, probably from bedrooms. I felt the striking contrast between the silence of this majestic stream, whose banks are populous with men and women and children, and flocks and herds—between the silence by night of this peopled river, and the ceaseless noise, and uproar, and loud agitations of the desolate solitude of the ocean. The passengers below had all retired to their beds; and I felt the interest of this quiet scene the more deeply from the circumstance of having just quitted them. For the Prussian had during the whole of the evening displayed all his talents to captivate the Dane, who had admitted him into the train

[1] Facing upstream. This and the preceding sentence are taken from *CN* I 335 and the beginning of a letter to Mrs C 18 Sept 1798: *CL* I 415.

of his dependents. The young Englishman continued to interpret the Prussian's jokes to me. They were all without exception profane and abominable, but some sufficiently witty, and a few incidents, which he related in his own person, were valuable as illustrating the manners of the countries in which they had taken place.

Five o'clock on Wednesday morning we hauled the anchor, but were soon obliged to drop it again in consequence of a thick fog, which our captain feared would continue the whole day; but about nine it cleared off, and we sailed slowly along, close by the shore of a very beautiful island, forty miles from Cuxhaven, the wind continuing slack. This holme or island is about a mile and a half in length, wedge-shaped, well wooded, with glades of the liveliest green, and rendered more interesting by the remarkably neat farm house on it. It seemed made for retirement without solitude—a place that would allure one's friends while it precluded the impertinent calls of mere visitors. The shores of the Elbe now became more beautiful, with rich meadows and trees running like a low wall along the river's edge; and peering over them, neat houses and (especially on the right bank) a profusion of steeple-spires, white, black, or red. An instinctive taste teaches men to build their churches in flat countries with spire-steeples, which as they cannot be referred to any other object, point as with silent finger to the sky and stars,[1] and sometimes when they reflect the brazen light of a rich though rainy sun-set, appear like a pyramid of flame burning heavenward. I remember once, and once only, to have seen a spire in a narrow valley of a mountainous country. The effect was not only mean but ludicrous, and reminded me against my will of an *extinguisher*;[2] the close neighbourhood of the high mountain, at the foot of which it stood, had so completely dwarfed it, and deprived it of all connection with the sky or clouds. Forty-six English miles from Cuxhaven, and sixteen from Hamburg, the Danish village Veder ornaments the left bank with its black steeple, and close by it the wild and pastoral hamlet of Schulau. Hitherto both the right and left bank, green to the very brink, and level with the river, resembled the shores of a park

[1] Cf WW's use of C's phrase in *Excursion* vi 19 and his note on it. *WPW* v 187, 456. (*F*).

[2] The large metal cone fixed to railings in front of a house in which the light-boy put out the torch he carried to light people home in the days before street lighting.

canal. The trees and houses were alike low, sometimes the low
trees overtopping the yet lower houses, sometimes the low houses
rising above the yet lower trees. But at Schulau the left bank rises
at once forty or fifty feet, and stares on the river with its perpendicular fassade [1] of sand, thinly patched with tufts of green.
The Elbe continued to present a more and more lively spectacle
from the multitude of fishing boats and the flocks of sea gulls
wheeling round them, the clamorous rivals and companions of the
fishermen; till we came to Blankaness,[2] a most interesting village
scattered amid scattered trees, over three hills in three divisions.
Each of the three hills stares upon the river, with faces of bare
sand, with which the boats with their bare poles, standing in files
along the banks, made a sort of fantastic harmony. Between each
fassade lies a green and woody dell, each deeper than the other.
In short it is a large village made up of individual cottages, each
cottage in the centre of its own little wood or orchard, and each
with its own separate path: a village with a labyrinth of paths, or
rather a *neighbourhood*[3] of houses! It is inhabited by fishermen
and boat-makers, the Blankanese boats being in great request
through the whole navigation of the Elbe. Here first we saw the
spires of Hamburg, and from hence as far as Altona the left bank
of the Elbe is uncommonly pleasing, considered as the vicinity of
an industrious and republican city—in that style of beauty, or
rather prettiness, that might tempt the citizen into the country,
and yet gratify the taste which he had acquired in the town.
Summer houses and Chinese show-work are every where scattered
along the high and green banks; the boards of the farm-houses left
unplaistered and gaily painted with green and yellow; and scarcely
a tree not cut into shapes and made to remind the human being of
his own power and intelligence instead of the wisdom of nature.
Still, however, these are links of connection between town and
country, and far better than the affectation of tastes and enjoyments for which men's habits have disqualified them. Pass them
by on Saturdays and Sundays with the burgers of Hamburg smoking
their pipes, the women and children feasting in the alcoves of box
and yew, and it becomes a nature of its own. On Wednesday, four

---

[1] C uses the German spelling.
(F).

[2] Blankenese. (F).

[3] The word for C implies a group-
ing without close connection of a
spiritual or governmental character.
See *Friend* (*CC*) I 200n.

o'clock, we left the vessel, and passing with trouble through the huge masses of shipping that seemed to choke the wide Elbe from Altona upward, we were at length landed at the Boom House,[1] Hamburg.

[1] Low German for toll-house. (*F*).

LETTER II (To a Lady) [1]

Meine liebe Freundin,

See how natural the German comes from me, though I have not yet been six weeks in the country!—almost as fluently as English from my neighbour the Amptschreiber (or public secretary) who as often as we meet, though it should be half a dozen times in the same day, never fails to greet me with—"* * *ddam your ploot unt eyes, my dearest Englander! vhee goes it!*"—which is certainly a proof of great generosity on his part, these words being his whole stock of English. I had, however, a better reason than the desire of displaying my proficiency: for I wished to put you in good humour with a language, from the acquirement of which I have promised myself much edification and the means too of communicating a new pleasure to you and your sister, during our winter readings. And how can I do this better than by pointing out its gallant attention to the ladies? Our English affix, *ess,* is, I believe, confined either to words derived from the Latin, as *actress, directress,* &c. or from the French, as *mistress, duchess,* and the like. But the German, *in,* enables us to designate the sex in every possible relation of life. Thus the Amptman's lady is the Frau Amptman*in*—the secretary's wife (by the bye the handsomest woman I have yet seen in Germany) is Die allerliebste Frau Amptschreiber*in*—the colonel's lady, Die Frau Obrist*in* or colonel*lin*—and even the parson's wife, die frau pastor*in*. But I am especially pleased with their *freundin,* which, unlike the *amica* of the Romans, is seldom used but in its best and purest sense. Now, I know, it will be said, that a friend is already something more than a friend, when a man feels an anxiety to express to himself that this friend is a female; but this I deny—in that sense at least in which the objection will be made. I would hazard the impeachment of heresy, rather than abandon my belief that there is a sex in our SOULS as well as in their perishable garments; and he who does not feel it, never truly loved a sister—nay, is not capable even of loving a wife as she deserves to be loved, if she indeed be worthy of that holy name.

---

[1] The "Lady" is Mrs C. The following (from *Friend* No 16) is a pastiche of letters to Poole 26 Oct and to Mrs C 8 Nov 1798, to whom C had promised to write alternately twice a week. *CL* I 430–40. (*F*).

Now I know, my gentle friend, what you are murmuring to yourself—"This is so like him! running away after the first bubble, that chance has blown off from the surface of his fancy; when one is anxious to learn where he is and what he has seen." Well then! that I am settled at Ratzeburg, with my motives and the particulars of my journey hither, —————[1] will inform you. My first letter to him, with which doubtless he has edified your whole fireside, left me safely landed at Hamburg on the Elbe Stairs, at the Boom House. While standing on the stairs, I was amused by the contents of the passage boat which crosses the river once or twice a day from Hamburg to Haarburg.[2] It was stowed close with all people of all nations, in all sorts of dresses; the men all with pipes in their mouths, and these pipes of all shapes and fancies—straight and wreathed, simple and complex, long and short, cane, clay, porcelain, wood, tin, silver, and ivory; most of them with silver chains and silver bole-covers. Pipes and boots are the first universal characteristic of the male Hamburgers that would strike the eye of a raw traveller. But I forget my promise of journalizing as much as possible.—Therefore, *Septr. 19th Afternoon.* My companion[3] who, you recollect, speaks the French language with unusual propriety, had formed a kind of confidential acquaintance with the emigrant, who appeared to be a man of sense, and whose manners were those of a perfect gentleman. He seemed about fifty or rather more. Whatever is unpleasant in French manners from excess in the *degree*, had been softened down by age or affliction; and all that is delightful in the *kind*, alacrity and delicacy in little attentions, &c. remained, and without bustle, gesticulation, or disproportionate eagerness. His demeanour exhibited the minute philanthropy of a polished Frenchman, tempered by the sobriety of the English character disunited from its reserve. There is something strangely attractive in the character of a *gentleman* when you apply the word emphatically, and yet in that sense of the term which it is more easy to *feel* than to define. It neither includes the possession of high moral excellence, nor of necessity even the ornamental graces of manner. I have now in my mind's eye a parson whose life would scarcely stand scrutiny even in the court of honour, much less in that of conscience; and his manners, if nicely observed, would of the two excite an idea of awkwardness

[1] Poole. Actually the first letter was not to him but to Mrs C. (*F*).
[2] Harburg. (*F*).
[3] WW. (*F*).

rather than of elegance: and yet every one who conversed with him felt and acknowledged *the gentleman*. The secret of the matter, I believe to be this—we feel the gentlemanly character present to us, whenever under all the circumstances of social intercourse, the trivial not less than the important, through the whole *detail* of his manners and deportment, and with the ease of a habit, a person shews respect to others in *such a way*, as at the same time implies in his own feelings an habitual and assured anticipation of re-ciprocal respect from them to himself. In short, the *gentlemanly* character arises out of the feeling of Equality acting, as a Habit, yet flexible to the varieties of Rank, and modified without being disturbed or superseded by them. This description will perhaps explain to you the ground of one of your own remarks, as I was englishing to you the interesting dialogue concerning the causes of the corruption of eloquence.[1] "What perfect gentlemen these old Romans must have been! I was impressed, I remember, with the same feeling at the time I was reading a translation of Cicero's philosophical dialogues and of his epistolary correspondence: while in Pliny's Letters I seemed to have a different feeling—he gave me the notion of a very *fine* gentleman."[2] You uttered the words as if you had felt that the adjunct had injured the substance and the encreased degree altered the kind. Pliny was the courtier of an absolute monarch—Cicero an aristocratic republican. For this reason the character of gentleman, in the sense to which I have confined it, is frequent in England, rare in France, and found, where it is found, in age or the latest period of manhood; while in Germany the character is almost unknown. But the proper *antipode* of a gentleman is to be sought for among the Anglo-American democrats.

I owe this digression, as an act of justice, to this amiable French-man, and of humiliation for myself. For in a little controversy between us on the subject of French poetry, he made me feel my own ill behaviour by the silent reproof of contrast, and when I afterwards apologized to him for the warmth of my language, he answered me with a chearful expression of surprize, and an imme-diate compliment, which a gentleman might both make with dignity and receive with pleasure. I was pleased, therefore, to find it agreed on, that we should, if possible, take up our quarters in the same

[1] Tacitus *Dialogus de oratoribus.* (*F*). See ch 3, above, ı 56 and n 1.
[6] The quoted passage is not in the original letters to Mrs C and Poole but was presumably a later inter-polation for *Friend* No 16. (*F*).

house. My friend went with him in search of an hotel, and I to deliver my letters of recommendation.

I walked onward at a brisk pace, enlivened not so much by any thing I actually saw, as by the confused sense that I was for the first time in my life on the *continent* of our planet. I seemed to myself like a liberated bird that had been hatched in an aviary, who now after his first soar of freedom poises himself in the upper air.[1] Very naturally I began to wonder at *all* things, some for being so like and some for being so unlike the things in England—Dutch women with large umbrella hats shooting out half a yard before them, with a prodigal plumpness of petticoat behind—the women of Hamburg with caps plaited on the caul with silver or gold, or both, bordered round with stiffened lace, which *stood out* before their eyes, but not lower, so that the eyes sparkled through it— the Hanoverian women with the fore part of the head bare, then a stiff lace standing up like a wall perpendicular on the cap, and the cap behind *tailed* with an enormous quantity of ribbon which lies or tosses on the back:

> Their visnomies seem'd like a goodly banner
> Spread in defiance of all enemies.
> S P E N S E R .[2]

——The ladies all in English dresses, all *rouged*, and all with bad teeth: which you notice instantly from their contrast to the almost *animal*, *too* glossy mother-of-pearl whiteness and the regularity of the teeth of the laughing, loud-talking country-women and servant-girls, who with their clean white stockings and with slippers without heel-quarters tripped along the dirty streets, as if they were secured by a charm from the dirt: with a lightness too, which surprized me, who had always considered it as one of the annoyances of sleeping *in an Inn*, that I had to clatter up stairs in a pair of them. The streets narrow; to my English nose sufficiently offensive, and explaining at first sight the universal use of boots; without any appropriate path for the foot-passengers; the gable ends of the houses all towards the street, some in the ordinary triangular form and *entire* as the botanists say,[3] but the greater number notched and scolloped with more than Chinese grotesqueness. Above all,

---

[1] On C's self-identification with birds, see Introd, above, I xlvii, and *C Life* (B) 58, 111, 122. Cf C's letter to Stuart 11 Sept 1809: *CL* III 222.

[2] *Amoretti* v 11–12 (var). (*F*).

[3] Cf "entire" in *OED* (which cites C): "having an unbroken outline, without notches or indentions".

I was struck with the profusion of windows, so large and so many, that the houses look all glass. Mr. Pitt's Window Tax,[1] with its pretty little *additionals* sprouting out from it like young toadlets on the back of a Surinam toad,[2] would certainly improve the appearance of the Hamburg houses, which have a slight summer look, not *in keeping*[3] with their size, incongruous with the climate, and precluding that feeling of retirement and self-content, which one wishes to associate with a house in a noisy city. But a conflagration would, I fear, be the previous requisite to the production of any architectural beauty in Hamburg: for verily it is a filthy town. I moved on and crossed a multitude of ugly bridges, with huge black deformities of water wheels close by them. The water intersects the city every where, and would have furnished to the genius of Italy the capabilities of all that is most beautiful and magnificent in architecture. It might have been the rival of Venice, and it is huddle and ugliness, stench and stagnation. The Jungfer Stieg[4] (i.e. young Ladies Walk) to which my letters directed me, made an exception. It is a walk or promenade planted with treble rows of elm trees, which being yearly pruned and cropped remain slim and dwarf-like. This walk occupies one side of a square piece of water, with many swans on it perfectly tame, and moving among the swans shewy pleasure boats with ladies in them, rowed by their husbands or lovers. **********

(Some paragraphs have been here omitted.)[5]

**** thus embarrassed by sad and solemn politeness still more than by broken English, it sounded like the voice of an old friend when I heard the emigrant's servant enquiring after me. He had come for the purpose of guiding me to our hotel. Through streets and streets I pressed on as happy as a child, and, I doubt not, with a childish expression of wonderment in my busy eyes, amused by

---

[1] "By 1766 the elder Pitt's government succeeded in raising the tax that had been levied on houses containing fifteen or more windows and lowering to seven the number of windows that made a house taxable. Householders began to brick up and plaster-and-lath their excess windows. C is probably thinking of the younger Pitt's window tax of 1797, which trebled his earlier (1792) graduated window tax." (*F*).

[2] Cf the letter to Sotheby 28 Apr 1808: ". . . My Thoughts are like Surinam Toads—as they crawl on, little Toads vegetate out from back & side, grow quickly, & draw off the attention from the mother Toad—." *CL* III 94–5.

[3] Cf ch 14, above, II 15 and n 3.

[4] Jungfernstieg in Hamburg. (*F*).

[5] Containing minor details. *CL* I 432. (*F*).

the wicker waggons with moveable benches across them, one behind the other, (these were the hackney coaches;) amused by the sign-boards of the shops, on which all the articles sold within are painted, and that too very exactly, though in a grotesque confusion (a useful substitute for language in this great mart of nations) amused with the incessant tinkling of the shop and house door bells, the bell hanging over each door and struck with a small iron rod at every entrance and exit;—and finally, amused by looking in at the windows, as I passed along; the ladies and gentlemen drinking coffee or playing cards, and the gentlemen all smoking. I wished myself a painter, that I might have sent you a sketch of one of the card parties. The long pipe of one gentleman rested on the table, its bole half a yard from his mouth, fuming like a censer by the fish pool—the other gentleman, who was dealing the cards, and of course had both hands employed, held his pipe in his teeth, which hanging down between his knees, smoked beside his ancles. Hogarth himself never drew a more ludicrous distortion both of attitude and physiognomy, than this effort occasioned: [1] nor was there wanting beside it one of those beautiful female faces which the same Hogarth, in whom the satyrist never extinguished that love of beauty which belonged to him as a poet, so often and so gladly introduces as the central figure in a crowd of humourous deformities, which figure (such is the power of true genius!) neither acts, nor is *meant* to act as a contrast; but diffuses through all, and over each of the group, a spirit of reconciliation and human kindness; and even when the attention is no longer consciously directed to the cause of this feeling, still blends its tenderness with our laughter: and thus prevents the instructive merriment at the whims of nature or the foibles or humours of our fellow-men from degenerating into the heart-poison of contempt or hatred.

Our hotel DIE WILDE MAN, (the sign of which was no bad likeness of the landlord, who had engrafted on a very grim face a restless grin, that was at every man's service, and which indeed, like an actor rehearsing to himself, he kept playing in *expectation* of an occasion for it)—neither our hotel, I say, nor its landlord

[1] "Shakespear! Milton Fuller! Defoe! Hogarth!—As to the remaining Host of our great Men, other Countries have produced something like them—but these are uniques—England may challenge the world to shew a correspondent name to either of the Five . . .". Annotation on Thomas Fuller *History of the Worthies of England* (2 vols 1811) I vii: *CM* (*CC*) II; quoted in *Misc C* 273.

were of the genteelest class. But it has one great advantage for a stranger, by being in the market place, and the next neighbour of the huge church of St. Nicholas: a church with shops and houses built up against it, out of which *wens* and *warts* its high massy steeple rises, *necklaced* near the top with a round of large gilt balls. A better pole-star could scarcely be desired. Long shall I retain the impression made on my mind by the awful echo, so loud and long and tremulous, of the deep-toned clock within this church, which awoke me at two in the morning from a distressful dream,[1] occasioned, I believe, by the feather bed, which is used here instead of bed clothes. I will rather carry my blanket about with me like a wild Indian, than submit to this abominable custom. Our emigrant acquaintance was, we found, an intimate friend of the celebrated Abbé de Lisle:[2] and from the large fortune which he possessed under the monarchy, had rescued sufficient not only for independence, but for respectability. He had offended some of his fellow-emigrants in London, whom he had obliged with considerable sums, by a refusal to make further advances, and in consequence of their intrigues had received an order to quit the kingdom. I thought it one proof of his innocence, that he attached no blame either to the alien act, or to the minister who had exerted it against him; and a still greater, that he spoke of London with rapture, and of his favourite niece, who had married and settled in England, with all the fervor and all the pride of a fond parent. A Man sent by force out of a country, obliged to sell out of the stocks at a great loss, and exiled from those pleasures and that style of society which habit had rendered essential to his happiness, whose predominant feelings were yet all of a private nature, resentment for friendship outraged, and anguish for domestic affections interrupted—such a man, I think, I could dare warrant guiltless of *espionage* in any service, most of all in that of the present French Directory. He spoke with extacy of Paris under the Monarchy:

---

[1] Cf *Christabel* lines 555–8:
I woke; it was the midnight hour,
The clock was echoing in the tower;
But though my slumber was gone by,
This dream it would not pass away—

PW (EHC) I 232. (*F*).

[2] Jean Baptiste Isoard (1743–1816), who gave himself the surname Delisle de Sales, a prolific writer of dramas, history, and moral philosophy, remembered especially for his *De la philosophie de la nature* (1769).

and yet the particular facts, which made up his description, left as deep a conviction on my mind, of French worthlessness, as his own tale had done of emigrant ingratitude. Since my arrival in Germany, I have not met a single person, even among those who abhor the Revolution, that spoke with favor, or even charity, of the French emigrants. Though the belief of their influence in the origination of this disastrous war, (from the horrors of which, North Germany deems itself only reprieved, not secured) may have some share in the general aversion with which they are regarded; yet I am deeply persuaded that the far greater part is owing to their own profligacy, to their treachery and hard-heartedness to each other, and the domestic misery or corrupt principles which so many of them have carried into the families of their protectors. My heart dilated with honest pride, as I recalled to mind the stern yet amiable characters of the English patriots, who sought refuge on the Continent at the Restoration! O let not our civil war under the first Charles be parallelled with the French revolution! In the former, the chalice overflowed from excess of principle; in the latter, from the fermentation of the dregs! The former, was a civil war between the virtues and virtuous prejudices of the two parties; the latter, between the vices. The Venetian glass of the French monarchy shivered and flew asunder with the working of a double poison.[1]

*Sept. 20*th. I was introduced to Mr. Klopstock,[2] the brother of the poet, who again introduced me to professor Ebeling,[3] an intelligent and lively man, though deaf: so deaf, indeed, that it was a painful effort to talk to him, as we were obliged to drop all our pearls into a huge ear-trumpet. From this courteous and kind-hearted man of letters, (I hope, the German literati in general may resemble this first specimen) I heard a tolerable Italian pun, and an

---

[1] The passage "My heart di-lated . . ." to end of paragraph, which does not appear in the original letters, was probably added in 1809.
[2] Victor Klopstock (1744–1811), whom C in his original letter de-scribed as "a sort of Merchant in the agency Line", was the younger brother of the poet and editor of the Hamburg *Neue Zeitung* and the *Adresskomptoirnachrichten. CN* I 337n. For C's meeting with the

Klopstock brothers, see also *CN* I 337 and Reed I 250–2.
[3] Christoph Daniel Ebeling (1741–1817), professor of Greek and history at the Hamburg Aka-demisches Gymnasium and (1799) librarian of the Stadtbibliothek there; author of a work on the geography and history of North America, *Erdbeschreibung und Geschichte von Amerika* (1787). *CN* I 337 and n.

interesting anecdote. When Buonaparte was in Italy, having been irritated by some instance of perfidy, he said in a loud and vehement tone, in a public company—" 'tis a true proverb, *gli Italiani tutti ladroni* (i.e. *the Italians all plunderers.*) A Lady had the courage to reply, "Non tutti; ma BUONA PARTE," (*not all, but a good part,* or *Buonaparte.*)[1] This, I confess, sounded to *my* ears, as one of the many good things that *might have been* said. The anecdote is more valuable; for it instances the ways and means of French insinuation. HOCHE[2] had received much information concerning the face of the country from a map of unusual fullness and accuracy, the maker of which, he heard, resided at Düsseldorf. At the storming of Düsseldorf by the French army, Hoche previously ordered, that the house and property of this man should be preserved, and entrusted the performance of the order to an officer on whose troop he could rely. Finding afterwards that the man had escaped before the storming commenced, Hoche exclaimed, "HE had no reason to flee! it is *for* such men, not *against* them, that the French nation makes war, and consents to shed the blood of its children." You remember Milton's sonnet—

> The great Emathian conqueror bid spare
> The house of Pindarus when temple and tower
> Went to the ground————————————[3]

Now though the Düsseldorf map-maker may stand in the same relation to the Theban bard, as the snail that marks its path by lines of film on the wall it creeps over, to the eagle that soars sunward and beats the tempest with its wings; it does not therefore follow, that the Jacobin of France may not be as valiant a general and as good a politician, as the madman of Macedon.[4]

From Professor Ebeling's, Mr. Klopstock accompanied my friend and me to his own house, where I saw a fine bust of his brother. There was a solemn and heavy greatness in his countenance which corresponded to my preconceptions of his style and genius.—I saw there, likewise, a very fine portrait of Lessing, whose works are at present the chief object of my admiration. His eyes were uncommonly like mine, if any thing, rather larger and

---

[1] Cf *CN* I 342 and n.
[2] Lazare Hoche (1768–97), the brilliant young general of the Revolution; "Pacificator of the Ven- dée"; briefly Minister of War (1797) before his death at twenty-nine. (*F*).
[3] Sonnet VIII ("Captain or Col- onel . . .") lines 10–12. (*F*).
[4] Alexander the Great.

more prominent. But the lower part of his face and his nose—O what an exquisite expression of elegance and sensibility!—There appeared no depth, weight, or comprehensiveness, in the forehead.—The whole face seemed to say, that Lessing was a man of quick and voluptuous feelings; of an active but light fancy; acute; yet acute not in the observation of actual life, but in the arrangements and management of the ideal world, i.e. in taste, and in metaphysics. I assure you, that I wrote these very words in my memorandum book with the portrait before my eyes,[1] and when I knew nothing of Lessing but his name, and that he was a German writer of eminence.

We consumed two hours and more over a bad dinner, at the table d'Hote. "PATIENCE *at a German ordinary, smiling at time.*"[2] The Germans are the worst cooks in Europe. There is placed for every two persons a bottle of common wine—Rhenish and Claret alternately; but in the houses of the opulent during the many and long intervals of the dinner, the servants hand round glasses of richer wines. At the Lord of Culpin's they came in this order. Burgundy—Madeira—Port—Frontiniac—Pacchiaretti—[3] Old Hock—Mountain—Champagne—Hock again—Bishop, and lastly, Punch. A tolerable quantum, methinks! The last dish at the ordinary, viz. slices of roast pork (for all the larger dishes are brought in, cut up, and first handed round and then set on the table) with stewed prunes and other sweet fruits, and this followed by cheese and butter, with plates of apples, reminded me of Shakespeare * and Shakespeare put it in my head to go to the French comedy.[5]

* * *

Bless me! why it is worse than our modern English plays! The first act informed me, that a court martial is to be held on a Count Vatron, who had drawn his sword on the Colonel, his brother-in-

---

* "*Slender.* I bruised my shin with playing with sword and dagger for a dish of stewed prunes, and by my troth I cannot abide the smell of hot meat since." So again, *Evans.* "I will make an end of my dinner: there's pippins and cheese yet to come."[4]

[1] *CN* I 337.

[2] Cf Shakespeare *Twelfth Night* II iv 113–14: "She sat like Patience on a monument, | Smiling at grief." Cf *CN* I 339. (*F*).

[3] Actually "Pajarete," a sweet dessert wine from southern Spain. *CN* I 371n.

[4] *Merry Wives of Windsor* I i 254–8 (var), I ii 10–11. (*F*).

[5] The play was a French translation (*Le Comte de Waltron*) of *Der Graf von Walltron oder die Subordination* (1776) by Heinrich Friedrich Möller (1745–98). *CN* I 337n.

law. The officers plead in his behalf—in vain! His wife, the
Colonel's sister, pleads with most tempestuous agonies—in vain!
She falls into hysterics and faints away, to the dropping of the
inner curtain! In the second act sentence of death is passed on the
Count—his wife, as frantic and hysterical as before: more so
(good industrious creature!) she could not be. The third and last
act, the wife still frantic, very frantic indeed! the soldiers just about
to fire, the handkerchief actually dropped, when reprieve! reprieve!
is heard from behind the scenes: and in comes Prince somebody,[a]
pardons the Count, and the wife is still frantic, only with joy; that
was all!

O dear lady! this is one of the cases, in which laughter is followed by melancholy: for such is the *kind* of drama, which is now
substituted every where for Shakespeare and Racine.[1] You well
know, that I offer violence to my own feelings in joining these
names. But however meanly I may think of the French serious
drama, even in its most perfect specimens; and with whatever
right I may complain of its perpetual falsification of the language,
and of the connections and transitions of thought, which Nature
has appropriated to states of passion; still, however, the French
tragedies are consistent works of art, and the offspring of great
intellectual power. Preserving a fitness in the parts, and a harmony
in the whole, they form a nature of their own, though a false
nature. Still they excite the minds of the spectators to active
thought, to a striving after ideal excellence. The soul is not stupe-

[a] BL (1817) omits comma

[1] Cf WW's remark in Preface to
LB (1800): "The invaluable works
of our elder writers . . . are driven
into neglect by frantic novels, sickly
and stupid German Tragedies, and
deluges of idle and extravagant
stories in verse." *W Prose* I 128.
Friend II 216n points out that the
following discussion of drama is not
in the original letters but notes the
conclusion of Lect 5 of 11 Nov 1813
in Bristol, which refers to the general
attitude and also to the anecdote in
the previous paragraph. In that lecture C spoke of the "degree of excitement, which was the object of the
German drama; and concluded . . .

with reading some observations he
penned, after being present at the
representation of a play in Germany,
in which the wife of a colonel who
had fallen into disgrace, was frantic
in the beginning, middle, and end;
frantic first for grief, and afterwards
for joy. A distortion of feeling was
the feature of the modern drama of
Kotzebue, and his followers; its
heroes were generous, liberal, brave,
and noble, just so far as they could,
without the sacrifice of one christian
virtue—its misanthropes were tender-
hearted, and its tender-hearted were
misanthropes." *Sh C* II 284–5.

fied into mere sensations, by a worthless sympathy with our own ordinary sufferings, or an empty curiosity for the surprising, undignified by the language or the situations which awe and delight the imagination. What (I would ask of the crowd, that press forward to the pantomimic tragedies and weeping comedies of Kotzebue and his imitators) what are you seeking?[1] Is it comedy? But in the comedy of Shakespeare and Molière[2] the more accurate my knowledge, and the more profoundly I think, the greater is the satisfaction that mingles with my laughter. For though the qualities which these writers pourtray are ludicrous indeed, either from the kind or the excess, and exquisitely ludicrous, yet are they the natural growth of the human mind and such as, with more or less change in the drapery, I can apply to my own heart, or at least to whole classes of my fellow-creatures. How often are not the moralist and the metaphysician obliged for the happiest illustrations of general truths and the subordinate laws of human thought and action to quotations not only from the tragic characters but equally from the Jaques, Falstaff, and even from the fools and clowns of Shakespeare, or from the Miser, Hypochondriast, and Hypocrite, of Molière! Say not, that I am recommending abstractions: for these class-characteristics, which constitute the instructiveness of a character, are so modified and particularized in each person of the Shakesperian Drama, that life itself does not excite more distinctly that sense of individuality which belongs to real existence. Paradoxical as it may sound, one of the essential properties of geometry is not less essential to dramatic excellence, and (if I may mention his name without pedantry to a lady) Aristotle has accordingly required of the poet an involution of the universal in the individual.[3] The chief differences are, that in geometry it is

---

[1] August Friedrich Ferdinand von Kotzebue (1761–1819), whose numerous plays were popular in England as well as Germany. C speaks of him as "the German Beaumont and Fletcher, without their poetic powers and without their *vis comica*". *Sh C* I 60. (*F*). Möller's *Graf von Walltron* was less an "imitation" than a forerunner of Kotzebue's plays. *CN* I 337n.

[2] Cf C's praise of Molière as being among the great French writers who are "*ultimi Gothorum,*

the last in whom the Gothic predominated over the Celtic". Samuel Pepys *Memoirs* (2 vols 1825) II i 254: *CM* (*CC*) III; in *Misc C* 286 (*F*). *CN* III 4264 and n.

[3] C refers to *Poetics* 9.1–4 (see ch 17, above, II 46 and n 2), but with an emphasis on the organic interrelation ("involution") that is common in German criticism, especially in A. W. and Friedrich Schlegel. *CN* I 943n also suggests that C is recalling a key passage in Pomponatius (Pietro Pomponazzi,

the universal truth itself, which is uppermost in the consciousness, in poetry the individual form in which the Truth is cloathed. With the Ancients, and not less with the elder dramatists of England and France, both comedy and tragedy were considered as kinds of *poetry*. They neither sought in comedy to make us laugh merely, much less to make us laugh by wry faces, accidents of jargon, slang phrases for the day, or the clothing of common-place morals in metaphors drawn from the shops or mechanic occupations of their characters; nor did they condescend in tragedy to wheedle away the applause of the spectators, by representing before them fac-similies of their own mean selves in all their existing meanness, or to work on their sluggish sympathies by a pathos not a whit more respectable than the maudlin tears of drunkenness.[1] Their tragic scenes were meant to affect us indeed, but within the bounds of pleasure, and in union with the activity both of our understanding and imagination. They wished to transport the mind to a sense of its possible greatness, and to implant the germs of that greatness during the temporary oblivion of the worthless "thing, we are"[2] and of the peculiar state, in which each man *happens* to be; suspending our individual recollections and lulling them to sleep amid the music of nobler thoughts.

Hold! (methinks I hear the spokesman of the crowd reply, and we will listen to him. I am the plaintiff, and be he the defendant.)

DEFENDANT. Hold! are not our modern sentimental plays filled with the best Christian morality?

PLAINTIFF. Yes! just as much of it, and just that part of it which you can exercise without a single Christian virtue—without a single sacrifice that is really painful to you!—just as much as *flatters* you, sends you away pleased with your own hearts, and quite reconciled to your vices, which can never be thought very ill of, when they keep such good company, and walk hand in hand with so much compassion and generosity; adulation so loathsome, that you would spit in the man's face who dared offer it to you in a private company, unless you interpreted it as insulting irony, you appropriate with infinite satisfaction, when you share the garbage with the whole stye, and gobble it out of a common trough. No

---

1462–1525) in *Tractatus de immor- talitate animae* (1534) 59. Cf *Misc C* 44 and *Friend* (*CC*) I 457.

[1] Cf C's attack, in his letter to RS 9 Feb 1813, on the deliberate use of dramatic pathos: *CL* III 434.

[2] Shakespeare *Rape of Lucrece* line 149. (*F*).

Cæsar must pace your boards—no Antony, no royal Dane, no Orestes, no Andromache!—

D. No: or as few of them as possible. What has a plain citizen of London, or Hamburg, to do with your kings and queens, and your old school-boy Pagan heroes? Besides, every body knows the *stories*: and what curiosity can we feel————

P. What, Sir, not for the *manner*? not for the delightful language of the poet? not for the situations, the action and reaction of the passions?

D. You are hasty, Sir! the only curiosity, we feel, is in the story: and how can we be anxious concerning the end of a play, or be surprized by it, when we know how it will turn out?

P. Your pardon, for having interrupted you! we now understand each other. You seek then, in a tragedy, which wise men of old held for the highest effort of human genius, the same gratification, as that you receive from a new novel, the last German romance, and other dainties of the day, which *can* be enjoyed but once.[1] If you carry these feelings to the sister art of Painting, Michael Angelo's Sistine*a* Chapel, and the Scripture Gallery of Raphael, can expect no favour from you. *You know all about them before-hand*; and are, doubtless, more familiar with the subjects of those paintings, than with the tragic tales of the historic or heroic ages. There is a consistency, therefore, in your preference of contemporary writers: for the great men of former times, those at least who were deemed great by our ancestors, sought so little to gratify *this* kind of curiosity, that they seemed to have regarded the *story* in a not much higher light, than the painter regards his canvass: as that *on*, not *by*, which they were to display their appropriate excellence. No work, resembling a tale or romance, can well shew less variety of invention in the incidents, or less anxiety in weaving them together, than the Don Quixote of CERVANTES.[2] Its admirers feel the disposition to go back and re-peruse some preceding chapter, at least ten times for once that they find any eagerness to hurry forwards: or open the book on those parts which they best recollect, even as we visit those friends oftenest

a BL (1817): Sestine

[1] "Not the poem which we have *read*, but that to which we *return* ... claims the name of *essential poety*." Above, I 23.

[2] For detailed discussion of *Don Quixote*, see Lect 8 of 20 Feb 1818: *Misc C* 98–103; *CN* III 4503 (notes for Lect 7 of 25 Mar 1819).

whom we love most, and with whose characters and actions we are the most intimately acquainted. In the divine ARIOSTO, (as his countrymen call this, their darling poet) I question whether there be a single *tale* of his own invention, or the elements of which, were not familiar to the readers of "old romance." [1] I will pass by the ancient Greeks, who thought it even necessary to the fable of a tragedy, that its substance should be previously known. That there had been at least fifty tragedies with the same title, would be one of the motives which determined Sophocles and Euripides, in the choice of Electra, as a subject. But Milton—

D. Aye Milton, indeed! but do not Dr. Johnson, and other great men tell us, that nobody now reads Milton but as a task? [2]

P. So much the worse for them, of whom this can be truly said! But why then do you pretend to admire *Shakespeare*? The greater part, if not all, of *his* dramas were, as far as the names and the main incidents are concerned, already stock plays. All the *stories*, at least, on which they are built, pre-existed in the chronicles, ballads, or translations of contemporary or preceding English writers. Why, I repeat, do you pretend to admire *Shakespeare*? Is it, perhaps, that you only *pretend* to admire him? However, as once for all, you have dismissed the well-known events and personages of history, or the epic muse, what have you taken in their stead? Whom has *your* tragic muse armed with her bowl and dagger? the sentimental muse I should have said, whom you have seated in the throne of tragedy? What heroes has *she* reared on her buskins?

D. O! our good friends and next-door-neighbours—honest tradesmen, valiant tars, high-spirited half-pay officers, philanthropic Jews, virtuous courtezans, tender-hearted braziers, and sentimental rat-catchers! (a little bluff or so, but all our very generous, tender-hearted characters *are* a little rude or misanthropic, and all our misanthropes very tender-hearted.)

[1] On Ariosto, see esp *Misc C* 148–9; *TT* 12 Jul 1827. (*F*). Cf ch 15, above, II 22.

[2] An exaggeration, extrapolating one remark from what is the first great critique of Milton. Speaking of the "defects" of *Paradise Lost,* Johnson mentions the lack of "human interest" in the characters and states that it is a book that the general reader "admires and lays down. . . . Its perusal is a duty rather than a pleasure." But he also adds that "he who can put in balance [the "defects" of that "wonderful performance"] with its beauties must be . . . pitied for want of sensibility". *Lives* "Milton" I 183, 188.

P. But I pray you, friend, in what actions great or interesting, can such men be engaged?

D. They give away a great deal of money: find rich dowries for young men and maidens who have all other good qualities; they browbeat lords, baronets, and justices of the peace, (for they are as bold as Hector!)—they rescue stage coaches at the instant they are falling down precipices; carry away infants in the sight of opposing armies; and some of our performers act a muscular able-bodied man to such perfection, that our dramatic poets, who always have the actors in their eye, seldom fail to make their favourite male character as strong as Samson.[a] And then they take such prodigious leaps!! And what is *done* on the stage is more striking even than what is acted. I once remember such a deafening explosion, that I could not hear a word of the play for half an act after it: and a little real gunpowder being set fire to at the same time, and smelt by all the spectators, the naturalness of the scene was quite astonishing!

P. But how can you connect with such men and such actions that dependence of thousands on the fate of one, which gives so lofty an interest to the personages of Shakespeare, and the Greek Tragedians? How can you connect with them that sublimest of all feelings, the power of destiny and the controlling might of heaven, which seems to elevate the characters which sink beneath its irresistible blow?

D. O mere fancies! We seek and find on the present stage our own wants and passions, our own vexations, losses, and embarrassments.

P. It is your own poor pettifogging nature then, which you desire to have represented before you? not human nature in its heighth and vigour? But surely you might find the former with all its joys and sorrows, more conveniently in your own houses and parishes.

D. True! but here comes a difference. Fortune is blind, but the poet has his eyes open, and is besides as complaisant as fortune is capricious. He makes every thing turn out exactly as we would wish it. He gratifies us by representing those as hateful or contemptible whom we hate and wish to despise.

P. (*aside*) That is, he gratifies your envy by libelling your superiors.

[a] *BL* (1817): Sampson.

D. He makes all those precise moralists, who affect to be better than their neighbours, turn out at last abject hypocrites, traitors, and hard-hearted villains; and your men of spirit, who take their girl and their glass with equal freedom, prove the true men of honour, and (that no part of the audience may remain unsatisfied) reform in the last scene, and leave no doubt on the minds of the ladies, that they will make most faithful and excellent husbands: though it does seem a pity, that they should be obliged to get rid of qualities which had made them so interesting! Besides, the poor become rich all at once; and in the final matrimonial choice the opulent and high-born themselves are made to confess, that VIRTUE IS THE ONLY TRUE NOBILITY,[1] AND THAT A LOVELY WOMAN IS A DOWRY OF HERSELF!![2]

P. Excellent! But you have forgotten those brilliant flashes of loyalty, those patriotic praises of the king and old England, which, especially if conveyed in a metaphor from the ship or the shop, so often solicit and so unfailingly receive the public plaudit! I give your prudence credit for the omission. For the whole system of your drama is a moral and intellectual *Jacobinism* of the most dangerous kind, and those common-place rants of loyalty are no better than hypocrisy in your playwrights, and your own sympathy with them a gross self-delusion. For the whole secret of dramatic popularity consists with you, in the confusion and subversion of the natural order of things, their causes and their effects; in the excitement of surprise, by representing the qualities of liberality, refined feeling, and a nice sense of honour (those things rather, which pass among you for such) in persons and in classes of life where experience teaches us least to expect them; and in rewarding with all the sympathies that are the dues of virtue, those criminals whom law, reason, and religion, have excommunicated from our esteem!

And now good night! Truly! I might have written this last sheet without having gone to Germany,[3] but I fancied myself talking to you by your own fire-side, and can you think it a small pleasure to me to forget now and then, that I am *not* there. Besides, you and my other good friends have made up your minds to me as I am, and from whatever place I write you will expect that part of my "Travels" will consist of the excursions in my own mind.

[1] Juvenal 8.20. (*F*).
[2] Shakespeare *King Lear* I i 241 ("She is herself a dowry"). (*F*).

[3] It was indeed written afterwards, possibly for the 1808 lectures or for *Friend* No 16 (*F*).

LETTER III[1]

RATZEBURG

No little fish thrown back again into the water, no fly unimprisoned from a child's hand, could more buoyantly enjoy its element, than I this clean and peaceful house, with this lovely view of the town, groves, and lake of Ratzeburg, from the window at which I am writing. My spirits certainly, and my health I fancied, were beginning to sink under the noise, dirt, and unwholesome air of our Hamburg hotel—I left it on Sunday, Sept. 23d. with a letter of introduction from the poet Klopstock, to the Amptman of Ratzeburg.[2] The Amptman received me with kindness, and introduced me to the worthy pastor, who agreed to board and lodge me for any length of time not less than a month. The vehicle, in which I took my place, was considerably larger than an English stage coach, to which it bore much the same proportion and rude resemblance, that an elephant's ear does to the human. Its top was composed of naked boards of different colours, and seeming to have been parts of different wainscots. Instead of windows there were leathern curtains with a little eye of glass in each: they perfectly answered the purpose of keeping out the prospect and letting in the cold. I could observe little, therefore, but the inns and farm houses at which we stopped. They were all alike, except in size: one great room, like a barn, with a hay-loft over it, the straw and hay dangling in tufts through the boards which formed the ceiling of the room, and floor of the loft. From this room, which is paved like a street, sometimes one, sometimes two smaller ones, are enclosed at one end. These are commonly floored. In the large room the cattle, pigs, poultry, men, women, and children, live in amicable community: yet there was an appearance of cleanliness and rustic comfort. One of these houses I measured. It was an hundred feet in length. The apartments were taken off from one corner. Between these and the stalls there was a small interspace, and here the breadth was forty-eight feet, but thirty-two where the stalls were; of course, the stalls were on each side eight feet in depth. The faces of the cows, &c. were turned towards the room; indeed they were in it, so that they had at least the comfort of seeing each other's

[1] Revised slightly from *Friend* No 18 (21 Dec 1809), which in turn is a pastiche of two letters to Mrs C and two to Poole. *CL* I 445–9, 460–1, 453–8, 441–5. (*F*).

[2] "Amtman Braunes". *CL* I 448. (*F*).

faces. Stall-feeding is universal in this part of Germany, a practice concerning which the agriculturalist and the poet are likely to entertain opposite opinions—or at least, to have very different feelings. The wood work of these buildings on the outside is left unplaistered, as in old houses among us, and being painted red and green, it cuts and tesselates the buildings very gaily. From within three miles of Hamburg almost to Molln, which is thirty miles from it, the country as far as I could see it, was a dead flat, only varied by woods. At Molln it became more beautiful. I observed a small lake nearly surrounded with groves,[1] and a palace in view belonging to the king of Great Britain, and inhabited by the Inspector of the Forests. We were nearly the same time in travelling the thirty-five miles from Hamburg to Ratzeburg, as we had been in going from London to Yarmouth, one hundred and twenty-six miles.

The lake of Ratzeburg runs from south to north, about nine miles in length, and varying in breadth from three miles to half a mile. About a mile from the southernmost point it is divided into two, of course very unequal, parts by an island, which being connected by a bridge and a narrow slip of land with the one shore, and by another bridge of immense length with the other shore, forms a complete isthmus. On this island the town of Ratzeburg is built. The pastor's house or vicarage, together with the Amptman's, Amptschreiber's, and the church, stands near the summit of a hill, which slopes down to the slip of land and the little bridge, from which, through a superb military gate, you step into the island-town of Ratzeburg. This again is itself a little hill, by ascending and descending which, you arrive at the long bridge, and so to the other shore. The water to the south of the town is called the Little Lake, which however almost engrosses the beauties of the whole: the shores being just often enough green and bare to give the proper effect to the magnificent groves which occupy the greater part of their circumference. From the turnings, windings, and indentations of the shore, the views vary almost every ten steps, and the whole has a sort of majestic beauty, a feminine grandeur. At the north of the Great Lake, and peeping over it, I see the seven church towers of Lubec,[2] at the distance of twelve or thirteen miles, yet as distinctly as if they were not three. The

---

[1] Möllner See. (*F*).　　　　　　[2] Those of the Domkirche, Marienkirche, and Holsten-Tor. (*F*).

only defect in the view is, that Ratzeburg is built entirely of red bricks, and all the houses roofed with red tiles. To the eye, therefore, it presents a clump of brick-dust red. Yet this evening, Oct. 10th. twenty minutes past five, I saw the town perfectly beautiful, and the whole softened down into *complete keeping*,[1] if I may borrow a term from the painters. The sky over Ratzeburg and all the east, was a pure evening blue, while over the west it was covered with light sandy clouds.[2] Hence a deep red light spread over the whole prospect, in undisturbed harmony with the red town, the brown-red woods, and the yellow-red reeds on the skirts of the lake. Two or three boats, with single persons paddling them, floated up and down in the rich light, which not only was itself in harmony with all, but brought all into harmony.

I should have told you that I went back to Hamburg on Thursday (Sept. 27th.) to take leave of my friend, who travels southward, and returned hither on the Monday following.[3] From Empfelde, a village half way from Ratzeburg, I walked to Hamburg through deep sandy roads and a dreary flat: the soil every where white, hungry, and excessively pulverized; but the approach to the city is pleasing. Light cool country houses, which you can look through and see the gardens behind them, with arbours and trellis work, and thick vegetable walls, and trees in cloisters and piazzas, each house with neat rails before it, and green seats within the rails. Every object, whether the growth of nature or the work of man, was neat and artificial. It pleased me far better, than if the house and gardens, and pleasure fields, had been in a nobler taste: for this nobler taste would have been mere apery. The busy, anxious, money-loving merchant of Hamburg could only have *adopted*, he could not have *enjoyed* the simplicity of nature. The mind begins to love nature by imitating human conveniences in nature; but this is a step in intellect, though a low one—and were it not so, yet all around me spoke of innocent enjoyment and sensitive comforts, and I entered with unscrupulous sympathy into

[1] For "keeping" see ch 14, above, II 15 and n 3, and "Satyrane's Letters" II, above, II 178.

[2] Here and in the next two sentences C, for *The Friend*, had drawn on *CN* I 357 (see 357n).

[3] WW, learning from C on 27 Sept that Ratzeburg was expensive, decided the next day to find lodgings southward and settled on Goslar, where he and DW stayed from 6 Oct until late Feb 1799, afterwards travelling until they left for England in Apr. Meanwhile C and John Chester departed again for Ratzeburg on 30 Sept. Reed I 252–67.

the enjoyments and comforts even of the busy, anxious, money-loving merchants of Hamburg. In this charitable and *catholic* mood I reached the vast ramparts of the city. These are huge green cushions, one rising above the other, with trees growing in the interspaces, pledges and symbols of a long peace. Of my return I have nothing worth communicating, except that I took extra post, which answers to posting in England. These north German post chaises are uncovered wicker carts. An English dust-cart is a piece of finery, a chef d'oeuvre of mechanism, compared with them: and the horses! a savage might use their ribs instead of his fingers for a numeration table. Wherever we stopped, the postilion fed his cattle with the brown rye bread of which he eat himself, all break-fasting together, only the horses had no gin to their water, and the postillion no water to his gin. Now and henceforward for subjects of more interest to you, and to the objects in search of which I left you: namely, the literati and literature of Germany.

Believe me, I walked with an impression of awe on my spirits, as W————[1] and myself accompanied Mr. Klopstock to the house of his brother, the poet, which stands about a quarter of a mile from the city gate.[2] It is one of a row of little common-place summer-houses, (for so they looked) with four or five rows of young meagre elm trees before the windows, beyond which is a green, and then a dead flat intersected with several roads. What-ever beauty (thought I) may be before the poet's eyes at present, it must certainly be purely of his own creation. We waited a few minutes in a neat little parlour, ornamented with the figures of two of the muses and with prints, the subjects of which were from Klopstock's odes.[3] The poet entered. I was much disappointed in his countenance, and recognized in it no likeness to the bust. There was no comprehension in the forehead, no weight over the eye-brows, no expression of peculiarity, moral or intellectual,[a] on the eyes, no massiveness in the general countenance. He is if any thing

[a] *BL* (1817) omits comma

[1] WW.

[2] For C's opinion of Klopstock's *Messias* (1748–73) see ch 22, above, II 133–4 and n 4. From here to the end of the letter cf generally WW's own notes on the conversations with Klopstock, from which C later quotes directly. *W Prose* I 91–8.

After their visit of 21 Sept WW had two further interviews with Klopstock on 26 Sept. (See below, II 199). With C's original letter to Poole (*CL* I 441–5) cf *CN* I 339.

[3] Presumably the ode *Die beyden Musen: Oden* (1771) 150–3. (F).

rather below the middle size. He wore very large half-boots which his legs filled, so fearfully were they swoln. However, though neither W——— nor myself could discover any indications of sublimity or enthusiasm in his physiognomy, we were both equally impressed with his liveliness, and his kind and ready courtesy. He talked in French with my friend, and with difficulty spoke a few sentences to me in English. His enunciation was not in the least affected by the entire want of his upper teeth. The conversation began on his part by the expression of his rapture at the surrender of the detachment of French troops under General Humbert.[1] Their proceedings in Ireland with regard to the committee which they had appointed, with the rest of their organizing system, seemed to have given the poet great entertainment. He then declared his sanguine belief in Nelson's victory,[2] and anticipated its confirmation with a keen and triumphant pleasure. His words, tones, looks, implied the most vehement Anti-Gallicanism. The subject changed to literature, and I enquired in Latin concerning the History of German Poetry and the elder German Poets.[3] To my great astonishment he confessed, that he knew very little on the subject. He had indeed occasionally read one or two of their elder writers, but not so as to enable him to speak of their merits. Professor Ebeling, he said, would probably give me every information of this kind: the subject had not particularly excited his curiosity. He then talked of Milton and Glover,[4] and thought Glover's blank verse superior to Milton's. W——— and myself expressed our surprise: and my friend gave his definition and notion of harmonious verse, that it consisted (the English iambic blank verse above all) in the apt arrangement of pauses and cadences, and the sweep of whole paragraphs,

[1] Jean Joseph Amable Humbert (1767–1823) led a French force of about a thousand soldiers in Aug 1798 to support an Irish rebellion, and then surrendered 8 Sept to a superior force led by Lord Cornwallis. (*F*).

[2] Aboukir Bay 1 Aug 1798. (*F*).

[3] "He answered in French, & Wordsworth interpreted it to me". *CL* I 442. (*F*).

[4] Richard Glover (1712–85), the son of a Hamburg merchant, is remembered especially for his blank-verse epic *Leonidas* (1737), later enlarged (1770). The first version was tr into French in 1738 and into German in 1766. He also wrote other less successful blank-verse poems, notably *London, or the Progress of Commerce* (1739) and an enormous epic in thirty books, *Athenaid* (1787), as well as two plays on classical themes, *Boadicea* (1753) and *Medea* (1761).

——————— with many a winding bout
Of linked sweetness long drawn out,[1]

and not in the even flow, much less in the prominence or antithetic
vigour, of single lines, which were indeed injurious to the total
effect, except where they were introduced for some specific purpose. Klopstock assented, and said that he meant to confine
Glover's superiority to single lines. He told us that he had read
Milton, in a prose translation, when he was fourteen.*[2] I understood him thus myself, and W——————— interpreted Klopstock's
French as I had already construed it. He appeared to know very
little of Milton—or indeed of our poets in general. He spoke with
great indignation of the English prose translation of his Messiah.[3]
All the translations had been bad, very bad—but the English was
no translation—there were pages on pages not in the original:—
and half the original was not to be found in the translation.
W——————— told him that I intended to translate a few of his odes
as specimens of German lyrics[4]—he then said to me in English,
"I wish you would render into English some select passages of the
Messiah, and *revenge* me of your countryman!" It was the liveliest
thing which he produced in the whole conversation. He told us,
that his first ode was fifty years older than his last. I looked at him
with much emotion—I considered him as the venerable father of
German poetry; as a good man; as a Christian, seventy-four years
old; with legs enormously swoln; yet active, lively, chearful, and
kind, and communicative. My eyes felt as if a tear were swelling
into them. In the portrait of Lessing there was a toupee perriwig,
which enormously injured the effect of his physiognomy—Klopstock wore the same, powdered and frizzled. By the bye, old men
ought never to wear powder—the contrast between a large snow-
white wig and the colour of an old man's skin is disgusting, and

* This was accidentally confirmed to me by an old German gentleman at
Helmstadt, who had been Klopstock's school and bed-fellow. Among other
boyish anecdotes, he related that the young poet set a particular value on a
translation of the Paradise Lost, and always slept with it under his pillow.

[1] *L'Allegro* lines 139–40. (*F*).
[2] J. J. Bodmer's prose-translation
into German (1732), though Klopstock later defensively claimed he
had not read Milton before he had
"finished his plan" for his own epic.
See below, II 200.

[3] *The Messiah. Attempted from
the German of Mr. Klopstock* tr
Mary and Joseph Collyer (1763),
four eds of which appeared in the
next six years. (*F*).
[4] If C did compose any translations, they are not extant. (*F*).

wrinkles in such a neighbourhood appear only channels for dirt. It is an honour to poets and great men, that you think of them as parts of nature; and any thing of trick and fashion wounds you in them as much as when you see venerable yews clipped into miserable peacocks.—The author of the Messiah should have worn his own grey hair.—His powder and perriwig were to the eye what Mr. Virgil would be to the ear.

Klopstock dwelt much on the superior power which the German language possessed of concentrating meaning. He said, he had often translated parts of Homer and Virgil, line by line, and a German line proved always sufficient for a Greek or Latin one.[1] In English you cannot do this. I answered, that in English we could commonly render one Greek heroic line in a line and a half of our common heroic metre, and I conjectured that this line and a half would be found to contain no more syllables than one German or Greek hexameter. He did not understand me: * and I

* Klopstock's observation was partly true and partly erroneous. In the literal sense of his words, and if we confine the comparison to the average of space required for the expression of the same thought in the two languages, it is erroneous. I have translated some German hexameters into English hexameters, and find, that on the average three lines English will express four lines German. The reason is evident: our language abounds in monosyllables and dissyllables. The German, not less than the Greek, is a polysyllable language. But in another point of view the remark was not without foundation. For the German possessing the same unlimited privilege of forming compounds, both with prepositions and with epithets as the Greek, it can express the richest single Greek word in a single German one, and is thus freed from the necessity of weak or ungraceful paraphrases. I will content myself with one example at present, viz. the use of the prefixed particles *ver, zer, ent,* and *weg*:[2] thus, reissen to rend, verreissen to rend away, zerreissen to rend to pieces, *entreissen* to rend off or out of a thing, in the active sense: or schmelzen to melt—ver, zer, ent, schmelzen—and in like manner through all the verbs neuter and active. If you consider only how much we should feel the loss of the prefix *be*, as in bedrop, besprinkle, besot, especially in our poetical language, and then think that this same mode of composition is carried through all their simple and compound prepositions, and many of their adverbs; and that with most of these the Germans have the same privilege as we have of dividing them from the verb and placing them at the end of the sentence; you will have no difficulty in comprehending the reality

[1] Cf C's own remarks on the "Superior advantages of the German in the imitation of the ancient metres". *CN* III 3450.

[2] Cf C's note of Sept 1807: "O for the power to persuade all the writers of G. B. [Great Britain] to adopt the ver, zer, and ab of the German—why not verboil, zerboil? versend, zersend? I should like the very words verflossen, zerflossen, to be naturalized—and as I look, now feels my Soul creative Throes, And now all Joy, all sense, Zerflows." *CN* II 3160 and n. (*F*).

who wished to hear his opinions, not to correct them, was glad
that he did not.

We now took our leave. At the beginning of the French Revolution Klopstock wrote odes of congratulation. He received some
honorary presents from the French Republic (a golden crown I
believe) and, like our Priestley,[a][2] was invited to a seat in the
legislature, which he declined. But when French liberty metamorphosed herself into a fury, he sent back these presents with a
palinodia, declaring his abhorrence of their proceedings: and since
then he has been perhaps more than enough an Anti-Gallican.
I mean, that in his just contempt and detestation of the crimes and
follies of the Revolutionists, he suffers himself to forget that the
revolution itself is a process of the Divine Providence; and that
as the folly of men is the wisdom of God,[3] so are their iniquities
instruments of his goodness. From Klopstock's house we walked to
the ramparts, discoursing together on the poet and his conversation, till our attention was diverted to the beauty and singularity
of the sunset and its effects on the objects round us. There were
woods in the distance. A rich sandy light (nay, of a much deeper
colour than sandy) lay over these woods that blackened in the
blaze. Over that part of the woods which lay immediately under
the intenser light, a brassy mist floated. The trees on the ramparts,

---

and the cause of this superior power in the German of condensing meaning,
in which its great poet exulted. It is impossible to read half a dozen pages of
Wieland[1] without perceiving that in this respect the German has no rival but
the Greek. And yet I seem to feel, that concentration or condensation is not
the happiest mode of expressing this excellence, which seems to consist not so
much in the less time required for conveying an impression, as in the unity
and simultaneous with which the impression is conveyed. It tends to
make their language more picturesque: it *depictures* images better. We have
obtained this power in part by our compound verbs derived from the Latin:
and the sense of its great effect no doubt induced our Milton both to the use
and the abuse of Latin derivatives. But still these prefixed particles, conveying no separate or separable meaning to the mere English reader, cannot
possibly act on the mind with the force or liveliness of an original and
homogeneous language such as the German is, and besides are confined to
certain words.

[a] *BL* (1817): Priestly

[1] See below, II 202–3.
[2] Joseph Priestley (1733–1804),
the famous scientist and philosopher,
systematiser of David Hartley's work
on association of ideas, liberal in his
political and religious views. Cf
above, ch 6, I 110, and ch 8, I 136.
[3] Cf *Friend* (*CC*) I 184 and n 2,
which cites 1 Cor and Berkeley
Alciphron.

and the people moving to and fro between them, were cut or divided into equal segments of deep shade and brassy light. Had the trees, and the bodies of the men and women, been divided into equal segments by a rule or pair of compasses, the portions could not have been more regular. All else was obscure. It was a fairy scene! and to encrease its romantic character among the moving objects thus divided into alternate shade and brightness, was a beautiful child, dressed with the elegant simplicity of an English child, riding on a stately goat, the saddle, bridle, and other accoutrements of which were in a high degree costly and splendid. Before I quit the subject of Hamburg, let me say, that I remained a day or two longer than I otherwise should have done, in order to be present at the feast of St. Michael, the patron saint of Hamburg,[1] expecting to see the civic pomp of this commercial Republic. I was however disappointed. There were no processions, two or three sermons were preached to two or three old women in two or three churches, and St. Michael and his patronage wished elsewhere by the higher classes, all places of entertainment, theatre, &c. being shut up on this day. In Hamburg, there seems to be no religion at all: in Lubec it is confined to the women. The men seem determined to be divorced from their wives in the other world, if they cannot in this. You will not easily conceive a more singular sight, than is presented by the vast aisle of the principal church at Lubec seen from the organ-loft: for being filled with female servants and persons in the same class of life, and all their caps having gold and silver cauls, it appears like a rich pavement of gold and silver.

I will conclude this letter with the mere transcription of notes, which my friend W———— made of his conversations with Klopstock, during the interviews that took place after my departure.[2] On these I shall make but one remark at present, and that will appear a presumptuous one, namely, that Klopstock's remarks on the venerable sage of Koenigsberg[a] are to my own knowledge injurious and mistaken; and so far is it from being true, that his system is now given up, that throughout the Universities of Germany there is not a single professor who is not, either a

[a] *BL* (1817): Koenigsburg

[1] 29 Sept (though St Michael is not the patron saint of Hamburg). Cf *CN* i 347 and n.

[2] For the complete text of WW's "Conversations with Klopstock" with notes see *W Prose* i 91–8. The selection C prints is almost verbatim.

Kantean; or a disciple of Fichte, whose system is built on the Kantean, and presupposes its truth; or lastly who, though an antagonist of Kant as to his theoretical work, has not embraced wholly or in part his moral system, and adopted part of his nomenclature. "Klopstock having wished to see the Calvary of Cumberland, and asked what was thought of it in England, I went to Remnant's (the English bookseller) where I procured the Analytical Review, in which is contained the review of Cumberland's Calvary.[1] I remembered to have read there some specimens of a blank verse translation of the Messiah. I had mentioned this to Klopstock, and he had a great desire to see them. I walked over to his house and put the book into his hands. On adverting to his own poem, he told me he began the Messiah when he was seventeen: he devoted three entire years to the plan without composing a single line. He was greatly at a loss in what manner to execute his work. There were no successful specimens of versification in the German language before this time. The first three cantos he wrote in a species of measured or numerous prose. This, though done with much labour and some success, was far from satisfying him. He had composed hexameters both Latin and Greek as a school exercise, and there had been also in the German language attempts in that style of versification. These were only of very moderate merit.—One day he was struck with the idea of what could be done in this way—he kept his room a whole day, even went without his dinner, and found that in the evening he had written twenty-three hexameters, versifying a part of what he had before written in prose. From that time, pleased with his efforts, he composed no more in prose. To-day he informed me that he had finished his plan before he read Milton.[2] He was enchanted to see an author who before him had trod the same path. This is a contradiction of what he said before. He did not wish to speak of his poem to any one till it was finished: but some of his friends who had seen what he had finished, tormented him till he had

---

[1] For Richard Cumberland's *Calvary* (1792) see ch 22, above, ii 133–4 n 4. The review of the work in *Analytical Review* xiii (1792) 121–38, a copy of which WW picked up from the bookseller William Remnant, speaks disparagingly of the Collyer prose translation of Klopstock's *Messias* and provides specimen translations in Miltonic blank verse (presumably by the reviewer "R. R.") that would better fit the original. *W Prose* i 97.

[2] See above, ii 196 and n 2.

consented to publish a few books in a journal.[1] He was then I believe very young, about twenty-five. The rest was printed at different periods, four books at a time. The reception given to the first specimens was highly flattering. He was nearly thirty years in finishing the whole poem, but of these thirty years not more than two were employed in the composition. He only composed in favourable moments; besides he had other occupations. He values himself upon the plan of his odes, and accuses the modern lyrical writers of gross deficiency in this respect. I laid the same accusation against Horace: he would not hear of it—but waived the discussion. He called Rousseau's Ode to Fortune a moral dissertation in stanzas.[2] I spoke of Dryden's St. Cecilia;[3] but he did not seem familiar with our writers. He wished to know the distinctions between our dramatic and epic blank verse. He recommended me to read his Herman[4] before I read either the Messiah or the odes. He flattered himself that some time or other his dramatic poems would be known in England. He had not heard of Cowper. He thought that Voss in his translation of the Iliad had done violence to the idiom of the Germans, and had sacrificed it to the Greek, not remembering sufficiently that each language has its particular spirit and genius.[5] He said Lessing was the first of their dramatic writers. I complained of Nathan as tedious.[6] He said there was not enough of action in it; but that Lessing was the most chaste of their writers. He spoke favourably of Goethe; but said that his 'Sorrows of Werter' was his best work,[7] better than

[1] Cantos 1–3 appeared in *Bremer Beiträge* (1748), reprinted (with Cantos 4–5) as Vol I (1751). Cantos 1–10 were then issued in 1755, Cantos 11–15 in 1768, and Cantos 16–20 in 1773. *W Prose* I 97.

[2] Jean Baptiste Rousseau (1671–1741) *Ode à la fortune: Odes* II 6. *Oeuvres complètes* (Paris 1797) I 107–13. (*F*).

[3] *A Song for St. Cecilia's Day* (1687).

[4] Klopstock's play *Hermanns Schlacht* (1769).

[5] Johann Heinrich Voss (1751–1826), rector of the Gymnasium at Eutin, wrote original poems in the classical vein, contributed to the new

interest in myth in his *Mythologische Briefe* (2 vols 1794), and translated several classical poets. He is best known for his translations of the *Odyssey* (1781) and the *Iliad* (1793), which C in 1816 described to J. H. Frere as "truly marvellous Translations". *CL* IV 655. (*F*). Cf *Misc C* 387.

[6] Lessing's *Nathan der Weise* (1778–9), based on Boccaccio's *Decameron* I 3. WW read it in the translation by either R. E. Raspe (1781) or William Taylor (priv pr 1791, pub 1805). *W Prose* I 97.

[7] *Die Leiden des jungen Werthers* (1774). By "first written" (below) among Goethe's dramas, Klopstock

any of his dramas: he preferred the first written to the rest of Goethe's dramas. Schiller's 'Robbers' he found so extravagant that he could not read it. I spoke of the scene of the setting sun.[1] He did not know it. He said Schiller could not live. He thought Don Carlos the best of his dramas; but said that the plot was inextricable.[2]—It was evident, he knew little of Schiller's works: indeed he said, he could not read them. Bürger[a] he said was a true poet, and would live;[3] that Schiller, on the contrary, must soon be forgotten; that he gave himself up to the imitation of Shakespeare, who often was extravagant, but that Schiller was ten thousand times more so. He spoke very slightingly of Kotzebue, as an immoral author in the first place, and next, as deficient in power. At Vienna, said he, they are transported with him; but we do not reckon the people of Vienna either the wisest or the wittiest people of Germany. He said Wieland[4] was a charming author, and a sovereign master of his own language: that in this respect Goethe could not be compared to him, or indeed could any body else. He said that his fault was to be fertile to exuberance. I told him the Oberon had just been translated into English. He asked me, if I was not delighted with the poem. I answered, that I thought the story began to flag about the seventh or eighth book; and observed that it was unworthy of a man of genius to make the interest of a long poem turn entirely upon animal gratification.[5]

a BL (1817): Burgher

refers to *Götz von Berlichingen* (1773).

[1] *Die Räuber* (1781) III ii, in which Karl von Moor, moved by the beauty of the setting sun, thinks of his lost innocence; tr A. F. Tytler (1792).

[2] *Don Carlos* (1787) appeared in two translations in 1798, one by G. H. Noehden and J. Stoddart and one printed for W. J. and J. Richardson. *W Prose* I 98.

[3] Gottfried August Bürger (1747–94), whose ballad *Lenore* (1772) had been translated into English several times by 1798. Cf to Mrs C 8 Nov 1798: "Bürger of all the German Poets pleases me the most, as yet—the Lenore is greatly superior to any of the Translations."

CL I 438. WW thought less of the poem. Cf C's account of their disagreement about it in his letter to William Taylor 25 Jan 1800. *CL* I 565–6. (*F*).

[4] Christoph Martin Wieland (1733–1813), whose *Oberon* (1780), tr William Sotheby (1798), C himself had begun translating in Nov 1797. *CL* I 357.

[5] Cf "Instead of doing as Ariosto, or, in a still more offensive way, Wieland has done—degrading the struggles of passion into a low animal feeling, Shakespeare had dissipated the reader's attention by a thousand outward images . . .". Lect 4 of 28 Nov 1811: *Sh C* II 93. Cf the revision of this statement in ch 15, above, II 22.

He seemed at first disposed to excuse this by saying, that there are different subjects for poetry, and that poets are not willing to be restricted in their choice. I answered, that I thought the *passion* of love as well suited to the purposes of poetry as any other passion; but that it was a cheap way of pleasing to fix the attention of the reader through a long poem on the mere *appetite*. Well! but, said he, you see, that such poems please every body. I answered, that it was the province of a great poet to raise people up to his own level, not to descend to theirs. He agreed, and confessed, that on no account whatsoever would he have written a work like the Oberon. He spoke in raptures of Wieland's style, and pointed out the passage where Retzia is delivered of her child, as exquisitely beautiful.[1] I said that I did not perceive any very striking passages; but that I made allowance for the imperfections of a translation. Of the thefts of Wieland, he said, they were so exquisitely managed, that the greatest writers might be proud to steal as he did. He considered the books and fables of old romance writers in the light of the ancient mythology, as a sort of common property, from which a man was free to take whatever he could make a good use of. An Englishman had presented him with the odes of Collins, which he had read with pleasure. He knew little or nothing of Gray,[a] except his Elegy[b] in the churchyard. He complained of the fool in Lear. I observed, that he seemed to give a terrible wildness to the distress; but still he complained. He asked whether it was not allowed, that Pope had written rhyme poetry with more skill than any of our writers—I said, I preferred Dryden, because his couplets had greater variety in their movement. He thought my reason a good one; but asked whether the rhymes of Pope were not more exact. This question I understood as applying to the final terminations,[2] and observed to him that I believed it was the case; but that I thought it was easy to excuse some inacuracy in the final sounds, if the general sweep of the verse was superior. I told him that we were not so exact with regard to the final endings of

---

[a] *BL* (1817): Grey,   [b] *BL* (1817): Essay

[1] *Oberon* viii 4969–5064. *W Prose* i 98.

[2] The phrase "as applying to the final terminations" was replaced by "literally" and, in the phrase "final endings" in the next sentence, the superfluous "final" was deleted in the

errata at the end of *Friend* No 19 (the word is found in WW's text in both cases). Their reappearance here indicates that C, in incorporating "Satyrane's Letters" in *BL*, was in too much haste to check for errata.

lines as the French. He did not seem to know that we made no distinction between masculine and feminine (i.e. single or double,) rhymes: at least he put inquiries to me on this subject. He seemed to think, that no language could ever be so far formed as that it might not be enriched by idioms borrowed from another tongue. I said this was a very dangerous practice; and added that I thought Milton had often injured both his prose and verse by taking this liberty too frequently. I recommended to him the prose works of Dryden as models of pure and native English. I was treading upon tender ground, as I have reason to suppose that he has himself liberally indulged in the practice.

"The same day I dined at Mr. Klopstock's, where I had the pleasure of a third interview with the poet. We talked principally about indifferent things. I asked him what he thought of Kant. He said that his reputation was much on the decline in Germany. That for his own part he was not surprised to find it so, as the works of Kant were to him utterly incomprehensible—that he had often been pestered by the Kanteans; but was rarely in the practice of arguing with them. His custom was to produce the book,[1] open it and point to a passage, and beg they would explain it. This they ordinarily attempted to do by substituting their own ideas. I do not want, I say, an explanation of your own ideas, but of the passage which is before us. In this way I generally bring the dispute to an immediate conclusion. He spoke of Wolfe as the first Metaphysician they had in Germany.[2] Wolfe had followers; but they could hardly be called a sect, and luckily till the appearance of Kant, about fifteen years ago,[3] Germany had not been pestered by any sect of philosophers whatsoever; but that each man had separately pursued his enquiries uncontrolled by the dogmas of a Master. Kant had appeared ambitious to be the founder of a sect, that he had succeeded: but that the Germans were now coming to their senses

---

[1] Probably Kant's *Kritik der reinen Vernunft* (Riga 1781) or one of the later eds, though the dating of what Klopstock calls Kant's "appearance" (see n 3, below) could suggest other works that Klopstock found equally "incomprehensible".

[2] Christian von Wolff (1679–

1754), who systematised some aspects of Leibniz's rationalism into a near orthodoxy for eighteenth-century German thought until the influence of Kant became strongly felt. See ch 8, above, I 131.

[3] WW's text states "ten years ago" (i.e. about 1788).

again. That Nicolai[1] and Engel[2] had in different ways contributed to disenchant the nation; but above all the incomprehensibility of the philosopher and his philosophy. He seemed pleased to hear, that as yet Kant's doctrines had not met with many admirers in England—did not doubt but that we had too much wisdom to be duped by a writer who set at defiance the common sense and common understandings of men. We talked of tragedy. He seemed to rate highly the power of exciting tears—I said that nothing was more easy than to deluge an audience, that it was done every day by the meanest writers."

I must remind you, my friend, first, that these notes, &c. are not intended as specimens of Klopstock's intellectual power, or even *"colloquial prowess,"* to judge of which by an accidental conversation, and this with strangers, and those too foreigners, would be not only unreasonable, but calumnious. Secondly, I attribute little other interest to the remarks than what is derived from the celebrity of the person who made them. Lastly, if you ask me, whether I have read the Messiah, and what I think of it? I answer—as yet the first four books only: and as to my opinion (the reasons of which

[1] Christoph Friedrich Nicolai (1733–1811), prolific author and bookseller, who indeed (in contrast to J. J. Engel, see n 2, below) attacked Kant as well as many other leading German minds of the period (e.g. Goethe, Schiller, Herder, and Fichte), wildly misrepresenting all of them. In his copy of Nicolai's *Über meine gelehrte Bildung . . .* (Berlin and Stettin 1799) C wrote of him as a "Gander arching its neck in imitation of the Swans"; "Hoot! Pretty Poll! . . ."; "old Nic. the Berlin book-scribling Bookshopster & Book-monger". (*F*).

[2] Johann Jakob Engel (1741–1802), remembered primarily for his *Der Philosoph für die Welt* (1775–8) and *Anfangsgründe einer Theorie der Dichtungsarten* (1783), was hardly an attacker of Kant in the sense that Nicolai was. SC cites a section of *Der Philosoph* (II Stück 31 "Zwei Gespräche den Werth der Kritik betreffend"). See *BL* (1847) II 254. But the misgivings expressed there about "Kritik" apply to analytic criticism of the arts generally, in contrast to the importance of "feeling", rather than to Kant's first *Kritik*, which appeared later anyway. In mentioning that Engel helped to "disenchant" the nation of Kant, Klopstock was probably referring to the general tenor of his thinking, which reflects a strong eighteenth-century British influence: empirical, at times quasi-utilitarian, emotionalist, and, in aesthetics, stressing the creative, organic, and vital. Hence C's special interest in him, his thought (1801) of translating Stück VI of *Der Philosoph,* and his use of him especially in *The Friend.* Cf *CN* I 930 and n, III 3585 and n; *Friend* (*CC*) I 370n, 451n, and ch 17, above, II 53 n 1. For general discussion see Ernst Paepke *J. J. Engel als Kritiker* (Freiburg 1928).

hereafter) you may guess it from what I could not help muttering to myself, when the good pastor this morning told me, that Klopstock was the German Milton—"a very *German* Milton indeed!!!" —Heaven preserve you, and

S. T. COLERIDGE

CHAPTER 23[1]

Quid quod præfatione præmunierim libellum, quâ conor omnem offendiculi ansam præcidere? Neque quicquam addubito, quin ea candidis omnibus faciat satis. Quid autem facias istis, qui vel ob ingenii pertinaciam sibi satisfieri nolint, vel stupidiores sint quam ut satisfactionem intelligant? Nam quem ad modum Simonides dixit, Thessalos hebetiores esse quam ut possint a se decipi, ita quosdam videas stupidiores quam ut placari queant. Adhæc, non mirum est, invenire quod calumnietur qui nihil aliud quærit nisi quod calumnietur.

ERASMUS *ad Dorpium, Theologum*[2]

[1] The following chapter is essentially a reprint of five letters contributed by C to the *Courier* 29 Aug and 7, 9, 10, and 11 Sept 1816, on the tragedy *Bertram* (1816) by the Irish novelist and playwright, Charles Robert Maturin (1782–1824).

Of these five letters, the first is here reproduced only in part. The omissions and changes are recorded in *EOT* (*CC*) II 435–40, which gives the first of the five letters. This letter and the remaining four are reprinted in App C, below.

In a letter to H. J. Rose 17 Sept 1816 C stated that he had dictated the letters to Morgan, though "I was not able to revise them or correct the style". *CL* IV 670. Cf the recently published letter to Morgan 24 Jun 1816. *CL* VI 1040–2. C was uneasy in his conscience about reviewing *Bertram* as he did. Hence his remark to Alexander Rae 15 Apr 1817, which is true only in the most narrowly literal sense, that the letters "were written by Mr Morgan", though the "Thoughts" were his own. *CL* IV 720. As David Erdman states, "C was attacking the work of a rival playwright, and engaged in what he considered the

immoral act of anonymous reviewing; hence it suited him to attribute to his amanuensis the responsibility —sometimes for flaws of 'style' (*CL* IV 670), sometimes for all but 'the thoughts' (720)". *EOT* (*CC*) II 435n; *SIR* I (1961) 53–6.

[2] From the letter to Dorpius (var) affixed to Erasmus *Moriae encomium* in many eds, including C's (Oxford 1668). C had entered this passage into a notebook Aug–Sept 1815: *CN* III 4262 and n. Tr: "What has been the use of forearming my little book [i.e. *Moriae encomium*] with a preface in which I try to cut off any handle for the least offence? [Sentence here omitted by C.] I have no doubt that it will satisfy everyone who is sincere. What, however, are you to do about those who either refuse to be satisfied out of natural stubbornness or who are too stupid to appreciate their own satisfaction? For even as Simonides said, 'The Thessalians are too dim-witted to be able to be deceived by me,' so you may see that some people are too stupid to be capable of being placated. Besides, it is not surprising that a man who searches only for something to abuse finds nothing else."

I N THE rifacciamento of T H E F R I E N D , I have inserted extracts from the Conciones ad Populum, printed, though scarcely published, in the year 1795, in the very heat and height of my anti-ministerial enthusiasm: these in proof that my principles of *politics* have sustained no change.[1]—In the present chapter, I have annexed to my Letters from Germany, with particular reference to that, which contains a disquisition on the modern drama, a critique on the Tragedy of Bertram, written within the last twelve months: in proof, that I have been as falsely charged with any fickleness in my principles of *taste*.—The letter was written to a friend:[2] and the apparent abruptness with which it begins, is owing to the omission of the introductory sentences.[3]

You remember, my dear Sir, that Mr. Whitbread,[4] shortly before his death, proposed to the assembled subscribers of Drury-Lane Theatre, that the concern should be farmed to some responsible individual under certain conditions and limitations: and that his proposal was rejected, not without indignation, as subversive of the main object, for the attainment of which the enlightened and patriotic assemblage of philo-dramatists had been induced to risk their subscriptions. Now this object was avowed to be no less than the redemption of the British stage not only from horses, dogs, elephants, and the like zoological rarities, but also from the more pernicious barbarisms and Kotzebuisms[5] in morals and taste. Drury-Lane was to be restored to its former classical renown; Shakspeare, Jonson, and Otway, with the expurgated muses of Vanburgh, Congreve, and Wycherly, were to be re-inaugurated in their rightful dominion over British audiences;[6] and the Herculean process was to commence, by exterminating the speaking monsters imported from the banks of the Danube, compared with which their mute relations, the emigrants from Exeter 'Change, and Polito (late Pidcock's)[7] show-carts, were tame and inoffensive. Could

---

[1] See *Friend* (*CC*) I 326–38.

[2] Actually "To the Editor of the Courier".

[3] I.e. after the opening original sentence (". . . conditions and limitations"). See App C, below.

[4] Samuel Whitbread (1758–1815). See ch 11, above, I 223 n 1, and *EOT* (*CC*) II 436 and n.

[5] On Kotzebue and C's opinion,

see "Satyrane's Letters" II, above, II 185.

[6] Bowdlerised versions of Restoration plays had become common on the London stage since the 1760s. See *EOT* (*CC*) II 437 n 8.

[7] Gilbert Pidcock's Museum, a menagerie in Exeter Change in the Strand, which exhibited exotic animals. It had recently been bought

an heroic project, at once so refined and so arduous, be consistently entrusted to, could its success be rationally expected from, a mercenary manager, at whose critical quarantine the *lucri bonus odor*[a][1] would conciliate a bill of health to the plague in person? No! As the work proposed, such must be the work-masters. Rank, fortune, liberal education, and (their natural accompaniments, or consequences) critical discernment, delicate tact, disinterestedness, unsuspected morals, notorious patriotism, and tried Mæcenasship, these were the recommendations that influenced the votes of the proprietary subscribers of Drury Lane Theatre, these the motives that occasioned the election of its Supreme Committee of Management.[2] This circumstance alone would have excited a strong interest in the public mind, respecting the first production of the Tragic Muse which had been announced under such auspices, and had passed the ordeal of such judgements: and the Tragedy, on which you have requested my judgement, was the work on which the great expectations, justified by so many causes, were doomed at length to settle.

But before I enter on the examination of *Bertram, or the Castle of St. Aldobrand,* I shall interpose a few words, on the phrase *German Drama,* which I hold to be altogether a misnomer. At the time of Lessing, the German stage, such as it was, appears to have been a flat and servile copy of the French. It was Lessing who first introduced the name and the works of Shakespeare to the admiration of the Germans; and I should not perhaps go too far, if I add, that it was Lessing who first proved to all thinking men, even to Shakespeare's own countrymen, the true nature of his apparent irregularities.[3] These, he demonstrated, were deviations only from

[a] *BL* (1817), *Courier*: ordor

by a man named Polito. *EOT* (*CC*) II 437 n 9.

[1] Juvenal 14.204. Tr: "Good smell of profit".

[2] On Whitbread's death (1815) the management of Drury Lane was taken over jointly by Thomas Dibden and Alexander Rae, assisted by a committee consisting of Lord Byron, Lord Essex, George Lamb, Douglas Kinnaird, and Peter Moore. *EOT* (*CC*) II 437 n 11.

[3] The latter part of the sentence is so completely at variance with the facts (the defence and understanding of Shakespeare's "apparent irregularities" are common in eighteenth-century English criticism, especially after 1765, the date of Johnson's Preface) that one can only assume that C at this moment is nodding or partly thinking of something else while dictating to Morgan. In fact, he was himself offended when WW ("Essay, Supplementary to the Preface" 1815) had implied that the Germans were in advance of the English in this respect, though in

the *Accidents* of the Greek Tragedy; and from such accidents as hung a heavy weight on the wings of the Greek Poets, and narrowed their flight within the limits of what we may call the *Heroic Opera*. He proved, that in all the essentials of art, no less than in the truth of nature, the Plays of Shakespeare were incomparably more coincident with the principles of Aristotle, than the productions of Corneille and Racine, notwithstanding the boasted regularity of the latter. Under these convictions, were Lessing's own dramatic works composed. Their deficiency is in depth and in imagination: their excellence is in the construction of the plot; the good sense of the sentiments; the sobriety of the morals; and the high polish of the diction and dialogue. In short, his dramas are the very antipodes of all those which it has been the fashion of late years at once to abuse and to enjoy, under the name of the German Drama. Of this latter, Schiller's *Robbers* was the earliest specimen; the first fruits of his youth (I had almost said of his boyhood) and as such, the pledge, and promise of no ordinary genius.[1] Only as *such*, did the maturer judgement of the author tolerate the Play. During his whole life he expressed himself concerning this production with more than needful asperity, as a monster not less offensive to good taste, than to sound morals; and in his latter years his indignation at the unwonted popularity of the *Robbers* seduced him into the *contrary* extremes, viz. a studied feebleness of interest (as far as the interest was to be derived from incidents and the excitement of curiosity); a diction elaborately metrical; the affectation of rhymes; and the pedantry of the chorus.

But to understand the true character of the *Robbers*, and of the countless imitations which were its spawn, I must inform you, or at least call to your recollection, that about that time, and for some years before it, three of the most popular books in the German language were, the translations of *Young's Night Thoughts*,

---

this case he may have sensed a tribute to the priority of A. W. Schlegel over himself. *CL* IV 839. For Lessing on the unities of time and place as mere consequences of the more important "unity of action", C may be thinking particularly of *Hamburgische Dramaturgie* No 46..

[1] Schiller's *Die Räuber* was published 1781, when he was twenty-two. *Wallenstein*, which C considered "the greatest of his works", appeared in 1798–9. "After this point it was that Goethe and other writers injured by their theories the steadiness and originality of Schiller's mind", leading to "fluctuations" in "principles of composition" such as the attempt to imitate Greek tragedy in *Die Braut von Messina* (1803). *TT* 16 Feb 1833.

Harvey's Meditations, and *Richardson's Clarissa Harlow.*[1] Now we have only to combine the bloated style and peculiar rhythm of Harvey, which is poetic only on account of its utter unfitness for prose, and might as appropriately be called prosaic, from its utter unfitness for poetry; we have only, I repeat, to combine these Harveyisms with the strained thoughts, the figurative metaphysics and solemn epigrams of Young on the one hand; and with the loaded sensibility, the minute detail, the morbid consciousness of every thought and feeling in the whole flux and reflux of the mind,[2] in short the self-involution and dreamlike continuity of Richardson on the other hand;[3] and then to add the horrific incidents, and mysterious villains, (geniuses of supernatural intellect, if you will take the author's words for it, but on a level with the meanest ruffians of the condemned cells, if we are to judge by their actions and contrivances)—to add the ruined castles, the dungeons, the trap-doors, the skeletons, the flesh-and-blood ghosts, and the perpetual moonshine of a modern author, (themselves the literary brood of the *Castle of Otranto,*[4] the translations of which, with the imitations and improvements aforesaid, were about that time beginning to make as much noise in Germany as their originals were making in England),—and as the compound of these ingredients duly mixed, you will recognize the so called *German* Drama. The *Olla Podrida*[5] thus cooked up, was denounced, by the best critics in Germany, as the mere cramps of weakness, and orgasms[6] of a sickly imagination on the part of the author, and the lowest provocation of torpid feeling on that of the readers. The old blunder however, concerning the irregularity and wildness of Shakespeare, in which the German did but echo the French, who again were but the echoes of our own critics, was still in vogue, and Shakespeare was quoted as authority for the most anti-

---

[1] Edward Young's (1683–1765) *The Complaint, or Night Thoughts on Life, Death, and Immortality* (1742–5) was translated into German in 1752; James Hervey's (1714–58) *Meditations among the Tombs* (1748) in 1755; and Richardson's *Clarissa* (1748) in 1748–52.

[2] On "flux and reflux" cf ch 22, above, II 147.

[3] For C's dislike of Richardson despite his admiration ("so oozy,

hypocritical, praise-mad, canting, envious, concupiscent"), see esp *CN* I 2471 and *TT* 5 Jul 1834.

[4] The famous "Gothic novel" (1765) by Horace Walpole (1717–97).

[5] A Spanish stew of meat and mixed vegetables.

[6] C, however indignant, is not using the word in the sense common now but as in *OED* 1 ("Immoderate or violent excitement; rage, fury").

Shakspearean Drama. We have indeed two poets who wrote as one, near the age of Shakespeare, to whom (as the worst characteristic of their writings), the Coryphæus[1] of the present Drama may challenge the honour of being a poor relation, or impoverished descendant. For if we would charitably consent to forget the comic humour, the wit, the felicities of style, in other words, *all* the poetry, and nine-tenths of all the genius of Beaumont and Fletcher, that which would remain becomes a Kotzebue.

The so-called *German* Drama, therefore, is *English* in its origin, *English* in its *materials*, and *English* by re-adoption; and till we can prove that Kotzebue, or any of the whole breed of Kotzebues, whether dramatists or romantic writers, or writers of romantic dramas, were ever admitted to any other shelf in the libraries of well-educated Germans than were occupied by their originals, and apes' apes in their mother country, we should submit to carry our own brat on our own shoulders; or rather consider it as a lackgrace returned from transportation with such improvements only in growth and manners as young transported convicts usually come home with.

I know nothing that contributes more to a clear insight into the true nature of any literary phenomenon, than the comparison of it with some elder production, the *likeness* of which is *striking*, yet only *apparent*: while the *difference* is *real*.[2] In the present case this opportunity is furnished us, by the old Spanish play, entitled *Atheista Fulminato*, formerly, and perhaps still, acted in the churches and monasteries of Spain, and which, under various names (*Don Juan, the Libertine, &c.*) has had its day of favour in every country throughout Europe.[3] A popularity so extensive, and

---

[1] The leader of the chorus in Greek drama. He is referring to Kotzebue, "the German Beaumont and Fletcher" but without their poetic and comic powers. See "Satyrane's Letters" II, above, II 185.

[2] On "likeness" and "difference" see ch 14, above, II 16–17 and nn 2, 7.

[3] C helped to popularise the idea that there was an early Spanish play of this title about Don Juan Tenorio. The story supposedly goes back to the fourteenth century, though Oscar Mandel *The Theatre of Don Juan* (Lincoln, Neb 1963) 3ff finds that that was a legend, propagated by L. Viardot with no basis in fact. Cf Shadwell *The Libertine* Preface: "The story from which I took the hint of this Play, is famous all over *Spain, Italy,* and *France* . . . And I have been told by a worthy Gentleman, that many years ago (when first a Play was made upon this Story in *Italy*) he had seen it acted there by the name of *Atheisto Fulminato,* in Churches, on *Sundays,* as a part of Devotion . . .". Gabriel Téllez (c 1583–1648), known as

of a work so grotesque and extravagant, claims and merits philosophical attention and investigation. The first point to be noticed is, that the play is throughout *imaginative*. Nothing of it belongs to the real world, but the names of the places and persons. The comic parts, equally with the tragic; the living, equally with the defunct characters, are creatures of the brain; as little amenable to the rules of ordinary probability, as the *Satan* of *Paradise Lost*, or the *Caliban* of the *Tempest*, and therefore to be understood and judged of as impersonated *abstractions*. Rank, fortune, wit, talent, acquired knowledge, and liberal accomplishments, with beauty of person, vigorous health, and constitutional hardihood,—all these advantages, elevated by the habits and sympathies of noble birth and national character, are supposed to have combined in *Don Juan*, so as to give him the means of carrying into all its *practical* consequences the doctrine of a godless nature, as the sole ground and efficient cause not only of all things, events, and appearances, but likewise of all our thoughts, sensations, impulses, and actions. Obedience to nature is the only virtue: the gratification of the passions and appetites her only dictate: each individual's self-will the sole organ through which nature utters her commands, and

> Self-contradiction is the only wrong!
> For by the laws of spirit, in the right
> Is every individual character
> That acts in strict consistence with itself.[1]

That speculative opinions, however impious and daring they

Tirso de Molina, created the character and legend of Don Juan, in his *El Burlador de Sevilla y convidado de piedra* (1630) (there is no basis to the assertion that the story of Don Juan being carried off to hell by the statue of his victim is found in *Las Cronicas de Sevilla*). The "legend" was later acted in Italy by the commedia dell' arte as *Convitato di pietra*. The title mentioned by C was of a seventeenth-century Italian version, also acted by the commedia dell' arte, *L'Ateista fulminato*. Enzo Petraccone *La Commedia dell' arte* (Naples 1927) 374–82; Georges Gendarme de Bévotte *La Légende de Don Juan* (Paris 1906) 21–30.

The Libertine (1675) of Thomas Shadwell (c 1642–92), from which C later quotes, is an English version of a slightly later date than the Italian, and some of C's information about the play, including the fact that the play was occasionally acted in churches, is taken from Shadwell's Preface. The classic treatments of the theme are Molière's *Don Juan, ou le festin de pierre* (1665) and Mozart's *Don Giovanni* (1787).

[1] *Piccolomini* IV vii 191–4: *PW* (EHC) II 703. C here puts the last of his four lines first and may be quoting from memory.

may be, are not always followed by correspondent conduct, is most true, as well as that they can scarcely in any instance be *systematically* realized, on account of their unsuitableness to human nature and to the institutions of society. It can be hell, only where it is *all* hell: and a separate world of devils is necessary for the existence of any one complete devil. But on the other hand it is no less clear, nor, with the biography of Carrier[1] and his fellow-atheists before us, can it be denied without wilful blindness, that the (so called) *system of nature*, (i.e. materialism, with the utter rejection of moral responsibility, of a present providence, and of both present and future retribution) may influence the characters and actions of individuals, and even of communities, to a degree that almost does away the distinction between men and devils, and will make the page of the future historian resemble the narration of a madman's dreams. It is not the *wickedness* of *Don Juan*, therefore, which constitutes the character an *abstraction*, and removes it from the rules of probability; but the rapid succession of the correspondent acts and incidents, his intellectual superiority, and the splendid accumulation of his gifts and desirable qualities, as co-existent with *entire* wickedness in one and the same person. But this likewise is the very circumstance which gives to this strange play its charm and universal interest. *Don Juan* is, from beginning to end, an *intelligible* character: as much so as the *Satan* of Milton. The poet asks only of the reader, what as a poet he is privileged to ask: viz. that sort of negative faith in the existence of such a being, which we willingly give to productions *professedly ideal*,[2] and a disposition to the same state of feeling, as that with which we contemplate the *idealized* figures of the Apollo Belvedere, and the Farnese Hercules. What the Hercules is to the *eye* in *corporeal* strength, *Don Juan* is to the *mind* in strength of *character*. The ideal consists in the happy balance of the generic with the individual.[3] The former makes the character representative and

---

[1] Jean Baptiste Carrier (1756–94), the French Revolutionist and Terrorist, who established the Legion of Marat in order to kill as quickly as possible the prisoners crowded in the jails, having many of them shot *en masse* and others sunk in the Loire. He was himself guillotined 16 Nov 1794.

[2] See esp ch 14, above, II 6–7 and n 2.

[3] Cf above, II 45–6, and *CN* II 2828 and n: "Ideal = the subtle hieroglyphical *felt*-by-all though not without abstruse and difficult analysis detected & understood, consonance of the *physiognomic* total & substance (Stoff) with the obvious

symbolical,[1] therefore instructive; because, *mutatis mutandis*, it is applicable to whole classes of men. The latter gives it[a] its *living* interest; for nothing *lives* or is *real*, but as definite and individual. To understand this compleatly, the reader need only recollect the specific state of his feelings, when in looking at a picture of the historic (more properly of the poetic or heroic) class, he objects to a particular figure as being too much of a *portrait*; and this interruption of his complacency he feels without the least reference to, or the least acquaintance with, any person in real life whom he might recognize in this figure. It is enough that such a figure is not *ideal*: and therefore not ideal, because one of the two factors or elements of the *ideal* is in excess. A similar and more powerful objection he would feel towards a set of figures which were *mere* abstractions, like those of Cipriani,[2] and what have been called Greek forms and faces, i.e. outlines drawn according to a recipe. *These* again are not *ideal*; because in these the *other* element is in excess. "*Forma formans per formam formatam translucens,*"[3] is the definition and perfection of *ideal* art.

---

[a] *BL* (1817) omits; in *Courier*

---

*Patho*gnomic . . .". "It was S[hakespeare]'s prerogative to have the *universal* which is potentially in each *particular,* opened out to him—the *homme generale* not as an abstraction of observation (from a variety of men,) but as the Substance capable of endless modifications of which his own personal Existence was but one—& to use *this one* as the eye that beheld the other, and as the Tongue that could convey the discovery". BM Add MS 34225 f 61ᵛ, used in Lect 7 of 17 Feb 1818, quoted (var) in *Misc C* 44. *Lects 1808–19* (*CC*) ms.

[1] Cf C's definition in *SM* of a true "symbol" as "characterized by a translucence of the Special in the Individual or of the General in the Especial or of the Universal in the General". *SM* (*CC*) 30.

[2] Giovanni Battista Cipriani (1727–85), Italian painter and engraver, who spent the latter half of his life in England and was noted for

his mannered, decorative style. Cf C's remark on the need of the artist to master the *natura naturans:* "If he proceeds from a Form, that answers to the notion of Beauty, namely, the many seen as one— what an emptiness, an unreality—as in Cipriani". *CN* III 4397 f 50ᵛ. Cf *PA: BL* (1907) II 257.

[3] "The forming form shining through the formed form". C probably uses Latin to give the remark aphoristic strength or authority. The concept, especially associated with Plotinus and enriched by the German organicists from Jakob Böhme to Schelling, is central to C's mature thinking about the arts. *BL* (1847) II 266 adds a footnote, presumably from an annotation on *BL* by C: "Better thus: *Forma specifica per formam individualem translucens:* or better yet—*Species individualizata, sive Individuum cuilibet Speciei determinatæ in omni parte correspondens et quasi versione*

This excellence is so happily achieved in the *Don Juan*, that it is capable of interesting without poetry, nay, even without words, as in our pantomime of that name.[1] We see clearly how the character is formed; and the very extravagance of the incidents, and the super-human *entireness* of *Don Juan's* agency, prevents the wickedness from shocking our minds to any painful degree. (We do not *believe* it enough for this effect; no, not even with that kind of temporary and negative belief or acquiescence which I have described above.) Meantime the qualities of his character are too desirable, too flattering to our pride and our wishes, not to make up on this side as much additional faith as was lost on the other. There is no danger (thinks the spectator or reader) of *my* becoming such a monster of iniquity as *Don Juan*! *I* never shall be an atheist! *I* shall never disallow all distinction between right and wrong! *I* have not the least inclination to be so outrageous a drawcansir[2] in my love affairs! But to possess such a power of captivating and enchanting the affections of the other sex! to be capable of inspiring in a charming and even a virtuous woman, a love so deep, and so entirely personal to *me*! that even my worst vices, (if I *were* vicious) even my cruelty and perfidy, (if I *were* cruel and perfidious) could not eradicate the passion! To be so loved for my *own self*, that even with a distinct knowledge of my character, she yet died to save me! this, sir, takes hold of two sides of our nature, the better and the worse. For the heroic disinterestedness, to which love can transport a woman, can not be contemplated without an honourable emotion of reverence towards womanhood: and on the other hand, it is among the mysteries,[a] and abides in the dark ground-work of our nature, to crave an

---

[a] *BL* (1817): miseries; *Courier*: mysteries

---

quadam eum interpretans et repetens." ("The specific form [form of the species] shining through the individual form" . . . "The Species made individual, or the Individual corresponding in every part to any determined Species, and as if by a kind of translation interpreting and repeating it.")
[1] The pantomime *Don Juan, or The Libertine Destroyed* (first produced by David Garrick) was often performed at Drury Lane Theatre.

See *An Historical Account of the Tragi-comic Pantomime, entituled Don Juan, or The Libertine Destroyed* (1782). There were several versions of the tale in pantomime performed at other theatres, e.g. at the Royalty Theatre in 1784, etc.
[2] A braggart in Buckingham's *Rehearsal* who ends up in battle killing all the combatants on both sides. Cf Byron *Don Juan* canto XI st 51 lines 1–2.

outward confirmation of that *something* within us, which is our *very self*, that something, not *made up* of our qualities and relations, but itself the supporter and substantial basis of all these. Love *me*, and not my qualities, may be a vicious and an insane wish, but it is not a wish wholly without a meaning.[1]

Without power, virtue would be insufficient and incapable of revealing its being. It would resemble the magic transformation of Tasso's heroine into a tree, in which she could only groan and bleed.[2] (Hence power is necessarily an object of our desire and of our admiration.) But of all power, that of the mind is, on every account, the grand desideratum of human ambition. We shall be as Gods in knowledge,[3] was and must have been the *first* temptation: and the co-existence of great intellectual lordship with guilt has never been adequately represented without exciting the strongest interest, and for this reason, that in this bad and heterogeneous co-ordination we can contemplate the intellect of man more exclusively as a separate self-subsistence, than in its proper state of subordination to his own conscience, or to the will of an infinitely superior being.

This is the sacred charm of Shakespeare's male characters in general. They are all cast in the mould of Shakespear's own gigantic intellect; and this is the open attraction of his *Richard, Iago, Edmund,* &c.[4] in particular. But again; of all intellectual power, that of superiority to the fear of the invisible world is the most dazzling. Its influence is abundantly proved by the one circumstance, that it can bribe us into a voluntary submission of our better knowledge, into suspension of all our judgment derived from

[1] Cf C on his love for SH: ". . . as if a human Soul were made like a watch, or loved for this & that tangible & verbally expressible quality!" *CN* III 3991; cf also 3442.

[2] Torquato Tasso *Gerusalemme liberata* XIII sts 38ff. *BL* (1847) II 267n. Cf C on his health in later life: "I . . . have felt, even in the intervals of Freedom from Pain and distressful Feelings, just as the imprisoned Spirit in the enchanted Wood of Tasso, or in Virgil's Tree—like a naked Intelligence, a Mind detached from Life". To C. A. Tulk 17 Aug 1826: *CL* VI 605.

[3] Cf Gen 3.5.

[4] Cf HCR's report of C's remarks on 23 Dec 1810: "Shakespeare, he said, delighted in portraying characters in which the intellectual powers are found in a pre-eminent degree, while the moral faculties are wanting, at the same time that he taught the superiority of moral greatness. . . . Iago's most marked feature is his delight in governing by fraud and superior understanding the noble-minded and generous Moor. In Richard III. cruelty is less the prominent trait than pride . . .". *CRD* I 309.

constant experience, and enable us to peruse with the liveliest interest the wildest tales of ghosts, wizards, genii, and secret talismans. On this propensity, so deeply rooted in our nature, a specific *dramatic* probability may be raised by a true poet, if the whole of his work be in harmony: a *dramatic* probability, sufficient for dramatic pleasure, even when the component characters and incidents border on impossibility.[1] The poet does not require us to be awake and believe; he solicits us only to yield ourselves to a dream; and this too with our eyes open, and with our judgment *perdue* behind the curtain, ready to awaken us at the first motion of our will: and meantime, only, not to *dis*believe. And in such a state of mind, who but must be impressed with the cool intrepidity of *Don John* on the appearance of his father's ghost:

> GHOST.—Monster! behold these wounds!
> D. JOHN.—I do! They were well meant and well performed, I see.
> GHOST.————Repent, repent of all thy villanies.
> My clamorous blood to heaven for vengeance cries,
> Heaven will pour out his judgments on you all.
> Hell gapes for you, for you each fiend doth call,
> And hourly waits your unrepenting fall.
> You with eternal horrors they'll torment,
> Except of all your crimes you suddenly repent.
> (Ghost sinks.)
> D. JOHN.—Farewell, thou art a foolish ghost. Repent, quoth he! what could this mean? our senses are all in a mist sure.
> D. ANTONIO.—(one of D. Juan's reprobate companions.)
> They are not! 'Twas a ghost.
> D. LOPEZ.—(another reprobate.) I ne'er believed those foolish tales before.
> D. JOHN.—Come! 'Tis no matter. Let it be what it will, it must be natural.
> D. ANT.—And nature is unalterable in us too.
> D. JOHN.—'Tis true! The nature of a ghost can not change our's.[2]

[1] C here repeats one of the basic tenets of Aristotle: "The poet should prefer probable impossibilities to improbable possibilities." *Poetics* 24.10. Thus a character such as Ariel or Caliban in *The Tempest* is "impossible" in real life, but their actions and statements are consistent with their characters if they did exist. Hence they are "probable impossi-bilities". On the other hand an "improbable possibility" would be a freak accident in the plot, which is not impossible, or a character who could indeed exist but whose actions and speech are poorly and "improbably" portrayed.

[2] Shadwell *The Libertine* II (with the omission of lines before and after the Ghost's "repent" speech).

Who also can deny a portion of sublimity to the tremendous consistency with which he stands out the last fearful trial, like a second Prometheus?

> Chorus of Devils.
>
> S T A T U E - G H O S T.—Will you not relent and feel remorse?
> D . J O H N.—Could'st thou bestow another heart on me I might. But with this heart I have, I can not.
> D . L O P E Z.—These things are prodigious.
> D . A N T O N.—I have a sort of grudging to relent, but something holds me back.
> D . L O P.—If we could, 'tis now too late. I will not.
> D . A N T.—We defy thee!
> G H O S T.—Perish ye impious wretches, go and find the punishments laid up in store for you!
> (Thunder and lightning. D. Lop. and D. Ant. are swallowed up.)
> G H O S T to D . J O H N.—Behold their dreadful fates, and know that thy last moment's come!
> D . J O H N.—Think not to fright me, foolish ghost; I'll break your marble body in pieces and pull down your horse.
> (Thunder and lightning—chorus of devils, &c.)
> D . J O H N.—These things I see with wonder, but no fear.
> Were all the elements to be confounded,
> And shuffled all into their former chaos;
> Were seas of sulphur flaming round about me,
> And all mankind roaring within those fires,
> I could not fear, or feel the least remorse.
> To the last instant I would dare thy power.
> Here I stand firm, and all thy threats contemn.[a]
> Thy murderer (*to the ghost of one whom he had murdered*)
> Stands here! Now do thy worst!
> (*He is swallowed up in a cloud of fire.*)[1]

In fine the character of *Don John* consists in the union of every thing desirable to human nature, as *means*, and which therefore by the well known law of association become at length desirable on their own account. On their own account, and in their own dignity they are here displayed, as being employed to *ends* so *un*human, that in the effect, they appear almost as *means* without an *end*. The ingredients too are mixed in the happiest proportion, so as to uphold and relieve each other—more especially in that

---

a BL (1817), *Courier*: condemn

[1] Shadwell *The Libertine* v ii   Don John's final speech).
(with the omission of a line before

constant interpoise of wit, gaiety, and social generosity, which prevents the criminal, even in his most atrocious moments, from sinking into the mere ruffian, as far at least, as our *imagination* sits in judgment. Above all, the fine suffusion through the whole, with the characteristic manners and feelings, of a highly bred gentleman gives life to the drama. Thus having invited the *statue-ghost* of the governor whom he had murdered, to supper, which invitation the marble ghost accepted by a nod of the head, *Don John* has prepared a banquet.

> D . J O H N .—Some wine, sirrah! Here's to Don Pedro's ghost—he should have been welcome.
> D . L o p .—The rascal is afraid of you after death.
> *(One knocks hard at the door.)*
>
> D . J O H N .—*(to the servant)*—Rise and do your duty.
> S E R V .—Oh the devil, the devil! *(marble ghost enters.)*
> D . J O H N .—Ha! 'tis the ghost! Let's rise and receive him! Come Governor,[a] you are welcome, sit there; if we had thought you would have come, we would have staid for you.
>
> *   *   *   *   *   *   *
>
> Here Governor, your health! Friends put it about! Here's excellent meat, taste of this ragout. Come, I'll help you, come eat and let old quarrels be forgotten.
> *(The ghost threatens him with vengeance.)*
>
> D . J O H N .—We are too much confirmed—curse on this dry discourse. Come,[a] here's to your mistress, you had one when you were living: not forgetting your sweet sister. *(devils enter.)*
> D . J O H N .—Are these some of your retinue? Devils say you? I'm sorry I have no burnt brandy to treat 'em with, that's drink fit for devils. &c.[1]

Nor is the scene from which we quote interesting, in *dramatic* probability alone; it is susceptible likewise of a sound moral; of a moral that has more than common claims on the notice of a too numerous class, who are ready to receive the qualities of gentlemanly courage, and scrupulous honor (in all the recognized laws of honor,) as the *substitutes* of virtue, instead of its *ornaments*.[2] This, indeed, is the moral value of the play at large, and that which

---

[a] *BL* (1817) omits comma; in *Courier*

[1] Shadwell *The Libertine* IV iv (var, with many omitted lines).
[2] C echoes the close of Burke's concluding speech to the House of Lords in the impeachment of Warren Hastings (16 Jun 1794): "May you stand, not as a substitute for virtue, but as an ornament of virtue . . .". *Works* (1865–7) XII 398.

places it at a world's distance from the spirit of modern jacobinism. The latter introduces to us clumsy copies of these showy instrumental qualities, in order to *reconcile* us to vice and want of principle; while the *Atheista Fulminato* presents an exquisite portraiture of the same qualities, in all their gloss and glow, but presents them for the sole purpose of displaying their hollowness, and in order to put us on our guard by demonstrating their utter indifference to vice and virtue, whenever these, and the like accomplishments are contemplated for themselves alone.

Eighteen years ago I observed,[1] that the whole secret of the modern jacobinical drama, (which, and not the German, is its appropriate designation,) and of all its popularity, consists in the confusion and subversion of the natural order of things in their causes and effects: namely, in the excitement of surprise by representing the qualities of liberality, refined feeling, and a nice sense of honour (those things rather which pass amongst us for such) in persons and in classes where experience teaches us least to expect them; and by rewarding with all the sympathies which are the due of virtue, those criminals whom law, reason, and religion have excommunicated from our esteem.

This of itself would lead me back to *Bertram*, or the *Castle of St. Aldobrand*; but, in my own mind, this tragedy was brought into connection with the *Libertine*, (Shadwell's adaptation of the *Atheista Fulminato* to the English stage in the reign of Charles the Second,) by the fact, that our modern drama is taken, in the substance of it, from the first scene of the third act of the *Libertine*. But with what palpable superiority of judgment in the original! Earth and hell, men and spirits, are up in arms against *Don John*: the two former acts of the play have not only prepared us for the supernatural, but accustomed us to the prodigious. It is, therefore, neither more nor less than we anticipate when the *Captain* exclaims: "In all the dangers I have been, such horrors I never knew. I am quite unmanned;" and when the *Hermit* says, "that he had beheld the ocean in wildest rage, yet ne'er before saw a storm so dreadful, such horrid flashes of lightning, and such claps of thunder, were never in my remembrance."[2] And *Don John's*

---

[1] In the letter later incorporated in "Satyrane's Letters" II, above, II 188–9.

[2] Shadwell *The Libertine* III i (var).

burst[a] of startling impiety is equally intelligible in its motive, as dramatic in its effect.

But what is there to account for the prodigy of the tempest at *Bertram's* shipwreck? It is a mere supernatural effect without even a hint of any supernatural agency; a prodigy without any circumstance mentioned that is prodigious; and a miracle introduced without a ground, and ending without a result. Every event and every scene of the play might have taken place as well if *Bertram* and his vessel had been driven in by a common hard gale, or from want of provisions. The first act would have indeed lost its greatest and most *sonorous* picture; a scene for the sake of a scene, without a word spoken; as *such*, therefore, (a rarity without a precedent) we must take it, and be thankful! In the opinion of not a few, it was, in every sense of the word, the best scene in the play. I am quite certain it was the most *innocent*: and the steady, quiet uprightness of the flame of the wax-candles which the monks held over the roaring billows amid the storm of wind and rain, was *really* miraculous.

The Sicilian sea coast: a convent of monks: night: a most portentous, unearthly storm: a vessel is wrecked: contrary to all human expectation, one man saves himself by his prodigious powers as a swimmer, aided by the peculiarity of his destination—

> Prior———— All, all did perish—
> 1st Monk—Change, change those drenched weeds—
> Prior—I wist not of them—every soul did perish—
> Enter 3d Monk hastily.
> 3d Monk—No, there was one did battle with the storm
> With careless desperate force; full many times
> His life was won and lost, as tho' he recked not—
> No hand did aid him, and he aided none—
> Alone be breasted the broad wave, alone
> That man was saved.[1]

Well! This man is led in by the monks, supposed dripping wet, and to very natural enquiries he either remains silent, or gives most brief and surly answers, and after three or four of these half-line courtesies, *"dashing off the monks"* who had saved him, he exclaims in the true sublimity of our modern misanthropic heroism—

[a] *BL* (1817), *Courier*: bursts

[1] *Bertram* I iii 2–9.

Off! ye are men—there's poison in your touch.
But I must yield, for this *(What?)* hath left me strengthless.[1]

So end the three first scenes. In the next (the Castle of St. Aldobrand,) we find the servants there equally frightened with this
unearthly storm, though wherein it differed from other violent
storms we are not told, except that Hugo informs us, page 9—

> Piet.—Hugo, well met. Does e'en thy age bear
> Memory of so terrible a storm?
> Hugo—They have been frequent lately.
> Piet.—They are ever so in Sicily.
> Hugo—So it is said. But storms when I was young
> Would still pass o'er like Nature's fitful fevers,
> And rendered all more wholesome. Now their rage
> Sent thus unseasonable and profitless
> Speaks like the threats of heaven.[2]

A most perplexing theory of Sicilian storms is this of old Hugo!
and what is very remarkable, not apparently founded on any great
familiarity of his own with this troublesome article. For when
Pietro asserts the *"ever more frequency"* of tempests in Sicily, the
old man professes to know nothing more of the fact, but by hearsay. "So it is said."—But why he assumed this storm to be unseasonable, and on what he grounded his prophecy (for the storm is
still in full fury) that it would be profitless, and without the physical
powers common to all other violent sea-winds in purifying the
atmosphere, we are left in the dark; as well concerning the particular points in which he knew it (during its continuance) to differ
from those that he had been acquainted with in his youth. We are
at length introduced to the Lady Imogine, who, we learn, had not
rested *"through"* the night,[3] not on account of the tempest, for

> Long 'ere the storm arose, her restless gestures
> Forbade all hope to see her blest with sleep.[4]

Sitting at a table, and looking at a portrait, she informs us—First,
that portrait-painters may make a portrait from memory—

> The limner's art may trace the absent feature.[5]

For surely these words could never mean, that a painter may have

1 I iii 39–40.   4 I iv 32–3.
2 I iv 12–20.   5 I v 2.
3 I iv 31.

a person sit to him who afterwards may leave the room or perhaps the country? Second, that a portrait-painter can enable a mourning lady to possess a good likeness of her absent lover, but that the portrait-painter cannot, and who shall—

> Restore the *scenes* in which they met and parted? [1]

The natural answer would have been—Why the scene-painter to be sure! But this unreasonable lady requires in addition sundry things to be painted that have neither lines nor colours—

> The thoughts, the recollections sweet and bitter,
> Or the Elysian dreams of lovers when they loved.[2]

Which last sentence must be supposed to mean; *when they were present, and* making love to each other.—Then, if this portrait could speak, it would "acquit the faith of womankind." [3] How? Had she remained constant? No, she has been married to another man, whose wife she now is. How then? Why, that, in spite of her marriage vow, she had continued to yearn and crave for her former lover—

> This has her body, that her mind:
> Which has the better bargain? [4]

The lover, however, was not contented with this precious arrangement, as we shall soon find. The lady proceeds to inform us, that during the many years of their separation, there have happened in the different parts of the world, a number of "*such things*"; even such, as in a course of years always have, and till the Millennium, doubtless always will happen somewhere or other. Yet this passage, both in language and in metre, is perhaps among the best parts of the Play. The Lady's loved companion and most esteemed attendant, Clotilda, now enters and explains this love and esteem by proving herself a most passive and dispassionate listener, as well as a brief and lucky querist, who asks by *chance*, questions that we should have thought made for the very sake of the answers. In short, she very much reminds us of those puppet-heroines, for whom the showman contrives to dialogue without any skill in

---

[1] *Bertram* I v 5 (var: "restore" from line 8).

[2] I v 6–7 (var).

[3] I v 12.

[4] William Congreve (1670–1729) "Song: Tell me no more I am de- ceived" lines 13–14 (altered): "I take her body, you her mind, | Who has the better bargain?" In *B Poets* VII 546. The song had been put to music by Henry Purcell.

ventriloquism. This, notwithstanding, is the best scene in the Play, and though crowded with solecisms, corrupt diction, and offences against metre, would possess merits sufficient to outweigh them, if we could suspend the moral sense during the perusal. It tells well and passionately the preliminary circumstances, and thus over-comes the main difficulty of most first acts, viz. that of retrospective narration. It tells us of her having been honourably addressed by a noble youth, of rank and fortune vastly superior to her own: of their mutual love, heightened on her part by gratitude; of his loss of his sovereign's favour: his disgrace; attainder; and flight; that he (thus degraded) sank into a vile ruffian, the chieftain of a murderous banditti; and that from the habitual indulgence of the most reprobate habits and ferocious passions, he had become so changed, even in his appearance and features,

> That she who bore him had recoiled from him,
> Nor known the alien visage of her child,
> Yet still *she* (Imogine) lov'd him.[1]

She is compelled by the silent entreaties of a father, perishing with "bitter shameful want on the cold earth,"[2] to give her hand, with a heart thus irrecoverably pre-engaged, to Lord Aldobrand, the enemy of her lover, even to the very man who had baffled his ambitious schemes, and was, at the present time, entrusted with the execution of the sentence of death which had been passed on Bertram. Now, the proof of "woman's love," so industriously held forth for the sympathy, if not the esteem of the audience, consists in this, that though Bertram had become a robber and a murderer by trade, a ruffian in manners, yea, with form and features at which his own mother could not but "recoil," yet she (Lady Imogine) "the wife of a most noble, honoured Lord,"[3] estimable as a man, exemplary and affectionate as a husband, and the fond father of her only child—that she, notwithstanding all this, striking her heart, dares to say to it—

> But thou art Bertram's still, and Bertram's ever.[4]

A Monk now enters, and entreats in his Prior's name for the wonted hospitality, and "free *noble usage*"[5] of the Castle of St. Aldo-brand for some wretched ship-wrecked souls, and from this we

---

[1] *Bertram* I v 67–9 (var).
[2] I v 108–9 (var).
[3] I v 120.
[4] I v 122.
[5] I v 153.

learn, for the first time, to our infinite surprize, that notwithstanding the supernaturalness of the storm aforesaid, not only Bertram, but the whole of his gang, had been saved, by what means we are left to conjecture, and can only conclude that they had all the same desperate swimming powers, and the same saving destiny as the Hero, Bertram himself. So ends the first act, and with it the tale of the events, both those with which the Tragedy begins, and those which had occurred previous to the date of its commencement. The second displays Bertram in disturbed sleep, which the Prior who hangs over him prefers calling a "starting trance,"[1] and with a strained voice, that would have awakened one of the seven sleepers,[2] observes to the audience—

> How the lip works! How the bare teeth *do* grind!
> And beaded drops course * down his writhen brow![5]

The dramatic effect of which passage we not only concede to the admirers of this Tragedy, but acknowledge the further advantage of preparing the audience for the most surprising series of wry faces, proflated mouths, and lunatic gestures that were ever "*launched*" on an audience to "† *sear the sense.*"

> * ———————— The big round tears
> Coursed one another down his innocent nose
> In piteous chase,[3]

says Shakespeare of a wounded stag hanging its head over a stream: naturally, from the position of the head, and most beautifully, from the association of the preceding image, of the chase, in which "the poor sequester'd stag from the hunter's aim had ta'en a hurt."[4] In the supposed position of Bertram, the metaphor, if not false, loses all the propriety of the original.

† Among a number of other instances of words chosen without reason, Imogine in the first act declares, that thunder-storms were not able to intercept her prayers for "the desperate man, in desperate *ways* who dealt"——

> Yea, when the launched bolt did sear her sense,
> Her soul's deep orisons were breathed for him;

i.e. when a red-hot bolt launched at her from a thunder-cloud had cauterized her sense, in plain English, burnt her eyes out of her head, she kept still praying on.

> Was not *this* love? Yea, thus doth woman[a] love![6]

> ᵃ *BL* (1817): women; *Courier*: woman

[1] *Bertram* II i 1.
[2] The seven Christian youths who fled the Decian persecution, were walled up in a cave, and slept for over two hundred years.
[3] Shakespeare *As You Like It* II i 38–40.
[4] Ibid II i 33–4 (var).
[5] *Bertram* II i 4–5.
[6] I v 77–9 (var).

> Prior.—I will awake him from this *horrid trance,*
> This is no natural sleep! Ho, *wake thee,* stranger![1]

This is rather a whimsical application of the verb reflex we must confess, though we remember a similar transfer of the agent to the patient in a manuscript Tragedy, in which the Bertram of the piece, prostrating a man with a single blow of his fist exclaims—"Knock me thee down, then ask thee if thou liv'st."—Well; the stranger obeys, and whatever his sleep might have been, his waking was perfectly natural, for lethargy itself could not withstand the scolding stentorship of Mr. Holland, the Prior. We next learn from the best authority, his own confession, that the misanthropic hero, whose destiny was incompatible with drowning, is Count Bertram, who not only reveals his past fortunes, but avows with open atrocity, his satanic hatred of Imogine's Lord, and his frantic thirst of revenge; and so the raving character raves, and the scolding character scolds—and what else? Does not the Prior *act*? Does he not send for a posse of constables or thief-takers to handcuff the villain, and take him either to Bedlam or Newgate? Nothing of the kind; the author preserves the unity of character, and the scolding Prior from first to last does nothing but scold, with the exception indeed of the last scene of the last act, in which with a most surprizing revolution he whines, weeps and kneels to the condemned blaspheming assassin out of pure affection to the high-hearted man, the sublimity of whose angel-sin rivals the star-bright apostate, (i.e. who was as proud as Lucifer, and as wicked as the Devil), and "had thrilled him," (Prior Holland aforesaid) with wild admiration.[2]

Accordingly in the very next scene, we have this tragic Macheath, with his whole gang, in the Castle of St. Aldobrand, without any attempt on the Prior's part either to prevent him, or to put the mistress and servants of the Castle on their guard against their new inmates, though he (the Prior) knew, and confesses that he knew that Bertram's "fearful mates"[3] were assassins so habituated and naturalized to guilt, that—

> When their *drenched hold* forsook both gold and gear,
> They griped their daggers with a murderer's instinct;[4]

and though he also knew, that Bertram was the leader of a band

---

[1] II i 6–7.
[2] III ii 68–71.
[3] III ii 40.
[4] III ii 43–4.

whose trade was blood. To the Castle however he goes, thus with the holy Prior's consent, if not with his assistance; and thither let us follow him.

No sooner is our hero safely housed in the castle of St. Aldobrand, than he attracts the notice of the lady and her confidante, by his "wild and terrible dark eyes," "muffled form," "fearful form," * "darkly wild," "proudly stern," [1] and the like common place indefinites, seasoned by merely verbal antitheses, and at best, copied with very slight change, from the CONRADE of Southey's Joan of Arc. [2] The lady Imogine, who has been (as is the case, she tells us, with all soft and solemn spirits,) *worshipping* the moon on a terrace or rampart within view of the castle, insists on having an interview with our hero, and this too tete-a-tete. [3] Would the reader learn why and wherefore the confidante is excluded, who very properly remonstrates against such "conference, alone, at night, with one who bears such fearful form," the reason follows— "why, *therefore* send him!" I say, *follows*, because the next line, "all things of fear have lost their power over me," [4] is separated from the former by a break or pause, and besides that it is a very poor answer to the danger, is no answer at all to the gross indelicacy of this wilful exposure. We must therefore regard it as a mere after-thought, that a little softens the rudeness, but adds nothing to the weight of that exquisite woman's reason aforesaid. And so exit Clotilda and enter Bertram, who "stands without looking at her," [5] that is, with his lower limbs forked, his arms akimbo, his side to the lady's front, the whole figure resembling an inverted Y. He is soon however roused from the state surly to the state frantic,

---

* This sort of repetition is one of this writer's peculiarities, and there is scarce a page which does not furnish one or more instances—Ex. gr. in the first page or two. Act I, line 7th, "and *deemed* that I might sleep."—Line 10, "Did rock and *quiver* in the bickering *glare*."—Lines 14, 15, 16, "But by the momently *gleams* of sheeted blue, Did the pale marbles *glare* so *sternly* on me, I almost *deemed* they lived."—Line 37, "The *glare* of Hell."—Line 35, "O holy Prior, this is no *earthly storm*."—Line 38, "This is no *earthly storm*."—Line 42, "*Dealing* with us."—Line 43, "*Deal* thus sternly."— Line 44, "Speak! thou hast *something seen*!"—"A *fearful sight*!"—Line 45, "What hast thou *seen*? A piteous, *fearful sight*."—Line 48, "*quivering gleams*."—Line 50, "In the hollow *pauses of the storm*."—Line 61, "The *pauses of the storm*, &c."

[1] *Bertram* II iii 39, 40 (var), 55, 60.
[2] *Joan of Arc* (Bristol 1796).
[3] *Bertram* II iii.
[4] II iii 54–6 (var).
[5] Stage direction after II iii 61.

and then follow raving, yelling, cursing, she fainting, he relenting, in runs Imogine's child, squeaks "mother!" He snatches it up, and with a "God bless thee, child! Bertram has kissed thy child,"— the curtain drops.[1] The third act is short, and short be our account of it. It introduces Lord Aldobrand on his road homeward, and next Imogine in the convent, confessing the foulness of her heart to the prior, who first indulges his old humour with a fit of senseless scolding, then leaves her alone with her ruffian paramour, with whom she makes at once an infamous appointment, and the curtain drops, that it may be carried into act and consummation.

I want words to describe the mingled horror and disgust, with which I witnessed the opening of the fourth act, considering it as a melancholy proof of the depravation of the public mind. The shocking spirit of jacobinism seemed no longer confined to politics. The familiarity with atrocious events and characters appeared to have poisoned the taste, even where it had not directly disorganized the moral principles, and left the feelings callous to all the mild appeals, and craving alone for the grossest and most outrageous stimulants. The very fact then present to our senses, that a British audience could remain passive under such an insult to common decency, nay, receive with a thunder of applause, a human being supposed to have come reeking from the consummation of this complex foulness and baseness, these and the like reflections so pressed as with the weight of lead upon my heart, that actor, author, and tragedy would have been forgotten, had it not been for a plain elderly man sitting beside me, who with a very serious face, that at once expressed surprize and aversion, touched my elbow, and pointing to the actor, said to me in a half-whisper— "Do you see that little fellow there? he has just been committing adultery!" Somewhat relieved by the laugh which this droll address occasioned, I forced back my attention to the stage sufficiently to learn, that Bertram is recovered from a transient fit of remorse, by the information that St. Aldobrand was commissioned (to do, what every honest man must have done without commission, if he did his duty) to seize him and deliver him to the just vengeance of the law; an information which (as he had long known himself to be an attainted traitor and proclaimed outlaw, and not only a trader in blood himself, but notoriously the *Captain* of a gang of

[1] Close of Act II.

thieves, pirates and assassins) assuredly could not have been new
to him. It is this, however, which alone and instantly restores him
to his accustomed state of raving, blasphemy, and nonsense. Next
follows Imogine's constrained interview with her injured husband,
and his sudden departure again, all in love and kindness, in order
to attend the feast of St. Anselm at the convent. This was, it must
be owned, a very strange engagement for so tender a husband to
make within a few minutes after so long an absence. But first his
lady has told him that she has "a vow on her," and wishes "that
black perdition may gulf her perjured soul,"[1]—(Note: she is
lying at the very time)—if she ascends his bed, till her penance
is accomplished. How, therefore, is the poor husband to amuse
himself in this interval of her penance? But do not be distressed,
reader, on account of[a] St. Aldobrand's absence! As the author has
contrived to send him out of the house, when a husband would be
in his, and the lover's way, so he will doubtless not be at a loss to
bring him back again as soon as he is wanted. Well! the husband
gone in on the one side, out pops the lover from the other, and
for the fiendish purpose of harrowing up the soul[2] of his wretched
accomplice in guilt, by announcing to her with most brutal and
blasphemous execrations his fixed and deliberate resolve to assassinate her husband; all this too is for no discoverable purpose on
the part of the author, but that of introducing a series of super-
tragic starts, pauses, screams, struggling, dagger-throwing, falling
on the ground, starting up again wildly, swearing, outcries for help,
falling again on the ground, rising again, faintly tottering towards
the door, and, to end the scene, a most convenient fainting fit of
our lady's, just in time to give Bertram an opportunity of seeking
the object of his hatred, before she alarms the house, which indeed
she has had full time to have done before, but that the author
rather chose she should amuse herself and the audience by the
above-described ravings and startings. She recovers slowly, and
to her enter Clotilda, the confidante and mother confessor; then
commences, what in theatrical language is called the madness, but
which the author more accurately entitles, delirium, it appearing
indeed a sort of intermittent fever with fits of light-headedness off
and on, whenever occasion and stage effect happen to call for it. A

---

[a] *BL* (1817), *Courier*: of the

[1] *Bertram* IV ii 159–60 (var).   [2] Shakespeare *Hamlet* I v 16
                                                   (var).

convenient return of the storm (we told the reader before-hand how it would be) had changed—

> The rivulet, that bathed the Convent walls,
> Into a foaming flood: upon its brink
> The Lord and his small train *do* stand appalled.
> With torch and bell from their high battlements
> The monks *do* summon to the pass in vain;
> He must return to-night.[1]

Talk of the devil, and his horns appear, says the proverb: and sure enough, within ten lines of the exit of the messenger, sent to stop him, the arrival of Lord St. Aldobrand is announced. Bertram's ruffian-band now enter, and range themselves across the stage, giving fresh cause for Imogine's screams and madness. St. Aldobrand having received his mortal wound behind the scenes, totters in to welter in his blood, and to die at the feet of this double-damned adultress.

Of her, as far as she is concerned in this 4th act, we have two additional points to notice: first, the low cunning and Jesuitical trick with which she deludes her husband into *words* of forgiveness, which he himself does not understand; and secondly, that every where she is made the object of interest and sympathy, and it is not the author's fault, if at any moment she excites feelings less gentle, than those we are accustomed to associate with the self-accusations of a sincere, religious penitent. And did a British audience endure all this?—They received it with plaudits, which, but for the rivalry of the carts and hackney coaches, might have disturbed the evening-prayers of the scanty week day congregation at St. Paul's cathedral.

Tempora mutantur, nos et mutamur in illis.[2]

Of the fifth act, the only thing noticeable (for rant and nonsense, though abundant as ever, have long before the last act become things of course,) is the profane representation of the high altar in a chapel, with all the vessels and other preparations for the holy

---

[1] *Bertram* IV ii 357–62 (var).

[2] Probably of mediaeval rather than Renaissance origin, the line (tr "Times change, and we change with them") first appears as a quotation in William Harrison (1534–93) *An Historicall Description of the Islande* of *Britayne* (1577) III iii 99 and thereafter in other sixteenth- and seventeenth-century writers. *Plays and Poems of Robert Greene* ed J. C. Collins (Oxford 1905) II 382. *BL* (1907) II 301. Cf *EOT* (*CC*) II 186 and n, *LS* (*CC*) 123.

sacrament. A hymn is actually sung on the stage by the choirister[a] boys! For the rest, Imogine, who now and then *talks* deliriously, but who is always light-headed as far as her *gown* and *hair* can make her so, wanders about in dark woods with cavern-rocks and precipices in the back-scene; and a number of mute dramatis personæ move in and out continually, for whose presence, there is always at least this reason, that they afford something to be *seen*, by that very large part of a Drury-lane audience who have small chance of *hearing* a word. She had, it appears, taken her child with her, but what becomes of the child, whether she murdered it or not, nobody can tell, nobody can learn; it was a riddle at the *representation*, and after a most attentive *perusal* of the Play, a riddle it remains.

> No more I know, I wish I did,
> And I would tell it all to you;
> For what became of this poor child
> There's none that ever knew.
> Wordsworth's Thorn.[1]

Our whole information * is derived from the following words—

> Prior.—Where is thy child?
> Clotil.—(Pointing to the cavern into which she has looked)
> Oh he lies cold within his cavern-tomb!
> Why dost thou urge her with the horrid theme?
> Prior.—(who will not, the reader may observe, be disappointed of his dose of scolding)
> It was to make (quere wake) one living cord o'th'heart,
> And I will try, tho' my own breaks at it.
> Where is thy child?
> Imog.—(with a frantic laugh)
> The forest-fiend hath snatched him—
> He (who? the fiend or the child?) rides the night-mare thro' the wizzard woods.[2]

Now these two lines consist in a senseless plagiarism from the counterfeited madness of Edgar in Lear, who, in imitation of the

---

* The child is an important personage, for I see not by what possible means the author could have ended the second and third acts but for its timely appearance. How ungrateful then not further to notice its fate?

[a] *BL* (1817), *Courier*: choirester

[1] Lines 144–7 (the first phrase was altered in 1827 to "More knew I not").   [2] *Bertram* v iii 39–46.

gipsey incantations, puns on the old word Mair, a Hag;[1] and the no less senseless adoption of Dryden's forest-fiend, and the wizzard-stream by which Milton, in his Lycidas, so finely characterises the spreading Deva, fabulosus Amnis.[2] Observe too these images stand unique in the speeches of Imogine, without the slightest resemblance to any thing she says before or after. But we are weary. The characters in this act frisk about, here, there, and every where, as teasingly as the Jack o'Lanthorn-lights which mischievous boys, from across a narrow street, throw with a looking-glass on the faces of their opposite neighbours. Bertram disarmed, out-heroding Charles de Moor in the Robbers,[3] befaces the collected knights of St. Anselm (all in complete armour,) and so, by pure dint of black looks, he outdares them into passive poltroons. The sudden revolution in the Prior's manners we have before noticed, and it is indeed so outré, that a number of the audience imagined a great secret was to come out, viz.: that the Prior was one of the many instances of a youthful sinner metamorphosed into an old scold, and that this Bertram would appear at last to be his son. Imogine re-appears at the convent, and dies of her own accord. Bertram stabs himself, and dies by her side, and that the play may conclude as it began, viz. in a superfetation of blasphemy upon nonsense, because he had snatched a sword from a despicable coward, who retreats in terror when it is pointed towards him in sport; this *felo de se*, and thief-captain, this loathsome and leprous confluence of robbery, adultery, murder, and cowardly assassination, this monster whose best deed is, the having saved his betters from the degradation of hanging him, by turning jack ketch[4] to himself, first recommends the charitable Monks and holy Prior to pray for his soul, and then has the folly and impudence to exclaim—

> I died no felon's death,
> A warrior's weapon freed a warrior's soul![5]

---

[1] See ch 18, above, II 70 and n 3.

[2] Dryden's *Theodore and Honoraria* (tr from Boccaccio's *Decameron*) published in his *Fables* (1700); and *Lycidas* line 55, of the river Dee, "the fabled torrent".

[3] Karl von Moor in Schiller's *Die Räuber*.

[4] The notorious hangman and executioner (d 1686), who dispatched Lords Russell and Monmouth and flogged Titus Oates, and whose name was given to the executioner in *Punchinello* and other puppet plays.

[5] *Bertram* final lines (var).

CHAPTER 24

CONCLUSION

I T sometimes happens that we are punished for our faults by incidents, in the causation of which these faults had no share: and this I have always felt the severest punishment. The wound indeed is of the same dimensions; but the edges are jagged, and there is a dull underpain that survives the smart which it had aggravated. For there is always a consolatory feeling that accompanies the sense of a proportion between antecedents and consequents. The sense of Before and After becomes both intelligible and intellectual when, and *only* when, we contemplate the succession in the relations of Cause and Effect, which like the two poles of the magnet manifest the being and unity of the one power by relative opposites, and give, as it were, a substratum of permanence, of identity, and therefore of reality, to the shadowy flux of Time.[1] It is Eternity revealing itself in the phænomena of Time: and the perception and acknowledgement of the proportionality and appropriateness of the Present to the Past, prove to the afflicted Soul, that it has not yet been deprived of the sight of God, that it can still recognize the effective presence of a Father, though through a darkened glass and a turbid atmosphere, though of a Father that is chastising it. And for this cause, doubtless, are we so framed in mind, and even so organized in brain and nerve, that all confusion is painful.—It is within the experience of many medical practitioners, that a patient, with strange and unusual symptoms of disease, has been more distressed in mind, more wretched, from the fact of being unintelligible to himself and others, than from the pain or danger of the disease: nay, that the patient has received the most solid comfort, and resumed a genial and enduring chearfulness, from some new symptom or product, that had at once determined the name and nature of his complaint,

[1] For C's Brunoesque concept of "polarity" and its relation to cause and effect see Barfield chs 3 and 4 passim, esp 138–41. Cf *Friend* (*CC*) i 94 and *TL* (1848) passim.

and rendered it an intelligible effect of an intelligible cause: even though the discovery did at the same moment preclude all hope of restoration. Hence the mystic theologians, whose delusions we may more confidently hope to separate from their actual intuitions, when we condescend to read their works without the presumption that whatever our fancy (always the ape, and too often the adulterator and counterfeit of our memory) has not made or cannot make a picture of, must be nonsense,—hence, I say, the Mystics have joined in representing the state of the reprobate spirits as a dreadful dream in which there is no sense of reality, not even of the pangs they are enduring—an eternity without time, and as it were below it—God present without manifestation of his presence. But these are depths, which we dare not linger over. Let us turn to an instance more on a level with the ordinary sympathies of mankind. Here then, and in this same healing influence of *Light* and distinct Beholding, we may detect the final cause of that instinct which in the great majority of instances leads and almost compels the Afflicted to communicate their sorrows. Hence too flows the alleviation that results from *"opening out* our griefs:"[1] which are thus presented in distinguishable forms instead of the mist, through which whatever is shapeless becomes magnified and (literally) *enormous.*[2] Casimir, in the fifth Ode of his third Book, has happily * expressed this thought.

* *Classically* too, as far as consists with the allegorizing fancy of the *modern,* that still *striving to project* the inward, contra-distinguishes itself from the seeming ease with which the poetry of the ancients *reflects* the world without. Casimir affords, perhaps, the most striking instance of this characteristic difference.—For his *style* and *diction* are really classical: while Cowley, who resembles Casimir in many respects, compleatly barbarizes *his* Latinity, and even his metre, by the heterogeneous nature of his thoughts. That Dr. Johnson should have passed a contrary judgement, and have even preferred Cowley's Latin Poems to Milton's, is a caprice that has, if I mistake not, excited the surprize of all scholars.[3] I was much amused last

[1] Cf "And now having for the very first time in my whole Life opened out my whole feelings & thoughts concerning my Past Fates & Fortunes". To Daniel Stuart 12 Sept 1814: *CL* III 533.
[2] From *e* (out of) + *norma* (the mason's or carpenter's square or pattern); hence departing from regular form. On the image of the magnifying mist cf *Conciones: Lects 1795*

(*CC*) 52 and n 5; *Watchman* (*CC*) 125; *EOT* (*CC*) II 283, 405, 462; *Wallenstein* IV iii 71–2: *PW* (EHC) II 787–8.
[3] *Lives* "Cowley" I 13. Johnson justifies his preference, the premise of which can certainly be disputed, with the thought that Cowley is more essentially "modern" as a Latin poet, and "without much loss of purity or elegance, accommodates the diction

Me longus silendi
Edit amor; facilesque Luctus
Hausit medullas. Fugerit ocius,
Simul negantem visere jusseris
Aures amicorum, et loquacem
Questibus evacuâris iram.

Olim querendo desinimus queri,
Ipsoque fletu lacryma perditur,
Nec fortis æquè, si per omnes
Cura volet residetque ramos.

Vires amicis perdit in auribus
Minorque semper dividitur dolor
Per multa permissus vagari
Pectora.—

Id. Lib. iii, Od. 5.[2]

summer with the laughable *affright,* with which an Italian poet perused a
page of Cowley's Davideis, contrasted with the enthusiasm with which he
first ran through, and then read aloud, Milton's Mansus and Ad Patrem.[1]

of Rome to his own conceptions",
whereas Milton "expresses the
thoughts of the ancients in their
language".

[1] For a quotation from Cowley's
Latin poem *Davideis* (unfinished, bk
I only, first published in *Works* 1668)
see *CN* II 3196 and n. The poem is
headed "Davideidos liber primus"
(the first book of the *Davideis*), following the normal convention with
Latin titles; it is correctly called
Davideis, but is not to be confused
with the English version, *Davideis, a
Sacred Poem of the Troubles of
David* (unfinished, bks I–IV, first
published 1656). Both are in C's ed
of Cowley *Works* (1681).

Could the "Italian poet" be Ugo
Foscolo (1778–1827)? He was stay-
ing with W. S. Rose at Mudeford
shortly after 17 Sept 1816, soon after
his arrival in England. C first met
Rose at Mudeford on 19 Sept (*CL* IV
671), and there was some social
intercourse between them thereafter.
The scene could have been Rose's
library (*CL* IV 684).

[2] Maciej Kazimierz Sarbiewski
(1595–1640), the Polish Jesuit poet

celebrated for the Horatian quality
of his style, *Carmina* (Paris 1759)
3.5 (Ad Publium Munatium) 11–24.
C begins *Me* ("me") instead of *Te*
("you"), probably by accident, since
the change of person is not carried
out throughout the quotation, nor
would the metre allow of this. Tr:
"A long-lasting passion for silence
has devoured [you] and grief has
consumed [your] soft marrows. It will
swiftly flee as soon as you command
it, refuse though it may, to visit
the ears of your friends and empty
out your anger in talk and lamenta-
tions. Often by complaining we cease
to complain, the tear dries in the
very act of weeping, nor is care so
strong if it takes wing and settles on
all the branches. Pain loses strength
in loving ears and ever grows less
by division, allowed to wander
through many breasts." In 1796 C
had written: "If we except Lucretius
and Statius, I know not of any
Latin Poet, ancient or modern, who
has equalled Casimir in boldness of
conception, opulence of fancy, or
beauty of versification." *Watchman*
(*CC*) 68, which also points out

I shall not make this an excuse, however, for troubling my Readers with any complaints or explanations, with which, as Readers, they have little or no concern. It may suffice (for the present at least) to declare that the causes that have delayed the publication of these volumes for so long a period after they had been printed off, were not connected with any neglect of my own; and that they would form an instructive comment on the Chapter concerning Authorship as a Trade, addressed to young men of genius in the first volume of this work.[1] I remember the ludicrous effect of[a] the first sentence of an Auto-biography, which happily for the writer was as meagre in incidents as it is well possible for the Life of an Individual to be—"The *eventful* Life which I am about to record, from the hour in which I rose into existence[b] on this Planet, &c."[2] Yet when, notwithstanding this warning example of Self-importance before me, I review my own life, I cannot refrain from applying the same epithet to it, and with more than ordinary emphasis—and no private feeling, that affected myself only, should prevent me from *publishing* the same, (for *write* it I assuredly shall, should life and leisure be granted me)[3] if continued reflection should strengthen my present belief, that my history would add its contingent to the enforcement of one important truth, viz. that we must not only love our neighbours as ourselves, but ourselves likewise as our neighbours; and that we can do neither unless we love God above both.[4]

---

[a] *BL* (1817): which   [b] *BL* (1817): exist

(n 4) that C in college had intended to include Casimir in his "Imitations of the Modern Latin Poets". One imitation is included in *Watchman* (*CC*) 69–70. Cf *CN* I 161 and n, III 3276 and n.

In *BL* (1847) II 295 there is a footnote to the word "fortis" in line 9 of the poem as quoted above, presumably an annotation by C on a copy of *BL: "Flectit,* or if the metre had allowed, *premit* would have supported the metaphor better." Instead of "nor is care so strong" C suggests "Nor does care bow us down (or oppress us) so much".

[1] Ch 11, above, esp I 223–5.

[2] Untraced.

[3] It was never written. Cf "He had even half promised himself to write his own biography, but the want of success in his literary labours, and the state of his health, caused him to think seriously that his life was diminishing too fast, to permit him to finish those great works, of which he had long planned the execution." *C Life* (G) 145–6. The remark in *BL,* as George Watson says, shows that he does not regard it as a real autobiography. *BL* (1975) 281n.

[4] Matt 22.39, 37. Cf *CN* III 3293 f 17ᵛ.

> Who lives, that's not
> Depraved or depraves? Who dies, *that bears*
> *Not one spurn to the grave—of their friends' gift?* [1]

Strange as the delusion may appear, yet it is most true that three years ago I did not know or believe that I had an enemy in the world: and now even my strongest sensations of gratitude are mingled with fear, and I reproach myself for being too often disposed to ask,—Have I one friend?—During the many years which intervened between the composition and the publication of the Christabel, it became almost as well known among literary men as if it had been on common sale, the same references were made to it, and the same liberties taken with it, even to the very names of the imaginary persons in the poem.[2] From almost all of our most celebrated Poets, and from some with whom I had no personal acquaintance, I either received or heard of expressions of admiration that (I can truly say) appeared to myself utterly disproportionate to a work, that pretended to be nothing more than a common Faery Tale. Many, who had allowed no merit to my other poems, whether printed or manuscript, and who have frankly told me as much, uniformly made an exception in favour of the CHRISTABEL and the Poem, entitled LOVE.[3] Year after year, and in societies of the most different kinds, I had been entreated to recite it: and the result was still the same in all, and altogether different in this respect from the effect produced by the occasional recitation of any other poems I had composed.—This before the publication. And since then, with very few exceptions, I have heard nothing but abuse, and this too in a spirit of bitterness at

[1] Shakespeare *Timon of Athens* I ii 140–2 (var):
>   Who lives that's not depraved
>   or depraves?
>   Who dies that bears not one
>   spurn to their graves
>   Of their friends' gifts?

[2] Composed 1797–1800, *Christabel* was published 1816. Among the many who had read the poem in ms or had heard it recited were Sir Walter Scott and Byron, the first of whom imitated some aspects of the style in *Lay of the Last Minstrel* (1805). Byron, in a note to *The Siege of Corinth* (1816) st xix lines 521–32, acknowledged "a close,

though unintentional, resemblance in these twelve lines to a passage in an unpublished poem of Mr. Coleridge, called 'Christabel.' It was not till after these lines were written that I heard that wild and singularly original and beautiful poem recited . . ." (by Scott).

[3] Written 1798–9; published (with additional stanzas) in *M Post* 21 Dec 1799 as "Introduction to the Tale of the Dark Ladie"; reprinted *LB* (1800). Cf ch 14, above, II 7–8 n 3. Charles James Fox, for one, had praised *Love;* see *CL* II 676n, III 325.

least as disproportionate to the pretensions of the poem, had it been the most pitiably below mediocrity, as the previous eulogies, and far more inexplicable. In the Edinburgh Review it was assailed with a malignity and a spirit of personal hatred that ought to have injured only the work in which such a Tirade was suffered to appear: and this review was generally attributed (whether rightly or no I know not) to a man, who both in my presence and in my absence, has repeatedly pronounced it the finest poem of its kind in the language.[1]—This may serve as a warning to authors, that in their calculations on the probable reception of a poem, they must subtract to a large amount from the panegyric, which may have encouraged them to publish it, however unsuspicious and however various the sources of this panegyric may have been. And, first, allowances must be made for private enmity, of the very existence of which they had perhaps entertained no suspicion— for personal enmity behind the mask of anonymous criticism: secondly, for the necessity of a certain proportion of abuse and ridicule in a Review, in order to make it saleable, in consequence of which, if they have no friends behind the scenes, the chance must needs be against them; but lastly and chiefly, for the excitement and temporary sympathy of feeling, which the recitation of the poem by an admirer, especially if he be at once a warm admirer and a man of acknowledged celebrity, calls forth in the audience. For this is really a species of Animal Magnetism,[2] in which the enkindling Reciter, by perpetual comment of looks and tones, lends his own will and apprehensive faculty to his Auditors.

[1] C was convinced that Hazlitt was the author of the crude and heavily sarcastic review in *Ed Rev* XXVII (1816) 58–67. Cf *CN* III 4323 and n. Hazlitt had already reviewed the work unfavourably but in a very different spirit and with some tribute to the poem's style in *Examiner* 2 Jun 1816 pp 348–9. The legend persisted that Hazlitt wrote the *Ed Rev* article, which was then revised by Jeffrey. But P. P. Howe, with good reason, refused to include it in *H Works*. Elisabeth Schneider "The Unknown Reviewer of *Christabel*" *PMLA* 20 (1955) 417–32 persuasively states the arguments against Hazlitt's authorship and suggests Thomas Moore. But there are indications that Moore, who thought the article "disgraceful", was not responsible, and the authorship still remains in doubt. *Letters of Thomas Moore* ed W. S. Dowden (Oxford 1964) I 395n, 407.

[2] The name first given to the influence by which the hypnotist operated on his subject, when F. A. Mesmer (1733–1815) popularised mesmerism or hypnotism. For C's interest in animal magnetism see *IS* 45–51 and *P Lects* Lect 2 (1949) 104–5, 423–4.

They *live* for the time within the dilated sphere of his intellectual Being. It is equally possible, though not equally common, that a reader left to himself should sink below the poem, as that the poem left to itself should flag beneath the feelings of the reader.—But in my own instance, I had the additional misfortune of having been gossipped about, as devoted to metaphysics, and worse than all to a system incomparably nearer to the visionary flights of Plato, and even to the jargon of the mystics, than to the established tenets of Locke. Whatever therefore appeared with my name was condemned before hand, as predestined metaphysics. In a dramatic poem, which had been submitted by me to a gentleman of great influence in the Theatrical world,[1] occurred the following passage.—

> O we are querulous creatures! Little less
> Than all things can suffice to make us happy:
> And little more than nothing is enough
> To make us wretched.[2]

Aye, here now! (exclaimed the Critic) here come Coleridge's *Metaphysics*! And the very same motive (that is, not that the lines were unfit for the present state of our immense Theatres; but that they were *Metaphysics* *) was assigned elsewhere for the rejection of the two following passages. The first is spoken in answer to a usurper, who had rested his plea on the circumstance, that he had been chosen by the acclamations of the people.—

> What people? How conven'd? Or if conven'd,
> Must not that magic power that charms together

* Poor unlucky Metaphysics! and what are they? A single sentence expresses the object and thereby the contents of this science. Γνῶθι σεαυτόν:[3] et Deum quantum licet et in Deo omnia scibis.[4] Know thyself: and so shalt thou know God, as far as is permitted to a creature, and in God all things.— Surely, there is a strange—nay, rather a too natural—aversion in many to know themselves.

[1] Byron, who was a member of the committee that helped to administer Drury Lane (see ch 23, above, II 209 n 2). *C Life* (B) 139–40; *C Life* (C) 271–3. The reference is to C's recently completed play *Zapolya* (1817), which a majority of the committee decided not to produce. Cf below, App C, II 293–4, 299.

[2] *Zapolya* pt II i i 23–6 (var): *PW* (EHC) II 902.

[3] See above, I 252 and n 1.

[4] In *BL* (1847) II 299 this has been put into verse:

> Nosce te ipsum
> Tuque Deum, quantum licet,
> inque Deo omnia noscas.

Source untraced, but SC may be here citing, from an annotation by C, a versified rendition by C himself. Cf C's poem *Self-knowledge: PW* (EHC) I 486.

Millions of men in council, needs have power
To win or wield them? Rather, O far rather,
Shout forth thy titles to yon circling mountains,
And with a thousandfold reverberation
Make the rocks flatter thee, and the volleying air,
Unbribed, shout back to thee, King Emerich!
By wholesome laws to embank the Sovereign Power;
To deepen by restraint; and by prevention
Of lawless will to amass and guide the flood
In its majestic channel, is man's task
And the true patriot's glory! In all else
Men safelier trust to heaven, than to themselves
When least themselves: even in those whirling crowds
Where folly is contagious, and too oft
Even wise men leave their better sense at home
To chide and wonder at them, when return'd.[1]

The second passage is in the mouth of an old and experienced Courtier, betrayed by the man in whom he had most trusted.

And yet Sarolta, simple, inexperienced,
Could see him as he was and oft has warn'd me.
Whence learnt she this? O she was innocent.
And to be innocent is Nature's wisdom.
The fledge dove knows the prowlers of the air
Fear'd soon as seen, and flutters back to shelter!
And the young steed recoils upon his haunches,
The never-yet-seen adder's hiss first heard!
Ah! surer than suspicion's hundred eyes
Is that fine sense, which to the pure in heart
By mere oppugnancy of their own goodness
Reveals the approach of evil![2]

As therefore my character as a writer could not easily be more injured by an overt act[a] than it was already in consequence of the report, I published a work, a large portion of which was professedly metaphysical.[3] A long delay occurred between its first annunciation and its appearance; it was reviewed therefore by anticipation with a malignity, so avowedly and exclusively personal, as is, I believe, unprecedented even in the present contempt of all common humanity that disgraces and endangers the liberty

---

a BL (1817): overt-act

[1] Prelude to *Zapolya* i 355–72 (var): *PW* (EHC) ii 895.
[2] Pt ii iv i 70–81 (var): *PW* (EHC) ii 939.
[3] *SM*, first of the two *Lay Sermons;* published Dec 1816.

of the press.[1] After its appearance, the author of this lampoon was chosen to review it in the Edinburgh Review: and under the single condition, that he should have written what he himself really thought, and have criticized the work as he would have done had its author been indifferent to him, I should have chosen that man myself both from the vigour and the originality of his mind, and from his particular acuteness in speculative reasoning, before all others.—I remembered Catullus's lines,

> Desine de quoquam quicquam bene velle mereri,
> Aut aliquem fieri posse putare pium.
> Omnia sunt ingrata: nihil fecisse benigne est:
> Imo, etiam tædet, tædet obestque magis.
> Ut mihi, quem nemo gravius nec acerbius urget
> Quam modo qui me unum atque unicum amicum habuit.[2]

But I can truly say, that the grief with which I read this rhapsody of predetermined insult, had the Rhapsodist himself for its whole and sole object: and that the indignant contempt which it excited in me, was as exclusively confined to his employer and suborner. I refer to this Review at present, in consequence of information having been given me, that the innuendo of my "potential infidelity,"[3] grounded on one passage of my first Lay Sermon, has been received and propagated with a degree of *credence*, of which I can safely acquit the originator of the calumny. I give the sentences as they stand in the sermon, premising only that I was speaking

[1] Hazlitt wrote an anticipatory review of *SM* when it was advertised, three months before it was published and at a time he himself had not seen it, in the *Examiner* 8 Sept 1816 pp 571–3. The attack was then continued by Hazlitt in actual reviews not only in *Ed Rev* XXVII (1816) 444–59 but also in *Examiner* 29 Dec 1816 pp 824–7. Cf *CN* III 4323 and n; *SM* (*CC*) xxxviii–xxxix and n.

[2] *Carmina* 73. The text of lines 3–4 of this poem is variously emended. C's version is that of many editions, including *Catulli Tibulli Propertii Opera* ed Edward Harwood (1774), which C owned. In this edition the poem is numbered LXXI, owing to the omission of two supposedly indecent poems. Tr LCL: "Leave off wishing to deserve any

thanks from anyone, or thinking that anyone can ever become grateful. All this wins no thanks; to have acted kindly is nothing, rather it is wearisome, wearisome and harmful; so is it now with me, who am vexed and troubled by no one so bitterly as by him who but now held me for his one and only friend." Cf C's letter to Brabant 5 Dec 1816: *CL* IV 693–4.

[3] Actually the phrase was C's own, speaking of "the plan of poisoning the children of the poor with a sort of *potential* infidelity under the '*liberal idea*' of teaching those points only . . . in which all denominations agree . . .". *SM* (*CC*) 40. Hazlitt, resenting the phrase, applied it back to C's own position. *Ed Rev* XXVII (1816) 451.

exclusively of miracles worked for the outward senses of men. "It was only to overthrow the usurpation exercised in and through the senses, that the senses were miraculously appealed to. REASON AND RELIGION ARE THEIR OWN EVIDENCE. The natural sun is in this respect a symbol of the spiritual. Ere he is fully arisen, and while his glories are still under veil, he calls up the breeze to chase away the usurping vapours of the night-season, and thus converts the air itself into the minister of its own purification: not surely in proof or elucidation of the light from heaven, but to prevent its interception.

"Wherever, therefore, similar circumstances co-exist with the same moral causes, the principles revealed, and the examples recorded, in the inspired writings render miracles superfluous: and if we neglect to apply truths in expectation of wonders, or under pretext of the cessation of the latter, we tempt God and merit the same reply which our Lord gave to the Pharisees on a like occasion." [1]

In the sermon and the notes both the historical truth and the necessity of the miracles are strongly and frequently asserted. "The testimony of books of history (i.e. relatively to the signs and wonders, with which Christ came) is one of the strong and stately *pillars* of the church; but it is not the *foundation!*" [2] Instead, therefore, of defending myself, which I could easily effect by a series of passages, expressing the same opinion, from the Fathers and the most eminent Protestant Divines, from the Reformation to the Revolution, I shall merely state what my belief is, concerning the true evidences of Christianity. 1. Its consistency with right Reason, I consider as the outer Court of the Temple—the common area, within which it stands. 2. The miracles, with and through which the Religion was first revealed and attested, I regard as the steps, the vestibule, and the portal of the Temple. 3. The sense, the inward feeling, in the soul of each Believer of its exceeding *desirableness*—the experience, that he *needs* something, joined with the strong Foretokening, that the Redemption and the Graces propounded to us in Christ are *what* he needs—this I hold to be the true FOUNDATION of the spiritual Edifice. With the strong

---

[1] *SM* (*CC*) 10. The reference in the last sentence is to Matt 12.39 and 16.4. For the first of the two paragraphs quoted, cf *CN* III 4489 and n.

[2] *SM* (*CC*) 55–6 (the parenthesis added).

a priori probability that flows in from 1 and 3 on the correspondent historical evidence of 2, no man can refuse or neglect to make the experiment without guilt. But, 4, it is the experience derived from a practical conformity to the conditions of the Gospel—it is the opening Eye; the dawning Light; the terrors and the promises of spiritual Growth; the blessedness of loving God as God, the nascent sense of Sin hated as Sin, and of the incapability of attaining to either without Christ; it is the sorrow that still rises up from beneath and the consolation that meets it from above; the bosom treacheries of the Principal in the warfare and the exceeding faithfulness and long-suffering of the uninterested Ally;—in a word, it is the actual *Trial* of the Faith in Christ, with its accompaniments and results, that must form the arched R O O F, and the Faith itself is the completing K E Y-S T O N E. In order to an efficient belief in Christianity, a man must have been a Christian, and this is the seeming argumentum in circulo, incident to all spiritual Truths, to every subject not presentable under the forms of Time and Space, as long as we attempt to master by the reflex acts of the Understanding what we can only *know* by the act of *becoming*.[1] "Do the will of my father, and ye shall K N O W whether I am of God."[2] These four evidences I believe to have been and still to be, for the world, for the whole church, all necessary, all equally necessary; but that at present, and for the majority of Christians born in christian countries, I believe the third and the fourth evidences to be the most operative, not as superseding but as involving a glad undoubting faith in the two former. Credidi, ideóque intellexi,[3] appears to me the dictate equally of Philosophy and Religion, even as I believe Redemption to be the antecedent of Sanctification, and not its consequent. All spiritual predicates

[1] Cf on "true knowledge": ". . . It is a form of BEING, or indeed it is the only knowledge that truly *is,* and all other science is real only as far as it is symbolical of this". *Friend* (*CC*) I 524. *BL* (1907) II 303. Cf *CN* III 4397 f 52ᵛ: "to know is to *resemble*"; and below, II 248 n 1.
[2] John 7.17. "If any man will do his will, he shall know of the doctrine, whether it be of God, or whether I speak of myself."

[3] These words not traced in St Augustine, but out of many other echoes of Isa (Septuagint version) 7.9 in Augustine cf *Sermones* 43.3.4, 9 and *In Joannis Evangelium tractatus* 29.6: "crede ut intelligas", "believe in order that you may understand". C's words tr: "I believed and therefore I understood". Cf also *CN* III 3888n; *Friend* (*CC*) I 427; *SM* (*CC*) 97 and n.

may be construed indifferently as modes of Action or as states of Being. Thus Holiness and Blessedness are the same idea, now seen in relation to act and now to existence. The ready belief which has been yielded to the slander of my "potential infidelity," I attribute in part to the openness with which I have avowed my doubts, whether the heavy interdict, under which the name of BENEDICT SPINOZA lies, is merited on the whole or to the whole extent.[1] Be this as it may, I wish, however, that I could find in the books of philosophy, theoretical or moral, which are alone recommended to the present students of Theology in our established schools, a few passages as thoroughly *Pauline*, as compleatly accordant with the doctrines of the established Church, as the following sentences in the concluding page of Spinoza's Ethics. Deinde quó mens amore divino seu beatitudine magis gaudet, eó plus *intelligit*, eó majorem in affectus habet potentiam, et eó minus ab affectibus, qui mali sunt, patitur: atque adeo ex eo, quód mens hoc amore divino seu beatitudine gaudet, potestatem habet libidines coercendi, nemo beatitudine gaudet quia affectus coercuit; sed contra potestas libidines coercendi ex ipsâ beatitudine oritur.[2]

With regard to the Unitarians, it has been shamelessly asserted, that I have denied them to be Christians.[3] God forbid! For how

[1] C may refer to the passage on Spinoza's *Ethics* in *Friend* No 3 (*CC*) II 48. Cf *CRB* I 112 and *CL* IV 548–9, 775.

[2] *Ethics* pt V prop 42 demonst (var, with omissions). Spinoza *Opera* ed H. E. G. Paulus (2 vols 1802–3) II 299. "Again, in proportion as the mind rejoices more in this divine love or blessedness, so does it the more understand . . . so much the more power has it over the emotions, and so much the less is it subject to those emotions which are evil; therefore, in proportion as the mind rejoices in this divine love or blessedness, so has it the power of controlling lusts. . . . No one rejoices in blessedness, because he has controlled his lusts, but, contrariwise, his power of controlling his lusts arises from this blessedness itself." Tr R. H. M. Elwes.

[3] Cf ". . . those, whose faith

few but themselves would honor with the name of Christianity; however reluctant we might be . . . to withhold from the persons themselves the title of Christians". *SM* (*CC*) 57. Cf C's remark to Anna Letitia Barbauld (1743–1825): "Walking across the room, she addressed him in these words:—'So, Mr Coleridge, I understand you do not consider Unitarians Christians.' 'I hope, Madam,' said he, 'that all persons born in a Christian country are Christians, and trust they are under the condition of being saved; but I *do* contend that Unitarian*ism* is not Christianity;' to which she replied, 'I do not understand the distinction.'" *C Life* (G) 164. *BL* (1907) II 303. For further distinctions between "Unitarians" and "Unitarianism" see *CN* III 3907 f 56 and n and *TT* 4 Apr 1832. In Hazlitt's review of *SM* the charge

should I know, what the piety of the Heart may be, or what Quantum of Error in the Understanding may consist with a saving Faith in the intentions and actual dispositions of the whole moral Being in any one Individual? Never will God reject a soul that sincerely loves him: be his speculative opinions what they may: and whether in any given instance certain opinions, be they Unbelief, or Misbelief, are compatible with a sincere Love of God, God only can know.—But this I have said, and shall continue to say: that if the Doctrines, the sum of which I *believe* to constitute the Truth in Christ, *be* Christianity, then Unitarian*ism* is not, and vice versâ: and that in speaking theologically and *impersonally,* i.e. of PSILANTHROPISM and THEANTHROPISM as schemes of Belief,[1] without reference to Individuals who profess either the one or the other, it will be absurd to use a different language as long as it is the dictate of common sense, that two opposites cannot properly be called by the same name. I should feel no offence if a Unitarian applied the same to me, any more than if he were to say, that 2 and 2 being 4, 4 and 4 must be 8.

> Ἀλλὰ βροτῶν
> Τὸν μὲν κενόφρονες αὖχαι
> Ἐξ ἀγαθῶν ἔβαλον·
> Τὸν δ' αὖ καταμεμφθέντ' ἄγαν
> Ἰσχὺν οἰκείων κατέσφαλεν καλῶν,
> Χειρὸς ἕλκων ὀπίσσω, Θυμὸς ἄτολμος.
>
> PINDAR. Nem. Ode xi.[2]

---

is not "asserted" but mildly implied. *Ed Rev* XXVII (1816) 451. Cf C's remark (to John May 27 Sept 1815), about the time he wrote the above chapter, that in his "Logosophia" he planned to devote Pt VI to "the Causes & Consequences of modern Unitarianism". *CL* IV 590.

[1] On "Psilanthropism" (the belief that Jesus Christ was "mere man"), a word coined by C from the Greek, see above, I 180, and *TT* 4 Apr 1832. For "Theanthropism", the doctrine that the human and divine are united in Christ, *OED* cites C as the first user, though "theanthropist" was common in seventeenth-century English religious writing.

[2] *Nemean Odes* 11.29–32 (var). (See next n, below.) C's κενόφρονες is not an error for κενεόφρονες, but is the reading in *Poetae graeci veteres* II 80. (The slip κατέσφαλεν for παρέσφαλεν occurs also in C's marginal note.) Tr LCL: "But, among mortals, *one* is cast down from his blessings by empty-headed conceit, whereas *another,* underrating his strength too far, hath been thwarted from winning the honours within his reach, by an uncourageous spirit that draggeth him back by the hand."

This has been my Object,[1] and this alone can be my Defence—and O! that with this my personal as well as my LITERARY LIFE might conclude! the unquenched desire I mean, not without the consciousness of having earnestly endeavoured to kindle young minds, and to guard them against the temptations of Scorners, by shewing that the Scheme of Christianity, as taught in the Liturgy and Homilies of our Church, though not discoverable by human Reason, is yet in accordance with it; that link follows link by necessary consequence; that Religion passes out of the ken of Reason only where the eye of Reason has reached its own Horizon; and that Faith is then but its continuation:[2] even as the Day softens away into the sweet Twilight, and Twilight, hushed and breathless, steals into the Darkness. It is Night, sacred Night! the upraised Eye views only the starry Heaven which manifests itself alone: and the outward Beholding is fixed on the sparks twinkling in the awful depth, though Suns of other Worlds,[3] only to preserve the Soul steady and collected in its pure *Act* of inward Adoration to the great I AM, and to the filial WORD that

[1] In this final paragraph, as George Whalley points out, C is using a marginal note he had written earlier in his copy of Böhme *Works* (1768–81) I i 47: "This alone be my Object, as this alone can be my Defence, the desire to kindle young minds, & to guard them against the temptation of the Scorners, by shewing that the Scheme of Christianity tho' not discoverable by reason, is yet accordant thereto—that Link follows Link by necessary consequence; that Religion passes out of the ken of Reason only where ⟨the Eye of⟩ Reason has reached its own Horizon; and that Faith is ⟨then⟩ but its *Continuation,* even as the Day softens away into the sweet Twilight, and Twilight ⟨hushed & breathless steals⟩ into the Darkness! It is Night, sacred Night! The upraised Eye views only the starry Heaven, which manifests only itself—and the outward Look gazes on the sparks, twinkling in the awful Depth, only

to preserve the Soul steady and con-centered in its Trance of inward Adoration. Θεῳ Μονῳ Δοξα!" *CM* (*CC*) I 576. The quotation from Pindar is also in the same annotation, as a footnote to an introductory sentence (not used in *BL*).

[2] C may be thinking, as *BL* (1907) II 304 suggests, of a remark of the Cambridge Platonist John Smith (1618–52): "When *Reason* once is raised by the mighty force of the Divine Spirit into a converse with God, it is turn'd into *Sense:* That which before was onely *Faith* well built upon sure Principles, (for such our *Science* may be) now becomes *Vision.*" *The True Way or Method of Obtaining Divine Knowledge* § II: *Select Discourses* (1660) 16. C had been reading the *Discourses* in 1804 (*CN* II 2164–2167 and nn), and later annotated it.

[3] Cf *CL* I 354, *CN* I 82 and n. McFarland 163; cf 358–9.

re-affirmeth it from Eternity to Eternity, whose choral Echo is the Universe.[1]

$$\Theta E \Omega \iota \quad M O N \Omega \iota \quad \Delta O \Xi A.^{2}$$

FINIS

[1] Cf ". . . that all knowledge is a striving toward community with the divine Being, and is a portion of that which is original knowledge, whose image is the visible universe and whose birthplace is the pinnacle of eternal power". Schelling *Vorlesungen* (1803) 17 (*SW* v 218). McFarland "SI" also cites Leibniz *Philosophische Schriften* ed K. I. Gerhardt (Berlin 1875–90) v 65.

[2] "Glory to God alone". The phrase, as *CN* III 3291 f 4n points out, does not occur exactly in this form in the NT; cf 1 Tim 1.17, Jude 25. G. Whalley notes (*CM—CC—*I 576n) that this formal doxology was sometimes placed at the end of a book in the seventeenth century.

EDITORS' APPENDIXES

APPENDIX A

UNACKNOWLEDGED USES OF
GERMAN WORKS
IN CHAPTERS 5–9, 12–13

UNACKNOWLEDGED USES OF
GERMAN WORKS
IN CHAPTERS 5–9, 12–13

AFTER studying the unacknowledged passages and comparing them against the originals (see Editors' Introduction, above, I cxiv–cxxvii), we have divided Coleridge's appropriations into four categories, explained under four headings in the table. The word counts are very close approximations; there are few grey areas. Another person compiling this table (or the same person compiling it yet again) would arrive at slightly different figures. But such differences would be slight. The table presents, as accurately as is feasible, a direct and complete measure of the unacknowledged material. Although no quantitative calculation can describe Coleridge's intellectual debts, it should answer some of the generalisations that have been made about Coleridge's use in the *Biographia* of his German reading.

Ch	Length	Direct Translation (occasional words and phrases altered or interpolated)	Close Paraphrase (sentence and phrase correspondence; some translation)	Loose Paraphrases (little if any translation; parallels in wording)	Material Summarised (but reworded)
5	3000	200 (7%)	320 (11%)	70 (2%)	195 (7%)
6	2285	260 (11%)	—	—	—
7	2475	—	—	—	—
8	1610	310 (19%)	90 (6%)	140 (9%)	—
9	4880	10/+290 * (6%) *	60 (1–2%)	20 (0–1%)	[35(?)]
12	12,100	1560/+960 * (13%)/+(8%) *	1070 (9%)	660 (5–6%)	490 (4%)
13 (epigraphs not included)	2290	110 (5%)	—	100 (4%)	265 (11%)
Total	28,640	2450/+1250 (9%)/+(4%) *	1540 (5–6%)	990 (3–4%)	950 (3%)

* Coleridge's attribution leaves unclear how much he is translating. It is not acknowledged specifically. See ch 9, I 147 n 5, ch 12, I 248 n 1.

THE CRITIQUE OF *BERTRAM*
IN THE *COURIER*

THE CRITIQUE OF *BERTRAM*
IN THE *COURIER*

C OLERIDGE'S critique of the Gothic tragedy *Bertram* (1816), by
Charles Robert Maturin (1772–1824), appeared in five issues of
The Courier (29 Aug and 7, 9, 10, and 11 Sept 1816) as a series of five
anonymous letters "To the Editor of the Courier". These letters are
reproduced here as more relevant to the *Biographia* than to *Essays on
His Times,* which consequently reprints only the first of the five letters.
Chapter 23 of the *Biographia,* as noted, is essentially a composite of
these letters. Only a fraction of the first letter is reproduced in Chapter
23, since the rest of it is largely an attack on the taste of the Drury
Lane management for producing the play. In the following four letters
only minor changes are made. Brief discussion of the background is
presented above in the Editors' Introduction and in the opening note
to Chapter 23 and therefore is not repeated here. Nor are the critical
notes to the body of the text repeated. Critical notes are offered only
for those parts of Letter I that Coleridge did not include in Chapter 23.

THE DRAMA.—BERTRAM.

To the Editor of the Courier.

a SIR—Mr. Whitbread, as it is well known,*b* shortly before his
death,[1] proposed to the assembled Subscribers of Drury-Lane Theatre,
that the concern should be farmed to some responsible individual under
certain conditions and *c* limitations. Whether he admitted, with regard
to the Body Theatric, what the ardent spirit of party, rendered more
intoxicating by the philter of popularity, had prevented him from
seeing in the body politic, namely: that the right of suffrage may be
too widely diffused, and the representatives in consequence too pro-

---

a–b BL (1817): You remember, my dear Sir, that Mr. Whitbread
c–a (p 258) BL (1817): limitations: and that his

[1] For Samuel Whitbread (1758–
1815), the noted reformer, who
became involved in the management
of Drury Lane, grew depressed, and
committed suicide, see also ch 11,
above, I 223. "C contrasts Whitbread's advocacy of Parliamentary
Reform . . . with his judgment as
manager of Drury Lane Theatre
(rebuilt in 1812). In Jul 1815 Byron
wrote to Tom Moore, 'Poor Whitbread died yesterday morning . . . I
perceive Perry [of the *M Chron*]
attributes his death to Drury-lane,—
a consolatory encouragement to the
new committee'. Byron *L&J* III 207–
8." *EOT* (*CC*) II 436n.

miscuous, we have not the means of ascertaining. But we have his authority for asserting, that his own experience had proved to him the necessity of concentrating the executive at least; in short, had forced the conviction upon him, that where there are many managers, there will be no management, or worse than none. On occasion of some general plaudit in the Athenian Forum while he was speaking, Phocion is related to have anxiously inquired of a friend, whether he had said any thing remarkably foolish.[1] The uncourteous sounds, or rather noises of general dislike or dissent must have been in such an audience not less novel and surprising to the British, than the shout of popular applause was to the Grecian Patriot. I dare not rest the appositeness of the story on the presumption, that the former felt himself as much flattered by the discourtesy, as the latter felt alarmed at the opposite occurrence, but had I happened to pass by, and had learnt only the name of the person so complimented, without having heard the speech, I should certainly have augured most favourably of its purpose, not without a feeling of regret, that I had lost the opportunity of seeing for the first time, Saul also amongst the Prophets. But different men, different minds! Wisdom is not for all audiences, any more than Caviare is for all palates! *De gustibus non est disputandum!* Mr. Whitbread's[a] proposal was rejected, not without indignation, as subversive of the main object, for the attainment of which, the enlightened and patriotic assemblage of Philo-dramatists had been induced to risk their subscriptions. Now this object was avowed to be no less, than the redemption of the British Stage [b](an allowable *pars in toto* for the largest and eldest of the two Metropolitan Theatres)[c] not only from horses, dogs, elephants, and the like Zoological rarities, but also from the more pernicious barbarisms and Kotzebuisms in morals and taste. Drury-Lane was to be restored to its former classical renown; Shakspeare, Jonson, and Otway, with the expurgated Muses of Vanburgh, Congreve, and Wycherly, were to be reinaugurated in their rightful dominion over British audiences; and the Herculean process was to commence, by exterminating the speaking monsters imported from the banks of the Danube, compared with which, their mute relations the emigrants from Exeter 'Change, and Polito [d]late Pidcock's[e] showcarts, were tame and inoffensive. Could an heroic project, at once so refined and so arduous, be consistently entrusted to—could its success be rationally expected from a mercenary Manager, at whose critical quarantine the *lucri bonus odor* would conciliate a bill of health to the plague in person? No! As the work proposed, such must be the workmasters. Rank, fortune, liberal education, and (their natural accom-

[1] Plutarch *Lives* "Phocion" 8.3. In presenting an argument in a public address, says Plutarch, Phocion, seeing that "all alike accepted his argument, turned to his friends and said: 'Can it possibly be that I am making a bad argument without knowing it?'" C's source may have been Bacon *Novum organum* I aphorism 77.

paniments or consequences), critical discernment, delicate tact, dis-interestedness, unsuspected morals, notorious patriotism, and tried Macænaship, these were the recommendations that influenced the votes of the proprietary subscribers of Drury-lane Theatre, *a* and in conse-quence *b* occasioned the election of its Supreme Committee of Man-agement. *c* These circumstances *d* alone would have excited a strong interest in the public mind, respecting the first production of the Tragic Muse which had been announced under such auspices, and had passed the ordeal of such *e* judgments. These alone would have compelled the attention of the *Courier* to the particular Drama, though, both from choice, and as an Evening Paper, it has been its plan to live on friendly terms, yet at a respectful distance from theatrical affairs; nay, on the score of public morals, and the tone of public feeling and sentiment (as closely connected with politics, and therefore in every point of view coincident with the plan and objects of the *Courier*), these circumstances alone would have imposed it as a duty on its conductor to have examined the work with unwonted earnestness, and to have laid before its readers the unbiassed result (at whatever length was requisite to do this), fully and fairly.— 1 *Bertram, or the Castle of St. Aldobrand*, a Tragedy,*f* was the work on which the great expectation,*g* justified by so many causes, were doomed at length to settle.*h* But the Committee did not trust to these causes alone, though strongly aided by the curiosity which the country and the profession of the author, as an Irish Clergyman, had raised, and still more by the prepossessions in favour of the first dramatic offspring produced by the praises that had been generally awarded to the *Family of Montorio*, a novel of no small reputation in the bold and terrific line.2 Every means which the daily and periodical press, or the authority of great names, or the conversation of those who had been

---

a–b BL (1817): these the motives that   *c–d* BL (1817): This circumstance
e–f BL (1817): judgements: and the Tragedy, on which you have requested my judgement,
        g BL (1817): expectations,   *h* BL (1817) omits the rest of the letter

---

1 "A moral difficulty C's criticism almost manages to surmount was his grievance as author of a drama recently *rejected*. The committee had considered producing C's *Zapolya* but had quarrelled among them-selves over it, first advising him to rewrite it as a melodrama and at length rejecting it altogether. The proposal to rewrite had reached C by 8 May; the next day, *Bertram* began its successful run—a speci-men, C felt, of what the committee really liked: an 'Abortion of Ignor-ance and Jacobinism . . . *got up*' in 'extreme splendor', as he com-plained two years later to Rae. C's *Remorse,* introduced by Byron, was still in the Drury-Lane repertory, but to the author it was 'a *depressive fact*' that the committee paid no attention to his one small request for a change in staging, yet lavished 'all the colors of the Rain-bow' on *Bertram. CL* IV 720. (A transcript of 'Bertram', from this sentence to the end of the article, is in VCL MS LT 84.)" *EOT* (*CC*) II 438n.

2 *The Fatal Revenge; or, the Family of Montorio* (1807) was published with the pseudonym "Dennis Jasper Murphy". His other early novels, *The Wild Irish Boy* (1808) and *The Milesian Chief* (1812), were "by the Author of 'Montorio' ".

favoured with the perusal of the Drama, could supply, were employed with unprecedented activity. The latter, swoln no doubt by the words of rumour which conveyed the trumpetry, was the most influensive, *"Præcurrebant^a laudes virorum laudatissimorum: inde ingens, immo^b incredibilis expectatio."* [1] It would be malignant to requote in detail the various comparisons, odious or panegyrical, which were thus circulated; now, with dramatic poets, whose reputation the agreeing suffrages of the good and wise in successive generations had fixed into fame, and now, with those whose names are yet probationary and militant. The purport of all may be comprised in one formula: as the principal actor to Garrick, so the author to Shakspeare and Otway. Some extravagance in the mode of commending a work of merit at its first appearance, is not only venial, but, from the counter activity of envy and wanton opposition, even amiable. Letting, therefore, all the fumes of exaggeration evaporate, moderate men, who judged soberly of Mr. Kean, expected to find, in *Bertram,* a dramatic poem of great defects, more than compensated by great and original excellence. To what extent these expectations were realized, I shall proceed to examine, dividing the characteristic merits and demerits of the tragedy into, first, the fable; second, the style and metre; third, originality; and lastly and chiefly, (as being in part the occasion and motive of the present critic,) its sentiments and morality. But I must beg leave to interpose a letter containing preliminary remarks and notices, the bearings of which will become evident to the reader in the letters that follow. The subjects of these remarks, meet only in their convergence to the same point: the illustration of the public taste, and the causes of its vitiation, and fall under three heads or titles: first, of the phrase German Drama; second, of the *Atheista Fulminato* as brought on the English stage in the reign of Charles II., by Thomas Shadwell, under the title of the *Libertine*; [2] third, of extra political jacobinism.

The present letter I will conclude by disclaiming all wish to detract from the merits of the actors, and, above all, by deprecating the application of any incidental passages to the general powers and qualities of Mr. Kean. On the contrary, I am fully convinced, not only that his mode of acting the part was in strict correspondence to the part itself, and the author's own conception of it, but that he could not have done less, or otherwise, without depriving the tragedy of its main support and interest. It is not of Mr. Kean,[3] as *Shylock, Sir*

---

^a *Courier: Precurrebant*   ^b *Courier: imo*

[1] "The praises of the most praised men were running ahead; hence great, nay rather, incredible expectation." Untraced. It is by no means improbable that the Latin quotation—as occasionally in other instances—is by C himself, and that the Ciceronian ring is intentional.

[2] For *Atheista fulminato* and Shadwell's *Libertine* (1676), discussed in C's second letter, see above, II 221.

[3] Edmund Kean (1787–1833), the noted Shakespearian actor, who had taken the rôle of Bertram.

Giles Overreach, &c. that I am to write; but of *Bertram*, as realized by Mr. Kean in a way which, in point of fact, did interest a succession of crowded audiences; and, in the belief and opinion of the most experienced judges, the only way in which such a part could have been rendered interesting. From this point of view, we may justifiably contemplate as matter of praise and admiration in his *Bertram*, what I should not hesitate to condemn as extravagance and debasement in *Othello* or *Richard the Third*.

THE DRAMA.—BERTRAM.

LETTER II.

TO THE EDITOR OF THE COURIER.

[a]SIR—Before[b] I enter on the examination of [c]*Bertram*, I beg leave to prefix[d] a few words, [e]according to my promise,[f] on the phrase *German Drama*, which I hold to be altogether a misnomer. At the time of Lessing, the German stage, such as it was, appears to have been a flat and servile copy of the French. It was Lessing first[g] introduced the name and the works of Shakespeare to the admiration of the Germans; and I should not perhaps go too far, if I add, that it was Lessing who first proved to all thinking men, even to Shakespeare's own countrymen, the true nature of his apparent irregularities. These, he demonstrated, were deviations only from the *Accidents* of the Greek Tragedy; and from such accidents as hung a heavy weight on the wings of the Greek Poets, and narrowed their flight within the limits of what we may call the *Heroic Opera*. In[h] all the essentials of art, no less than in the truth of nature, [i]he proved that the[j] Plays of Shakespeare were incompatibly[k] more coincident with the principles of Aristotle, than [l](notwithstanding their boasted regularity)[m] the productions of Corneille and Racine.[n] Under these convictions were Lessing's own dramatic works composed. Their deficiency is in depth and in imagination: their excellence is in the construction of the plot; the good sense of the sentiments; the sobriety of the morals, and the high polish of the diction and dialogue. In short, his dramas are the very antipodes of all those, which it has been the fashion of late years, at once to abuse and to enjoy, under the name of the German Drama. Of this latter, Schiller's *Robbers* was the earliest specimen; the first fruits of his youth (I had almost said of his boyhood), and as such, the pledge, and promise of no ordinary genius. Only as *such*, did the maturer judgment of the author tolerate the Play. During his whole life he expressed himself concerning this production with more than

[a-b] *BL* (1817): But before
[c-d] *BL* (1817): *Bertram, or the Castle of St. Aldobrand*, I shall interpose
[e-f] *BL* (1817) omits   [g] *BL* (1817): who first   [h] *BL* (1817): He proved, that in
[i-j] *BL* (1817): the   [k] *BL* (1817): incomparably   [l-m] *BL* (1817) omits
[n] *BL* (1817): Racine, notwithstanding the boasted regularity of the latter.

needful asperity, as a monster not less offensive to good taste than to sound morals; and in his latter years, his indignation at the unwonted popularity of the *Robbers,* seduced him into the *contrary* extremes, viz. a studied feebleness of interest (as far as the interest was to be derived from incidents and the excitement of curiosity); a diction elaborately metrical; the affectation of rhymes; and the pedantry of the chorus.

But to understand the true character of the *Robbers,* and of the countless imitations which were its spawn, I must inform you, or at least call to your recollection, that about that time, and for some years before it, three of the most popular books in the German language were, the translations of *Young's Night-Thoughts, Harvey's Meditations,* and *Richardson's Clarissa Harlow.* Now we have only to combine the bloated style and peculiar rhythm of Harvey, which is poetic only on account of its utter unfitness for prose; and might as appropriately be called prosaic, from its utter unfitness for poetry; we have only, I repeat, to combine these Harveyisms, with the strained thoughts, the figurative metaphysics and solemn epigrams of Young on the one hand; and with the loaded sensibility, the minute detail, the morbid consciousness of every thought and feeling in the whole flux and reflux of the mind, in short the self-involution and dreamlike continuity of Richardson on the other hand; and then to add the horrific incidents, the[a] mysterious villains, (geniuses of supernatural intellect, if you will take the author's word[b] for it, but on a level with the meanest ruffian[c] of the condemned cells, if we are to judge by their actions and contrivances) the[d] ruined castles, the dungeons, the trap-doors, the skeletons, the flesh-and-blood ghosts, and the perpetual moon-shine of a modern author, (themselves the literary brood of the *Castle of Otranto,* the translations of which, with the imitations and improvements aforesaid, were about that time beginning to make as much noise in Germany as their originals were doing[e] in England), and, as the compound to[f] these ingredients duly mixed, you will recognize the so called *German* Drama. The *Olla Podrida* thus cooked up, was denounced, by the best critics in *Germany,* as the mere cramps of weakness, and orgasms of a sickly imagination on the part of the authors,[g] and the lowest provocation of torpid feeling on that of the readers. The old blunder, however, concerning the irregularity and wildness of Shakespeare, in which the German did but echo the French, who again were but the echoes of our own critics, was still in vogue, and Shakespeare was quoted as authority for the most anti-Shakespearean Drama. We have indeed two poets who wrote as one, near the age of Shakespeare, to whom (as the worst characteristic of their writings), the Coryphæus[h] of the present Drama may challenge the honour of being a poor relation, or impoverished descendant. For if we would charitably consent to forget the comic

[a] *BL* (1817): and   [b] *BL* (1817): words   [c] *BL* (1817): ruffians
[d] *BL* (1817): —to add the   [e] *BL* (1817): making   [f] *BL* (1817): of
[g] *BL* (1817): author,   [h] *Courier* misprints: Coryphaelus

humour, the wit, the felicities of style, in other words, *all* the poetry and nine-tenths of all the genius of Beaumont and Fletcher, that which would remain becomes a Kotzebue.

The so-called *German* Drama, therefore, is *English* in its *origin*, *English* in its *materials*, and *English* by re-adoption; and till we can prove that Kotzebue, or any of the whole breed of Kotzebues, whether dramatists or romantic writers, or writers of romantic dramas, were ever admitted to any other shelf in the libraries of well-educated Germans than were occupied by their originals, and apes' apes in their own[a] country, we should submit to carry our own brat on our own shoulders; or rather consider[b] as a Lack-grace returned from transportation with such improvements only in growth and manners, as young transported convicts usually come home with.

I know nothing that contributes more to a clear insight into the true nature of any literary phenomenon, than the comparison of it with some elder production, the *likeness* of which is *striking*, yet only *apparent*: while the *difference* is *real*. In the present case this opportunity is furnished us, by the old Spanish play, entitled *Atheista Fulminato*, formerly, and perhaps still, acted in the churches and monasteries of Spain, and which, under various names *(Don Juan, the Libertine,* &c.) has had its day of favour in every country throughout Europe. A popularity so extensive, and of a work so grotesque and extravagant, claims and merits philosophical attention and investigation. The first point to be noticed is, that the play is throughout *imaginative*. Nothing of it belongs to the real world, but the names of the places and persons. The comic parts, equally with the tragic; the living, equally with the defunct characters, are creatures of the brain; as little amenable[c] to the rules of ordinary probability, as the *Satan* of *Paradise Lost*, or the *Caliban* of the *Tempest*, and therefore to be understood and judged of as impersonated *abstractions*. Rank, fortune, wit, talent, acquired knowledge, and liberal accomplishments, with beauty of person, vigorous health, and constitutional hardihood,[d] elevated by the habits and sympathies of noble birth and natural[e] character, are supposed to have combined in *Don Juan*, so as to carry[f] into all its *practical* consequences the doctrine of a godless nature, as the sole ground and efficient cause [g]of, not only[h] all things, events, and appearances, but likewise of all our thoughts, sensations, impulses, and actions. Obedience to nature is the only virtue: the gratification of the passions and appetites her only dictate: each individual's self-will the sole organ through which nature utters her commands, and

> "Self-contradiction is the only wrong,
> For by the laws of spirit, in the right

[a] *BL* (1817): mother   [b] *BL* (1817): consider it
[c] *Courier* misprints: untenable   [d] *BL* (1817: hardihood,—all these advantages,
[e] *BL* (1817) national   [f] *BL* (1817): give him the means of carrying
[g-h] *BL* (1817): not only of

Is every individual character
That acts in strict consistence with itself."

That speculative opinions, however impious and daring they may be, are not always followed by correspondent conduct, is most true, as well as that they can scarcely in any instance be *systematically* realised, on account of their unsuitableness to human nature and to the institutions of society. It can be hell, only where it is *all* hell: and a separate world of devils is necessary for the existence of any one complete devil. But on the other hand it is no less clear, nor, with the biography of Carrier and his fellow-atheists before us, can it be denied without wilful blindness, that the (so called) *system of nature* (i.e. materialism, with the utter rejection of moral responsibility, of a present providence, and of both present and future retribution) may influence the characters and actions of individuals, and even of communities, to a degree that almost does away the distinction between men and devils, and will make the page of the future historian resemble the narration of a madman's dreams. It is not the *wickedness* of *Don Juan*, therefore, which constitutes the character an *abstraction*, and removes it from the rules of probability; but the rapid succession of the correspondent acts and incidents, his intellectual superiority, and the splendid accumulation of his gifts and desirable qualities, as co-existent with *entire* wickedness in one and the same person. But this likewise is the very circumstance which gives to this strange play its charm and universal interest. *Don Juan* is, from beginning to end, an *intelligible*[a] [b]character. As[c] much so as the *Satan* of Milton. The poet asks only of the reader, what as a poet he is privileged to ask; viz. that sort of negative faith in the existence of such a being, which we willingly give to productions *professedly ideal*, and a disposition to the same state of feeling, as that with which we contemplate the *idealized* figures of the Apollo Belvidere, and the Farnese Hercules. What the Hercules is to the *eye*, in *corporeal* strength, *Don Juan* is to the *mind* in strength of *character*. The ideal consists in the happy balance of the generic with the individual. The former makes the character representative and symbolical, therefore instructive; because, *mutatis mutandis*, it is applicable to whole classes of men. The latter gives it[d] its *living* interest; for nothing *lives*, or is *real*, but as definite and individual. To understand this compleatly, the reader need only recollect the specific state of his feelings, when in looking at a picture of the historic (more properly of the poetic or heroic) class, he objects to a particular figure as being too much of a *portrait*; and this interruption of his complacency he feels without the least reference to, or the least acquaintance with any person in real life whom he might recognize in this figure. It is enough that such a figure is not [e]*ideal*, for[f] one of the two factors or elements of the *ideal* is in excess. A similar and more powerful objection he would feel towards a set of figures which were mere[g]

---

[a] *Courier* misprints: *intellible*   [b-c] *BL* (1817): character: as   [d] *BL* (1817) omits
    [e-f] *BL* (1817): *ideal*: and therefore not ideal, because   [g] *BL* (1817): *mere*

abstractions, like those of Cipriani, and what have been called Greek forms and faces, i.e. outlines drawn according to a recipe. These[a] again are not *ideal*; for[b] the *other* element is in excess. *"Forma formans per forman* [c]*formatam*: or, *"Norma specifica per faciem individualam translucent,"* [d] is the definition and perfection of *ideal* art.

This excellence is so happily achieved in the *Don Juan*, that it is capable of interesting without poetry, nay, even without words, as in our pantomime of that name. We see clearly how the character is formed; and the very extravagance of the incidents, and the superhuman *entireness* of *Don Juan's* agency, prevents the wickedness from shocking our minds to any painful degree. (We do not *believe* it enough for this effect; no, not even with that kind of temporary and negative belief or acquiescence which I have described above). Meantime the qualities of his character are too desirable, too flattering to our pride and our wishes, not to make up on this side as much additional faith as was lost on the other. There is no danger (thinks the spectator or reader) of *my* becoming such a monster of iniquity as *Don Juan! I* never shall be an athiest! *I* shall never disallow all distinction between right and wrong! *I* have not the least inclination to be so outrageous a drawcansir in my love affairs! But to possess such a power of captivating and enchanting the affections of the other sex! to be capable of inspiring in a charming and even a virtuous woman, a love so deep, and so entirely personal to *me!* that even my worst vices, (if I *were* vicious), even my cruelty and perfidy, (if I *were* cruel and perfidious), could not eradicate the passion! To be so loved for my *own self*, that even with a distinct knowledge of my character, she yet died to save me! this, Sir, takes hold of two sides of our nature, the better and the worse. For the heroic disinterestedness to which love can transport a woman, can not be contemplated without an honourable emotion of reverence towards womanhood, and on the other hand, it is among the mysteries,[e] and abides in the dark ground-work of our nature to crave an outward confirmation of that *something* within us, which is our *very self*, that sympathy,[f] not made up[g] of our qualities and relations, but itself the supporter and substantial basis of all these.[h]

(Letter the Third on Monday.)

[a] *BL* (1817): *These*   [b] *BL* (1817): because in these
[c-d] *BL* (1817): *formatam translucens,"*
[e] *BL* (1817): miseries,   [f] *BL* (1817): something,   [g] *BL* (1817): *made up*
[h] *BL* (1817) adds: Love *me*, and not my qualities, may be a vicious and an insane wish, but it is not a wish wholly without a meaning.

THE DRAMA.—BERTRAM.

LETTER III.

TO THE EDITOR OF THE COURIER.

SIR.—[a]Without power, virtue would be inefficient [b] and incapable of revealing its being. It would resemble the magic transformation of Tasso's Heroine into a tree, in which she could only groan and bleed. (Hence power is necessarily an object of our desire and of our admiration.) But of all power, that of the mind is, on every account, the grand desideratum of human ambition. We shall be as Gods in knowledge, was and must have been the *first* temptation: and the co-existence of great intellectual lordship with guilt, has never been adequately represented without exciting the strongest interest, and for this reason, that in this bad and heterogeneous society[c] we can contemplate the intellect of man more exclusively as a separate and[d] self-subsistence, than in its proper state of subordination to his own conscience, or to the will of an infinitely superior Being.[e]

This is the sacred charm of Shakspeare's male characters in general. They are all cast in the mould of Shakspeare's own gigantic intellect; and this is the open attraction of his *Richard, Iago, Edmund,* &c. in particular. But again; of all intellectual power, that of superiority to the fear of the invisible world is the most dazzling. Its influence is abundantly proved by the one circumstance, that it can bribe us into a voluntary submission of our better knowledge, into suspension of all our judgment derived from constant experience, and enable us to peruse with the liveliest interest the wildest tales of ghosts, wizards, genii, and secret talismans. On this propensity, so deeply rooted in our nature, a specific *dramatic* probability may be raised by a true poet, if the whole of his work be in harmony: a *dramatic* probability, sufficient for dramatic pleasure, even when the component characters and incidents border on impossibility. The poet does not require us to be awake and believe; he solicits us only to yield ourselves to a dream; and this too with our eyes open, and with our judgment *perdue* behind the curtain, ready to awaken us at the first motion of our will: and meantime, only, not to *dis*believe. And in such a state of mind, who but must be imprest[f] with the cool intrepidity of *Don John* on the appearance of his father's ghost:

"GHOST.—Monster! behold these wounds!"

"D. JOHN.—I do! They were well meant and well performed, I see."

"GHOST.———— Repent, repent of all thy villanies.

My clamourous blood to heaven for vengeance cries,

Heaven will pour out his judgments on you all.

Hell gapes for you, for you each fiend doth call,

---

[a] *BL* (1817) omits   [b] *BL* (1817): insufficient   [c] *BL* (1817): co-ordination

[d] *BL* (1817) omits   [e] *BL* (1817): being   [f] *BL* (1817): impressed

And hourly waits your unrepenting fall.
You with eternal horrors they'll torment,
Except of all your crimes you suddenly repent."

(Ghost sinks).

"D. JOHN.—Farewell, thou art a foolish ghost. Repent, quoth he! what could this mean? our senses are all in a mist sure."

"D. ANTONIO—(one of D. Juan's reprobate companions). They are not! 'Twas a ghost."

"D. LOPEZ—(another reprobate). I ne'er believed those foolish tales before."

"D. JOHN.—Come! 'Tis no matter. Let it be what it will it must be natural."

"D. ANT.—And nature is unalterable in us too."

"D. JOHN.—'Tis true! The nature of a ghost can not change our's."

Who also can deny a portion of sublimity to the tremendous consistency with which he stands out the last fearful trial, like a second Prometheus?

"Chorus of Devils."

"STATUE-GHOST.—Will you not relent and feel remorse?"

"D. JOHN.—Could'st thou bestow another heart on me I might. But with this heart I have, I can not."

"D. LOPEZ.—These things are prodigious."

"D. ANTON.—I have a sort of grudging to relent, but something holds me back."

"D. LOP.—If we could, 'tis now too late. I will not."

"D. ANT.—We defy thee!"

"GHOST.—*a* Perish ye impious wretches, go and find,
    The punishments laid up in store for you! *b*

(Thunder and lightning. D. Lop. and D. Ant. are swallowed up.)

"GHOST to D. JOHN.—Behold their dreadful fates and know, that thy last moment's come!"

"D. JOHN.—Think not to fright me, foolish Ghost; I'll break your marble body in pieces and pull down your horse."

(Thunder and lightning   Chorus of Devils, &c.)

"D. JOHN.—These things I see with wonder, but no fear.
    Were all the elements to be confounded,
    And shuffled all into their former chaos;
    Were seas of sulphur flaming round about me,
    And all mankind roaring within those fires,
    I could not fear, or feel the least remorse.
    To the last instant I would dare thy power.
    Here I stand firm, and all thy threats condemn.
    Thy murderer *(to the Ghost of one whom he had murdered.)*
    Stands here! Now do thy worst!"

(*He is swallowed up in a cloud of fire*)

a–b BL (1817) does not arrange as verse

In fine, the character of *Don John* consists in the union of every thing desirable to human nature, as *means*, and which therefore by the well-known law of association become at length desirable on their own *ᵃ*account: on*ᵇ* their own account, and in their own dignity they are here displayed, as being employed to *ends* so *un*human, that in the effect, they appear almost as *means* without an *end*. The ingredients too are mixed in the happiest proportion, so as to uphold and relieve each other—more especially in that constant interpoise of wit, gaiety, and social generosity, which prevents the criminal, even in his most atrocious moments, from sinking into the mere ruffian, as far at least as our *imagination* sits in judgment. Above all, the fine suffusion through the whole, with the characteristic manners and feelings of a highly bred gentleman gives life to the drama. Thus having invited the *Statue-Ghost* of the Governor whom he had murdered to supper, which invitation the marble-ghost accepted by a nod of the head, *Don John* has prepared a banquet.

"D. J O H N—Some wine, sirrah! Here's to Don Pedro's ghost—He should have been welcome."

"D. L O P.—The rascal is afraid of you after death."

(One knocks hard at the door.)

"D. J O H N *(to the Servant)*—Rise and do your duty."

"S E R V.—Oh the Devil, the Devil." *(Marble ghost enters).*

"D. J O H N—Ha! 'Tis the Ghost! Let's rise and receive him! Come Governor, you are welcome, sit there; if we had thought you would have come, we would have staid for you.

* * * * * * *

Here Governor! your health! Friends put it about! Here's excellent meat, taste of this ragout. Come, I'll help you, come eat, and let old quarrels be forgotten."

(The Ghost threatens him with vengeance.)

"D. J O H N—We are too much confirmed—Curse on this dry discourse. Come, here's to your Mistress, you had one when you were living: not forgetting your sweet Sister." *(Devils enter).*

"D. J O H N—Are these some of your retinue? Devils say you? I'm sorry I have no burnt brandy to treat 'em with, that's drink fit for Devils," &c.

Nor is the scene from which we quote interesting, in *dramatic* probability alone; it is susceptible likewise of a sound moral; of a moral that has more than common claims on the notice of a too numerous class, who are ready to receive the qualities of gentlemanly courage, and scrupulous honor (in all the recognized laws of honor), as the *substitutes* of virtue, instead of its *ornaments*. This, indeed, is the moral value of the play at large, and that which places it at a world's distance from the spirit of modern jacobinism. The latter introduces to us, clumsy copies of these showy instrumental qualities, in order to *reconcile* us to vice and want of principle; while the *Atheista Fulminato* presents

ᵃ⁻ᵇ BL (1817): account. On

an exquisite portraiture of the same qualities, in all their gloss and glow, but presents them for the sole purpose of displaying their hollowness, and in order to put us on our guard by demonstrating their utter indifference to vice and virtue, whenever these, and the like accomplishments are contemplated for themselves alone.

[a] A contemporary here well observes,[b] that the whole secret of the modern jacobinical drama, (which, and not the German, is its appropriate designation,) and of all its popularity consists in the confusion and subversion of the natural order of things in their causes and effects: namely, in the excitement of surprise by representing the qualities of liberality, refined feeling, and a nice sense of honour (those things rather which pass amongst us for such) in persons and in classes where experience teaches us least to expect them; and by rewarding with all the sympathies which are the due of virtue, those criminals whom law, reason, and religion have excommunicated from our esteem.

This of itself would lead me back to *Bertram*, or the *Castle of St. Aldobrand*; but, in my own mind, this tragedy was brought into connection with the *Libertine*, (Shadwell's adaptation of the *Atheista Fulminato* to the English stage in the reign of Charles the Second), by the fact, that our modern drama is taken, in the substance of it, from the first scene of the third act of the *Libertine*. But with what palpable superiority of judgment in the original! Earth and hell, men and spirits, are up in arms against *Don John*: the two former acts of the play have not only prepared us for the supernatural, but accustomed us to the prodigious. It is, therefore, neither more nor less than we anticipate when the *Captain* exclaims: "In all the dangers I have been, such horrors I never knew. I am quite unmanned;" and when the *Hermit* says, "that he had beheld the ocean in wildest rage, yet ne'er before saw a storm so dreadful, such horrid flashes of lightning, and such claps of thunder, were never in my remembrance." And *Don John's* bursts of startling impiety is equally intelligible in its motive, as dramatic in its effect.

But what is there to account for the prodigy of the tempest at *Bertram's* shipwreck? It is a mere supernatural effect without even a hint of any supernatural agency; a prodigy without any circumstance mentioned that is prodigious; and a miracle introduced without a ground, and ending without a result. Every event and every scene of the Play might have taken place as well; if *Bertram* and his vessel had been driven in by a common hard gale, or from want of provisions. The first act would have indeed lost its greatest and most *sonorous* picture; a scene for the sake of a scene, without a word spoken; as *such*, therefore, (a rarity without a precedent) we must take it, and be thankful! In the opinion of not a few, it was, in every sense of the word, the best scene in the Play. I am quite certain it was the most *innocent*, and the steady, quiet uprightness of the flame of the wax-

---

[a-b] *BL* (1817): Eighteen years ago I observed,

candles which the monks held over the roaring billows amid the storm of wind and rain, were[a] *really* miraculous.

[b]Having interposed these remarks, I shall proceed in my next letter, to the merits of the *Bertram* itself, which, indeed, need no comparison to illustrate them.[c]

THE DRAMA.—BERTRAM.

Letter IV.

To the Editor of the Courier.

Sir—[d]The Sicilian sea coast: A convent of Monks: Night: A most portentous, unearthly storm: A vessel is wrecked: Contrary to all human expectation, one man saves himself by his prodigious powers as a swimmer, aided by the peculiarity of his destination—

> Prior ——— ——— "All, all did perish—
> 1st Monk—Change, change those drenched weeds—
> Prior—I wist not of them:—every soul did perish—
>   Enter 3d Monk hastily.
> 3d Monk—No, there was one did battle with the storm
> With careless desperate force; full many times
> His life was won and lost, as tho' he wrecked[e] not—
> No hand did aid him, and he aided none—
> Alone he breasted the broad wave, alone
> That man was saved."

Well! This man is led in by the Monks, supposed dripping wet, and to very natural enquiries he either remains silent, or gives most brief and surly answers, and after three or four of these half-line courtesies, *"dashing off the Monks"* who had saved him, he exclaims in the true sublimity of our modern misanthropic Heroism—

> "Off! ye are men—there's poison in your touch,
> But I must yield, for this *(What?)* hath left me strengthless."

So end the three first scenes. In the next (the Castle of St. Aldobrand), we find the servants there equally frightened with this unearthly storm, tho' wherein it differed from other violent storms we are not told, except that Hugo informs us, page 9—

> Piet.—"Hugo, well met. Does e'en thy age bear
> Memory of so terrible a storm?
> Hugo—They have been frequent lately.
> Piet.—They are ever so in Sicily.
> Hugo—So it is said. But storms when I was young
> Would still pass o'er like Nature's fitful fevers,

---

[a] *BL* (1817): was   [b-c] *BL* (1817) omits
[d] *BL* (1817) omits   [e] *BL* (1817): recked

> And rendered all more wholesome. Now their rage
> Sent thus unseasonable and profitless
> Speaks like the threats of Heaven."

A most perplexing theory of Sicilian storms is this of old Hugo,[a] and what is very remarkable not apparently founded on any great familiarity of his own, with this troublesome [b]article, for[c] when Pietro asserts the *"ever more frequency"* of tempests in Sicily, the old man professes to know nothing more of the fact, but by hearsay. "So it is said"—But why he assumed this storm to be unseasonable, and on what he grounded his prophecy (for the storm is still in full fury) that it would be profitless, and without the physical powers common to all other violent sea-winds in purifying the atmosphere, we are left in the dark; as well concerning the particular points in which he knew it (during its continuance) to differ from those that he had been acquainted with in his youth. We are at length introduced to the Lady Imogine, who, we learn, had not rested *"through"* the night, not on account of the tempest, for

> "Long ere the storm arose, her restless gestures
> Forbade all hope to see her blest with sleep."

Sitting at a table, and looking at a portrait, she informs us—First, that portrait-painters may make a portrait from memory—

> "The limner's art may trace the absent[d] feature;"

for[e] surely these words could never mean, that a painter may have a person sit to him who afterwards may leave the room or perhaps the [f]country: second,[g] that a portrait-painter can enable a mourning lady to possess a good likeness of her absent lover, but that the portrait-painter cannot, and who shall—

> "Restore the *scenes* in which they met and parted?"

The natural answer would have been—Why the scene-painter to be sure! But this unreasonable lady requires in addition sundry things to be painted that have neither lines nor colours—

> "The thoughts, the recollections sweet and bitter,
> Or the Elysian dreams of lovers when they loved."

Which last sentence must be supposed to mean; *When they were present, and* making love to each other.—Then, if this portrait could speak, it would "acquit the Faith of Womankind." How? Had she remained constant? No, she has been married to another man, whose wife she now is. How then? Why, that, in spite of her marriage vow, she had continued to yearn and crave for her former lover—

> "This has her body, that her mind,[h]
> Which has the better bargain."[i]

[a] *BL* (1817): Hugo!
[b-c] *BL* (1817): article. For   [d-e] *BL* (1817): feature." For
[f-g] *BL* (1817): country? Second,   [h] *BL* (1817): mind: [i] *BL* (1817): bargain?

a The lover, however, was not contented with this precious arrangement, as we shall soon find. The Lady proceeds to inform us, that during the many years of their separation, there have happened in the different parts of the world a number of *"such things;"* even such, as in a course of years always have, and till the Millennium, doubtless always will happen somewhere or other. Yet this passage, both in language and in metre, is perhaps among the best parts of the Play. The Lady's loved companion and most esteemed attendant, Clotilda, now enters, and explains this love and esteem by proving herself a most passive and dispassionate listener, as well as a brief and lucky querist, who asks by *chance*, questions that we should have thought made for the very sake of the answers. In short, she very much reminds us of those puppet-heroines, for whom the showman contrives to dialogue without any skill in ventriloquism. This, notwithstanding, is the best scene in the Play, and though crowded with solecisms, corrupt diction, and offences against metre, would possess merits sufficient to outweigh them, if we could suspend the moral sense during the perusal. It tells well and passionately the preliminary circumstances, and thus overcomes the main difficulty of most first acts, viz. that of retrospective narration. It tells us of her having been honourably addressed by a noble youth, of rank and fortune vastly superior to her own; of their mutual love, heightened on her part by gratitude; of his loss of his sovereign's favour; his disgrace; attainder; and flight; that he (thus degraded) sank into a vile ruffian, the chieftain of a murderous banditti; and that from the habitual indulgence of the most reprobate habits and ferocious passions, he had become so changed, even in his appearance and features,

> "That she who bore him had recoiled from him,
> Nor known the alien visage of her child,
> Yet still *she* (Imogine) lov'd him."

b She is compelled by the silent entreaties of a Father, perishing with "bitter, shameful want on the cold earth," to give her hand, with a heart thus irrecoverably pre-engaged, to Lord Aldobrand, the enemy of her lover, even to the very man who had baffled his ambitious schemes, and was, at the present time, entrusted with the execution of the sentence of death which had been passed on Bertram. Now, the proof of "woman's love," so industriously held forth for the sympathy, if not the esteem of the audience, consists in this, that though Bertram had become a robber and a murderer by trade, a ruffian in manners, yea, with form and features at which his *own mother* could not but "recoil," yet she (Lady Imogine) "the wife of a most noble, honoured Lord," estimable as a man, exemplary and affectionate as a husband, the*c* fond father of her only child, that she, notwithstanding all this, striking her heart, dares to say to it—

> "But thou art Bertram's still, and Bertram's ever."

a BL (1817) begins new paragraph   *b BL* (1817) begins new paragraph
c BL (1817): and the

A Monk now enters, and entreats in his Prior's name for the wonted hospitality, and "free *noble usage*" of the Castle of St. Aldobrand for some wretched ship-wrecked souls, and from this we learn, for the first time, to our infinite surprize, that notwithstanding the supernaturalness of the storm aforesaid, not only Bertram, but the whole of his gang, had been saved, by what means we are left to conjecture, and can only conclude that they had all the same desperate swimming powers, and the same saving destiny as the Hero, Bertram himself. So ends the first act, and with it the tale of the events, both those with which the Tragedy begins, and those which had occurred previous to the date of its commencement. The second displays Bertram in disturbed sleep, which the Prior who hangs over him prefers calling a "starting trance," and with a strained voice, that would have awakened one of the seven sleepers, observes to the audience—

> "How the lip works! How the bare teeth *do* grind!
> And beaded drops course * down his writhen brow!"

The dramatic effect of which passage, we not only concede to the admirers of this Tragedy, but acknowledge the further advantage of preparing the audience for the most surprising series of wry faces, proflated mouths, and lunatic gestures that were ever "*launched*" on an audience to "† *sear the sense*."

> Prior—"I will awake him from this *horrid trance*,
> This is no natural sleep! Ho, *wake thee*, stranger!"

This is rather a whimsical application of the verb reflex we must confess, though we remember a similar transfer of the agent to the patient in a manuscript Tragedy, in which the Bertram of the piece,

> * ———————————— "The big round tears
> Coursed one another down his innocent nose
> In piteous chase,"

says Shakespeare of a wounded stag hanging its head over a stream, naturally, from the position of the head, and most beautifully, from the association of the preceding image, of the chase, in which "the poor sequester'd stag from the hunter's aim had ta'en a hurt." In the supposed position of Bertram, the metaphor, if not false, loses all the propriety of the original.

† Among a number of other instances of words chosen without reason, Imogine in the first act declares, that thunder-storms were not able to intercept her prayers for "the desperate man, in desperate *ways* who *dealt*" ——

> "Yea, when the launched bolt did sear her sense,
> Her soul's deep orisons were breathed for him;"

i.e. when a red-hot bolt launched at her from a thunder-cloud had cauterized her sense, in plain English, burnt her eyes out of her head, she kept still praying on.

> "Was not *this* love? Yea thus doth woman [a] love!"

[a] *BL* (1817): women

prostrating a man with a single blow of his fist[a] exclaims—"Knock me thee down, then ask thee if thou liv'st."—Well; the stranger obeys, and whatever his sleep might have been, his waking was perfectly natural, for lethargy itself could not withstand the scolding stentorship of Mr. Holland, the Prior. We next learn from the best authority, his own confession, that the misanthropic hero, whose destiny was incompatible with drowning, is Count Bertram, who not only reveals his past fortunes, but avows with open atrocity, his satanic hatred of Imogine's Lord, and his frantic thirst of revenge; and so the raving character raves, and the scolding character scolds, and what else? Does not the Prior *act*? Does he not send for a posse of constables or thief-takers to handcuff the villain, and take him either to Bedlam or Newgate? Nothing of the kind; the author preserves the unity of character, and the scolding Prior from first to last does nothing but scold, with the exception indeed of the last scene of the last act, in which with a most surprising revolution he whines, weeps and kneels to the condemned blaspheming assassin out of pure affection to the high hearted man, the sublimity of whose angel-sin rivals the star-bright apostate, (i.e. who was as proud as Lucifer, and as wicked as the Devil), and, "had thrilled him", (Prior Holland aforesaid) with wild admiration.

Accordingly in the very next scene, we have this tragic Macheath, with his whole gang, in the Castle of St. Aldobrand, without any attempt on the Prior's part either to prevent him, or to put the mistress and servants of the Castle on their guard against their new inmates, tho' he (the Prior) knew, and confesses that he knew that Bertram's "fearful mates" were assassins so habituated and naturalized to guilt, that—

> "When their *drenched hold* forsook both gold and gear,
> They griped their daggers with a murderer's instinct;"

and tho' he also knew, that Bertram was the leader of a band whose trade was blood. To the Castle however he goes, thus with the holy Prior's consent, if not with his assistance; and [b]in our next essay we shall follow him thither.[c]

THE DRAMA.—BERTRAM.

LETTER V.

TO THE EDITOR OF THE COURIER.

No sooner is our Hero safely housed in the Castle of St. Aldobrand, than he attracts the notice of the Lady and her confidante, by his "wild and terrible dark eye,"[a] "muffled form," "fearful form," * "darkly wild," "proudly stern," and the like common place indefinites, seasoned by merely verbal antitheses, and at best, copied with very slight change, from the Conrade of Southey's Joan of Arc. The Lady Imogine, who has been (as is the case, she tells us, with all soft and solemn spirits), worshipping[d] the moon on a terrace or rampart within view of the Castle, insists on having an interview with our Hero, and this too [e]tete-a-tete; would[f] the reader learn why and wherefore the confidante is excluded, who very properly remonstrates against such "Conference, alone, at night, with one who bears such fearful [g]form." The[h] reason follows—"Why *therefore* send [i]him"—for[j] the next line, "All things of fear have lost their power o'er[k] me," is separated from the former by a break or pause, and besides that it is a very poor answer to the danger, is no answer at all to the gross indelicacy of this wilful [l]exposure, and we[m] must therefore regard it as a mere after-thought, that a little softens the rudeness, but adds nothing to the weight of that exquisite woman's reason aforesaid. And so exit Clotilda and enter Bertram, who "stands without looking at her," that is, with his lower limbs forked, his arms akimbo, his side to the Lady's front, the whole figure resembling an inverted Y. He is soon however roused from the state surly, to the state frantic, and then follow, raving, yelling, cursing, she fainting, he relenting, in runs Imogine's child, squeaks "Mother!" He snatches it up, and with a "God bless thee, child, Bertram has kissed thy child,"—the curtain

---

* This sort of repetition is one of this writer's peculiarities, and there is scarce a page which does not furnish one or more instances—Ex. gr. The[b] first page or two. Act 1, line 7th, "and *deemed* that I might *sleep*." Line 10, "Did *rock* and *quiver* In the bickering *glare*." Lines 14, 15, and[c] 16, "But by the momently *gleams* of sheeted blue, Did the pale marbles *glare so sternly* on me, I almost *deemed* they lived"—Line 37, "The *glare* of Hell," Line 35, "O holy Prior, this is no *earthly storm*."—Line 38, "This is no *earthly storm*."—Line 42, "*Dealing* with us."—Line 43, "*Deal* thus sternly." —Line 44, "Speak! thou hast *something seen!*"—"A *fearful sight!*"—Line 45, "What hast thou *seen?* A piteous, *fearful sight*."—Line 48, "*quivering gleams*."—Line 50, "In the hollow *pauses of the storm*."—Line 61, "The *pauses of the storm*," &c.

[a] *BL* (1817): eyes,"
[b] *BL* (1817): in the   [c] *BL* (1817) omits
[d] *BL* (1817): *worshipping*   [e-f] *BL* (1817): tete-a-tete. Would
[g-h] *BL* (1817): form," the   [i-j] *BL* (1817): him!" I say, *follows*, because
[k] *BL* (1817): over   [l-m] *BL* (1817): exposure. We

drops. The third act is short, and short be our account of it. It introduces Lord St. Aldobrand on his road homeward, and next Imogine in the Convent, confessing the foulness of her heart to the Prior, who first indulges his old humour with a fit of senseless scolding, then leaves her alone with her ruffian paramour, with whom she makes at once an infamous appointment, and the curtain drops, that it may be carried into act and consummation.

I want words to describe the mingled horror and disgust, with which I witnessed the opening of the fourth Act, considering it as a melancholy proof of the depravation of the public mind. The shocking spirit of Jacobinism seemed no longer confined to politics. The familiarity with atrocious events and characters appeared to have poisoned the taste, even where it had not directly disorganized the moral principles, and left the feelings callous to all the mild,[a] and craving alone for the grossest and most outrageous stimulants. The very fact then present to our senses, that a British audience could remain passive under such an insult to common decency, nay, receive with a thunder of applause a human being supposed to have come reeking from the consummation of this complex foulness and baseless,[b] these and the like reflections so pressed as with the weight of lead upon my heart, that actor, author, and tragedy would have been forgotten, had it not been for a plain elderly man sitting beside me, who with a very serious face, that at once expressed surprize and aversion, touched my elbow, and pointing to the actor, said to me in a half whisper—"Do you see that little fellow there,[c] he has just been committing adultery!" Somewhat relieved by the laugh which this droll address occasioned, I forced back my attention to the stage sufficiently to learn, that Bertram is recovered from a transient fit of remorse, by the information that St. Aldobrand was commissioned (to do, what every honest man must have done without commission, if he did his duty) to seize him and deliver him to the just vengeance of the law; an information which (as he had long known himself to be an attained traitor and proclaimed outlaw, and not only a trader in blood himself, but notoriously the *Captain* of a gang of thieves, pirates and assassins) assuredly could not have been new to [d]him: it[e] is this however which alone and instantly restores him to his accustomed state of raving, blasphemy and nonsense. Next follows Imogine's constrained interview with her injured husband, and his sudden departure again, all in love and kindness, in order to attend the feast of St. Anselm at the Convent. This was, it must be owned, a very strange engagement for so tender a husband to make within a few minutes after so long an absence. But first his lady has told him that she has "a vow on her," and wishes "that black perdition may gulf her perjured soul,"—(Note: she is lying at the very time)—if she ascends his bed, till her penance is accomplished. How, therefore, is the poor husband to amuse himself in this interval of her penance? But do not be distressed, reader, on account of the St. Aldobrand's [f]absence, for[g] as the author has contrived to send him out of the

[a] *BL* (1817): mild appeals, [b] *BL* (1817): baseness [c] *BL* (1817): there?
[d-e] *BL* (1817): him. It [f-g] *BL* (1817): absence! As

house, when a husband would be in his, and the lover's way, so he will doubtless not be at a loss to bring him back again as soon as he is wanted. Well! the husband gone in on the one side, out pops the lover from the other, and for the fiendish purpose of harrowing up the soul of his wretched accomplice in guilt, by announcing to her with most brutal and blasphemous execrations, his fixed and deliberate resolve to assassinate her husband; all this too is for no discoverable purpose on the part of the author, but that of introducing a series of super-tragic starts, pauses, screams, struggling, dagger-throwing, falling on the ground, starting up again wildly, swearing, outcries for help, falling again on the ground, rising again, faintly tottering towards the door, and, to end the scene, a most convenient fainting fit of our lady's, just in time to give Bertram an opportunity of seeking the object of his hatred, before she alarms the house, which indeed she has had full time to have done before, but that the author rather chose she should amuse herself and the audience by the above-described ravings and startings. She recovers slowly, and to her enter Clotilda, the confidante and mother-confessor; then commences, what in theatrical language is called the madness, but which the author more accurately entitles, delirium, it appearing indeed a sort of intermittent fever with fits of lightheadedness off and on, whenever occasion and stage effect hap-pens[a] to call for it. A convenient return of the storm (we told the reader before-hand how it would be) had changed—

> "The rivulet that bathed the Convent walls,
> "Into a foaming flood, upon its brink
> "The Lord and his small train *do* stand appalled.
> "With torch and bell from their high battlements
> "The monks *do* summon to the pass in vain;
> "He must return to-night"—

Talk of the Devil, and his horns appear, says the proverb: and sure enough, within ten lines of the exit of the messenger, sent to stop him, the arrival of Lord St. Aldobrand is announced. Bertram's ruffian-band now enter, and range themselves across the stage, giving fresh cause for Imogine's screams and madness. St. Aldobrand having received his mortal wound behind the scenes, totters in to welter in his blood, and to die at the feet of this double-damned Adultress.

Of her, as far as she is concerned in this 4th act, we have two additional points to notice: First,[b] the low cunning and Jesuitical trick with which she deludes her husband into *words* of forgiveness, which he himself does not understand; and secondly, that every where she is made the object of interest and sympathy, and it is not the author's fault, if at any moment she excites feelings less gentle, than those we are accustomed to associate with the self-accusations of a sincere, religious penitent. And did a British audience endure all this?—They received it with plaudits, which, but for the rivalry of the carts and hackney coaches, might have disturbed the evening-prayers of the scanty week-day congregation at St. Paul's cathedral.

Tempora mutantur, nos et mutamur in illis.

Of the fifth act, the only thing noticeable (for rant and nonsense, tho' abundant as ever, have long before the last act become things of course), is the profane representation of the high altar in a chapel, with all the vessels and other preparations for the holy *ᵃ* sacrament; a *ᵇ* hymn is actually sung on the stage by the choirester-boys! For the rest, Imogine, who now and then *talks* deliriously, but who is always light-headed as far as her *gown* and *hair* can make her so, wanders about in dark woods with cavern-rocks and precipices in the back scene; and a number of mute dramatis personæ move in and out continually, for whose presence, there is always at least this reason, that they afford something to be *seen*, by that very large part of a Drury-lane audience who have small chance of *hearing* a word. She had, it appears, taken her child with her, but what becomes of the child, whether she murdered it or not, nobody can tell, nobody can learn; it was a riddle at the *representation*, and after a most attentive *perusal* of the Play, a riddle it remains.

> "No more I know, I wish I did,
> And I would tell it all to you;
> For what became of this poor child
> There's none that ever knew."
> WORDSWORTH'S THORN.

our *ᶜ* whole* information *ᵉ* is derived from the following words—

> "Prior.—Where is thy child?
> Clotid.*ᶠ*—(Pointing to the cavern into which she has looked)
> Oh he lies cold within his cavern-tomb!
> Why dost thou urge her with the horrid theme?
> Prior.—(who will not, the reader may observe, be disappointed
>   of his dose of scolding)
> It was to make (quere wake) one living cord o'th'heart,
> And I will try, tho' my own breaks at it.
> Where is thy child?
> Imog.—(with a frantic laugh)
> The forest-fiend hath snatched him—
> He (who? the fiend or the child?) rides the night-mare thro'
>   the wizzard woods."

Now these two lines consist in a senseless plagiarism from the counterfeited madness of Edgar in Lear, who, in imitation of the gypsey incantations, puns on the old word Mair, a Hag; and the no less

* The child is an important personage, for I see not by what possible means the author could have ended the second and third acts but for its timely appearance. How ungrateful then not further to notice its fate.*ᵈ*

ᵃ⁻ᵇ *BL* (1817): sacrament. A   ᶜ⁻ᵉ *BL* (1817): whole information *
ᵈ *BL* (1817): fate?
ᶠ *BL* (1817): Clotil.

senseless adoption of Dryden's forest-fiend, and the wizzard-stream by which Milton, in his Lycidas, so finely characterises the spreading Deva, *fabulosus Amnis*. Observe too these images stand unique in the speeches of Imogine, without the slightest resemblance to any thing she says before or after. But we are weary. The characters in this act frisk about, here, there, and every where, as teasingly as the Jack o' Lanthorn-lights which mischievous boys, from across a narrow street, throw with a looking-glass on the faces of their opposite neighbours. Bertram disarmed, outheroding Charles de Moor in the Robbers, befaces the collected knights of St. Anselm (all in complete armour), and so, by pure dint of black looks, he outdares them into passive poltroons. The sudden revolution in the Prior's manners we have before noticed, and it is indeed so outré, that a number of the audience imagined a great secret was to come out, viz.: that the Prior was one of the many instances of a youthful sinner metamorphosed into an old scold, and that this Bertram would appear at last to be his son. Imogine re-appears at the convent, and dies of her own accord. Bertram stabs himself, and dies by her side, and that the Play may conclude as it began, viz. in a superfetation of blasphemy upon nonsense, because he had snatched a sword from a despicable coward, who retreats in terror when it is pointed towards him in sport; this *felo de se*, and thief-captain, this loathsome and leprous confluence of robbery, adultery, murder and cowardly assassination, this monster whose best deed is, the having saved his betters from the degradation of hanging him, by turning jack ketch to himself, first recommends the charitable Monks and holy Prior to pray for his soul, and then has the folly and impudence to exclaim—

> "I died no felon's death,
> A warrior's weapon freed a warrior's soul!—"

APPENDIX C
LETTERS CONCERNING
THE PUBLICATION OF
THE *BIOGRAPHIA*

My dear Hood /   Calne August 10th 1815 —

    At length I am enabled to send you 57
sides of C's work — the ... full 100 sides is finished,
and not finished — that is, there is a metaphysical part
of about 5 or 6 sheets which must be revised or
rather re-written — this I trust will be done in a
few days, and the next parcel (coming I think
certainly next week) will contain the whole of
prefacing work (for you will see how ridiculous
it wod be to call it preface preface) and those
poems which he means to publish besides those
you already have, and their proper order. I assure
you that ever since I wrote to you on the subject
I think there has been but one day & half lost;
and that was owing to Mr Bowles insisting on taking
me to Bath to see Keane; and C: can not work
without me — but you need no assurances from me.
I am no dreamer, my facts are not ideas you know.
C do wonders ... X mas.

2. A letter from John James Morgan to William Hood 10 August 1815 concerning the writing and printing of the *Biographia*. See p. 283

LETTERS CONCERNING
THE PUBLICATION OF
THE *BIOGRAPHIA*

VCL MSS F7.1–5, 7–14
(omitting F7.6, printing bills from John Evans & Co)

1. John James Morgan to William Hood 10 August 1815. Addressed "Wm Hood Esqr | Brunswick Square | Bristol | In his absence to be opened by Mr Kiddell".

Calne August 10th 1815—

My dear Hood/

At length I am enabled to send you 57 sides of C.'s work—the rest (full 100 sides) is finished, and not finished—that is, there is a metaphysical part of about 5 or 6 sheets which must be revised or rather re-written—this I trust will be done in a few days, and the next parcel (coming I think certainly next week) will contain the whole of prefacing work (for you will see how ridiculous it wo^d be to call it ~~preface~~ preface) and those poems which he means to publish besides those you already have, and their proper order. I assure you that ever since I wrote to you on the subject I think there has been but one day & half lost; and that was owing to Mr Bowles insisting on taking me to Bath to see Keane; and C: can not work without me—but you need no assurances from *me*. I am no dreamer, my *facts* are not *ideas* you know.

Col: wo^u have written himself but that he intends writing a long letter to you with the next parcel—So to go on now ~~but~~ to what is absolutely necessary for you & the correction of the Press to know.

C: wishes it printed in the size of Wordsworth's last edition. of Poems &c. the prefatory remarks same sized type. ~~&c~~ ⟨as Wordsworth's *last* preface, not his old preface⟩ and if Mr Gutch will be kind enough, he can correct the press which will sa~~mov~~ve much trouble & expense—the number printed must be left to your ⟨& your friends⟩ judgement. I do think it not at all hazardous to make it a pretty large Edition—you know the press being once set, the additional paper is the only risk—wherever the mark § occurs, it denotes a direction for new paragraph. The Notes & quotations must be printed in somewhat smaller type than the text and on the note on back of 14th page of Manuscript, you

283

will find 3 Sonnets of Nehem^h Higginbottoms partially quoted, because we did not remember all of them & co^d not get the book here. I think Kiddell has it: (2 number of Monthly Magazine) pray let them be printed in full, as directed in that note. I do not recollect any thing else necessary, except that Col: wishes the title page to be left till you hear from us again. If any thing sho^d arise [which] you want to ask, you can write.

And now I want to give you a hint from myself. only indeed as a subject for you to think and consult on: Do you not think that an engraving of Wade's picture wo^d contribute to sell the book? the expence I sho^d reckon at about 30 pound. Would it pay or not? I have a bust ⟨of Col:⟩ done by Dawe the R: Accademitian—an engraving of *that* ('tis a very fine one as to expression) would not cost half the money—it might be done like C Foxs at the head of his historical work & that looks very fine—pray think of this. I send the parcel by the mail with this letter. if you sho^d not get it (by any accident) pray write for I can't book it here. If you don't write I shall conclude it has come safe—Yours very truly—with my & our best love to Kiddell & all friends—J J Morgan. If Col: goes on but half as well as he has done the last 6 weeks, we shall do wonders by Xmas.

P.S. to make all easy, you had better write & acknowledge the receipt.

2. John James Morgan to William Hood 14 August 1815. Addressed "Wm Hood Esqr | Brunswick Square | Bristol".

> Calne Monday night.
> 14 Augt 1815

My dear Hood—

Just received your's—and was about to write ~~to~~ in order to explain, what I believe needed explanation, the directions for the size of the type for C's preface. Col: means it to be printed like, in all respects, Mr Wordsworth last edition ~~of Poems~~ entitled *"Poems by Wm Wordsworth including Lyrical Ballads and the miscellaneous pieces of the author with additional ~~notes~~ poems a new preface and a supplementary essay"*. The preface to these 2 volumes: that preface which ~~goes~~ precedes the poem, is the one which he has fixed on as a prototype for his preface. You know there is at the end of the first volume *"the supplementary essay"* in small type—'tis not that which he means—there is likewise at the end of Vol: 2nd the preface to the former edition of Lyrical Ballads, now reprinted, also in small type—tis not that either, but tis the preface entitled preface prefixed to the poems in the 1st Vol: Excuse my ~~p~~ circumstantiallity about this. I know well that I am apt to write in an almost unintelligible way sometimes, and you know this is a particular *thing*. I expect to be at Ashton at Wm Morgan's cottage on Thursday next, and by that time I sho^d think you will have received the rest of the preface. If it however should not be done, it will be done soon after, for I shall stay out but a day & do not intend coming in to Bristol at all: ~~for because~~ for you know if I see one I must see *all* my friends. and I can't spare the time, not only because Col: will not, nor can not work, to any purpose at least, without me, but because I must return my horse (i e Bowles' horse who lends it to his curate every sunday) ~~be~~ by or before that time.

Can you contrive to see W^m or John Morgan & tell him I hope to dine with him on Thursday next 3 o'Clock. perhaps you may have occasion to ask me something or other about the work. it can be done through him. you will find me at Ashton Friday morn^g though I will if possible just shake you by the hand at your counting house. you won't I know ask me (under these particular circumstances) to do more. Will you place the insurance receipt in my cousins hand—*General Peachy* ⟨who is now here⟩ will convey it to Mrs Coleridge for us.

The occasion of my hasty visit ⟨to Ashton⟩ is, that a young ⟨Irish⟩ man whose family behaved extremely well to me in Ireland, is come over to marry one of my little cousins, and as he can't come to Calne, (for I believe the match is to take place almost immediately) it wo^d be highly ungrateful for me not to go to see him.

Don't be afraid—you may go boldly on with the printing, if not by Thursday, depend on my word: we *shall have soon done quite.* I am no poet no day-dreamer you know.

In your absence am I to write to Kiddell about this business, or to whom else?

Think about the bust—shall I write to Dawe. Yours sincerely &c J J Morgan—

Write me a short note by my cousin—can you spare time to come to Ashton, or must I come to you by ~~wh~~ at what hour?—

3. John James Morgan to William Hood 17 August 1815. Addressed "Wm Hood—Esqr | Brunswick Square | Bristol".

Bath August 17 1815

My dear Hood/

Upon my arrival here, I found all my cousin's family assembled; and am well content to be spared a further ride. I think it proper however to give you a line in apology for not seeing you. The above stated circumstance will I doubt not be sufficient.

I don't know any thing particular to communicate on the affair of Col's book. The rest will be sent to you in a few days. If you wish it directed to any other person, pray write to me immediately. Do you wish me to write to Dawe about the Bust, or will you or your friends do it. his direction is George Dawe Esqr R.A. Newman St Oxford St London. If you write, I should think the best way would be to ask, first what ~~w~~ would be the expence of it? stating in what manner ⟨size and all) you wish it done and for him to execute & send to you a drawing of it prior to it's being engraved, so that you may be able then to judge, whether you will go to the expence of the engraving or no. The drawing you know, must be first done, at any rate, and there (it can't cost much) you may stop if you please. I should like to have it stated to Dawe, that in ~~the~~ Baking the Bust, the Forehead shrunk a little, and he could easily remedy that defect in the drawing. Of course any thing that I can do I will. pray tell us whom we are to write to ~~y~~ in your absence.

> I am your's in great haste
> Jn⁰ Jaˢ Morgan
> to my best love to Kiddell & all other friends.

4. William Hood to John Mathew Gutch 24 August 1815. Addressed "J M Gutch Esqʳ | Small Street".

> Filton Augᵗ 24 1815

Dear Sir—

I unfortunately was too late at your Office Monday & too early Tuesday to see you on the Subject of Coleridge's Work therefore inclose you three letters I have rec'd from Mʳ Morgan the Friend & Amanuensis of C regarding the mode & manner of publication to which I have nothing to add it being in such able Hands as to render any directions even were I enabl'd to give them needless

The private parts of these letters I am sure you will read only to forget & I therefore make no scruple of entrusting them to you   I hope to return in about a month when I shall do myself the pleasure of calling on you—I have requested Mʳ M to correspond with you & forward the further parts of the Work during my absence—

> Believe me
> Dear Sir
> Yours truly
> Wᵐ Hood

5. John James Morgan to John Mathew Gutch 6 May 1816. Addressed "J Gutch Esqʳ | Small Sᵗ | Bristol".

> London—Monday
> [6 May 1816]

Dear Sir/

By this day's carriage I send you *all* the Poetry we are able to collect—we have made many efforts to recover those pieces (not very small in number, & not deficient in ~~qua~~ quality of composition)—~~but~~

~~they~~ which are lost I fear for ever—the Volume must end there. Col: will prefix to it & send this week an essay on the imaginative in Poetry making the whole Volume about 350 pages quite large enough. We likewise return the two proofs.

I have consulted with Murry the bookseller—than whom no man in London knows better about those things. and he is decidedly of opinion that the work sho^d make three Volumes. If therefore you end the first Vol: with the last Copy I sent (I mean the distinction between the Fancy & the Imagination) you have but to alter the pages ~~of the~~ and the number of each Chapter of the ⟨prose⟩ proofs now returnd, and all will be well. making it page 1 Chapter I of 2nd Vol: The three Volumes then will be of nearly equal size.

Lord Essex & Douglas Kinnaird with whom I breakfasted on Friday last have promised ⟨me⟩ to bring ⟨out⟩ *part* of the Tragedy next season at D:L: You know they manage every thing, & lead the Committee entirely—I rely on their words—and am to dine with Honble D. Kinnaird one day this week to settle what alterations they wish—In the mean time the Play will be published as a Poem & be out in 1st June. I believe you know that the Play is divided into 2 parts like the Winter's tale—they take the last part 4 Acts—and add Songs & Music. I shall be glad if you will send (this letter if you please) to Mr Hood—he will rejoice at the news.

Christabel is sold to Murray exclusively till finished, therefore must not be inserted in the Vol: It will be out on Wensday. Direct to Me or S T Coleridge—at Mr Gillman's—Surgeon—Highgate—Col: goes on exceedingly well—he is reduced to 20 drops a dose—Yours in great haste

J J Morgan

Dawe is making a very fine drawing from the Bust. but declines putting his name, unless a *London* engraver be employed. The expence will be nearly the same.

6. William Hood to Samuel Taylor Coleridge 23 October 1816, Addressed "S T Coleridge Esqre".

Bristol Octr 23. 1816

My dear Coleridge—

Your letter of last Month did not receive until a few days ago or it would have been much earlier notic'd as when I left London it was impossible to say where I might be therefore could leave no directions how to forward any rec'd after my departure—You are quite in error when you imagine that any Calumnies could discolor my Mind towards you, & you may be assur'd that you have in Bristol some as warm & zealous Friends as you ever had & equally desirous of rendring you every service in their Power—You must be aware my dear Friend that we are considerably in advance on the faith of your compleating the

work undertaken by M.ʳ Gutch & I am confident You will not disappoint us in the performance of this undertaking—You certainly
have misunderstood M.ʳ Gutch whose feelings towards you are of the
most friendly nature—That he feels hurt at not having the necessary
matter from you to proceed with the work can excite no great surprise
as the press has been stop'd at a great ~~ee~~ inconvenience to him—He
complains particularly that the last Sheet he receiv'd & return'd you
as wanting the heading, of the Chapter was not again sent & by the
delay the paper which was prepar'd was render'd useless & compleatly
lost—I am so engag'd at the Moment that I cannot go into the full
contents of your Letter, but I only express the opinion of all your
Friends here that it is a duty you owe them to compleat the work
agreeable to your engagem.ᵗ & I have no doubt but by their exertions
you will be benefitted in a pecuniary Sense more than any other plan
you could adopt—Our Motive was in the first place to serve you in
undertaking the publication & that motive still exists as strong as ever
& I am assur'd you will instantly sett about compleating it & I request
it as a personal favor that you will send M.ʳ Gutch or me if you prefer
it the Sheet before alluded to & what may remain necessary to Compleat the work—

I should have been most happy to have seen you in Town & felt
considerable disappointment—I sincerely hope you will obtain all you
wish from your excursion to the Sea Coast & shall be rejoic'd to hear
your health is confirm'd by it—Let me hear from you as early as
possible & I am assur'd you will meet my wishes in the point I have
press'd on you—Your little favorite John is quite well & often talks
of you—M.ʳ Hood & all your Friends that I know desire their best
regards—I only ret.ᵈ last week & can give no news—Believe me to
continue

My dear Friend
Yours very truly
W.ᵐ Hood

7. Draft of Letter from John Mathew Gutch to Samuel Taylor
Coleridge c 18 December 1816. (For Coleridge's letter to Gutch
[6] August 1816 *see CL* iv 661–3.)

Sir,

It has been solely owing to the wish that your friends in Bristol who
~~are~~ joined ~~with~~ with me in an earnest wish that the work which has
been placed in my hands should be finished by me.
Sir,

Had not ⟨all⟩ your Bristol friends who are interested as well as
myself in the welfare of the publication of the work I am printing,
expressed a wish to me that I should suspend all communicatⁿ with you
on the subject, till they had seen or heard from you, I should not thus

long have been silent, after the receipt ~~of the contents~~ of your ~~strange~~
letter of the 7ᵗʰ of Augᵗ last.

As none of these Gentⁿ however can ~~either~~ gain any tidings of you
or have been able to see you, ~~Thereoof~~ I defer no longer to send you
my Account for printing &c. ~~the work placed in my hands~~—Such a
return as you have shewn both to myself and them for the motives
which alone induced me to have any thing to do with the printing of
~~your book~~ this book, I could not have thought it possible, we could
have experienced at your hands—Your angry letter as you call it calls
upon me for very little reply—I did not write to Mʳ Gillman to
enquire for you till you had kept a proof sheet 3 weeks without
assigning any reason for the delay, tho' twice requested to do it—~~nay~~
When you found a necessity to lengthen the Biographia Literaria to
make the two volumes more uniform in size, there was surely no
reason to keep the rest of the work standing still—At any rate you
~~know enough~~ are not so ignorant of printing ~~to~~ as not to know that in
a provincial printg off. at least 3 weeks delay in a sheet is no trifling
loss or inconvenience. But when you did condescend to return the
sheet, why omit to fill up the head of the Chapter, that was a blank—
And when I returned you this sheet again ~~for~~ to have this blank
supplied, why never return at all—It was from your friend Mʳ Morgan's visit to Bristol that the first idea of dividing the B. L. into 2 vols.
originated—we both ~~judged act~~ gave our opinion accordg to the best
of our judgment—which you ought to have given us credit for I think,
instead of upbraiding me in the manner you have done

~~There are some other parts of your letter~~ To   What you mean by
lending the sheets ~~by~~ to your enemies at Clifton ⟨during the [. . .] thru
the press⟩ I know not ~~then you cannot reply to~~

~~I only know I have now put you~~ With the full approbatⁿ of all those
Gentⁿ here who advanced you money upon the faith of being repaid
out of the produce of the book, I ⟨now⟩ send you my Account of
expences already incurred—If any London Bookseller will take it off
my hands & give me security for the printg Bill & what we have
advanced, I shall most gladly give it up together with the MS—But if
this is not to be ~~allo~~ accomplished, & you persist in ~~can be~~ continuing
silent to us all upon the subject, I shall immedʸ announce the book to
the public in the state in which it was placed in my hands & publish
it in the best manner I can to ~~defray~~ reimburse what I can out of
pocket

Mʳ S. T. Coleridge

To J. M. Gutch

1815 & 1816

To paper and printing of "Biographia Literaria"
&c 8vo size—demy paper ~~large primer~~ pica
body, long primer notes, Greek & Hebrew quotations ~~Vizt~~ 750 Copies—Vizᵗ

Vol. Sig. B to T. Eighteen sheets at £5. 3. 6.	93. 1. 0
U half a sheet	2.11. 9
Vol. 2—A.A. to ~~J.G.~~ H.H. ~~seven~~ eight sheets..	~~36. 4. 6~~
~~To composing sheet H.H. & ½ sheet I.I. of Vol~~ ⎫	41. 8. 0
~~when you stopped the work~~ .... ⎭	2.18. 6
To extra Corrections in both Vols.	1.13. 6
Vol. 3 "Poems" printing 750 in Small pica body, ⎫	
Brevier notes, Greek Quotations—Viz^t Sig. B ⎬	103. 1. 6
to U. 19 sheets at 5. 8. 6 .... ⎭	
Extra corrections & the pp cancelled	2.13. 8
Printg of 25 Cop. Royal at 13/6	30.14. 3
Post^s & lett^s	3.17. 8
	£279. 1. 4

8. John Mathew Gutch to Samuel Taylor Coleridge 18 December 1816. Addressed "Mr S. T. Coleridge".

Sir,

Had not all your Bristol friends, who are interested as well as myself in the welfare of the publication of the Work I am printing, expressed a wish to me, that I should suspend all communication with you on the subject, till they had seen or heard from you, I should not thus long have remained silent, after the receipt of those unjustifiable accusations contained in your letter of the 7th of August last.

As none of these Gent^n however can gain any tidings of you, or have been able to see you, I defer no longer to send you the account you desire for printing &c. Such a return of Kindness as you have shewn both to them & myself for the motives, which alone could ⟨have⟩ induced us to have undertaken the printing of this book, I could not have ~~it~~ thought it possible, we could have experienced from you—

Your angry letter, as you ~~called it~~ term it, calls upon me for very little explanation in reply—I did not write to Mr Gillman to enquire for you, till you had kept a proof sheet 3 weeks without assigning a reason for the delay, tho' twice requested to do it—When you saw the necessity to lengthen the Biographia Literaria, to make the two Volumes uniform in size, there was surely no reason to keep the rest of the Work standing still. At any rate, you are not so ignorant of printing, as not to know, that in a provincial printing Office at least, three weeks delay in a sheet is no trifling loss and inconvenience—And when you did [. . .] condescend to return the sheet, why omit to fill up the head of the chapter that was left blank? & when a 2^d time I sent the sheet for this sole purpose, why never return it at all—?

It was from your friend Mr Morgan's visit to Bristol, that the first idea originated of dividing the Biogr. Liter. into two volumes—we both gave our opinions according to the best of our judgment—for which I think, you might have given us credit, instead of upbraiding me in the manner you have done.

What you mean by accusing me of lending the sheets as they passed thro' the press to your enemies at Clifton, I know not—

With the full approbation of all those Gentlemen here, who advanced you money upon the faith of being repaid out of the produce of this book, I now enclose my account for the printing already done—If any London Bookseller will take it off my hands in its present state & give me security for the printing Bill & the money advanced to you, I shall most gladly relinquish all claims upon you—But if this is not speedily to be accomplished, & you persist in declining to finish the work as you intended, I shall immediately announce ~~the book to~~ it to the public, ~~aff~~ in the state in which it was placed in my hands, & publish it in the best manner I can to reimburse the expences already incurred—

Your obedient Servant
J. M. Gutch

Bristol 18th Dec. 1816

PS. The 25 Copies on royal paper were meant to be taken by myself & friends at an advanced price, and whoever finishes the Work, I shall feel myself accountable ~~for every loss~~ should any loss be incurred by them—

M^r S T Coleridge

To J. M. Gutch

1815 & 1816—To paper & printing of "Biographia Literaria" &c—8vo size—demy paper—Pica Body—long primer Notes, Greek & Hebrew quotations, 750 Copies—Viz^t		
Volume I—Signature B. to T. eighteen sheets at £5.3.6 per sheet—		93. 1. 0
Sig. U—half a sheet		2.11. 9
Volume II—Sig. A.A. to H.H. eight sheets, when you stopp'd the press		41. 8. 0
To extra Corrections in Vol^s 1 & 2 . . .		1.13. 6
Volume III "Poems"—Small Pica Body Brevier Notes, Greek Quotations—Viz^t Signature B. to U—19 sheets at 5.8.6.		103. 1. 6
To extra Corrections and 4 pages cancelled in proof		2.13. 8

41. 8
5. 3. 6
————
46.11. 6

30.14. 3	To Printing 25 ~~sheets~~ Copies of each ⎤	
.13. 6	Volume on royal paper—Viz.ᵗ 18½ ⎥	30.14. 3
	Vol. I—8 Vol. 2—& 19 Vol. 3—in all ⎥	
	45½ sheets a. 13/6 ⎦	
31. 7. 9	Postages of letters & carriages of par- ⎤	
	cels from Calne, London & Highgate ⎥	3.17. 8
	during the progress of the Work . . . . ⎦	

£279. 1. 4
5.13. 6
13. 6
284.18. 4

Mʳ Hood's Account
Cash advanced to S. T. Coleridge to be paid by sale of his book

1815

April— Paid his Annuity J. Hinckley & Co.
in London 27. 5. 6
His draft & Cash in Bristol . . . . . 45. 0. 0——72. 5. 6

Oct— Cash note to Calne to enable him to send⎤
his Son Hartley to Oxford . . . . ⎦ '0. 0. 0

Dec. 9. Paid his draft at 2 months dated Calne to⎤
relieve him from anxiety regarding some⎥
debts & to enable him thus to compleat his⎥ 25. 0. 0
work . . . . ⎦

£107. 5. 6

9. Gale & Fenner to John Mathew Gutch 14 January 1817

London, 14 Janʸ 1817.

D Sir/

Will you have the goodness to state the amount of *Advances* to Mʳ Coleridge on the "Lit'y Life &c." and the printing Charges—perhaps, from home, you may not be able to say exactly as to the latter; but you may remember the general Amount of the Advances, of which we wish some idea before we can look at the thing; and remain,

Dʳ Sir,
Your mo. obed Servᵗˢ
Gale & Fenner

10. Draft of a letter from John Mathew Gutch to Gale & Fenner c January 1817

Gent^n

Much as I ~~may~~ might have felt feel inclined to have ~~make a~~ made a trifling sacrifice, if such had occurred, bet^n ⟨my own &⟩ your Estimate—~~for~~ of ~~print~~ the Paper & Printing of M^r C's Work, ~~& my own~~ I cannot in justice to my feelings as a fair tradesman submit to the deduction, which you propose. In the first place ~~upon~~ there exists a very mat^l ~~alt~~ error in your calculat^n of the Paper. Instead of its taking 1½ ream for ~~the pr~~ 750 ~~Sheets~~ it takes 32 quires & 6 processed paper, which makes the charge for Paper 2.14 per sheet, instead of 2.5.0 as you state—In the next place as to the 2 Vol^s of pica, I refer you for any charge to page 188 shown—2^d charge for notes, which ~~are~~ certainly run very heavy throughout the Vol (you will then find 2.10.6 per sheet is the price agreed upon—In regard to the Small pica Vol. shown makes the difference bet^n us, rather more in my favor—& as to the alteration for the ~~demy~~ 25 royal Copies, there is not I am sure a printer of any conscience but would admit my charge to be highly reasonable. As they were not ordered by Mr Coleridge, however, ~~I w~~ but done at my own risk, I should not be so very ~~sure in~~ firm in adhering to my mode of charging upon this part of the Work, as you ~~shall be upon~~ will find me upon the other The ~~Bills~~ 9. & 12 mo^s Bills ~~are~~ is a mode of payment after the delays I have already experienced that I must object to. Their dates must be altered to 3 & 6 mo^s. If you feel inclined to continue the negotiat^n subject to their ~~alte~~ revisions, I shall be glad to hear further from you.

I remain
Your

11. Thomas Curtis to Samuel Taylor Coleridge 4 March 1817.
Addressed "S. T. Coleridge, Esq | J. H. Gillman, Esq | Highgate".

Pat^r Row
Tuesday Morning.
[4 March 1817]

Dear Sir/

I *will* not be staggered by any thing I may learn of your Transactions of business, until I have an opportunity of seeing you from head to foot;—or find that impracticable.—But I cannot undertake to preserve any second mind in this state; and next to the pain of believing wrong of a friend, is that of the incapability of doing away an *alleged* wrong.

Thinking the Zapolya might command such a momentary Sale as to replace the house in funds advanced on the other works—I was requested to call on Mr *Murray* as I had done on Messrs Longman & C to ask the exact situation in which he felt himself toward that Poem. *Mr Murray states that he has advanced £100 on it and on the "Life 3 vols." together!* He behaved with great civility and liberality with regard to the mode of re-payment, but frankly gave this as his claim: £100. Now—Dr Sir, Messrs Gale & Fenner have *engaged* to pay Mr Gutch for the Life. To hear of *£100* where you had named but *£50*, and of any other individual being promised the publication of the Life after all that has occurred—look at it, Dr Sir.————You much mistake me if you suppose I am in the habit of receiving hasty impressions to the disadvantage of any one.————If I were to die without hearing any explanation of this matter, I should be determined to believe you could have given it—but while *exposed* to such representations as these from men who have an honorable character with the world—you never can sustain the good name you ought.

Do not—I would still say—let the expression of these plain things incapacitate you for action, or lead you to suppose Mr Murray either unjust or unkind (as far as I c^d see) toward you. He appeared much otherwise, and I have no doubt of settling the matter in time with him, satisfactorily—should we get into Funds, but these Gentlemen below stairs have been exposed to offering this 2nd Work ("The Life") in a public Saleroom on which a Brother Tradesman claims a serious Advance, and ⟨of⟩ which he may yet prevent the publication; and they have repaid another an excessive Charge. (Mr Gutch)

I shall be here on *Thursday* and on *Saturday* for a couple of hours in the middle of the day. Have you any digested thoughts upon our last important Conversation—I should be happy either of those days (and most satisfied at the earliest opportunity to do away *the pain* the foregoing matter has given me) to see you; & believe me

Ever Dr Sir,
Faithfully Yours
Thos Curtis

PS. If Messrs Gale & C give Mr Murray their Note for this £100 it will be *necessary* you sh^d see them on Thursday.—But they have not concluded to do this. For your own sake see Mr Fenner early;—and do—do let us know the last of these things.

12. Gale & Fenner to John Mathew Gutch 5 March 1817

London Mar. 5. 1817

Sir,

As we understand every thing is now completely arranged respecting Mr Coleridges work we beg to know wherein the delay now exists, as we expected to have had tidings of its being on the road ere this.

We are
Sir
Your Mo Obed Sev^s
Gale & Fenner

To
   Mr Gutch
   Bristol.

13. John Mathew Gutch to Gale & Fenner c March 1817

Gentⁿ

In the early part of ~~the~~ our Correspondence, I stated to you, that I held Mr Coleridge's Work as a security for some sums of money advanced to him by some of his friends in Bristol—Some of these debts have been relinquished by some of the Gentlemen—My own advance of £14. he has desired me to draw for upon you, which I suppose he has requested you to accept. There is however another sum of £14. which is due to a Gentleman [Le Breton], who has written to Mr Coleridge to say that he shall ~~ins~~ not relinquish his demand, & till this is satisfied he has informed me that he must look to me as having ~~the~~ Mr. C's work as a. security in my hands to repay him—This is the sole cause of the delay; the work is packed up for sending off, & as soon as this little debt is adjusted so as to exonerate me from any claim, the Work shall be instantly forwarded to your address by the first Waggon—

Your obed^t Servt
J. M. Gutch

PS. Please inform me, if I am correct in drawing upon you for the £14. 0. 0—

14. Gale & Fenner to John Mathew Gutch 13 May 1817. Addressed "Mr J. M. Gutch | Printer | Bristol".

London May 13th 1817

Sir

We have only just finished gathering and collating Coleridge's Life and Poems—& from the slovenly & careless way in which they came packed to us very many of the sheets are spoild—so that the Number perfect are as follows

727	Coleridge's Life		vol 1	demy 8vo
739	————————		vol 2	————
714	————————	Poems	demy 8vo	
24	————————	Life	vol 1,	royal 8vo
25	————————		vol 2	————
23	————————	Poems	———	royal 8vo

the damaged & overplus Sheets we would recommend sending back—that you may complete them up to No. charged—we at the same time beg to mention that it is usual in printing a work with the London Trade to have a certain No of overplus Books say 10 or 12 or a like No delivered gratis—and we ought certainly to look for that proportion or a deduction to the Amount—independent of this we have incurred a charge for gathering &c of £5. 0. 0 which must be deducted from the amount of Invoice—

Waiting your reply in course

> We remain Sir
> Yrs respectfully
> Gale & Fenner

15. John Mathew Gutch to Gale & Fenner 14 May 1817

Gent[n]

Had I been aware of the difficulties I find I am likely to meet with in arranging with you a Settlement about M[r] Coleridge's Work, I would have put it behind the fire rather than have subjected myself to such repeated disappointments, expences & delay—Will you by return of post inform me, if I accede to ~~your new~~ the fresh deductions you have proposed, whether there are others yet in reserve—You have the Work in hand & it seems I am now at your mercy—My ~~Composite~~ Pressmen are ready to make oath, that as far they can swear considering accidents, that they worked off 756 Copies of each Sheet for 750—M[r] Coleridge at different times had 3 or 6 Copies of the Work sent to him or his friends, you had another; On the whole I can account for 9 or 10 taken from the number by his directions—Make allowances for these & tell me what future deductions you intend to make. & rather than fur[r] altercation bet[n] us sho[d] arise, I will take your acceptance as agreed upon for the press amount specified, if it is at all within just bounds—

16. Gale & Fenner to John Mathew Gutch 16 May 1817. Addressed "Mr Gutch | Printer | Bristol".

London May 16th 1817

Sir

In reply to yours of the 14th we hand the annexed statement of Coleridge's Life & Poems—and you may draw for the Balance at agreed dates—which shall be immediately accepted.—

As to the difference between the No. charged & what were delivered as saleable—it is easily accounted for, by the improper mode of packing, and if an agreed no. of any work is published that quantity most certainly is expected to be delivered or accounted for at *Sale price*—: our claim to the overplus copies we have given up—although the custom of the Trade would justify a charge for the usual no del^d over & above a like impression

We are Sir

Yrs respectfully

Gale & Fenner

Dr Mr Gutch   in a/c with Gale and Fenner, C^o

1817

Mar. 27	To Carriage	5 11 6	Mar 27	By Amount	
	" 23 Life &c 2v			of Invoice	
	8vo a. 14/–			for Cole-	
	damaged &	16 2 –		ridge 3	
	short in No			vols: royal	
	" 36 Poems 8vo			& demy	265–4
	do 7/–	12 12 –			
	" Life 2v royal	1 – –			
	" 2 Poems royal				
	10/–	1 – –			
	" Gathering &				
	collating the				
	whole	5 – –			
	" Balance	223 14 10			
		£265 – 4			265–4

Balance 223 14 10

The gathering & collating employed our Warehouseman upwards of 4 weeks—

17. Thomas Curtis to Samuel Taylor Coleridge 21 June 1817. Addressed "Mr Coleridge, | J. H. Gillmans Esq | Highgate". (For Coleridge's letter to Curtis and Rest Fenner 18 June see *C L* IV 740–1.)

Pat^r Row
Saturday, 21 June

Dear Sir/

Your Letter which reached me on Thursday Evening I was anxious to compare with Mr Fenner's recollection of the matters you think "understood"—before I replied upon my own immediate ~~im~~ recollection of them. These are, *all that respects the* £300. in addition to what is stated in my Letter.

Now, Dear Sir, the advance of the £300 was only contemplated in the case of your being entirely given up to the Work, at Camberwell [*Encyclopaedia Metropolitana*]; and to the best of my recollection not *named* when it was agreed you should be paid for what you *wrote*, and as *you wrote it*. From whatever prejudice, miscalculation, or erroneous view of things the proprietors may judge as they judge of the difference of your being wholly given up to the thing near the Press, or as you will, perhaps, state you mean to be given up to it, at Highgate; that there was this difference in the propositions respecting your remuneration, I am clear. And Mr Fenner's recollect^n is the same. Your ~~at all ev~~ writing those distinct—[v]ery distinct views of things, to us, now—only shows the [fa]ct of delay in acknowledging Arrangements of this [m]agnitude.

To re-make the proposition of your coming over to the Press, after all that has been stated upon that subject, at this time, would be needless—though our mind is the same;—Mr Fenner would not feel himself justified in adding to his Engagements any undertaking beyond those contained in my last. He requests me to say he should be happy to see you here to talk this matter over, or any other on *Tuesday*— but the above is his final mind.

I am, Dear Sir,
Yours ever faithfully,
Thos Curtis.

18. Memorandum of Agreement Between Samuel Taylor Coleridge and Rest Fenner 18 August 1817

Agreement B—

London 18th August 1817

Memorandum of Agreement entered into this day between Mr Coleridge, of Highgate and Mr Fenner of Paternoster Row, Bookseller respecting the publishing and Copyright of Zapolya, a Poem, now ready for press, an Article to be called "Introduction" to the Encylopaedia Metropolitana, as specified in the Prospectus of that work now current, and Mr Coleridges remaining share of the Literary Life, 2 Vols, Sibylline Leaves, 1 Vol 8° the first and second Lay Sermons, and the Friend 3 Vol 8° now printing.—

That is to say, Mr Coleridge is to deliver immediately to Mr Fenner, complete, and ready for press the above Poem of Zapolya, which is to be published on the joint account of Half profit and Copyright as ⟨the above Works have been, and as⟩ stated in Agreement marked A signed also this day, but of which Poem, Mr Fenner is to have the entire Sale & Property until the Advance now contemplated and by this Agreement arranged to be made is repaid to him from Mr Coleridge's Half Share of the Profits of this poem, or from ⟨the⟩ Works which follow, That is to say further, Mr Fenner is also to retain the entire ~~possession~~ proceeds of the Literary Life, Sibylline Leaves, the first and second Lay Sermons and of the Friend 3 Vol 8 now printing, until the ⟨said⟩ Advance is repaid, and Mr Coleridge hereby agrees to write the above-named Article to be called the Introduction to the Encyclopaedia Metropolitana, at the rate of Ten Guineas per Sheet, (and making Six Sheets demy 4to) and to deliver it complete to Mr Fenner on or before the Eighteenth of October next ensuing.—

Upon these Conditions Mr Fenner hereby agrees to advance to Mr Coleridge, the Sum of Three Hundred Pounds, in the following manner

     25 in Cash
     50 per Bill to be drawn by Mr Coleridge at 2 Months
   225 per Bill Due 18th Jany 1818
   —
£300

for which as before stated, all his Works now in hand are to remain in pledge, the Zapolya to be immediately given over in addition, and the Introduction to the Encyclopaedia Metropolitana to be written/

Rest Fenner

INDEX

INDEX

303

faith
  analogon of [2]134; vs historic belief
  [2]134; irrationality of article of
  [1]204; keystone of Christianity [2]244;
  life of [1]203; negative [2]6n, 134, 214,
  216, 264, 265; not commanded by
  conscience [1]135; poetic [2]6, 6n;
  reason and [1]156n, [2]247, 247n; saving [2]246; its sensorium in heart
  [1]122; total act of being/soul [1]122,
  122n; what is [1]242n
falsehood
  fiction as [2]133, 134; half truths and
  144n; truth and [2]83
Falstaff (Shakespeare) [1]cx, [2]53n,
  185
fame, vs reputation [1]33, 33n, [2]36*,
  158, 260
familiar, to bestow novelty to [2]5n
familiarity, film of [1]80n, [2]7, 7n
family, of authors [1]225
fanatic(s)/fanaticism
  bees, as image of [1]30, 30n, 197n;
  democratic [1]199; enthusiasm and
  [1]31, 31n, 47, 147; magic rod of
  [1]197; mystics as [1]149; and persecution [1]198; queen bee in hive of
  party [1]197; and superstition [1]30–1;
  treatise of religious [1]232–3, 232n;
  verbal precision in exclusion of
  [2]143
fancy
  aggregative and associative power
  [1]ciii, civ, 105, 293, 294, 294n, 305,
  [2]16n; ape of memory [1]ciii, [2]235;
  allegorizing [2]235*; and artificial
  memory [1]127–8, 127n; drapery of
  poetry [2]18, 18n; excess of f. is
  delirium [1]ciii, 84n; image-forming
  power [1]288n; imagination vs [1]1, liii,
  liv, lx, lxxxiii, xcvii–civ, cxxi, cxxx,
  cxxxiv–cxxxv, 36n, 82–8 and nn,
  89n, 99, 99n, 169n, 173n, 291n,
  294, 304–5, 304n–5, [2]15, 16n, 49n,
  87, 127, 151, 287; and mental
  abandon [1]84n; mode of memory
  [1]305, 305n; passive [1]104; poetry
  addressed to [1]18; vs wit [1]ciii, 287n
Farington, Joseph (1748–1820) *Diary*
  ed James Greig q [1]39n
farmers
  and church property [1]227–8; and
  poor [2]45; talk of [2]53n

farmhouses, German [2]191–2
Farnese Hercules [2]214, 264
fashion, fairies of [2]83
fast-days [1]185n
fate [2]189
  and idea of God [1]201
Father, God as [2]234
faults
  vs beauties *see* defects; genius clears
  itself of [1]78; punished for [2]234;
  seductive [1]74, 74n
Fawkes, Francis (1721–77) [2]34n
fear 272
  and anger [1]30n, 31, 31n, 71; of
  invisible world [2]217–18, 266; per-
  plexity and [1]71
feather bed [2]180
Federalist Papers [1]219n
federal journals of America, C's
  essays reprinted in [1]219, 219n
feeling(s)
  alienation/aloofness of, in poet
  [2]22, 22n; bad writing was bad
  [1]224n; of childhood into powers of
  manhood [1]80–1, 81n; dim ideas and
  vivid [2]70n; and effect of metre 266;
  electric force of [1]199; and fixed
  opinions [1]190; intensity of f. disproportionate to object [2]136; language of natural [2]55; natural f. in
  poetry [2]40n, 42, 43; obscure f. and
  words [2]169; personal or domestic f.
  in poetry [2]20; poetry spontaneous
  overflow of [2]71; in public discussion
  [1]197; tautologies of [2]57, 57n; and
  thoughts and images 143–4; under-
  current of [1]23; union of f. and
  thought [1]80
Feinagle, Gregor von (c 1765–1819)
  [1]127n, 128n
  The New Art of Memory [1]127n
Felix Farley's Bristol Journal [1]xlix,
  170n
feminine, vs effeminate [1]36n
Fenner, Rest (fl 1817) [1]lxiv, [2]294,
  298
Fenwick, Isabella (1783–1816) [1]79n,
  [2]7n, 120n, 126n, 147n
Ferdinand VII, King of Spain (1784–
  1856) [1]190n
Ferguson, Adam (1723–1816) [2]90n
ferment, of genius [1]78

Stoddart, Sir John (1773–1856) *see* Schiller *Don Carlos*

Stoics, and necessary connection [1]245n, 246–7

story, in poetry and painting [2]187–8

Strada, Famiano (1572–1649) [1]56n
De bello belgico [1]56n; *Prolusiones academicae* [1]56, 56n

Strassburg [1]149n

streams, two rapid s. meeting [2]26

Strozzi, Filippo (fl 1593) [2]34*

Strozzi, Giovanni Battista, the Elder (1504–71) [2]34n
Madrigali [2]34*–6, tr 35*, q 36*–9, tr 37n

Strozzi, Leone (fl 1580) [2]34*

Strozzi, Lorenzo (fl 1593) [2]34*

structuralism [1]xlii, cvi

Stuart, Daniel (1766–1846) [1]xlvi, 136n, 212n, 214n, 215n, [2]6n, 157n, 177n, 235n

Studies in Bibliography [1]li n

Studies in Romanticism [2]107n, 207n

Studium [2]19n

style(s)
austere, natural [1]8; conditions and criteria of poetic [1]23; damnatory s. of *Ed Rev* [2]108; differences of, in poetry [2]83; disharmony in [2]123, 123n; epigrammatic [1]39, 39n; essentially different [2]62–3; humblest vs highest [1]56; to identify s. of prose and verse [2]79; inconstancy of, in WW [2]121–6; neutral s. between prose and verse [2]78, 89–97, 98–9, 121; prosaic [2]77; simplicity of [1]39n; unpoetic [2]76–7; untranslatableness as test of [1]cviii, cxi, [1]0n, 23, [2]142; vicious [2]88; words and [1]cx, [2]61

subintellegitur [1]267

subject
equivalent to mind [1]253; essence of [2]62–3; not presentable under time and space [2]244; and object [1]cxxi, coincidence of, basis of knowledge [1]252–4, 252n–3, 271, 271n–2, identity of [1]276n, 279, 279n, 285

subjective
and objective [1]168n, 172, 172n–3, 253n, 255–60 and nn, 285; self or intelligence and [1]253n, 255

subjects (of poetry)
choice of [1]8, and genius [1]44n, [2]20–2, 21n; novelty of [2]32; from ordinary life [2]6, 8; thoughts and images too great for [2]136–42

sublime, the [2]16n

subscription list, to periodical [1]175

substance(s)
essence of [2]62–3; intercommunion between [1]117; modification and one only [2]140; and shadows [1]301

substrate/substratum [1]cxxi, 130n, 143, 143n
of body and spirit [1]130, 130n

subsumption, principle of [1]lxxv–lxxvi

succession, reduced to instant (simultaneous) [2]23, 25

suffering, passion as [2]82n

suffictions [1]102, 102n, 258

suffrage, right of [2]257–8

suggestiveness [1]cxi, [2]128n–9

Sulzer, Johann Georg (1720–79)
on imagination [1]lxxxviii, 305n
Allgemeine Theorie der schönen Kunste [1]lxxxviii

sum see I am

sun(s)
and earth [1]44*; horns of rising [2]116, 116n; of other worlds [2]247, 247n; said to extinguish household fires [2]134; symbol of spiritual [2]243

sunset, on landscape [2]5

superiors
imitation of inferiors [2]42–3; libelling [2]189

supernatural
experiences [1]232–3, 232n; illumination [1]232n; in nature, and elder poets [2]75–6; in poetry [1]xlvi, xlix, 306, 306n, [2]6, 7; and unnatural [2]116

superstition
and despotism [1]190; Egyptian [1]41*; and fanaticism [1]30–1; men prone to [2]49, 49n

Suphan, Bernhard Ludwig (1845–1911) *see* Herder *Sämmtliche Werke*

supposition(s) [1]101–2, 101n, 102n
arbitrary [1]258

Supreme Being
existence of [2]62, 62n, 140; idea of [1]200–1, 200n; intelligence and [1]201;

with dew on [1]186n–7, [2]145n; divine ventriloquist [1]cxviii, 164, 164n; dramatic [2]6; and effort of thought [1]167; establishment of [1]86n; and falsehood [2]83; half [1]44, 44n; hieroglyphic of [2]12n; of historians [2]127; vs illusion [1]262; its own predicate [1]268–9; make us free [1]179, 179n; mediate or immediate [1]cxxii, 265, 265n; of natural religion [1]200; to nature [2]5, 148–9; own higher evidence [2]83; paradoxes as [2]61–2; perception of new [1]85, 85n, 150; in philosophical sects [1]244–7; pleasure, not t., object of poem [1]cviii, 212–13, 12n, 130; plucked as growing [1]186n; poetry and [1]22, 212n; of poets [2]127; and prose [2]12, 12n; and prudence [2]156; rescued by genius [1]82; revelation and t. of religion [1]204, 204n; of science vs doctrines of religion [1]203; spiritual [2]244; and Supreme Being [1]142n–4, 143; symbols and [1]lxxv; unity of [2]11; unseen [1]244; veracity vs [1]157, 157n, 232n

tub, vs turtle shell, in WW *Blind Highland Boy* [2]123, 123n
tubes, nerves as hollow [1]101, 101n
Tucker, Abraham (1705–74)
on imagination [1]169n
The Light of Nature Pursued q [1]236n
Tulk, Charles Augustus (1786–1849) [1]lxx n, 224n, [2]75n, 217n
Turkey [1]100, 100n, [2]85n
turtle shell *see* tub
Tuscany, poets of [2]35*
twilight [2]247, 247n
Two Bills [1]185n
Tychsen, Thomas Christian (1758–1834) C studies Gothic and Old High German under [1]207–9, 207n
Tyrone's Rebellion [1]36n
Tyrtaeus (fl 650 B.C.) [2]140, 140n
Tyrwhitt, Thomas (1730–86) "Essays on the Language and Versification of Chaucer" [2]92n; *see also* Chaucer
Tytler, Alexander Fraser, Lord Woodhouselee (1747–1813) *see* Schiller *Die Räuber*

Ulfilas ("Ulphilas"), bp of Nicomedia (c 311–83) [1]207–8, 207n
Una (Spenser) [2]160n
unanimity, national [1]189, 190–1
unbelief [2]246
deserts of [1]152
unconditional, and conditional [1]265n, 267n, 268n, 270n, 271n
understanding
belief and [2]244, 244n; errors of/in [1]122, 122n, 217, [2]246; food for [2]143; function of [1]120–1; ignorant of a writer's [1]232, 232n, 233; and imagination [2]16, 16n, 46*, 186; reason and *see* reason; reflex acts of [2]244; regulative and realizing power [1]293
uneducated
man of genius [1]150–1; order of words of [2]58
Ungrund [1]146n
Unitarian(s)
as Christians [2]245–6, 245n; C as [1]179–80, 180n, 204–5
Unitarianism [1]136n
and Christianity [2]245–6, 245n–6; treatise on causes and consequences of [1]136n, [2]246n
United Provinces *see* Netherlands
unities, dramatic [1]34*, 34n, [2]210, 210n
unity
and diversity [2]73n; divine [1]226; end of thought and feeling [1]xciv; instinct to seek [2]72; multeity in [1]lxxvi, cxxxvi, [2]23n, 73n; of nature and experience [1]lxxvi–lxxvii; organic [1]cx; reducing multitude to [2]20, 23, 23n
universal
in individual [1]156n, 246*, 46n, 185, 185n; in particular [2]215n; reason 187*
universality, and law of association [1]111, 111n
universe
choral echo of filial Word [2]247–8; God and [1]203; image of divine Being [2]248n; incomprehensible property of [1]lxxix; matter and motion to construct [1]296–7, 297n; *see also* world(s)